BETRAYAL:
The Promise Never Kept

BETRAYAL:
The Promise Never Kept

Genocide And The West's Secret War For OIL!

Shahan Natalie
Soghomon Tehlirian
Armen Garo
Sylva Natalie Manoogian
Ara Khachig Manoogian

For more information about this book and related documentation, please visit www.snff.org

© 2019 Sylva Natalie Manoogian and Ara Khachig Manoogian
All Right Reserved

ISBN 978-1-950801-02-2

All rights reserved. No part of this book may be reproduced or transmitted in any form or by any means, electronic or mechanical, including photocopying, recording, or by any information storage and retrieval system, without permission in writing from the copyright owner.

For further detail please contact:
Shahan Natalie Family Foundation, Inc.
3727 West Magnolia Blvd., #215
Burbank, CA 91505 USA
Email: info@snff.org

This book is dedicated to the memory of
Shahan Natalie, Soghomon Tehlirian,
Aaron Sachaklian, all those who have
invested their time and energy for
the preservation of the Armenian people
without any expectation of personal
monetary gains, and to those who
may one day choose to do the same.

Contents

INTRODUCTION ix

Chapter 1: Ides of March 1
Chapter 2: The Birth of Nemesis 23
Chapter 3: Broken Promises of Reforms for the Ottoman Armenians 29
Chapter 4: Armenian Revolutionary Parties 37
Chapter 5: The Young Turks 43
Chapter 6: The Four Pashas 53
Chapter 7: Turks and Russians Vying for Armenian Support 63
Chapter 8: Turkish Resistance to the Young Turks 67
Chapter 9: German and Ottoman Genocidal Cooperation 73
Chapter 10: Russians Turned Bolshevik 81
Chapter 11: Secret Treaty 89
Chapter 12: Arming the Enemy 99
Chapter 13: Morgenthau 107
Chapter 14: Presenting the Armenian Case 133
Chapter 15: One Man Armenian Lobby 159
Chapter 16: British Spies 169
Chapter 17: ARF 9th General Assembly 181
Chapter 18: U.S. Mandate over Armenia 187
Chapter 19: The Treaty of Sèvres 191
Chapter 20: Wilsonian Armenia 201
Chapter 21: Joining the League of Nations 217
Chapter 22: Operation Nemesis 229
Chapter 23: Armen Garo 241
Chapter 24: Making deals with the Turks 259
Chapter 25: Soghomon 261
Chapter 26: Lausanne Treaties 273
Chapter 27: Chester Concessions 279
Chapter 28: Confession of a Rear Admiral 295

Contents

Chapter 29: The Bankers	305
Chapter 30: The Colt Memos and Letter	317
Chapter 31: Theodore Roosevelt Letters	325
Chapter 32: An Open Letter to President Wilson	339
Chapter 33: Still Arming the Enemy	347
Chapter 34: Genocide Recognition	353
Chapter 35: Talaat's Conclusion	369

ABOUT THE AUTHORS

Shahan Natalie (1884-1983)	375
Soghomon Tehlirian (1896-1960)	383
Garegin Pasdermadjian (1873-1923)	387
Sylva Natalie Manoogian (1937)	393
Ara Khachig Manoogian (1965)	395

Appendix I to XV is avalible in a separate paperback volume or in the original hardcover version.

INTRODUCTION

The genocide of the Armenian people, which took place from 1894 to 1923, included the forced conversion to Islam as well as the murder of approximately 2.5 million Christian Armenians living in the Ottoman Empire. It started with the orders of Sultan Abdul Hamid and continued under the leadership of the Committee of Union and Progress (C.U.P.), a well-organized group of revolutionaries conceived in the city of Salonica.

This book will share what was told to me by my grandfather, Shahan Natalie, the man behind Operation Nemesis. His work halted the Armenian Genocide before it could erase from the map what we know today as Armenia. Operation Nemesis also saved the lives of the few Armenians who remained in modern day Turkey.

In 1971, when my grandfather was 87 years old, he shared his extraordinary life story with my two brothers and me. I was 5 years old. This memorable experience was recorded on reel-to-reel tape by my father. It was the first time my grandfather would consent to making an incriminating recording of how he orchestrated the assassinations of some of the most powerful world leaders of that time.

My father had convinced him to tell his story on tape, explaining to my grandfather that his enemies within the Armenian community in the United States, Europe and the Middle East had their own version of Operation Nemesis and his role in it. They would lie about him in order to conceal their own misdeeds, which led to the murder of thousands of Armenians.

Shahan Natalie (1884-1983)

Although found guilty in a Turkish court for the mass murder of Armenian, Greek and Assyrian Christians, as well as respected Islamist leaders who opposed them, it was crystal clear to my grandfather that the western powers who claimed to want to hand down justice to the C.U.P. leaders were, in fact, making backroom deals with these convicted murderers.

These western powers were not alone. Even the newly formed Armenian Government, led by the Armenian Revolutionary Federation (A.R.F.), said they were not interested in holding these convicted murderers accountable. They reasoned that as a government they could no longer behave as a militant political movement and use their past methods. It was later discovered that this newly formed Armenian government had foolishly made secret deals with C.U.P. leaders in exchange for promises that were never fulfilled.

Shahan Natalie was a writer, poet, journalist, human rights activist and revolutionary. Although he loved literature from a very young age, and would have preferred a career as a writer, he felt compelled into revolutionary politics. In 1895, at the age of 11, Shahan Natalie's father and a dozen family members were murdered in the Hamidian massacres (so named after Sultan Abdul Hamid). Shahan and his mother dragged the body of his beheaded father to the family cemetery. With his bare hands the 11-year-old clawed out a shallow grave, wearing down the ends of his fingernails, cracking them open and causing them to bleed.

On his father's open grave, Shahan's mother imposed on him an oath to restore the family's honor and avenge the death of his beloved father, so that others would not experience the pain he would carry with him for the rest of his life.

My grandfather was my mentor. Before he died on April 19, 1983, when I was seventeen, he inspired me to continue his oath and carry on the spirit of his work. My first step to fulfilling my commitment was as a human rights activist.

Out of necessity I added investigative journalism to my repertoire, which I have been engaged in for more than 16 years. I discovered that most journalists wouldn't or couldn't cover controversial subjects. This skill has become particularly useful after finally gaining access to my grandfather's private archive, which contains volumes of unpublished memoirs documenting the lives of the Armenian people before, during and after the Armenian Genocide.

This book will present a concise history of the Armenian people that I believe has never been told before. It will not resemble anything I have seen which is publicly available today. It will not only address the atrocities my grandfather witnessed first-hand when he was eleven years old and the actions he took to end the Armenian Genocide, but will also present my own findings derived from decades of research made possible thanks to many clues my grandfather left me and that I've built on with information discovered in the most unlikely of places.

Most historians present the Armenian Genocide as a crime carried out by the Turks, Kurds and Germans. Although there is truth to this, their conclusion that it was a hate crime between religious groups is not entirely accurate. The mass murder of the Armenian, Greek and Assyrian Christians of the Ottoman Empire was a crime built to order by Western Powers who had little to lose and much to gain.

Like so many millions of Christians, I believe many Ottoman Muslims were victimized, as they had their culture, language—indeed, their alphabet— stolen from them. They also found themselves criminally liable for the genocide against the Armenian people. A genocide, like most, that the masses didn't gain from, but rather a few corrupt officials and those powers in the world who supported them, become wealthy and almost immune from the crime that they in fact orchestrated.

In the pages that follow, I will present evidence that will prove that the Armenian people were driven from the land they lived on for thousands of years, not because of ethnic and religious strife, but because the land they inhabited was believed to have one-sixth of the world's crude oil reserve and other valuable natural resources. European powers and the United States were competing for these resources, having entered into concession agreements with the Sultan, Abdul Hamid II, and then later with the corrupt ruling powers of the C.U.P.

The push for the creation of an autonomous Armenian state within the Ottoman Empire as allowed by its constitution would have spoiled these deals that promised the C.U.P. leadership great personal gain. Thus, with the support of the Western Powers, the Armenian people were driven from their land and massacred so they could never return to claim what is rightfully theirs.

Ara Khachig Manoogian
Los Angeles, CA
April 24, 2019

Chapter 1

Ides of March

No words were spoken. A single shot to the back of his head at close range, and Talaat Pasha, the chief perpetrator of the Armenian Genocide, lay in the pool of his own blood on a Berlin street, on March 15, 1921.

"All of a sudden I heard an explosion. I thought a tire had blown out nearby. But then I saw a man fall down in front of me and another began to flee," stated 32-year-old Boleslav Detnhicki, a witness. The assassin disposed of his German-made Luger pistol and ran. "I started to run after him. The defendant entered Fazanenstrasse from the left side but a number of people were in front of him in the street and he could not escape…From there we took the defendant to the precinct station next to the zoo."[1]

The following day in the Boston Post on page 9, printed the Associated Press' news release.

EX-TURK VIZIER ASSASSINATED
Slain in Berlin by Armenian Student

BERLIN, March 15 (by the Associated Press)-Talaat Pasha, former grand vizier and minister of finance of Turkey, was assassinated in Charlottenburg, a western suburb of Berlin, today. He was shot to death. The murderer, an Armenian student, was arrested."

Talaat Pasha, Enver Pasha and Djemal Pasha formed the triumvirate which controlled the Turkish government during World War I. In July, 1919 a Turkish court-martial, investigating the conduct of the Turkish government during the war period, condemned them to death. By the time a sentence was pronounced, however, Talaat had fled to Germany, and Enver Pasha and Djemal Pasha also took refuge there.

Responsibility for the massacres of the Armenians was thrown on Talaat Pasha.

Talaat Pasha was walking with his wife in Hardenberger Strasse when he was hailed by a student, who approached him from behind. As Talaat turned to return the greeting the stranger fired at the former grand vizier's head, killing him instantly. The second shot struck Talaat's wife.

The assassin threw away his weapon and attempted to escape, but a crowd of pedestrians captured him.[2]

Although the news release claimed Talaat's wife, Hayriye Talat Bafralı (1895-1983), had been shot, the Associated Press later retracted it, stating instead that she had been at home at that time and, upon learning the news of her husband's death, fainted.

Talaat had been found guilty of the Armenian Genocide, as it would

1   Vartkes Yeghiayan, *The Case of Soghomon Tehlirian*, (Los Angeles, CA: A.R.F. Varantian Gomideh, 1985)
2   Associated Press, *EX-TURK VIZIER ASSASSINATED – Slain in Berlin by Armenian Student*, (Boston, MA: Boston Post Newspaper, March 16, 1921), 9.

come to be known after the word 'genocide' was coined by Raphael Lemkin and adopted by the United Nations on December 11, 1948, in relation to the Convention on the Prevention and Punishment of Genocide.

During the speedy trial of June 2-3, 1921, Soghomon Tehlirian, the Armenian student accused of Talaat's murder, testified to the atrocities which befell him and his fellow Armenians in the city of Erzinga: "In the early part of June [1915], an order was issued for the people to get ready to leave the city. We were all told that money and valuables could be given to the government for safekeeping. Three days later, early in the morning, the people were taken out of the city... As soon as the group had gone a little distance from the city, it was stopped. The gendarmes began to rob us. They wanted to take our money and anything else of value that we had... While we were being plundered, they started firing on us from the front of the caravan. At that time, one of the gendarmes pulled my sister out and took her with him. My mother cried out, 'May I go blind.' I cannot remember that day any longer. I do not want to be reminded of that day. It is better for me to die than describe the events of that black day...I cannot say everything. Every time I relive those events . . . They took everyone away . . . and they struck me. Then I saw how they struck and cracked my brother's skull with an axe."

"Your sister, the one whom they pulled and took with them, did she return?" asked the presiding justice.

"Yes, they took my sister and raped her," Tehlirian said. "I was struck on the head and fell to the ground. I have no recollection of what happened after that."

Tehlirian claimed to have been shot and thought for dead. Later, he awoke with a terrible stench of decomposing human bodies in his nostrils. With many hardships, he effected his escape and returned to his home. Inside, he dug out the money his father had buried before the deportations. With 4,800 Turkish Pounds, he managed to escape to France and then travelled to Germany to acquire an education.

One day while walking in Berlin, Tehlirian recognized the elegant foreigner Talaat. At first, he had not thought of revenge. "Approximately two weeks before the incident. I was feeling very bad. I kept seeing over and over again the scenes of the massacres. I saw my mother's corpse. The corpse just stood up before me and told me, 'You know, Talaat is here and yet you do not seem to be concerned. You are no longer my son,' Tehlirian stated while under oath. [3]

Tehlirian knew what duty demanded of him. He rented out a room across the street from the sumptuous apartments where Talaat had been living under an assumed name.

One sunny March day, this Armenian youth saw Talaat walk out. He seized a revolver, dashed into the street and shot the convicted wholesale murderer.

"Any killing revolts a sense of order and justice, but since the days of Brutus or Willian Tell, had any manslaughter been more comprehensible, more nearly excusable, than this riding the earth of a monster, a hyena in human shape?" writes Germany's foremost publicist, Maximilian Harden in his June 4, 1921 article titled "Armenian Is Acquitted in Berlin for Murder of 'Unspeakable Turk.'" The German journalist has taken a note of an uncanny coincidence of

---

[3] Vartkes Yeghiayan, *The Case of Soghomon Tehlirian,* (Los Angeles, CA: A.R.F. Varantian Gomideh, 1985)

two murders committed on the same day, Ides of March, almost two thousand years apart — that of Julius Caesar and Talaat Pasha.

During Tehlirian's trial, the question of his own life and death hung by a slender thread, dependent on whether or not his epilepsy, caused by his experience in Erzinga, would in the jury's eyes absolve him from blame.

"Fortunately he was a acquitted. The slaughter of millions of innocent people in the war was considered a sacred duty. But the putting to death of the unspeakable, miserable Talaat was treated in this trial as a grave criminal offense." Harden concludes.[4]

Trial of Soghomon Tehlirian, June 1921, Berlin

The acquittal of Soghomon Tehlirian enraged Talaat's wife and his associates who attempted to file an appeal. But their cries landed on deaf ears. The prosecutor went on a vacation following the trial, while Tehlirian was deported from Germany and headed to the United States of America.

In press, there were, of course, also stories considering the trial unfair or a 'shipwreck of justice,' as Helen Waljeska quoted Deutsches Abendblatt in "How German Papers Censured Acquittal of Talaat Pasha's Slayer" published in the Baltimore Sun, on November 20, 1921.

In his article published in the Deutsche Zeitung, on June 7, Dr. Mansur Rifat stated that Turkish subjects living in Berlin had engaged counsel to safeguard their nation's interest at the trial, but were advised that no representative of Turkey would be admitted — the complicated Armenian question was not to be reopened, and the case was to be conducted as a murder trial only. In spite of this announcement, the case was conducted on political likes exclusively. Talaat, the murdered man, was the real accused; chief responsibility of the "Armenian atrocities" was laid at his door, yet to him no counsel was granted. The notorious Turkophobe Professor Lepsius and the Balkan Armenian Bishop from Manchester were allowed to testify, while important Turkish witnesses intimately acquainted with all phases of the Armenian question living in Berlin were passed over. Talaat's wife was prevented from taking the stand, and the murderer's story, sounding like a cheaply sentimental romance, was accepted by the court without analysis and would any attempt at verification.

Dr. Rifat asks: "Supposing that Hamar Greenwod had been shot in Paris by an Irishman—is it conceivable that the murderer would have been acquitted in France?" He continues, "History reserves for itself the right eventually to proclaim the truth, to show where the instigators of the Armenian and Turkish

---

4   Maximilian Harden, *Armenian Is Acquitted in Berlin for Murder of 'Unspeakable Turk'*, (Great Falls, MT, Great Falls Tribune, June 5, 1921) 1.

atrocities are to be found, and who are the actual murders of Talaat Pasha. Count Reventlow has recently written an article: 'Talaat Pasha—England's Hand.' There lies the Truth!"[5]

The Turkish journal, "Freedom of the East," which appears twice a month in Berlin, has a dignified editorial on the acquittal of Tehlirian in its issue of June 10. It says, in part: "We hear that during the trial of Talaat's murder someone ... went so far as to assert that Mohammed ordered his followers to murder the Christians.

... Our prophet Mohammed, all whose teachings are just and fair, has never ordered anything of the kind, but, on the contrary, has taught that, 'You shall grand safety to the strangers living within your borders, and shall consider their lives and fortune as entrusted to your care.' To be sure, he also said 'Whosoever attacks you or your country, incites mutiny or causes rebellion, him you shall punish and cast out.' But is not this law accepted in all your countries as well? ... The whole world has now understood that the Armenians were cheated by those Christian powers who, during the war, instigated them to attack Turkey. .. Many thousands of Turkish and Armenian men, women and children thus became the victims of the imperialistic ambitions of certain European powers. ... Clearly, these dramas were not in the spirit of Mohammed or Jesus. ... It is deeply to be regretted that religion of 400,000,000 Mohammedans was insulted and falsely accused in the open court of a friendly nation, and the ideal friendship between Islam and Germany polluted... "

The question must truly be asked - why did the trial of the murder of a world leader only take two days and the jury return with a not guilty verdict?

In 2012, Osik Moses, submitted a thesis for her partial fulfillment of the requirements for a degree of Master of Arts in History from California State University, Northridge, titled: "THE ASSASSINATION OF TALAAT PASCHA IN 1921 IN BERLIN -- A CASE STUDY OF JUDICIAL PRACTICES IN THE WEIMAR REPUBLIC" in which she uncovered important documents that shed light on why the trial was speedy and Tehlirian found not guilty.

"The trial took place on 2-3 June 1921, two and a half months after the assassination. While the defense counsel was trying to extend the process in order to collect additional evidence, the prosecuting authorities, together with the German Foreign Office, tried to hasten the proceedings and have a short trial and a quick verdict. Why?

The assassination served to remind Germany and the world of the horrific events that had taken place in the Ottoman Empire during World War I. It was during this time that the ethnic Armenian population in the Ottoman Empire was driven out of their homes to perish on their forced march into the Syrian Desert.

The Ottoman Empire had been Germany's ally during that war, and German military officials were stationed in every province of the empire. These officials witnessed the massacres and reported the events to their superiors as the horrors were unfolding. Though the Allied governments at the time accused Germany of taking part in the atrocities, no attempts were made by the German

---

5 Helen Waljeska, *How German Papers Censored Acquittal of Talaat Pasha's Slayer*(Baltimore, MD, The Baltimore Sun, November 20, 1921) 6.

government to exert any influence on its ally.

The assassination renewed those accusations. Many major newspapers worldwide began to report on the Armenian massacres again and on the fact that not only had Germany failed to prevent its ally from committing those acts, but also sheltered the perpetrators.

To counter the adverse publicity surrounding the case, Weimar officials resorted to every kind of strategy to hasten the proceedings and the trial and rid themselves of that "troublesome foreigner" ("lästigen Ausländer") Tehlirian. By reducing the political significance of the case and emphasizing its criminal aspect, they managed to obtain an acquittal and summarily deport the defendant before a proper appeal could be filed."[6]

The German courts would even go further to lay this case to rest. At the conclusion of the trial, the court transcript would be published. The actual court proceedings and what was actually published was not reflective of Tehlirian's testimony. It would seem that claims made by Tehlirian that could lead to further investigation were omitted. In fact this practice of omitting testimony from the transcript was not limited to only Tehlirian's testimony.

In a letter dated June 9/13, 1921, from Georg Elgard, Stenographer, was sent to one of the witnesses at the requested of Dr. v. Gordon, Head of the Classified Justice Council. A certified translation from German to English done by Mike Bortscheller (ATA Member #263976) is as follows:

Georg Elgard

Grunewald-Berlin, Humboldtstrasse 13
June 9/13, 1921.

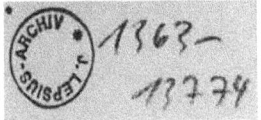

Seal: Archive
Handwriting: 1363-13774 (1)

Urgent!

Dear (illegible)

I am sending the statements made by you before the court, as recorded by the stenographer, in the case of Mr. Salomon Teilirian, with the request to communicate them to Dr. v. Gordon, Head of the Classified Justice Council, to view the content and return them to me as soon as possible (rest of clause redacted), to the Office of Judicial Council Chief Dr. Werthauer, Berlin, no. 24, Friedrichstrasse 120.

This is an urgent matter because Dr. v. Gordon is going on leave and wants to have the manuscript printed before he does. You are aware that the stenographic report has to be published and promulgated.

Please note that the changes made by you may only affect reports

---

6   Osik Moses, *THE ASSASSINATION OF TALAAT PASCHA IN 1921 IN BERLIN -- A CASE STUDY OF JUDICIAL PRACTICES IN THE WEIMAR REPUBLIC* (Northridge, CA, California State University, Northridge, 2012) v – vi.

and supplements to the stenography to your own statements and I am not authorized to record any new information that may have been stated, but was omitted.

Thank you for your time.
Sincerely yours,

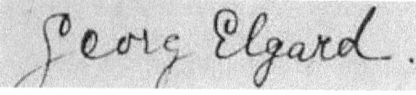

Page 6
Seal: Archive
Handwriting: 13774 (2)

...was victimized/sacrificed. The humanitarian reasons, the "Protection of Christians" were just an excuse. When Abdul Hamid signed the reform plan (illegible) to him by England, Russia, and France in 1895 and responded to it with a series of Armenian massacres, Lord Salisbury declared that the Armenian issue was settled in his opinion. (handwriting illegible). The 1894 massacre of Sassun caused by the reform plan cost 1000 Armenian lives, and that in 1895/96 - 100,000. The massacre of 1915-18 following the reform plan of 1913 claimed 1 million lives. This scale of 1894, 1895, and 1915: 1000, 100,000, and 1,000,000 was an event unmatched in its gruesomeness in the history of the world. In the meantime, the Cilician massacre of Adana claimed 25,000 victims in 1809.

Page 8
Seal: Archive
Handwriting: 13774 (3)

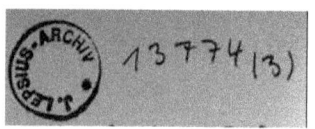

...Schefket Pascha, who was open to good advice, drafted a reform plan that entailed three general inspectorates - East, (illegible), West, with four sub-inspectorates. The Turkish general and deputy inspectors would each be assigned a European adviser. Mahmut Schefket Pascha wanted Englishmen as civil advisers and Germans as military advisers and approached Lord Grey with respect to the former. However, the German government didn't want to give Russia an occasion to intervene, and asked its ambassador Lichnowsky to raise the reform issue at the London Conference of Ambassadors at the beginning of June. The German government was convinced that Russia would not tolerate Englishmen in West Anatolia even as advisers unless Russians were appointed as advisers in East Anatolia and Frenchmen were appointed as advisers in Syria. Sassonow learned about the German's intentions in London and took measures in advance, authorizing the Russian ambassador from Giers in Constantinople to invite the local ambassador of the powers to a conference on the reform issue. At the same time, the Russian press (illegible) with a march of protest in Armenia unless the Armenian reforms demanded by the Berlin Congress were finally implemented.

To the chagrin of Ottoman Porte, the Armenian issue was raised before the six great powers yet again. An "Administration of East Anatolia by England", as you, honorable Emir, believe, would be tantamount to a waiver of Ottoman sovereignty and would unleash immediate war between Russia and England. This is all regarding your first "fact". Now to the second.

The committee sent Jhsan Bey to Smyrna at the beginning of May 1914 to organize a movement against the Greeks together with Vali. The outcome? Over 50,000 Greeks were driven away from the coastal areas, forced to flee to the islands or Piraeus. Their homes, land, tobacco and fig cultures were taken over by Mohadjirs (refugees from Macedonia). The Greek threat of war, the warning of the powers and the depletion of tax sources of the wealthy area Aidin brought the Porte to reflection. Talast Bey traveled around the area to...

Page 9

Seal: Archive
Handwriting: 13774 (4)

...Dr. Niemeyer, Defendant of the Classified Council: Isn't it true? The Armenians were the last Christians in the region enslaved by the Ottomans. All Balkan nations and other previously enslaved peoples had liberated themselves from Ottoman rule one by one. To keep the Armenians from doing so as well, the (Ottoman Empire) decided to destroy them. Would this view be correct?

Dr. Lepsius, Expert: Count Wetternich, the German ambassador to Constantinople in 1910, wrote in a report dated June 30: The Armenians are done. The young Turkish mob is feverishly prepared for the moment when Greece will succumb to Turkey. Greek individuality forms Turkey's culture element. It will be destroyed just like the Armenian one. Turkification means to drive away or kill everything that isn't Turkish and take possession violently. These were Count Wetternich's predictions for the outbreak of a war with Greece.

Page 8

Seal: Archive, J. Lepsius
Handwriting: 1363-13774 (5)

..."Official Journal" proof that dispatch of the young Turkish committee had been decided on and that Talaat Pascha, the soul and strongest member of the committee (illegible) and didn't do anything to prevent it. There is filed evidence of this based on German and Turkish documents.

I've made these statements to show that the game of diplomacy led the powers to an outcome where first Abdul Hamid and then the Young Turks became suspicious of the Armenians, ultimately reaching the conclusion that the best thing to do was destroy the Armenians. This annihilation was described by eyewitnesses in thousands, even tens of thousands of ways, and you've heard these stories from their own mouths.

Dr. Werthauer, Defendant, Judicial Council: You said the game of diplomacy between Russia and England contributed to the Armenian annihilation (genocide). Why?

Dr. Lepsius, Expert: Because the Turks were afraid they wanted to be free, which would threaten Turkey's existence in Asia.

Dr. Werthauer, Defendant, Judicial Council: (illegible) had heard earlier the reason was that Turks were Muslim and Armenians were Christian, and the (illegible)

Dr. Lepsius, Expert: The ludicrous idea of creating a pan-Turkish, pan-Islamic kingdom, in which there was no room for Christians, was that of the committee and Enver Pascha.

Dr. Werthauer, Defendant, Judicial Council: So if you said "all-German", "all-Russian", or "all-Turkish", you would mean annihilating everything that wasn't completely Turkish.

Dr. Lepsius, Expert: Yes.

A search of the officially published transcript for the above testimony reveals that the testimony had been omitted. Further investigation into omitted testimony led to the discovery of a newspaper article printed on August 7, 1921 in the Oregon Daily Journal, just two months after Tehlirian acquittal.

"Why I Destroyed the Greatest Murderer of Modern Times"
The heartrending Plea Which Won the Acquittal of the Young Armenian Who Killed Talaat Pasha on the Streets of Berlin After Being Pursued Day and Night by the Vision of the Cruel Slaughter of His Mother and Relatives

TALAAT PASHA was Grand Vizier of Turkey and planned the Armenian massacres during the war.

Solomon Teilirian, a young Armenian, killed Talaat Pasha on the streets of Berlin on March 15, this year.

A German Jury has just acquitted Teilirian of the murder, ostensibly because he was not responsible for this act, but really because he was avenging the massacre of his mother, his family and nation.

On the witness stand Teilirian described how the Turks wronged and killed his mother and sisters before his eyes, killed all his other relations and massacred all the people of his town – Erzingan.

Then he told how the ghost of his mother appeared to him in a vision and reproached him for letting Talaat live. It was that vision which decided the jury to aquit him promptly.

In the following columns are printed Teilirian's full testimony as brought out with the help of Armenian interpreters – one of the most terrible stories of human agony ever told.

Teilirian is slight of stature and delicate looking; his face is narrow, his forehead high, his melancholy dark eyes lie deep in the shadow cast by heavy crescent-shaped brows.

When Teilirian justified his plea of "not guilty" by the statement that his conscience was quite untroubled, the judge asked him how that was possible. And Teilirian answered: "At least I have not slaughtered an entire nation."

The prosecuting attorney, Dr. Gollnick, then began his examination.

Q. Surely you must realize that to kill a man as you have done is wrong?

A. If it is wrong to kill one man, how much more wrong is it to instigate the killing of a million people?

Q. How do you know that Talaat Pasha was responsible for the massacres?

A. Every Armenian knows it.

Q. How?

A. Certain dispatches were made public after the war. If there had been any doubt as to the origin of the cold-blooded villainy which has plunged an entire race into its death throes, those telegrams suffice to fasten the guilt upon Talaat and upon Enver.

Q. Of what dispatches are you speaking?

A. On September 15, 1915, I know that Talaat Pasha wired to Aleppo: "The Government has decided, by command of the Djernet, completely to exterminate all the Armenians living in Turkey." To the same address was sent on March 17, 1916, the following message was sent: "Under the pretext that they will be looked after by the administration as exiles, all the children who have been collected and are being cared for must without exciting suspicion, on the orders of the War Minister, be seized and exterminated."

One of the dispatches sent out by Talaat after the Young Turk Committee had decided in April, 1915, that the entire Armenian population must be deported, read: "Their destination is the No-Where."

Q. What did that mean – the No-Where?

A. Just what the words say.

Q. The words might be construed as meaning that their destination was to be kept quiet?

A. No, it meant nothing of the sort. It meant that we were not really to be deported. We were to be extirpated. The meaning of "deportation" under Turkish rule means deportation into the Beyond – in brief, into the No-Where.

Q. Why do you believe that such messages were sent?

A. I was shown authentic copies of the messages at Saloniki, in 1919. We few Armenian survivors all know that they were true.

Q. You admit, do you not, that you are incapable of considering Talaat impartially?

A. Do historians consider Nero impartially? Or Pontius Pilate?

Or Judas? Yet Nero caused only one city to be burned, while Talaat is responsible for the murder in cold blood of a million people.

Q. Did Talaat, to your knowledge, kill anyone with his own hands?

A. I do not know of any such case.

Q. But you admit that you killed Talaat with your own hands, don't you?

A. No, I did not kill him with my own hands. I killed him with a pistol. The pistol was my instrument of punishing him as the Turkish soldiers who massacred my countrymen and women were Talaat's instruments of murder.

(The court room suddenly rang with loud and sustained applause. Teilirian's pointed answer had aroused the enthusiasm of the Armenians, and nothing would quench it. In vain the judge threatened to clear the court room. The applause had to run its course. Slowly it died away.)

Q. I will word my question differently. It was your intention to kill Talaat Pasha, was it not?

A. Yes, of course. He's dead, isn't he?

Q. Then you do admit your guilt?

A. I do not say so. I am not guilty. My conscience is serene and clear.

Q. When did you first conceive the idea of murdering Talaat Pasha?

A. About two months before the shooting my mother appeared to me in a dream or vision. I had gone to bed and some time in the middle of the night I thought I woke up feeling very cold and terrified. It was bright moonlight and all around me as far as I could see were bodies stretched on the ground. At first I thought they were sleeping, and then I remembered that they were the dead bodies of my countrymen, as I had seen them when I escaped with my life. Hundreds of them lay with their throats cut. There were women and young girls who had undergone every indignity and atrocity before they were put to death.

The more I watched the more clearly the dreadful details appeared to me. Babies whose brains had been dashed out were lying across their dead mothers' bodies. Women and children who had been slashed to pieces were lying in their own blood.

Old, white-bearded patriarchs, several of them priests, were lying there with agony still on their faces, for they had been tortured to death.

Then, as I looked, some of the bodies seemed to be rolling their eyes and others were pointing their hands at me.

And on top of a heap of corpses there rose a woman's figure. I looked and I saw that it was my mother. She was dressed as I last saw her, when the Turks took her away to kill her. The blood was streaming down her face and there was a great wound in her breast. Her face was as pale as a sheet and she looked at me with eyes that burned into me. She pointed her finger. I could scarcely endure it for I was mad with agony and terror. She opened her lips and spoke to me.

Q. What did your mother say to you?

A. She said, "My son, you know that Talaat Pasha murdered your nation. You know that he murdered your father and your mother, your brother and your sisters. You know that he is living here in Berlin, and yet you are making no effort whatever to avenge the innocent blood of your Armenian compatriots, shed by this fiend in human form. I am ashamed to think that I bore such a cowardly creature,"You are no longer a son of mine!"

Q. You say you heard your mother say this? Did you really hear her voice?

A. I believed that I heard it. It was not like an ordinary dream. I knew that I had gone to sleep, but I believed that I woke and saw a vision of my mother right there before me. I went to sleep again and woke very tired and I immediately felt that my mother had been in the room.

Q. Did you decide at once to obey your mother's suggestions?

A. No, but my mother's spirit appeared to me again and again. Day and night I was haunted by the vision of my slaughtered mother and family. I felt that I was being driven on by a stronger power to do the will of God.

Q. Describe how you felt?

A. I felt as I had a million times before, that it is an unspeakable shame that Christian nations who profess to believe in the Saviour's golden Rule should stand idly by. And see a Christian nation exterminated – exterminated with as little mercy as would be shown to noxious vermin.

Q. had you not formed a desire for revenge on Talaat Pasha before this?

A. After I had received proof that my father and mother and my whole family had been killed by Talaat's orders I had longed to kill him. I wandered through Germany in search of him, but he was hard to find, for he concealed himself skillfully. I had time for reflection, and I began to wonder whether I would be wrong to kill him just on account of the wrongs to my family. I even began to think that he might be a wrong-headed man who was forced into crime by his fanatical countrymen.

But the vision of my mother appeared to me and convinced me that I should strike for the sake of my massacred fellow-countrymen.

Q. When did you make your first move toward carrying out your mother's suggestion?

A. One day when I visited the Zoological Garden, in Berlin, I heard some people back of me speaking Turkish, and presently the name of Talaat Pasha was spoken in addressing one of the party. I turned and recognized Talaat Pasha from pictures which I had seen of him. He was accompanied by a handsome and elegant young lady.

Q. did you decide then and there to murder him?

A. I hardly know. I only know that seeing at close range like that the man at whose door all the Armenian abominations can be laid stirred me as I have never been stirred before. My heart felt as if it was bursting. There he stood, smiling and speaking amiably with his companion the way any normal, decent-minded, kindhearted man would have done. I saw him stroke the head of a monkey, and when the keeper told him the animal as sick and had not long to live he actually showed concern. Think of it! The man who calmly asked, when telegraphic reports concerning the Armenian deportations began to come in, "How many are there still alive? Would show pity for a monkey because he was doomed soon to die.

I tell you, the blood pounded in my veins and hammered in my brain. And it came to me that it was a monstrous, a preposterous injustice that this man should be alive and happy, with an undisturbed conscience when the bones of millions of his victims lay bleaching in the desert sand or rotting at the bottom of the sea.

Q. But you said before that your conscience was untroubled, and yet you murdered him? How do you explain that?

A. The task has to be done. Fate assigned me the duty to do it. That's all.

Q. What do you mean by that – the task had to be done?

A. So long as Talaat Pasha was alive there was the possibility of his return to Turkey and to power. That would have been equivalent to the signing of the death warrant of every Armenian who had escaped so far. The fangs of the adder had to be drawn. It was a man's duty to draw them. I acted as the adder's dentist, and that is all.

Q. Then you admit that your resolution to kill Talaat hardened after you had seen him at the Zoological Garden?

A. Yes, I realized it had to be done.

Q. What move did you make next?

A. I found out where he lived and rented a room in the Hardenbergstrasse, right opposite to Talaat's dwelling, so that I was bale to observe him all the time.

Q. And then?

A. I was walking up and down my room one day when I saw Talaat leave his house. I was undecided what to do. Suddenly I heard the voice of my mother again very distinctly, telling me to cast aside my weakness and indetermination and to play my part like a man. Then I opened my trunk and took out my pistol and ran down the street after Talaat. When I caught up to him I walked up to him and covered him with my pistol. He could not escape me. I said to him, "Talaat Pasha, you shall have the same mercy you gave my dear ones and my countrymen – no more. My dead mother has commanded me to execute you – murderer of a nation, Coward that you are, you ran away from Turkey because you feared that justice would overtake you. Here and there through your wanderings I followed you, and at last I have found you. To-day, now, you die, I shoot you down as I would a dog!"

I fired at him once and missed him. I fired again immediately and he dropped dead.

He hated to die, for he had great wealth, many women and he still hoped to return to Turkey and rule as grand Vizier.

Q. What did you do after shooting Talaat?

A. First of all, I covered myself that he was really dead. I made sure that there was no fear of his coming back to life.

Q. And then?

A. I threw the pistol away and ran in the direction of the Fasanenstrasse.

Q. Why did you do that – run?

A. Oh, I dreaded getting caught in a crowd. I dislike mobs.

Q. But you didn't escape the crowd, did you?

A. No. People seemed to grow up out of the ground around me like mushrooms. They seemed very angry. Several-men began beating me. One man tried to stop the others, but they pushed him aside and struck at me again and again.

Q. Did they hurt you?

A. I didn't feel the blows. I was too much excited – too passionately excited. But I disliked seeing their hot, perspiring, anger-distorted faces so close to mine.

Q. What happened after then?

A. I was taken into custody.

Q. You made no resistance?

A. No.

Q. Had you hoped to make your escape after killing Talaat?

A. No. I did nothing wrong. There was nothing to be ashamed of.

Q. You had made no preparations for leaving Germany quickly after the murder?

A. Certainly not.

Q. You must have known that the police would get you?

A. If I had thought about it at all I would have known that, of course. But, you see, I didn't think about it. I had a certain work to do and I did it. It is all very simple.

Q. Where did you get the 12,000 marks which you had about your person when arrested?

A. My father was a very wealthy merchant. I carried 10,000 marks with me when I was driven from home. There is hidden treasure at home now, waiting to be unearthed. Some day I may be able to get it.

Q. But 12,000 marks is a very large sum. How is it that you did not spend what money you had in the course of your wanderings?

A. I did spend a lot of money – far more than the sum I still have or had.

Teilirian was then examined by the attorneys for the defense. Dr. von Gordon asked:

Q. Is Solomon Teilirian your right name?

A. Yes.

Q. Where were you born?

A. In Bekaritsch. But when I was quite a small boy my parents moved to Erzingan.

Q. How big was the family?

A. We were three boys and three girls.

Q. Do you remember Turkish persecution as a child?

A. My parents spoke of it to me as going on elsewhere. But our town was not molested until May, 1915. Then, by order of the Young Turk Committee, the schools were closed and a manifesto was read, stating that all prominent citizens – among whom my father was included – were to be deported. They were led away and butchered by the Turkish guards. My father was taken away to be killed before the rest of us were driven out into the desert.

Q. What did your mother do?

A. Like everybody else, we bought an ox-cart and a donkey and loaded the cart with such household necessities as simple cooking utensils, blankets, extra garments and all the provisions it would carry. We realized that we might be separated and my mother distributed among us what paper money we had in the house. Gold and silver, as well as valuables such as jewels and family heirlooms, we buried under the cellar of our house at dead of night.

Q. Where were you to be taken to?

A. We were not told. We had travelled only a day and a half when the guards attacked us and plundered us.

Q. Did this frighten you?

A. We had expected it, of course. That is why we had hidden away our principal treasures in the depths of the earth and had placed the paper money in odd places about our persons, where we hoped the guards would not look for it.

Q. What odd places, for instance?

A. Well, I had placed some of my paper money in between the soles of my shoes and the insoles, some in the lining of my cap, some in my vest lining.

Q. And the Turkish soldiers did not find your money?

A. Not the paper money – no. Some small coins they found which we jingled in our pockets purposely to mislead them. That they found and took.

Q. What did the Turks do after plundering you?

A. The caravan was about to start again when we became aware that there was a panic in front of us. I went to the top of a little hill and saw what was happening in the forward part of the caravan.

I saw five hundred Armenian men – about that number – tied together with ropes. The Turks then drove them into the river with swords and bayonets, some of the Armenians tried to struggle toward the shore and the Turks drove them back with swords and clubs.

Scores of women were then treated in an atrocious manner. Many of the older women and children were beaten to death and then left lying in their blood.

The prettiest girls were roped together and carried off to be sold into slavery in the harems of the Turks.

Presently it was the turn of my part of the column to be attacked. My brothers and I prepared to defend my mother and sisters, but we were unarmed and were practically helpless. I saw one Turkish brute split open the head of one of my brothers with an axe when he tried to save my youngest sister from the Turk's clutches. What became of my other brothers I do not know. Someone struck me on the head. Unhappily I was knocked senseless at once. Oh – I cannot go on!

(Teilirian suddenly interrupted himself and broke into sobs. It was the only time during the trial that the accused man broke down.)

I beg of you to spare me the agony of telling you in detail what happened. I would rather die on the spot than have to tell of the dreadful deeds that were done there – in my presence – while I was helpless to hinder what was going on!

Q. For your own good I must insist that you tell us the rest.

A. I was too weak to rise, much less to offer any resistance, and so I was forced to look on in half-consciousness while those devils violated my mother and sisters and then beat them to death. After that I fainted away.

Q. How long was it before you regained consciousness?

A. I cannot tell definitely, of course. But I think about forty-eight hours must have elapsed before I regained consciousness.

Q. What gives you the impression of that length of time?

(Teilirian could not reply to this question. The hunted, haunted look in hi eyes became intensified. His lips twitched. Counsel were obliged to give him time for rest. Dr. Niemeyer then took up the questioning.)

Q. When you awoke were you alone?

A. There were lots and lots of people lying around – as far as the eye could see they lay, under the white moonlight, asleep as I thought. Suddenly I realized that they were all dead.

Q. How did you realize this – was the moonlight strong enough to see by?

A. Oh, the moon was bright enough. But I did not need to look closely. I did not look closely. I knew – (Teilirian broke off for a moment and moistened his lips). I knew by the odor. The death-stench was all around me. It was that, too, that told me I had been unconscious for at least two days and two nights. It was that, too, I think, that finally brought me to.

Q. What did you do?

A. I crawled away from that field of unutterable horror as soon as I could. I think horror and disgust lashed me on and gave me the strength to move on which otherwise I might have lacked. I have only a very vague recollection of how long it took me to get away. I seemed to crawl along among corpses for an eternity. But when dawn broke I was clear of that field of decay and death and had reached a small village. No one wanted to give me shelter because the offense of succoring an Armenian is punishable with death. But an old Turkish woman took pity on me. She gave me refuge, hid me away and bathed and dressed my head-wounds. As soon as I was able to travel she supplied me with all the food I could carry and I set out at night.

Q. Where did you go?

A. I had disguised myself as as Kurd, hoping to make my way into Persia. But I lost my way. Finally I fell in with two other Armenians who had escaped death in pretty much the same way that I had.

Q. And then?

A. We wandered about for several weeks, traveling by night, sleeping in the woods through the day and living on herbs and wild berries and edible roots. Finally we found that we had crossed into the Russian lines and we knew that we were safe at last.

Q. Did any of the people in Erzingan escape massacre but yourself?

A. I learned afterward that only three escaped alive out of 20,000. Twenty-three of my own near relatives perished. I heard this from the other two survivors whom I met afterward in Russia.

Q. How long did you remain in Russia?

A. For about a year. Then Erzingan fell into Russian hands and I returned to my home town, hoping to be able to salvage our buried treasure. But I was unable to do so. Not a stone of our house was left standing. Only a few families remained – some twenty souls in all – and they had been forced to embrace the Mohammedan faith in order to save their lives.

Q. What happened then?

A. The Russians were driven away again and I was obliged to run. The Turks began to hunt down and massacre the few survivors of our race who were living in the empire.

Q. Where did you go then?

A. I wandered on foot into Persia, where, after nine months, I reached the British lines. Afterward I worked my way to Saloniki, where I knew I would meet some of my countrymen and perhaps a survivor of my own family. When peace was declared I went to Germany.

Q. Did you go with the intention of killing Talaat Pasha?

A. No. it seemed to me that my footsteps were guided by a higher power.

Q. Did you know that Talaat Pasha was direct author of the Armenian massacres – not merely an agent of the Sultan?

A. Yes. I was shown a letter in his own handwriting in which he said, "The Armenian nation must be exterminate in the interests of the future of Turkey and the Young Turk party. As long as any Armenians survive as an organized community they will rebel against us and embroil us with foreign Powers. The memory of the old massacres will always serve as an excuse to incite them to rise against us or to bring outsiders to their help. We need their territory for our own population and for our allies.

"The inhabitants of the Armenian settlements will be escorted by our troops into desert places and there will be lost to sight and cease to trouble us and the world."

Teilirian's testimony alone was sufficient to convince the jury that he ought not to be punished for his act. Other witnesses summoned fully corroborated his heartrending evidence concerning the Armenian massacres. Ferri Baschian, the wife of an Armenian cigarette maker and one of the three survivors, of the Erzingan massacres, gave a particularly moving story of the dreadful scenes she passed through.

Professor Lepsius, a well-known German historian and expert on the East, gave a general confirmation of Teilirian's story and described the Armenian massacre policy carried out by the Turks in the late war. The German public had hitherto been ignorant of these massacres and this testimony produced amazement in court.

General Liman von Sanders, the German military commander in Turkey during the World War, sat through the trial with the pretty blonde "widow" of Talaat, who was walking with him when Teilirian shot him. The general gave rather shamefaced evidence seeking to excuse the Turkish Government.

Teilirian had three lawyers. The second, Dr. Werthauer, made a particularly eloquent defense. He compared Teilirian to Willhelm Tell, Switzerland's great hero, who killed his country's oppressor.

"Could any court of justice be found on earth, now or then, that would condemn Wilhelm Tell?" Dr. Werthauer demanded of the jury. "You know that that would be quite impossible. You know that no twelve right-minded men, possessing even an elementary sense of higher justice, would have condemned Wilhelm Tell. And compared to Teilirian's provocation to killing Talaat how insignificant was the provocation suffered by Wilhelm Tell? Gessler, to punish Tell for his patriotism, commanded him to shoot an apple from the head of his – Tell's – son with a bow-and-arrow, a form of shooting in which Wilhelm Tell was an expert. Wilhelm Tell seemingly acquiesced, but instead of shooting the apple from his own son's head, he waited for Gessler in a sequestered spot and sped the arrow through the tyrant's heart instead.

"And now, take the case of Teilirian. If you require a personal motive, gentlemen of the jury, Teilirian had it in abundance. It was not the possible death of one of his relatives that confronted him. He had actually witnessed the doing to death under the most revolting circumstances of five of his nearest relatives, his mother, his two brothers, his three sisters – the women, naturally, suffering the usual outrage before being killed.

"But to Teilirian's undying honor be it said that the doing to death of his own relatives was not chief motive in killing the monster in human form who called himself Talaat. Not even the foul wrongs sustained by his entire race formed the principal motivation for his deed; rather he hoped to prevent a recurrence of the Armenian horrors, to save what remained of his own people from Talaat's abominations in the future, in the event that that future should again invest Talaat with power for mischief.

"Under such circumstances it seems almost a travesty of justice to even arraign this man before a tribunal. His innocence is so self-evident."

Dr. von Gordon, Teilirian's first counsel, was the most famous of the three able attorneys delegated by Germany to defend the Armenian patriot. Dr. von Gordon achieved considerable notoriety before the war because of his willingness to undertake the defense of foreign spies before the imperial courts.

Teilirian's defense was conducted by von Gordon along entirely different lines. Dr. von Gordon cited paragraph 51, of the Penal code, which states that no man shall be held accountable for a crime committed in a state of mental irresponsibility or at a moment when his freedom of will has been impaired by untoward circumstances or undue emotional strain.

"As a famous writer has put it," von Gordon said, "a man who does not lose his mind in suffering certain injuries has no mind to lose."

Compared to the impassioned fervor of the three men summoned to defend Teilirian, the arraignment of the persecuting attorney, Dr. Gollnick, seemed weak and ineffectual.

"We must not lose sight of the fact," he said, "that this crime was the direct outcome of political hatred. Turkey was Germany's staunch ally during the war and Talaat Pasha was one of Turkey's greatest citizens. That he was done to death while seeking refuge in Germany, which along with his own country he had so ably served in the past, makes it imperative for us to deal courageously with his murderer, no matter how unpopular an unfavorable the verdict may be."

Dr. Gollnick's words made little impression upon the people in the court room. The only persons who seemed to be seriously affected by them was the widow of Talaat Pasha and her friends.

When all the testimony was in the jury withdrew. They were out only one hour and fifteen minutes. They returned with a verdict of "not guilty" on the ground that Teilirian's wrongs and sufferings had made him not responsible for his act. The Armenians in court went wild with joy. They applauded, hurrahed, clapped their hands. They crowded around Teilirian. Some embraced him, some kissed his hands. Teilirian, smiling sadly, his face a trifle flushed, received the ovation in dignified silence.

Like the search of the stenographers request to the witness did not appear in the official published transcript, the same held true for the testimony published on August 7, 1921 in the Oregon Daily Journal.

One explanation to this mystery might answered in the 1971 recording my father made of Shahan Natalie:

SHAHAN: I told those under my supervision that I am going to Berlin… I mean Rome. It seemed that, over there, in a hotel, you know… Over there, since a lot of Turks had gotten together, overfilled the place, there was a conference. Undoubtedly, it was going to be held at one of the best hotels, you know. I wanted to find that hotel and go. It might be a good opportunity for me to recognize Talaat. Everything, had to be directed at recognizing Talaat, to make sure we don't kill someone other than him. Because killing someone else other than Talaat, would simply be a catastrophe, according to our decision, which was to that the list should start with Talaat to resonate throughout the entire world. Do you understand? And so? At the same time, after assassinating Talaat, there is no escaping. He is going to stand on the body.

KHACHIG: This is the decision.

SHAHAN: The decision is this. To let the police arrive, catch and take you away. And there must be a trial! A trial! In a court! If the first time, upon assassination… If the second time, during the trial… a lot of propaganda against the Turks and in our favor. So that… All we needed was a brave boy. See? And there were a lot of them. But it happened to be Soghomon's destiny. It was a matter of luck, you know. And Soghomon – oh, how I love his soul – just as instructed… Only what he did was, after firing a shot, when he shot at him, and he fell, he stood there next to him with the gun in his hand. Then [makes a sound of kissing] he kisses the gun and places it on the dead body. And he stands there, but… It was a beautiful noon weather. On the 15th of March. A wonderful spring day! Wonderful! Such nice weather. He looks around. It was quite a wide street, you know, busy! He stood on that street and sees passers-by, you know. There are people! It was a busy one. But every one of them remained frozen. And it was quite a human thing to do, because they didn't realize what had happened. All they saw is that someone fired a shot, the other fell. And he stood there. Everyone did the same thing. What just happened? And carefully… The thing… and it happened instantly. When something like this happens, the assailant usually flees, opposite to his instructions not to flee. And it was at the corner of the street. The street is like this. This street was like this street. It was at this corner that he shot him dead.

KHACHIG: Do you remember the name of the street, grandfather?

SHAHAN: Of course, I know it. I have a photo. So, he runs away. As soon as he starts running, the people who had stood there frozen, all of them shouted: "Murderer! Murderer! Murderer!" They shouted: "Catch him!" So, everybody chased him. Those running towards him, those running after him and so on. This boy is crazy! Why are you running? But, you see, it's also a matter of luck. It's a sheer matter of luck. The mission was so divinely just that every unplanned incident that you didn't expect… was such that makes you think that there was divine intervention ["God's finger was in it"]. As a result of his escape, those running toward him and those from behind catch him and begin punching Soghomon's head. They are beating up Soghomon. And because of that beating he sustains wounds on his head and body, stiches and so on and so forth. And so, they restrain him. They catch the murderer. In the meantime, the corpse is lying farther away. The police arrive and take him away. Now what happens is that when they take him to the police station, they dress his wound on the forehead, you see. He is covered with blood and badly bruised. They dress him at the police station. And when they interrogate him for the first… When they conduct the first interrogation, he says I killed, he says. He says it in such a manner in response to their question… He knows only a few words in German, you see.

KHACHIG: Oh, so, he didn't speak German.

SHAHAN: Where would he know it from? Neither he spoke nor I. At least I was taking some German classes in those days. I had hired a female tutor who taught me and so on... so I could know. You aren't always accompanied by someone. And so, he knew so much as to say while they were beating him: "Ich ausländer, er ausländer," which means 'I'm a foreigner, non-German' I'm an ausländer. He wants to say, he [Talaat] is not a German, he is a foreigner, an ausländer. That is to say, it's none of your business! I killed... Yes, what?

KHACHIG: All right, but did they understand what he was saying?

SHAHAN: What?

KHACHIG: What did they do? What was their response to what he said?

SHAHAN: No. Now look. During the first interrogation he gives such an answer that, you see, that it appeared to be premeditated murder. An intentional one, a planned one. Got it? And if you have premeditated it, then it's a grave crime. See? Now! There was an interpreter, since he didn't know, right? They find an Armenian interpreter, bring him over. A young man, who Soghomon knows, you know, in Berlin.

KHACHIG: Luck.

SHAHAN: No, it was not by luck. When they came... because back then, in Berlin, there were Armenians, too, Armenian youth and so on.

SYLVA: No, I understand. But the police brought him. How did they know that... How did they know the police were going to bring him?

SHAHAN: No. That wasn't... It wasn't anything particular. It happened by chance. So, there were Armenians... "Are you Armenian." "Yes." "Do you know German? Let's go! Interpret for us." That's how the police...

SYLVA: Ok.

SHAHAN: And so... This guy tells him you shouldn't say it that way. And then later, in court... Then the second time, when the legal defense... when the attorneys... We hired them and so on, they were there. At that time, it's not going to be said that it is "premeditate," otherwise you'll be found guilty. Instead! Instead... without having it in my mind, but because Talaat is the one responsible for the massacre of my entire family: my father, sister, mother, brothers. When I saw him... I don't know.

SYLVA: I don't remember. Insanity.

SHAHAN: And a story, you know, an emotional one, that if it were premeditated, then it is immediately implied to have been organized. And our plan is to make it appear to be on personal grounds. It's not organized.

KHACHIG and SYLVA: It's an act of revenge.

SHAHAN: Since it's an act of revenge just on personal grounds. Because if it is discovered that there is an organization, and that this man has been a tool in the hands of that organization, then our subsequent missions would become more difficult. The next one in our project it won't come to an end. You see?

SYLVA: That's right. Two more were left.

SHAHAN: Yes. So, during the second interrogation, which was interpreted, it was explained to him that he must not say it was premeditated. When they ask him again, the police, he says: "I don't remember what I said. I don't know what I said with my head bandaged, my head was broken" so on and so forth. "I don't remember what I said." Let's say...

SYLVA: Amnesia.

SHAHAN: Yes. And so, they removed the "intentionally." It's not a murder! It's a personal revenge. And his attorneys... The attorneys... In all of Germany, we hired Germany's three most notable attorneys. And those days were favorable for us, during Talaat's times. These remarkable attorneys advised him on what to say, you know... because these attorneys believed that he had done the right thing, you see. And he should be set free. There is no such a thing in Germany. This is not the old Kaiser's Germany, right? And by luck, that those were not the Kaiser's time, it was the republic, right? The war had been over, hadn't it? It was 1921. And... the thing... the court... the court minister... the court minister was a... our notable German... Lepsius! The court minister was Lepsius' nephew (sister's son). And the Prosecutor General, who was from the Government, that Prosecutor General had been a student of these attorneys, our defense attorneys, which ties his [Prosecutor General's] hands with loyalty to them. You see? Even though on the day... he demands punishment with his stuff, he does this... He is the... District Attorney. So, these are the circumstance we have. And a dream in order to... No... with... He is not responsible, they [the attorneys] made up a dream for him [he laughs]. And it's mentioned in his book, in his memoirs. "At night I saw my mother in a dream," he says. "At night, I saw my mother in a dream."

KHACHIG: Vratsyan says that supposedly he had seen a dream.

SYLVA: No, it was not Vratsyan.

SHAHAN: Soghomon says that.

KHACHIG: Soghomon! Sorry. Soghomon.

SHAHAN: Yes. "I saw a dream." And he says: "In my dream, my mother said: 'You saw Talaat and didn't kill him. You are not my son.'" You underatand? So, Talaat from Bolis [Constantinople] – his [Soghomon's] brothers, this one, that one, his father, mother, his family... It is true that his, Soghomon's brothers were killed, his mother was killed. But he mixes in his father, whereas he has a store in Romania. Do you understand? He has a coffee store. But this is how we had the story created. The whole purpose was to make it appear as a stand-alone case. A person who acted on his own.

Soghomon Tehlirian's memoirs were published in Cario in 1956. The author of the preface, Vahan Navassartian, a member of the executive bureau of the Armenian Revolutionary Federation (A.R.F.) wrote:

> The memoirs of Soghomon Tehlirian are not the true and full story of the death of Talaat. The time has not yet come to give the public the true history of terrorism. That will be the work of the next generation. But the future historian of the great April catastrophe will be able to find some important document and the ramifications of the attack on Talaat in the Party's secret archives. Tehlirian's memoirs will be able to serve as a basis for this story...[7]

In the chapters that follow, we will open to the public for the first time in almost 97 years parts of the archive of Shahan Natalie, which are the secret archives of the Party Navassartian refers to, and that the A.R.F. has never before been able to access.

---

7   Jacques Derogy, *Resistance & Revenge* (New Brunswick, NJ, Transaction Publishers, 2013) 104.

Chapter 2

The Birth of Nemesis

The story which Soghomon had shared with the court closely resembled that of my grandfather's who, at the age of 11, had lost his father to the 1894-1896 Hamidian massacres. This is the most appropriate starting point to introduce Operation Nemesis. Shahan had shared this story with Soghomon before Talaat's assassination.

Shahan Natalie was born Hagop Der Hagopian in December of 1884. He was the middle child and the only boy of five children. His father was a tax collector and mother, as almost all Armenian woman of the time, a housewife. Their family also included Hagop's grandfather, who at the time of the massacre that took his life, was 105-years-old.

Just prior to the attack on Hagop's village of Husenik, Harpout, his father gathered the family and instructed them that Kurdish bandits would be coming to their village. He explained that when they arrived, all the children were to hold hands and walk to the cemetery on the hilltop, which overlooks their village. They were supposed to leave the front door of their home open, lest it should be broken down. From the cemetery, they could watch the Kurdish bandits pillage the homes. After the pillage, the family was instructed to return to their home, where their mother would make bread with the well hidden flour. Having had a meal, they were going to rebuild their lives once again. My grandfather told us that pillaging by Kurds were common, however, never before had it claimed lives, as far as he could remember.

Hagop Der Hagopian and his father Garabed

As anticipated, the Kurdish bandits showed up the day after. However, it was not a customary pillage, as everyone had been expecting. Rather than allowing the Armenians to walk away and allow the bandits to take whatever they want without harming anyone, shots were fired, and the Armenians were being brutally massacred. Before he could hold hands with his sisters, per his father's instruction, Hagop was snatched away by a neighbor, an older Armenian boy. Hagop's father had been watching this boy's family while his father was in America. Hagop was then forcibly pulled away and taken to the plantation of a wealthy Turk, for whom the neighbor boy worked. Behind high walls, in the garden, there were many frightened Armenians hiding from the massacre. Hagop remained on the plantation for three days before he was allowed to return to his home.

Similar massacres had happened in the surrounding villages, as well as the city of Harpoot, where there was an American College run by American missionaries. The Americans bore witness to the blood bath and their testimony was published in the December 16, 1895 issue of *The Saint Paul Globe* newspaper:

KILLED BY KURDS.
SLAUGHTER OF ARMENIAN AT HARPOOT STARTED BY BRIGANDS.
SOILDIERS STOOD IDLY BY
WHILE THE MOSLEMS RABBLE JOINED IN THE MASSACRE.
MISSIONARIES LOST THEIR ALL.
Protection By the Government as Sham-Two Score Villages Sacked.
BOSTON, Mass., Dec. 15.—Letters at hand from correspondents at Harpoot, Eastern Turkey, gave detailed account of the scenes and incidents attending the recent massacre of Armenians there, as well as of the massacre itself.

"The first excitement," says the writer, "over Turkish atrocities was dying out, and tranquility was pretty well restored, when the Dersim Kurds began to plunder the villages right and left, and six of which were in the immediate vicinity of Harpoot, the nearest one being within two hours of the city. The whole city was tossed with apprehension, and citizens were expecting an attack. Some said the Kruds had government sanction, other that the Turks in the city were in league with them. The Kurds, while plundering the villages, were heard to say 'We are going to Harpoot.' The Turks in the city said, 'The Kurds are coming here to plunder the Christian quarter.' One Agha, when appealed to to use means for the defense of the city, said, 'Why should we protect the Giaours? Let them be killed.'

"The governor of Malatia telegraphed here that 2,000 Kurds had come there and that he could not cope with them. That threw the responsibility upon the Harpoot government. The leading men of Arabrik went to the governor and asked for protection. They were treated with contempt. These disturbances could not have happened if strong orders had been sent to the governors general to preserve order at any cost.

"The terror and distress of the devastated villages can scarcely be pictured. Those who escaped with their live have been stripped of everything else with winter just at their doors. Where the Kurds alone have devastated, the loss of life is not great, but the TURKS KILL IN COLD BLOOD and in

The Birth of Nemesis

any way suggested by the arch fiend himself.

"The idea of an uprising among the Armenians is absurd. They are in terror of their lives. They are prepared to surrender all their possessions if only their lives can be spared."

Another writer, describing the attack upon the city, says: "The first attack began on Sunday, Nov. 10, by a few Kurds. These were easily driven off. Monday there was another attack in the morning, which was also repelled. Later Monday the Kurds and Turks from the surrounding region attacked Husenik. Several were killed. The soldiers went down the road to meet the, and some of the principal Moslems also went down. They had a conference with the Kurds. Then the bugle blew, and the soldiers, led by the commander, withdrew to the city, dragging their cannon in a very leisurely fashion. After the soldiers had reached the city the Kurds and Turks came in yelling and firing. The soldiers made no attempt to stop them. They fired tier cannon once harmlessly into the air towards the city and then over the heads of the enemy. The Turks of the city joined the plunder and attack. The Armenian school was first set on fire, then the greater part of the Christian quarter. Christians were shot down everywhere.

"I saw all these things myself, for I watched things with a field glass until it became perfectly plain that the whole thing was definitely planned and arranged. The Christians had give up their harms and cast themselves on the protection of the government. No Christian fired on the assailants. The MISSIONARIES TOOK REFUGE in the girls' school until that was attacked, and the mission house of Rev. O. P. Allen and wife was burned and the school set on fire. Then they gathered in the yard, prepared to die. Dr. Barnum spoke to the military commander and he sent soldiers, but only two remained to protect the missionaries, and they demanded money or they would go away as their comrades had done. The missionaries decided to go into the college building. As they left the school yard, a Turk fired upon them from across the yard twice, first at Mr. Allen and then at Rev. C. Frank Gates, but he was a very bad marksman and no one was hit. The family of Mr. Gates was the last to leave the yard. Soon after the missionaries got into the school building the officers sent for them to come out. The missionaries refused to do so, saying they had no confidence in the chief and the Mufti, and if they wished to offer protection they could protect them where they were. If they did not, the missionaries would die there.

"At last the Alai Bey (Mohomet Bay), a Circassian, arrived. He was the first and only man who acted as if he meant to do anything for the missionaries. He called back the soldiers who had been sent by the military commander. The missionaries at once came out and began to fight the fires that had been sent. Alai Bey helped them. The house of President Gates, the house of Dr. Barnum, the normal school building and the college building were saved, but eight of the buildings were burned. All the houses were plundered and the soldiers made no attempt to stop it. The missionaries were stripped of everything by the clothes they wore. The Turks of the city were very much disappointed that any of the missionary buildings were spared. Tuesday the Kurds returned to the attack. An order came to stop them and permission was given to SHOOT THE KURDS.

"When the order came, two soldiers laid down their arms. None Kurds were killed that day at Mezreh and five at Harpoot. That finished the attack of the Kurds, but there was still danger from the Turks, and there is now.

"The missionaries put themselves under the protection of the government again, but the protection was a sham. They and the leading men of the city and the Ulema or hierarchy of religion assured Dr. Barnum that no Krud should enter the city. The chief of defense told Dr. Barnum that until he was cut to pieces not a Kurd should enter the city, and not a hair of the head of the missionaries be injured, but he stood quietly looking on while the attack was made and offered not even a show of resistance. The missionaries had the best possible opportunity for observing the hollowness of the professions."

As a result of the massacres, the writer adds, "from Diarbekir to Talatia, Arabkir to Peri, the whole region is a desolation. I counted twenty-one ruined villages, and there are said to be thirty-five of them in the Char Sandjak alone. The missionaries my not escape with their lives."

To give a better idea as to what was going on prior to the attack on Hagop's village and why the world allowed such inhumane acts to go unchecked, a letter sent to any news media willing to listen was published in *The Leighton News* (Leighton, Alabama) front page, on January 3, 1896, tells a very revealing insight of world politics:

EUROPE'S DISGRACE.

Holding Up Hands in Holy Horror While Butchery Goes On.

A Voice from the Vale of Blood that Should Make the Civilized World Ashamed – Is America Entirely Blameless?

LONDON, Dec. 30. - Dr. Henry S. Lunn, editor of the Review of the Churches, and Percy W. Bunting, editor of the Contemporary Review, have addressed the following communication to "All Editors of England and America:"

"We enclose extracts from a letter from a private friend who spent several months of this year in Armenia and who is one of the first authorities on the question, as indeed you would admit were we at liberty to publish his name. May we beg you to insert these in the next issue of your paper?

"Yours, faithfully,
[Signed] "HENRY S. LUNN,
"Editor of the Review of the Churches .
"PERCY W. BUNTING,
"Editor of the Contemporary Review."
Any allusion to Armenia upsets me. I am ashamed, excited, indignant when I think of what I saw in that country and of the confidence with which I consoled quailing women and weeping men with hopes that England would see them through their difficulties, and the words of heartfelt thanks they

uttered, often on their knees in the fields or on the hillsides; and the childlike messages of anticipatory gratitude which they asked me to deliver to the English people new burn and rankle within me like an envenomed wound.

"The European powers are playing a farcical representation round the graves of a Christian people. If conduct similar to theirs were to be pursued by an individual in private life, it would be visited with social ostracism, and would brand him with an indelible Cain's mark of infamy. Fancy a man's neighbors parading about the doors of his house while he and his children rush frantically from room to room and from window to window, imploring them to save them from the devouring flames. We have pity on a rat, if we hear of its protracted and hopeless efforts to escape from the burning, but men and women, boys and girls who are killed piecemeal are laughed at – this is what it has come to.

The governments of Europe are a spectacle to make angles weep. They guard the gates of Turkey so to say, solemnly declaring that whatever may happen to the Christians, however diabolically they may be tortured to death, nothing shall happen to the Turks – they at any rate must and will be preserved from harm. Is it a wonder then that the Turks should set about fulfilling their threat of wiping out Armenia in Armenian blood.

Every one knew that the threat would be fulfilled. Consuls reported to their governments that the departure of the European delegates from Moush would mark the beginning of the blood bath, and newspapers gave the prophecy publicity. Appeals to the public to insist on precautionary measures were multiplied, and at last mere verbal warning gave place to unmistakable signs and ominous preparations.

But diplomacy turned a deaf ear (the Armenians are nobody's kith and kin). Were they Greeks or Bulgarians, Magyars or Serb, they would have high and powerful protectors who talk of the primary duty of protecting brothers and Christians. Even Abysinians are brethren and orthodox when political calculations come in. But they are Armenians; and so none of these governments insisted on the execution or even dismissal of Zekki Pasha and the authors of the Sassoun savagery. Nay, they were decorated and honored by the sultan as an encouragement to others to go and do likewise.

And now others have gone out and have outeroded Herod, and no one seems shocked. People are only interested to get the latest news of Sivas or Trebizond, or wherever the latest massacres have occurred, at their breakfast table early. Few persons take even a remote interest in the Armenian question on the continent, and those few are the advocates of Turkey. The Austrian press, said to be paid by the Turkish government, impudently denies the Sassoun massacre and accuses the Armenians of having attempted to butcher the Kurds and Turks. The German press is the bearer of the same kind of culture to its readers, and in both those countries the public knows positively nothing about the present status of the Armenian question.

The Russian papers, beginning with the Novoya Vremyra, cracks jokes at the Armenians, and in the last numbers I have read, ask: "Why should we Russians sacrifice a single soldier for the sake of Armenian bankers an millionaires, whoare much better off than we are ourselves, to say nothing of

British and American agitators, who have so cleverly got up the Armenian comedy."

A couple of regiments of British soldiers or Cossacks is what is wanted. They would set matters right in a few days. But even if the whole English-speaking people should arise and demand this, would it be accepted?

Upon returning home three days later, my grandfather found his mother grieving over his father's beheaded corpse. Together they dragged the body of his beloved father to the family cemetery, where Hagop clawed the dirt with his bare hands to dig his father a proper grave. As he dug, the tips of his fingers wore down to his flesh and began to bleed. Once the body was entombed, Hagop's devastated mother had the partially orphaned boy take an oath on his father's grave to take revenge on those who had been responsible for their loss and do his utmost to make sure no one else would endure what was going to haunt him for the rest of his life.

A year after the gruesome murder of my great-grandfather, Hagop was sent to an orphanage in Constantinople to lighten the family's burden. More importantly, he was expected receive proper education that would one day help him fulfill the oath he took on his father's grave.

After studying for a year at Kharberd's Euphrates College, together with other orphans, Hagop was sent to the St. James Orphanage in Constantinople. He did not want to stay there, so he himself found an Armenian rug merchant living in New York to adopt him so he could attend the famed Berberian Academy, where he studied until 1900. His teacher was the Academy's director, Reteos Berberian, the noted pedagogue and philosopher.

The young Hagop's love of culture, art, beauty, goodness, truth and justice were imprinted in his very essence. In 1901, he returned to his birthplace, where for three years he served on the local school's teaching staff, at the same time studying the provincial dialect of Kharberd. This philological study earned him a special honor in Patriarch Madteos Izmirlian's literary competition. But the trauma from his father's brutal murder and the plight of the Armenian people always molded his decisions and activities. And he was soon to take active steps to fulfill his oath.

Hagop Der Hagopian - 1901

Chapter 3

Broken Promises of Reforms for the Ottoman Armenians

To better understand why the habitual pillaging of the Armenian population in the Ottoman Empire eventually transformed into the unbridled bloodbath of the Hamidian massacres that shook the European and the U.S. press, it is necessary to go a few years back, specifically the Russo-Turkish War of 1877-1878 and some events preceding it.

In 1860, prominent representatives of the Armenian intelligentsia, Krikor Odian, Nahapet Rusinian, Dr. Servichen, Diran Nazariantz, Nigoğayos Balyan, and Krikor Margosian, penned the Armenian National Constitution that defined the powers of the Armenian National Assembly and the Patriarch in the Ottoman Empire. It was sanctioned three years later by Sultan Abdülaziz. The Assembly was soon flooded with complaints from the provinces, requesting a resolution to the mistreatment from the Kurds, Turks, and Circassians. But no particular measures were taken.

A little more than a decade later, in 1876, Grand Vizier, Midhat Pasha (1822-1883) introduced the Ottoman Constitution. It was written by Krikor Odian (1834-1887), an advisor to the Grand Vizier and the above mentioned co-author of the Armenian National Constitution of 1863.[8]

The new Ottoman Constitution granted equal rights to all citizens without distinction of race or creed, abolished slavery, sanctioned independent judiciary based on civil (rather than religious) law, secured universal elementary education, and established a bicameral parliament, with a Senate appointed by the Sultan and a directly-elected Chamber of Deputies.

Krikor Odian

The Armenians hoped that this liberal Constitution would finally bring relief to the Christians. However, the support for the Constitution began to waiver when it became known that it granted equal rights to non-Muslims. The *softas* (fanatic religious students) who had been Midhat Pasha's supporters months earlier, became largely opposed.[9] The Constitution,

---

8 Kurkjian, Vahan M. (2008). A history of Armenia. Los Angeles, CA: Indo-European Publishing. p. 338.

9 Victor Roudometof (2001). Nationalism, Globalization, and Orthodoxy: The Social Origins of Ethnic Conflict in the Balkans. Greenwood Publishing Group. p. 87.

Ottoman Parliament 1877

unfortunately, survived only a few months. It was soon replaced by the absolute rule of the newly enthroned Sultan, Abdul Hamid II.[10]

On April 24, 1877, when hostilities broke out between Russia and Turkey, the harsh living conditions of Armenians had already reached a peak. At the onset of the Russo-Turkish War (1877-1878), the Russian troops were able to make rapid advances on Turkish territory. The victorious Russian army included many Russian Armenians, including high-ranking military leaders. The Turks suspected that the Turkish-Armenians had provided assistance to the advancing Russian forces. Thus, after the Russian troops ceded some of their territorial gains as a result of the Congress of Berlin in 1878, the Turks sought vengeance, allowing Kurds and Circassians to pillage Armenian villages.[11]

The Russo-Turkish War concluded on March 3, 1878. The Turks defeated, the Armenians hoped to benefit from this favorable political situation, bidding on the Russian protection. Hitherto, four principal political factions existed among the Armenians. These groups were unorganized, but included a large number of Russophiles; Anglophiles, who were anti-Russian; Catholics, who were also anti-Russian, and who had hopes that Italy and France would come forth as protectors of the Ottoman Armenians; and the Turkophiles, whose number had considerably dwindled after the Russian victory. These differences in orientation were now put aside, and all the factions united for the protection of common national interests and the solution of the Armenian Question.[12]

In article XVI of the Treaty of San Stefano (March 3, 1878), which concluded the Russo-Turkish War, the central Ottoman government, a.k.a the Sublime Porte, agreed ". . . to carry out, without further delay, the ameliorations and reforms demanded by local requirements in the provinces inhabited by the Armenians, and to guarantee their security against the Kurds and Circassians."[13]

The Great Powers were unhappy with the growing influence of the Russian Empire under their nose, in Europe, as well as the Caucasus, as

---

10 William L. Langer, The Diplomacy of Imperialism 1890-1902 (2d ed.; New York, 1951), pp. 161, 203; A. J. P. Taylor, The Struggle for the Mastery in Europe 1848-1918 (Oxford, 1954), p. 359; Morris Wee, "Great Britain and the Armenian Question 1878-1914" (unpublished Ph.D. dissertation, University of Wisconsin, 1938), p. 283.

11 "Soc. Dem. Hunch. Kus. Amer-i Sherdjani" ["Social Democrat Hunchakian Party of America"], Hunchak Taregirk [Hunchak Yearly], October 20, 1895.

12 Nurhan Lusinian, "Zeytuni Tjakatamarte*' ["The Battle of Zeitun"], Hisnameak, p. 136.

13 Avetis Nazarbek, "Zeitun," Contemporary Review, LXIX (April 1896), 516.

evidenced by the Treaty of San Stefano Treaty. Thus, a few months later, Great Britain, Austria-Hungary, and Germany organized the Congress of Berlin to revise some of the articles. Archbishop Mkrtich Khrimian participated in the Congress to promote the Armenian interests. Consequently, the Treaty of Berlin was signed on July 13, 1878. As far as the Caucasus was concerned, Article XVI of the San Stefano Treaty was replaced with Article LXI in this new treaty, which read:

> The Sublime Porte engages to realize, without further delay, the ameliorations and the reforms demanded by local requirements in the provinces inhabited by the Armenians and to guarantee their security against the Circassian and the Kurds. She will periodically render account of measures taken with this intent to the Powers, who will supervise them.

Thereby the Treaty of Berlin transferred the supervision of the Armenians' security from the Russian Empire to the European Powers. Moreover, if the Treaty of San Stefano stipulated the eventual withdrawal of the Russian forces from the Western Armenian territories as a condition for Sublime Porte's meaningful reforms and security, the Berlin document implied unconditional withdrawal of the Russian forces laying the responsibility of supervision on the European Powers without specifying who they were going to superintend the application of said reforms.

The Armenians soon learned the hard way that the promises for reforms made at the Congress of Berlin and the Cyprus Convention existed only on paper. One of the spokesmen for the Armenians at Berlin, Archbishop Khrimian, who had just returned from the Congress, gave a sermon to a large crowd gathered in the Armenian Cathedral in Constantinople, where he famously described the bitter outcome of his mission with a striking metaphor. With a petition for reforms which was merely a piece of paper, he watched as the diplomats of the European Powers, who had placed on the table before them a "Dish of Liberty," allowed the Bulgarians, Serbians, and Montenegrins with their iron spoons, scooped into the delicious dish, taking out a portion for themselves. When it came turn for the Armenians, having only the paper on which the petition was written, he dipped into the dish on the table and watched as his paper spoon gave way and crumpled, leaving the Armenians without their share of the luscious treat.

Archbishop Khrimian (1820-1907)

Before the Berlin Congress, the provisions of the secret Cyprus (Anglo-

Turkish) Convention signed on June 4, 1878, were announced. In it, Sublime Porte promised the British to introduce reforms into Armenia.[14] While this Convention was taking place, the Kurds had been taking advantage of the evacuation of the Russians from Turkish Armenia and had resumed their pillaging.[15] Khrimian's participation in the Berlin Congress infuriated Sultan Hamid. When he learnt about the Armenian delegation's visit to Berlin, he reportedly commented: "Such great impudence... Such great treachery toward religion and state... May they be cursed upon by God."[16]

The prevalent lawlessness and the attacks by the Kurds and the Circassians induced thousands of Armenians to emigrate to Russia.[17] The Sultan's rage culminated in the form of Hamidian massacres of 1894-1896 costing the lives of over 300,000 people and earning him the nickname 'Bloody Sultan'[18].

A letter written to *The New York Times* that was published on November 29, 1895, provides insight into the circumstances surrounding the Hamidian massacres. It also documents that the Young Turks, who a few years later dethroned the Sultan and came to power, were active at the time of the Hamidian massacres. What gives this letter a greater value is that it shows that what happened back in 1895 is similar to what has been happening until today and will probably continue for generations to come should we fail to learn from our history.

THE ANARCHY IN TURKEY
Sultan's Antiquated Principle of Dividing in Order to Reign.
ASININITY OF PUBLIC SUBMISSION
Young Turkey Party Has Not the Force or the Ability to Renovate the Empire.
HOW THE TROUBLE BECAN AT MARASH
Terrible Scenes of Cruelty, Murder, Destitution, and Utter Helplessness Recorded at Erseroum.

---

14 Ministere des affaires etrangeres, op. cit., no. 184. M. P. Cambon, Ambassadeur de la Republique francaise a Constantinople, a M. Berthelot, Ministre des affaires Etrangeres, p. 214.

15 Gurgen Tahmazian, "Hambardzum Poyadjian (Murat)," Hisnameak —1887-1937— Sots. Demokrat Hunchakian Kusaktsuthian [The Fiftieth Anniversary of the Social Democrat Hunchakian Party, 1887- 1937], published by the Sots. Dem. Hunchakian Kus. Kedr. Vartchuthium [Central Committee of the Social Democrat Hunchakian Party] (Providence, 1938), pp. 149.

16 Quoted in Stephan Astourian, "On the Genealogy of the Armenian-Turkish Conflict, Sultan Abdülhamid, and the Armenian Massacres," *Journal of the Society for Armenian Studies* 21 (2012), p. 185.

17 Manoug C. Gismegian, Patmuthiun Amerikahai Kaghakakan Kusaktsuthiants 1890-1925 [The History of the Armenian-American Political Parties 1890-1925] (Fresno, 1930), pp. 53.

18 Balakian, Peter (2003). *The Burning Tigris: The Armenian Genocide and America's Response.* New York: HarperCollins., pp. 35.

CONSTANTANOPLE, Nov. 15.—Discussion of the reasons for the present frenzy of slaughter in Turkey seems a waste of time. There are the natural Turkish ferocity, the oppression of the Armenians, the Sassoun massacres, and the revolutionary movement inextricably mingled with it all; there are the wrath of English interference, and the vague spectre of purely religious fanaticism urging the Turk to proclaim war on all Christians. The elements of the strife are already known. The reason for all the horrible events that have shocked the world is the Turk and his four centuries of denial of civil rights to his Christian subjects. But in dealing with Turkey, generalizations are certain to be partial and misleading.

The Turk is not merely and universally the brute that he sometimes seems to be. During these very horrors of the last few weeks, plenty of instances have occurred where Turks have saved Christians at great personal risk, and have suffered punishment for it too. The only Turks arrested for their acts in the Constantinople massacres were those who harbored Armenians and refused to give them up to the mob. The Governor of Geiveh, in the district of Nicomedia, stopped the massacre of Ak Hissar by throwing himself alone between the Moslems and their victims when bullets were flying as in a battle: and the next week he was removed from office by order of the Sultan, and is now eating the bread of repentance at Constantinople.

At Trebizond, when the infuriated mob, having pillaged all the Armenian shops in the city, made a rush for the Armenian villages on the mountain side, a Turkish village opened its doors to the Armenian fugitives and its men went out and drove off the marauders from the Armenian houses, so that in one village, at least, the Armenians found their houses unpillaged after the store passed. There are good Turks beside the dead Turks. Win the confidence of a Turk of the class which has a smattering of education—the censors will not permit more than a smattering if they can help it—and which has read some of the better French literature; ask his views on current events, and you will receive enlightenment of the eyes.

There is a fundamental principle of Turkish statesmanship in internal affairs, to which are ascribed nearly all of the abnormal monstrosities of the present administration. From the first the sole principle has been "Divide the people whom you would govern." From this principle arises the fabric of dual government by which the Palace discredits the Porte before the people by overthrowing with hasty decrees sent out independently decisions of the Ministry taken carefully and promulgated with the Sultan's approval.

Under this principle the highest functionaries are constantly insulted and humiliated in having to endure ignoble and incapable clerks and secretaries placed close to their persons solely to worry them and to spy upon them. Under this principle the governing power had labored during five years past to maintain between the various sections of the population enmities which at all the rest of the world are dying out; carefully teaching for this end to the Moslem peasantry that their worst enemies are their Christian neighbors, whose prosperity tends to give them control of the country.

This principle places the police as a barrier between Turks and

Christians, as a skeleton at the feast in all large social functions among Turks and themselves, or among Christians by themselves, and as a ceil, with its censorship and prohibitions between the subjects of Turkey and the interests and aims, the culture and progress of all the other nations of the world. Number of intelligent Turks observe with anger the use made of this principle, fortified by religious precept, to defend the inertia of the worn-out system against the encroachments of the nineteenth century. It is not fair to exclude them from sympathy. Ask your progressive Turkish friend of the cause of the epidemic of bloodshed and rapine and outrage which is now sweeping over the empire, to destroy the real springs of its wealth in destroying the Christian, industrial, and agricultural classes. He will tell you of the villainy of Armenian revolutionists who seek to exasperate their Turkish neighbors by petting crimes and by coldblooded murders of individuals. He will swear at his Armenian compatriots with fervor; he will exhaust his copious vocabulary of vituperative epithets on England, and he will tell you that even far-off America has had a hand in this misery by educating the Christian clodhoppers until they have become insubordinate. But after all this he will say: **Stupidity of Submission to Sultan.**

"They are all asses, and the others are asses, and we are asses, for we submit to that blessed man on the hall who knows nothing but to skin his people and to set them all by the ears, that they may not unite against him." He will tell you, in short, that all the evil in the country originates at the Palace of Yildiz. Far beyond any Armenian he will go in denunciation of the Sultan. It is from Turks that one learns the degree of falsehood used in the official reports of recent outbreaks in various parts of the country in order that the people may have the impression that they are conflicts between Armenians and Moslems, instead of being great Moslem massacres, for which some crime of an individual served as an excuse. It is form Turks, whose hearts burn with shame at the comments of the European press upon Turkish turpitude, that one hears the fiercest curses upon the ruler who had brought the proud old empire to such a pas that any clown in all the wide world who kicks at it can find a crowd to cheer him.

Of such men is composed the so-called "Young Turkey" Party, the party of patriotism which has been expected, in some quarters, to make strong utterances in this time of disaster and bewilderment. The members of this party are men who have been shelved because they are honest, or because they are progressive. They are mean who have been insulted, who have been robbed, who have been pursued, even into the paths of business, by the emissaries of the palace, and have felt the grip of the sty in the household, in social life, in literary pursuits, in scientific culture, claiming to denounce as illegal every though and every action which has not been first authorized by special edict of this Majesty the Sultan.

But it is a great mistake to speak of the great multitude of Turks within and without Constantinople who long for the deposition of the Sultan as a party. They agree in the one desire, but nothing eles. There is no unity, no organization, no leadership. And it must be added that there is little spirit of self-denial and less idea of fixed principle, aside from discontent, to transform the throngs of individual jrumblers into a compact organization.

And there is no courage of conviction, so are visible, to elevate any among them into leaders. Some wish to unite with the Armenian revolutionists; some have seized upon the notion of demanding separately a Parliament and Constitutional; some think to restore Murad V. to the throne; some to do away with two or three of the brothers and raise a younger one to the Caliphate.

Others there are who have taken eagerly the idea carefully circulated in all these years that all will be will if the Christians of the empire are first made way with or at least stripped of their property and power. This section of the malcontent can hardly be called of truth a portion of the young Turkey party, but, with its eager adoption of the idea of reform by the sward and torch, it is the force now most to be feared by the Sultan and the palace party. All less violent members of the crowd that clamor for a change seem to be reduced to inertia appalled by this appeal to fanaticism and by the tremendous energy of cunning by which the Sultan ferrets out all schemes to attack him.

They hopelessly declare that he was born three days before the devil, and it is useless to try to circumvent him. The educated, gentlemanly, but somewhat effeminate young Turk is a charming man to meet in society, but he has not the qualities, intellectual, moral, or physical, which fit him to become savior of the empire. He will continue to rant against the tyranny, cruelty, and corruption that have befouled the Turkish name. He will in kindly way interfere now and then to save Christians from butchery. Possibly he may become some day desperate enough to hurl a bomb which will end the question, or to join a mob that will sweep all before it. But his is not the man to risk his life for liberty and justice, or to endure long the strain of following unflinchingly a great aim. The "young Turkey" party is a symptom, not a delivering force.

When a Turkish ship of the model of four hundred years ago, high of poop and round of bow, is coming down the Bosphorus, it often happens that she becomes unmanageable among the currents at the mouth of the Golden Horn. She will drift towards vessels lying at anchor, or threaten to wreck herself upon some projecting point of quay. Then a strange spectacle delights the eyes of him who is there to see. Every man of the crew of thirty or forty begins to bawl orders to his mates respecting the action to be taken.

Some will rush to the Captain, unbraiding him and gesticulating as if they were about to throw him overboard. Others will brace around the yards or let go sheets and lower sails and hoist them again at the most unexpected moment and upon the spur of some passing conviction. In the moment of crisis there are forty Captains, and no one of them is command of more than a limited section of the ship. Meanwhile the Captain is bawling as loud as any cursing, arguing, giving order which no one obeys, and seeming to render his clothes in despair. But he keeps firm hold of the helm and seeks to make the best of the various strange predicaments into which he is brought by the energy of his panic-stricken crew. At length some one takes a notion to let go the anchor, and if 'kismet' is favorable, the danger of disaster is averted, and the Captain has time to take a leisurely survey of the situation, and to find means to bring his ship to the place where she was to have been tied up.

It is always a marvel that these vessels reach their mooring without greater loss than the temper of the ship's company. Something of this nature is now going on in Turkey. The various discordant voices and violent efforts which attract our attention threaten ruin because no one principle guides them. A cheerful willingness exists to throw the Captain overboard; the turmoil is sure to result in some damage; it may end in terrible disaster. The one thought to be made prominent is such case is that if they safety of this ship and its passengers, and especially the safety of the neighboring vessels is to be secured, it must be by some combined effort from outside. The only hope of escape from being involved in some way is the ruin of Turkey is form the powers to drop dissension among themselves, and to control her course by irresistible united action. Risk of European war is, of course, involved. But European war is certain to follow a policy of non-intervention which merely postpones the assumption of control now sure sooner or later to be forced upon Europe. The following is a copy of a letter from Rev. L. O. Lee of Marash, under date of Oct. 30:

"Mr. Peet's and Mr. Terrell's answer to our telegram came promptly Sunday morning, the 27th. The next day came a telegram to the same effect from Mr. Marnham, the English Consul at Aleppo. We are safe and comfortable. The Government has given us repeated assurances of its protection, and the barracks near are ordered to look after us. Not a sign of danger has been seen near us, although we live on the outside of a Muslim suburd, with open country beyond.

Chapter 4

Armenian Revolutionary Parties

This historic sermon by Archbishop Khrimian was an indirect appeal for the use of arms — "iron spoons" — the means successfully adopted by Balkan revolutionaries. The results of the Congress of Berlin showed that "Christian" and "civilized" Europe had abandoned the Armenians and had left them to their own resources. This was not a new experience. For centuries they had appealed their cause to Europe to no avail. Khrimian's lamentation did not fall on deaf ears. In less than a decade, Armenian political parties sprouted, all of which aimed at armed self-denfense and the eventual liberation of Armenia.

Armenakan Party

Responding to Archbishop Khrimian's call by, the first of the organized secret revolutionary groups, the Armenakan Party, was founded in Van, Western Armenia, in 1885 by Mekertich Portukalian, Setrak Gabudian, and Hampig Der Hampartsoumian[19]. By the turn of the century, the party had cells in other towns and provinces including Trabzon and Constantinople. Their military structure was developed in Russian Transcaucasia, Persia, and the United States. They carried out military activities in the Ottoman Empire during the Defense of Van, in June 1896, and the Siege of Van, from April 19 to May 6, 1915. During the Armenian Genocide, the Armenakans had fighting groups attacking the Turks engaged in massacring the Armenians. In 1921, in Constantinople, after the fall of First Republic of Armenia as a result of the the Bolshevik invasion, Amenakans joined the Reformed Hunchakians (which is discussed in detail below), and the Constituent Democratic Party to form the Armenian Democratic Liberal Party (ADL), known in Armenian as the Ramgavar's. Of the three larger political/revolutionary parties, the Ramgavar's could be called the mildest, advocating liberalism and capitalism.

Hunchakian Party

The second party that took shape was the Hunchakian Party. Although the popular history of the Hunchaks is that it was founded in August 1887 by a group of students in Geneva, Switzerland, it was

---

[19] Talai, Vered Amit; Amit, Vered (1989). Armenians in London: The Management of Social Boundaries. Manchester University Press.

the first socialist party to operate in the Ottoman Empire and in Persia; all seven founders of the party were Russian-Armenian Marxists from affluent bourgeois families, who had never lived under the Turkish flag, but were driven to act out of concern for the well-being of their oppressed fellow Armenians. Their original goal was to attain Armenia's independence from the Ottoman Empire during the Armenian national liberation movement. The founders were influenced by social-democratic revolutionary ideology of Friedrich Engels, Georgi Plekhanov, and, later, Vladimir Lenin. The party's manifesto, printed in the first issue of Hunchak journal, contained the following slogan: "Those who cannot attain freedom through revolutionary armed struggle are unworthy of it."[20] It seems that the real history of this organization became public knowledge thanks to a police investigation following the murder of a Constantinople-based Armenian millionaire in May of 1906. Particularly, the early years of the Hunchakian Party were marred by extortions, blackmail, and murders in Europe and the U.S. More details are available in Appendix I, entitled "The Murderous Beginnings of the Hunchakian Party".

Armenian Revolutionary Federation (Dashnagtzoutune)

The last revolutionary organization to answer the Archbishop Khrimian's call was the Armenian Revolutionary Federation (ARF), a.k.a. Dashnaktsutiun, in 1890 Tiflis, Russian Empire, by Christapor Mikaelian, Stepan Zorian, and Simon Zavarian. After the assassination of Apik Effendi ordered by the Reformed Hunchakian Party in 1906, *The Evening Star* newspaper described the ARF as, "a reputable organization which does not believe in blackmail or assassination, and is endeavoring in improving the conditions of Armenia by other means."

In 1904, in Harpoot, my grandfather, Hagop, joined the Armenian Revolutionary Federation. As part of his revolutionary activities and to fulfill the oath he took on his father's grave, Hagop and his fellow revolutionaries would go out at night to the neighboring villages that had once been inhabited by Armenians prior to the Hamidian Massacres and terrorized the squatters living in the victims' homes. Hagop believed that if one takes something from someone unjustly, one should not enjoy it and must suffer lest others dare do the same. These early years of terrorist activities helped Hagop learn what later came in handy in the times of the Armenian people's greatest tragedy.

The same year, Hagop was identified as one of the night raiders. Before he could be caught, Hagop managed to emigrate and settle in the United States, where for three years he worked as a laborer at the Hood Rubber factory.

What made the ARF different from the other revolutionary societies

---

20 This echoes one of the striking statements made by a principal character in *The Fool*, a novel by Raffi: "[...] he who doesn't know how to use a weapon, who is not capable of shedding blood and killing people, he is told you have no right to be free."

was that they had worked together with the Young Turks to bring Talaat Pasha to power in 1908 with strong objections and warnings by General Antranik Ozanian, who would resign from the ARF because of this support for Talaat.

To best describe the history of the ARF, we have included two books in the appendix of this manuscript. The first one, *Patriotism Perverted: A discussion of the deeds and the misdeeds of the Armenian Revolutionary Federation, the so-called Dashnagtzoutune* can be found in Appendix II. It was written in 1934 following the murder on December 24, 1933, of Archbishop Leon Tourian, Primate of the Armenian Church in North and South America, by orders of the ARF. The second book, *The Armenian Revolutionary Federation Has Nothing Left to do*, was written in 1923 by Hovhannes Katchaznouni, First Prime Minister of the Independent Armenian Republic. It was presented to the Convention of foreign branches of the Armenian Revolutionary Federation, which convened during the month of April, 1923. This book is found in Appendix III.

The one thing that the ARF has in common with all the other Armenian revolutionary societies is that they had at one time or another been infiltrated by paid agents of governments. Alternatively, their own rank and file had been recruited by governments or opposing organizations.

My grandfather told us about spies in the early period of the ARF party, who reported back to their keepers, causing loyal members' deaths and internal conflicts that harmed and paralyzed the federation. This was one of the reasons why my grandfather resigned from the ARF in October of 1919, yet his resignation was never accepted, since the ARF constitution and by-laws don't allow a member to resign. The only way out of the ARF was expulsion, assassination or death. In my grandfather's case, before and after he was expelled, the ARF had attempted to assassinate him at least twice. In both cases, my grandfather had been warned of what was to come by ARF members loyal to my grandfather for which he was able to take countermeasures.

The first known assassination attempt was a young Italian hitman the leadership had hired. My grandfather had been told of the place and time by his informant within the ARF. When the hitman showed up to carry out his dubious deed, he was invited to the table my grandfather and his bodyguards were sitting. With their guns drawn under the tablecloth, my grandfather convinced the hired assassin that what they were doing would be detrimental to their own health. After conversing with the hitman, it was discovered that he had been misinformed about my grandfather. The assassin changed sides vowing his allegiance to my grandfather and offering to kill those who had hired him. My grandfather declined the offer.

The second known attempt was to be carried out by an ARF member. The man who knew my grandfather showed up to my grandfather's office. He knocked on the door and entered the room. My grandfather already knew that a man would be visiting and invited him in. My grandfather asked the man to sit, but the man refused. Then the man pulled out a revolver and told my grandfather he had been sent to kill him by the order of the ARF, but that he couldn't carry out the assassination. The man placed the revolver on the table and left.

During World War II, when the war had separated my grandfather from my grandmother, aunt, and mother, the ARF attempted to silence my grandfather and terrorize my grandmother who lived in France. Once they attempted to kidnap my mother. Fortunately, my grandmother had been warned and was able to take her children on a vacation in the south of France until the danger passed. The ARF would also send letters to both of my grandparents notifying one about the other's demise. This harassment lasted until they were able to reunite in the United States after the war, in 1946.

Although this volume primarily consists of that which was found in my grandfather's archive, I feel that it is helpful to close this chapter with something I found in a book that was published long after his death which documented cases of the ARF being infiltrated by the Soviet Union's famous KGB.

With the fall of the Soviet Union, one of the influential Soviet spies, Oleg Kalugin, wrote a book titled *Spymaster: My Thiry-Two Years in Intelligence and Espionage Agaisnt the West*. On page 221, Kalugin wrote of his infiltrating the ARF:

> Though it didn't play a pivotal role in our struggle with U.S. intelligence agencies, we carried on a low-level campaign to infiltrate numerous anti-Soviet émigré organizations, as well as so-called centers of ideological diversion. Virtually all of the large national groups in the Soviet Union—Ukrainians, Armenians, Lithuanians, Latvians, and Estonians—had vocal émigré organizations abroad that fought for the independence of their countrymen at home. Our job in KGB foreign counterintelligence was to insinuate agents into these groups who would keep abreast of émigré activities, let us know which leaders were likely targets for recruitment, and, if possible, soften the anti-Soviet thrust of these usually rabid anti-Communist organizations. Our ultimate goal in working with these groups was to find agents who might eventually go to work for Western intelligence and security services.
>
> We enjoyed some success in penetrating the Baltic émigré organizations, particularly in Sweden. And we had a good network of agents among the Ukrainian émigrés, particularly in Canada, where several million Ukrainians had settled. But the émigré organization we most thoroughly infiltrated was the Armenian exile group, Dashnaktsutyun. Once it had been a staunchly nationalist group that campaigned for an independent Armenian state. Over time, we placed so many agents there that several had risen to positions of leadership. We succeeded in effectively neutralizing the group, and by the 1980s Dashnaktsutyun had stopped fighting against Soviet power in Armenia. The organization and some of its members had been coopted by the KGB.

Years later, in 1992, when Dashnak Tsutyun leaders and other Armenian nationalists were attacking Armenian President Levon Ter-Petrosyan for not being sufficiently nationalist, I got a call from the president, with whom I had had several friendly conversations, at my Moscow apartment. He asked me for help in fending off the attacks by Dashnak Tsutyun, and I provided him and the Armenian press with information about the KGB's deep penetration of that émigré group in the 1970s.

Chapter 5

The Young Turks

> *"Turkish Republic, as it is today, as it stays today, was established by the party that organized the Armenian Genocide. We have a continuity of the party C.U.P. (Committee of Union and Progress). It is the same party today in Turkey we call it the Turkish the people's party, this is the C.H.P. (The Republican People's Party, founded in September 7, 1919, by Mustafa Kemal Atatürk) and the individuals who organized the Armenian Genocide, they became important officers during the Republic period. So, there is a continuity in the ruling that comes all the way today."*
>
> - Dr. Taner Akçam, Clark University – Lecture at Rowan Center for Holocaust and Genocide Studies and the History Department, March 7, 2019.

As history has proven, the Young Turks were the driving force of the Armenian Genocide, as well as the genocide of the Assyrians, atrocities against the Greeks and it can even be argued, the cultural genocide of the Turkish people themselves with the loss of their culture and written language.

The Young Turks Movement was believed to have its origins from Salonica, Ottoman Empire (presently, Thessaloniki, Greece).

According to popular claims, the Young Turks Movement was a reaction to the abolishment of the Ottoman Constitution of 1876, which had been introduced by the Grand Vizier, Midhat Pasha (1822-1883). The Ottoman constitution of 1876 was written by an Armenian named Krikor Odian (1834-1887), an advisor to the Grand Vizier. As mentioned in the previous chapter, Odian was also one of the authors of the Armenian National Constitution approved by the sultan in 1863.

Appointed Grand Vizier for the second time on December 23, 1876, Midhat Pasha replaced Mehmed Rushdi Pasha (1811-1882). Midhat Pasha announced that a constitution would be promulgated and a representative parliament established. This new form of governance was modeled after the Armenian National Constitution.

The Ottoman constitution of 1876 granted equal rights to all citizens without distinction of race or creed, abolished slavery, sanctioned independent judiciary based on civil (rather than religious) law, secured universal elementary education, and established a bicameral parliament, with a Senate appointed by the Sultan and a directly-elected Chamber of Deputies.[21]

On February 5, 1877, the Sultan, Abdul Hamid II, who had no real interest

---
21 Zvi Yehuda Hershlag (1980). Introduction to the Modern Economic History of the Middle East. Brill Archive. pp. 36–37.

in constitutionalism, exiled Midhat Pasha.

Following the end of the Russo-Turkish war of 1877-78, which the Turks lost, the Sultan dismissed the government and returned to despotic rule.[22]

The best evidence available as to finding when the Young Turks were founded indicates that they had come into existence as early as 1876. They were mentioned in *The Standard* (London, Greater London, England) newspaper on June 2, 1876, page 6, in which their demands for change were noted. The article in part reported:

> "The party of the 'Old Turks,' who are opposed to foreign loans and the bastard combinations which clothe Easter Corruption with European varnish, and the 'Young Turks,' who wish to remodel the Empire after a new plan, and endow it with institutions similar to those of Western States. The essential point on which all those parties were in accord was the wretched incapacity of the existing administration, which Moslemand rayahs found equally intolerable. On the one hand, the Old Turks, relying on the law of Islam, acknowledged that Christians were entitled to fairer treatment. On the other hand, the Young Turks thinking that rayahs can be easily satisfied if they are given rights that will make them citizens of the Turkish Empire and place them on the same footing as the true believers. They are further of the opinion that this would save the Empire from impeding ruin."

In terms of their documented connection with the Armenians, just one week before the attack on Shahan Natalie's village of Husenik, the Young Turks had been active in plotting atrocities that would bring "disgrace" to the Armenians. *The San Francisco Examiner* (San Francisco, California) reported on Oct 24, 1895, page 11:

> **COW THE YOUNG TURKS**
>
> Vigorous Action of the Sultan Thought to Have Prevented an Outbreak Just Now.
>
> LONDON, October 23.—A Constantinople dispatch to the "Standard" says: Sinister stories are afloat regarding the vengeance wreaked on members of the young Turkish party. A leading Musselman lawyer named Izzet (whose arrest was reported some time since) was tortured and died in Yl Dez Prison on proof of corresponding with the party.
>
> There is an unconfirmed rumor that fifty leaders of the party were arrested Saturday and were summarily tried and executed on a charge of excess during the recent Armenian riots. The Young Turks continue vehement talk among themselves, but it is believed the Sultan's vigor has nipped the agitation against the Palace Government. He has further, had his two brothers, Reshad and Murad, brought to Yl Dez and kept there till matter have calmed down.
>
> A dispatch from Constantinople last Saturday told of a warning received by the British Ambassador, Sir Philip Currie, from an Armenian source, that there was a plot by the Young Turkey party to kill him and thus bring

---

22 Selçuk Akşin Somel (2010). The A to Z of the Ottoman Empire. Rowman & Littlefield. P.188

disgrace upon the Armenian people.

First congress of Ottoman oppositin – Paris, 1902

The Young Turks participated in the first congress of the Ottoman opposition of 1902, held in Paris. They had a direct connection with the Committee of Union and Progress (CUP), which began as a secret society (originally known as "Committee of Ottoman Union") in Istanbul on February 6, 1889. In 1895, the society established contact with Ottoman liberals in European exile. The CUP transformed into a political organization (and later an official political party), aligning itself with the Young Turks in 1906.

In his memoirs, *Ben Kendim, A Record of Eastern Travel*, the British spy, Aubrey Herbert, writes the following with regard to the Young Turks of Salonika (pages 15-16) :

> Salonika, by the blue sea and amongst the cypresses, is only a poor footstool for Olympus. It is a town of intrigues and persecutions. In the days of my first visit it was more free than Constantinople; there was not the same vigilance, and the Jews, who are the majority of its inhabitants, have always enjoyed a greater liberty than any other subject race in Turkey. They have, indeed, shared with the greatest heartiness in assisting other people to massacre the Greeks and Armenians, who are their commercial rivals.
>
> The coming storm had not yet broken, but already its mutterings were to be heard. The Grand Orient[23] was at work. There were links between New York and the bootblacks of Salonika, and again between Salonika and the unruly Albanians. Talaat was studying the literature of the French Revolution; Karasso was engaged in Freemasonry; Enver, in the mountains of Macedonia or in a sailing boat in the Gulf, was engrossed in tactics.
>
> The Jews of Salonika, generally known as Dönmeh (converts), were the real parents of the Turkish revolution. They are a definite people--Hebrews, but indefinable as to creed. The popular verdict was that they were only nominal Moslems and were true followers of the Pentateuch, bowing their heads in the temple of Rimmon for the sake of profit. At that time, only the most industrious students of the Near East knew of their existence. There was no man to prophesy that the Dunmes were to be the chief authors of a revolution whose results were to shake the world.

---

23 The Chief Masonic Lodge of the Near East.

In order to give a fair look as to who the Young Turks were, I turn to Reverend Joseph K. Greene, D.D., who was a resident of Turkey for 51 years. He published a book titled *Leaving the Levant,* in 1916. This book serves as witness to his life in the Ottoman Empire and, compared with historical documents available today, can be deemed an accurate account of events in the time period he reports on. Below is a fragment from the book (pages 38 to 48):

> In the summer of 1908 the city of Samokov in Bulgaria afforded my wife and myself a delightful retreat from the heats of Constantinople. While there the report reached us that, as the result of a revolutionary movement, a constitutional government had been proclaimed in Turkey, and on our return to the capital we found abundant and gratifying evidence that such was the fact. Such a change of government, utterly unexpected, was a great and glad surprise. The men who brought about this revolution called themselves Young Turks. Who then were the Young Turks? The curious fact is that most of the leaders in the movement were not Turks at all, but Mohammedans whose ancestors were Christians. Until the recent war (1912-13) there were in the Balkan peninsula some 2,000,000 Mohammedans, most of whom in origin were neither Turks nor Arabs, but descended from the early Christian nations inhabiting the land. After the Turkish invasion, 550 years ago, many Greeks, Albanians, Bosnians, Servians, and Bulgarians professed themselves Mohammedans in order to save their lives, their honor, and their property; and their descendants are now, for the most part, the Mohammedans of the Balkan peninsula. They changed their religion, but to the present time have retained, each nation, its mother tongue, its traditions and customs; hence they are allied, not to Asiatics, but to Europeans.
>
> Now for many years the Turkish government has maintained two divisions of its army, numbering 60,000 men, in what was called European Turkey. These troops were very largely recruited from the European Mohammedans, and the great body of the officers came from the same peoples. Some of the officers received their education, in part, in the military and other schools of Europe, and became familiar with one or more of the European languages. For many years many young officers were ashamed and aggrieved on account of the unhonored position of their country, and were embittered by the despotism of Sultan Abdul Hamid and by the corruption of his ministers. Some of the officers were suspected by the Turkish authorities, and in order to escape arrest, imprisonment, exile, and, possibly, death, they fled to Europe. They congregated in Paris, Geneva, and other cities, formed secret committees and inaugurated a revolutionary propaganda. For years they carried on this propaganda with infinite secrecy and success, distributing their revolutionary documents in other divisions of the army and among the civil population, and gained many adherents.
>
> Finally, when their plans were completed and preparations made, on July 23, 1908, telegrams were sent from many places in European Turkey to Sultan Abdul Hamid, in the palace of Yildiz, Constantinople, demanding from him the proclamation of a constitution, the summoning of a parliament, the dismissal of his corrupt ministers, and other reforms, and threatening

that, unless these demands were immediately acceded to, they would march upon Constantinople with 60,000 men. The Sultan at once called his ministers to the palace, and they passed a very anxious night. The upshot of their conference was that not one of the ministers was able to guarantee the safety of the Sultan's life. Hence on the morning of July 24, by command of the Sultan, telegrams were sent to all divisions of the army and to the governors of the provinces, announcing that his Imperial Majesty, Sultan Abdul Hamid, was graciously pleased to proclaim a constitutional form of government. The people were dazed and bewildered, not knowing what to believe, and when reassured their outbursts of joy defied description. Turks, Christians, and Jews joined indiscriminately in their joyful demonstrations.

The Young Turks thought it best to leave Sultan Abdul Hamid upon the throne, he solemnly swearing that he would rule as a constitutional sovereign, and so he appeared to be doing. At the same time the wily and perfidious man began to prepare for a reaction. By means of the chief eunuch and other servants of the palace, by means of religious teachers, called imams, whom he hired, and by the use of unlimited sums of money, in the course of nine months, Sultan Abdul Hamid had deceived, seduced and bribed half the garrison of Constantinople, say 12,000 men. On the night of April 13, 1909, these mutinous soldiers rose upon their young officers, killing many of them and imprisoning others in their rooms, marched into the streets, crossed the bridge over the Golden Horn to Stamboul, took possession of the parliament house, killed several members of the new government, and in the course of the day secured control of the city. Sultan Abdul Hamid thought that he had carried the day, but he counted without his host. Within one week the Young Turks rallied, and by means of two lines of railway brought from Thrace and Macedonia and Albania some 45,000 troops, with artillery, ammunition and provisions to the gates of Constantinople. This army took possession, first, of a fortification called Chatalja on the line of the Roumelian railway, 25 miles from the city, and day by day captured without much fighting, the outlying fortifications. On Friday, the 23rd of April, the commander of the Young Turkey Army, General Mahmoud Shevket Pasha, received information that Sultan Abdul Hamid, in disappointment and rage, had planned for the following day a general massacre of Christians and of his opponents in the capital. Thereupon, General Mahmoud during Friday afternoon and night moved his army into the city in two divisions. One division, after some fighting, occupied the old city, Stamboul. The other division swept around the Golden Horn and, on Saturday, advanced upon Pera, the European quarter. Here, there were very strong barracks, occupied by the mutinous soldiers, and severe fighting ensued, with a loss on both sides of some 2,000 men. By night, however, the Young Turkey Army prevailed and had possession of the city. On Monday, the army surrounded the hill of Yildiz, situated three-quarters of a mile from the shore of the Bosphorus and separated from Pera by a valley. This hill, of 1,000 acres, was surrounded by a high wall and contained the palace of the Sultan, a palace for his wives, and another palace for the entertainment of European sovereigns, a porcelain factory, a theater, stables, and barracks for his bodyguard. Cannons were placed on the surrounding heights so as to command this hill, and on the morning of Tuesday the Sultan, seeing that his game was up, surrendered. The bodyguard was marched out and new troops were sent in. That night several young officers went to the palace of the Sultan and summoned him to their presence. He came in, pale as a sheet, trembling like a leaf, and begging for his life. He was told that his life would be spared, but that for the good of the country he must leave the city that night. The Young Turks dealt mercifully with the cruel monarch and allowed him to choose as his companions in exile eleven women, one child, two eunuchs, and five servants! These were placed in carriages, and after midnight were driven to the railway station in Stamboul, sent by special train 300 miles west to Salonica, and were consigned to a strong house prepared for them. Such was the end of a traitorous attempt to reestablish the old system of absolutism, and the alacrity and determination with which the Young Turks met and crushed the mutiny, and thereby saving Constantinople itself from a general massacre, deserved all praise.

It may be added that on the same day as the mutiny in Constantinople the Moslem population of the city and province of Adana, instigated from Constantinople, rose upon their Christian fellow-subjects and, in the course of a few days, robbed and murdered 20,000 Armenians, destroyed a large number of Christian villages, churches, and schools, and killed many religious teachers, including two American missionaries and 20 Protestant pastors and preachers and one college professor. Had the mutiny in Constantinople succeeded, the wave of destruction, as in 1895, would no doubt have swept over all Asia Minor. By order of the government, 70 men, found guilty of complicity in the massacre, most of whom were Turks, were hanged in Adana. The mutiny and the massacre were the last stroke of the dying monster, Sultan Abdul Hamid. Such in brief is the story of the revolution of 1908 and of the reaction of 1909.

The significance of the revolution of the Young Turks is found in the fact that, so far as we know, it was the first real attempt among Mohammedans to establish a constitutional government. For 1,300 years every Mohammedan ruler had been an absolute and irresponsible despot, the character of each reign being determined by the special traits of the sovereign. Revolutions without number had occurred in Mohammedan countries, but in every case the change had been from one despotism to another. The Young Turks of 1908, however, seemed to have learned the true idea of a constitutional government, with the Sultan as chief executive with a responsible ministry and a parliament, each department of the government loyally supplementing the other departments, and altogether constituting a government of the people, for the people, and by the people.

What now has been the issue of the government so hopefully begun?

First, it is but fair to say that the Young Turks made a good beginning. At the peril of their lives they accomplished a revolution which was almost bloodless. In place of the cruel monarch Hamid, they put upon the throne his brother, Reshid Effendi, the legitimate heir, under the name of Mohammed the Fifth, a man now 70 years old, without force or initiative, but mild-mannered and well-disposed. They inaugurated a constitutional government in all its forms. They had command of the army and navy, and for at least a few years they had the confidence and support of 5,000,000 Christians and Jews, who, after the Balkan war of 1912-13, constituted nearly one-third of all the subjects of Turkey outside of Arabia. Moreover they had a powerful secret committee, called the Committee of Union and Progress, which formulated the policy and controlled all the movements of the Young Turk party both in the administration and parliament.

The trouble with the Young Turks was that they had no leaders who truly comprehended and heartily adopted the fundamental principle upon which a real constitutional government is based. (None of the leaders had had an American college training as the leaders in Bulgaria had.) That principle is the equality in civil affairs of all the subjects of the state, with impartial justice and equal opportunities for all. This principle the Young Turks adopted in theory, and for political reasons professed to follow, but in fact they were a small minority, perhaps 20 per cent of the whole Mohammedan population, and were soon confronted by the old traditionary sentiment which demanded Mohammedan supremacy. In short, the everlasting controversy between the new and the old, between equal rights and special privilege, be- tween tolerance and fanaticism, between liberty and despotism asserted itself, and the intolerant Mohammedan sentiment triumphed. The Young Turks wished to maintain their power, and, while acting under constitutional forms, themselves became a despotism.

To attain *eclat* among their countrymen, in 1914, they, all of a sudden, denounced and abrogated the Capitulations, that is, the ancient treaties made with the European Powers, for the safeguarding of the persons and property of foreigners residing in Turkey. In consequence of the protests and threats of England, France, and Russia, and in order to secure support in the controversies with those Powers which they knew were sure to follow; in order also at the same time to thwart any further opposition at home, the Young Turks, contrary to the wishes of the great majority of the people, plunged into the great European war.

Still further to consolidate their power in Asia Minor and to obviate any interference of Europe in behalf of the Christian subjects of Turkey, following the example of Sultan Abdul Hamid, they adopted measures— measures the most cruel and diabolical—for the extermination of the Armenian people. First, they drafted into the army all able-bodied Armenian men; then they seized, imprisoned and secretly killed the remaining men and boys; then they drove from their homes the rest of the people, the young and the old, the rich and the poor, the sick and the well, and started them on foot from all points of Asia Minor on a journey of hundreds of miles, towards the deserts of Arabia, to die by the way from hunger and thirst, from weariness and exposure, while thousands of women and girls were forced into a life of shame and slavery in Moslem tents and huts and houses. Of course the goods and property of all these people—perhaps 1,000,000 in number—were seized and confiscated. These cruelties and crimes were explicitly ordered by the leaders of the Young Turks at Constantinople and executed by the regular Turkish officials. We are glad to be able to add, however, that some officials refused to execute the infamous orders and gave up their posts, and we have reason to believe that a large part of the Mohammedan population did not approve of them. Alas! that the movement of the Young Turks, begun so hopefully, should issue in such crimes. Alas! that the Young Turks should thus have blackened their name with infamy, and should have rendered themselves unworthy of the recognition of any self-respecting nation on the face of the earth.

But the Turks say, "The Armenians are rebels. Witness what they did in Van ! Did not the *Outlook* newspaper some months ago print a picture of the barricades which the Armenians built in the streets of that city?" Such was the statement of a Turk in a letter published in the *New York Times* of October 18, 1915. We reprint the picture.

Well, what are the facts? In April and May, 1915, Turkish soldiers, and Kourds made savage assaults on the Armenian towns and villages within a circuit of 50 miles of Van. With merciless cruelty they killed thousands of helpless people, multitudes of girls and women they carried away to a life of shame and slavery; they drove away the flocks and herds, and stole whatever they could carry off; and, finally, they burned the houses of the villagers and left the land waste and desolate. Some poor wretches escaped to Van, and they brought to the American hospital women with breasts cut off and children so mutilated that decency forbids description.

In the large town of Agantz, only 40 miles from Van, all the Armenian men were ordered to come to the Government Building "to hear an important proclamation." Those who hesitated were forced to come by the police. When they were all within the enclosure, they were divided into groups of 50, they were bound and were all shot to the number of 2,500. The women and children and the houses with all their contents were then given over to the Turks and Kourds.

On April 20, by command of Jevdet Bey, the governor of Van, Turkish soldiers began an attack on Van, the ancient capital of the Armenian kingdom, and at the time a city of 50,000 inhabitants, three-fifths of whom were Armenians, and the remainder Turks. Thereupon some 3,000 Armenians, seeing the awful fate which threatened them and their families, determined to defend themselves with such weapons as they had and such barricades as they could hastily erect, and until the middle of May they held back, with small loss of life, several thousand Turkish troops. On May 16, the Turks and Kourds, hearing that a Russian force was approaching, raised the siege and fled towards Bitlis, taking with them from a Turkish hospital Miss McLaren, an American nurse, and Schwester Martha, a German nurse, to tend sick officers. In their flight the Turks left behind 25 Turkish soldiers, too ill to travel, and 1,000 destitute women and children, many of them dangerously ill with typhus fever. All these forsaken people the Armenians, by permission of the missionaries, brought within the mission compound, where they were lodged in the mission school buildings and hospital, and were fed and tended until near the end of July, at the peril of the lives of the missionary attendants. Indeed, early in July Dr. Ussher, the leading physician, and his wife, Mr. and Mrs. Yarrow, and Miss Rogers, the principal of the girls' school, were taken with the dreaded disease, and on July 13 Mrs. Ussher died, and was buried in the missionary graveyard, while her husband and Mr. Yarrow were too ill to be informed of the sad event. When, near the end of July, a larger Turkish force approached Van, the entire Armenian population and 15 American missionaries, including children, fled, and after weeks of incredible hardship and no little loss reached the Russian border. Mrs. Raynolds, whose leg was broken in the flight, utterly exhausted, died in Tiflis on August 12, 1915, two days before the arrival of her husband from America, and after 47 years of missionary service.

It may be added that after the flight of the Armenians, the Turks and Kourds plundered the city of Van and burned a good part of it, including the mission hospital and church and several other buildings. Subsequently the Russians re- turned in larger force, and again the Turks fled, and Van is again in Russian hands.

Such is the history, in brief, of the so-called rebellion of the Van Armenians. It was an attempt to defend themselves and their families from sure outrage and death, and this attempt occurred only after the Young Turkish leaders in Constantinople had for months been sending into merciless deportation and destruction hundreds of thousands of innocent men, women, and children! Out of one body of Armenians numbering 5,000, deported from Harpout, only 213 survived to reach Aleppo, and these, almost naked and famished, were to be driven forward to the desert of Mesopotamia.

Are the few Young Turks who are responsible for such diabolical revenge the fitting representatives of their nation? We do not believe it. Is such action the end of the splendid attempt at constitutional government in Turkey? By the favor and mercy of God, we hope not.

Chapter 6

The Four Pashas

In this chapter we will take a close look at the Young Turk top leaders, Talaat, Enver and Jemal, who spearheaded the Armenian Genocide. These names were at the top of Shahan Natalie's list of persons to be assassinated for their crimes against the Armenian people. Talaat Pasha, whom my grandfather dubbed 'number one' was at the very top.

In this chapter we will also examine Mustapha Kemal Pasha, and his leading role in the Young Turk Movement. Mustapha Kemal later became known as Ataturk, the father of Modern Turkey.

Mehmed Talaat Pasha (1874-1921)

Mehmed Talaat Pasha

Mehmed Talaat was born in Kırcaali town of Edirne Vilayet, Ottoman Empire (modern Kardzhali, Kardzhali Province, Bulgaria) in 1874. He claimed to be from a family of Pomak[24] and Turkish decent.[25]

As a student attending a civil preparatory school, the young Talaat, whose manners were gruff, had a conflict with his teacher and left the school without a certificate. Without earning a degree, he became a postal clerk for the telegraph in Edirne. To supplement his meager salary, he worked as a Turkish language teacher at the Alliance Israelite School, which served the Jewish community of Edirne.[26]

At the age of 19, he claimed to have had a love affair with the daughter of the Jewish headmaster for whom he worked for. He was caught sending a telegram saying "Things are going well. I'll soon reach my goal." With two of his friends from the post office, he was charged with tampering with the official telegraph and arrested in 1893. He claimed that the message in question was to his girlfriend. The Jewish girl came forward to defend him. He was sentenced to two years in jail, but was pardoned and exiled to Salonika.

---

24 A term used for Slavic Muslims inhabiting Bulgaria, northeastern Greece and northwestern Turkey.

25 Taner Timur, Türkler ve Ermeniler: 1915 ve Sonrası, İmge Kitabevi, 2001, p. 53

26 Mango, Andrew (2004). Atatürk. London: John Murray. p. 67.

From 1898 to 1908 Talaat served as a postman on the staff of the Salonika Post Office. Eventually, after serving 10 years, he became the head of the post office.[27]

On March 19, 1910, he married Hayriye Hanim, a young girl from Ioinnina (located in northwestern Greece, 260 kilometers) southwest of Salonika.

When the 1908 Young Turk Revolution deposed the Sultan with a force dispatched from Salonika, Talaat had been allegedly dismissed from membership of the CUP. At that time, the CUP would end its secret existence, yet it would wait to take charge of the government due to the central committee, which was dominated by "ethnic Turks" of Salonika, including Talaat, who remained exclusive and its proceedings clandestine.[28]

Following the 1908 revolution, Talaat became the deputy of Edirne in the Ottoman Parliament. In July of that same year, he as appointed Minister of Interior Affairs. He became minister of post, and then secretary-general of the CUP in 1912.

After the assassination of the grand vizier, Mahmud Şevket Pasha, on June 11, 1913, Talaat once again became Minister of Interior Affairs in July of 1913.

On October 29, 1914, following the Black Sea Raid, which was an Ottoman naval sortie against Russian ports in the Black Sea and supported by Germany which, in turn, led the Ottoman Empire into World War I, the Minister of Finance, Mehmet Cavit Bey, resigned. Talaat, the then Minister of Interior Affairs, was appointed Minister of Finance while maintaining his position as Minister of Interior Affairs. As Minister of Interior Affairs, Talaat would issue orders that would start one of the darkest chapters in Armenian history. He ordered the arrests of Armenian intellectuals and community leaders on April 24, 1915. With the removal of Grand Vizier, Said Halim Pasha (1865-1921), on February 4, 1917, Talaat Pasha would rise to the most powerful post in the Ottoman Empire until the end of the war and his arrest on October 8, 1918.

Original copy of instructions from Talaat Pasah on April 24, 1915 to arrest Armenian intellectuals and community leaders.

---

27 http://www.telekomculardernegi.org.tr/haber-2730-iz-birakan-ptt%E2%80%99ciler--1--talat-pasa-.html

28 https://www.encyclopedia.com/humanities/encyclopedias-almanacs-transcripts-and-maps/committee-union-and-progress

On March 7, 2007, Dr. Taner Akçam, the renouned Turkish historian, presented a lecture at Harvard University, Center for Government and International Studies, in which he stated:

> "There is a very important document. This is hardly used in Turkish sources also. Even though if you look at Turkish books, published by mostly the others who support the Turkish thesis, you can find a reference to that document. This is an official letter written by Talaat Pasha, 26 May 1915. He wrote a lengthy letter, almost if you transcribe into modern Turkish or English, it is 4-5 pages a letter. He tires to explain the policy of the Ottoman government and in this letter, we learn the main policy of the Union and Progress Party and the government. It is very important this document, because we haven't published this in entirety in none of the languages we have. I have this and plan to publish in all entirety. In this document if you read why Talaat, explains that Armenian had to be deported, you read no one single word related to war. War is not reason for the deportation. In his letter he says, beginning of the war, we took some temporary measures to solve this issue, but it was not enough. Now it is time to solve this issue. Now I'm quoting from his letter. He wrote [on] 1915, 26th May: "The necessary preparation have been discussed and taken for the complete and fundamental elimination of these concern [the Armenian], which occupies an important place in the exalted states list of vital issues." And in the document, he made a summary of Armenians reform problem beginning of end of 19th century. For him, the basic problem was the "Armenian Reform Issue". And this issue must be solved because it gives the Allied power opportunity to intervene the domestic affairs to Ottoman Empire and against the national security interest of the state. So, this is the important connection, national security of Ottomans and national security policy of today's Turkey."

Held in pre-trial detention on the island of Malta under the watchful eye of the British, as a result of the Turkish courts martial convened in 1919-1920, Talaat Pasha, along with others found guilty of war crimes, including the systematic murders of the Armenian people of the Ottoman Empire, were secretly released. He and 6 of the other convicts, including Enver Pasha and Djemal Pasha, boarded a German torpedo boat, the Lorelei, on the night of November 1, 1918. Their final destination was Berlin, Germany, where they planned their return to power under the protection of the German government.

Ottoman Court Tribunal - 1919

Talaat was assassinated in Berlin, Germany, on March 15, 1921, by Soghomon Tehlirian.

Ahmed Djemal Pasha (1872-1922)

Ahmed Djemal was born in Mytilene, Lesbos, to Mehmet Nesip Bey, a military pharmacist. Destined for the army, Djemal transferred from Kuleli Military High School in 1890. He went on to the Military Academy (Mektebi Harbiyeyi Şahane) in 1893, the staff college in Istanbul. He was posted to serve with the 1st Department of the Imperial General Staff (Seraskerlik Erkânı Harbiye), and then he worked at the Kirkkilise Fortification Construction Department bound to Second Army. Djemal was assigned to the II Corps in 1896; being appointed two years later, the staff commander of Novice Division, stationed on the frontier Salonica.

Ahmed Djemal Pasha

Djemal sympathized with the reforms of Committee of Union and Progress (CUP) on military issues. In 1905, Djemal was promoted to major and designated Inspector of Roumelia Railways. The following year he joined the Ottoman Liberty Society. He became influential in the department of military issues of the Committee of Union and Progress. He became a member of Board of the III Corps, in 1907, working with future Turkish statesmen Major Fethi (Okyar) and Mustafa Kemal (Atatürk).[29] Between 1908 and 1918, Djemal was one of the most important leaders of the Ottoman government.

On July 21, 1922, at the age of 50, Djemal Pasha was assassinated on a Tbilisi, Georgian street by Stepan Dzaghigian, Artashes Gevorgyan, and Petros Ter Poghosyan, under the direction of my grandfather, Shahan Natalie. Djemal's remains were brought to Erzurm and buried there.

Ismail Enver Pasha (1881-?)

Enver was born in Constantinople on November 22, 1881. Enver's father, Ahmed (1860–1947), was a Gagauz Turk. He was either a bridge-keeper in Monastir[30] or a small town public prosecutor in the Balkans.[31] He was also the cook for the Sultan. Enver's mother Ayşe, was an Albanian.[32]

Enver's uncle was Halil Pasha (1881-1957), the regional governor and

---

29 Muammer Kaylan. The Kemalists: Islamic Revival and the Fate of Secular Turkey. Prometheus Books, Publishers. p. 77.

30 Kaylan, Muammer (2005), The Kemalists: Islamic Revival and the Fate of Secular Turkey, Prometheus Books, p. 75.

31 Akmese, Handan Nezir (2005), The Birth of Modern Turkey: The Ottoman Military and the March to WWI, IB Tauris, p. 44.

32 Mazower, Mark (2004), Salonica, City of Ghosts: Christians, Muslims and Jews 1430–1950, HarperCollins, p. 255.

military commander who was one of the main organizers of the Armenian and Assyrian genocides in Bitlis, Mush, and Beyazit. Halil Pasha also had crossed into neighboring Persia and massacred Armenians, Assyrians and Persians.[33] Halil Pasha was famously known for his declaration made during a meeting at Yerevan in the summer of 1918 which he was quoted as saying: "I have endeavored to wipe out the Armenian nation to the last individual."[34]

Ismail Enver Pasha

Enver was an Ottoman military officer and leader of the 1908 Young Turk Revolution. During the Balkan Wars (1912-1913) and in World War One (1914-1918), he became a top military leader, eventually securing the post of Minister of War on January 4, 1914. This was made possible thanks to the Ottoman coup d'état that resulted in the assassination of the Minister of the Navy, Hüseyin Nazim Pasha (1848-1913) and the eventual forced resignation 19 days later of the Grand Vizier, Mehmed Kâmil Pasha (1833-1913). On June 11, 1913, Kâmil Pasha CUP successor to the premiership, Mahmud Shevket Pasha (1856-1913) was assassinated by a relative of Nazim Pasha to avenge his death. The CUP leader Djemal Pasha (1872-1922) indicated to Kâmil's family that he had to leave the Ottoman Empire or he would be arrested. Kâmil Pasha, who had been under house arrest, 5 weeks prior to the assassination of Kâmil Pasha, had made his way to his native Cyprus and while making plans to visit England in 1914, he was reported to have died on November 14, 1913 of Syncope.

Prior to World War One, Enver Pasha was hailed "Hero of the Young Turk Revolution" and "Hero of Liberty".[35] Germans often referred to Ottoman Turkey as "Enverland".[36]

U.S. Ambassador Henry Morgenthau described Enver: "His nature had a remorselessness, a lack of pity, a cold-blooded determination, of which his clean-cut, handsome face, his small but sturdy figure and his pleasing manners gave no indication."[37]

33 Gaunt, David (2006). Massacres, resistance, protectors: muslim-christian relations in Eastern Anatolia during world war I (1st Gorgias Press ed.). Piscataway, NJ: Gorgias, p. 109.

34 Winter, J. M. (2003). America and the Armenian Genocide of 1915. Cambridge University Press. p. 65.

35 Asia, Journal of the American Asiatic Association, Volume 18, December 1918, p. 1052, 1054.

36 Asia, Journal of the American Asiatic Association, Volume 18, November 1918, p. 923.

37 The Enquirer, *AN UNCHANGED SCOUNDREL: Enver Pasha Was the Brains of Turkish Atrocities;* (Cincinnati, OH, June 19, 1919), p.4.

Like Talaat and many of the other leaders within the Ottoman Empire during the war, Enver Pasha was arrested on October 8, 1918, held in pretrial detention on the island of Malta under the watchful eye of the British and secretly released on November 1, 1918, with the eventual destination of Berlin, Germany.

Enver left Germany and made his way to Moscow, where he would become a representative for the Turkish Nationalist Movement. He would represent Mustafa Kemal Pasha, who was leading the movement in Turkey.

Although Enver's story could fill an entire book, I will only conclude with his alleged assassination, which although he was near the top of my grandfather's list of 100, I can say that it was not *Operation Nemesis* that killed him. In fact and although history has been recorded that Enver was killed in Bukharan People's Soviet Republic, (present-day Tajikistan) on August 4, 1922 at the age of 40, there is evidence to indicate that he was not killed by the Red Army Dashnakist band of soldiers.

Enver Bey (center) talking to the British attaché and press in Constantinople immediately after seizing power in the 1913 Raid on the Sublime Porte, also known as the 1913 Ottoman coup d'état.

On October 11, 1922, *The Age* newspaper of Melbourne, Australia, ran a story on page 11 titled "The Fate of Enver Pasha," which reads:

LAHORE, 10th October.

All Central Asia news continue to dwell upon the fate of Enver Pasha. It is impossible to ascertain whether he is alive or dead. Travelers from Badakshan tell circumstantial stories of the arrival in Khamaba of Enver's servants bringing his personal effects, including a coat with a bullet hole in it. It is stated that he was wearing this coat when he met his death. On the other hand equally credible stories state that he has retired with the remnants of his defeated forces into the wilds of Fershana. A third rumor is that peace has been signed between the insurgents and the Bolshevists, and that Enver is once more the ally of Russia.

On October 23, 1922, the *Selma Times Journal* ran a story on page 2, titled, "Enver Pasha Not Dead As Reported":

CONSTANTINOPLE, Oct. 23—Enver Pasha, former Turkish war minister is in excellent health at Samarkand, but he has given up his struggle against the Soviet, the Associated Press was informed by his emissary, Mufid Bey, just arrived from Tiflis. He quickly denied the various reports that Enver Pasha has died.

On August 22, 1922, more than 2 weeks following the alleged death of Enver, a story appeared on page 12 of the morning edition of the *Shreveport Times*, Karl H. Von Wiegand, Universal Service Staff Correspondent, wrote an article titled, "WOULD CARVE NEW EMPIRE: Enver Pasha Has Dreams of Becoming 'George Washington' of East":

> Berlin, Aug. 21.—Enver Pasha, whose aspirations to become "George Washington" of the Moslem world, has made him the most romantic figure in the eyes of the Mohammedans since the days of Saladin, is trying to carve out a new empire for himself.
>
> Deposer of the notorious Sultan Abdul Hamid, then military chieftain of the powerful Senusal tribe of Arabs against the Italians in the Tripoli war, minister of war and commander-in-chief of the Turkish armies in the World war, held coresponsible for Armenian massacres with Talaat Pasha, then ally of the Bolsheviki in Moscow, Enver Pasha has selected as stage for this new most romantic fiction like activities Turkestan and the Pamir region.
>
> Enver, the son of lowly parents, married the Princess Sultana, niece of the late Sultan of Turkey, shortly before the war broke out.
>
> According to information received here by his friends, Enver is trying to make some changes in the map of Asia all by himself. He is seeking to create an empire-like unity of Turkestan, Chiva and Bokara. With an army of 50,000 Muhammedans, he recently inflicted a severe defeat upon General Budjienny, commander of the Bolsheviki forces in Turkestan.

ENVER PASHA

> "Isvestijia," the official organ of the soviet government in Moscow, charges that Enver conspired to remove the Emir of Bokhara through assassination in order that he himself might succeed him, but that was frustrated.
>
> Enver Pasha is today in command of the only military forces making open war on the Bolsheviki.
>
> The Princess Sultana, Enver's wife, is still in Berlin, waiting for the new "Saladin" to conquer a throne for her.

If Enver were still alive after his alleged death on August 4, 1922, as the newspapers had been reporting, this would not be unusual for Enver to stage. During the war, in March of 1916, reports of Enver's death had been reported in the news. But, on March 16, 1916, the *Montana Standard* ran a story on page 14, with a picture of the very much alive Enver Pasha titled "ATHENS DECLARES ENVER PASHA IS STILL ALIVE":

> London—According to reports from the Turkish legation of Athens, there is no truth in the story that Enver Pasha, Turkish war minister, was attacked by a would-be assassin or that he died from his wounds.
>
> Previous dispatches told of rumors of Enver Pasha's death. One report stated that he had been attacked by an assassin in Jerusalem.

If these articles are accurate and I will add that I have dozens of articles that have Enver sightings all the way up to 1927, when Enver visits the Shah of Iran, then when did Enver finally die? Could this explain why his remains were not moved to Turkey as were Talaat's when Adolf Hitler was in power? Why only in 1996 was Enver laid to rest in the same lands where scores of Armenians were buried in mass graves because of him?

The *Gaurdian of London* newspaper ran a story on August 5, 1996 on page 9, written by Chris Nuttall, titled "Reburial restores Enver Pasha to his true glory":

> The remains of the Turkish revolutionary Enver Pasha were laid to rest in Istanbul yesterday, far from the plains of Central Asia where he died fighting the Soviet Union in 1922.
>
> Prayers were offered at the Sisli mosque before the reburial, with full military honours, in a mausoleum at Eternal Freedom Hill, where other leaders of the Young Turks revolution lie. They ended the rule of the Sultans over the Ottoman empire.
>
> President Suleyman Demirel, who arranged for the remains to be retrieved from Tajikistan, attended with descendants of Enver. He had been given the honorific title, Pasha, meaning general or commander.
>
> After helping to depose Sultan Abdul-Hamid II in 1909, Enver led a coup in 1913 which brought his Committee of Union and Progress to power. He ruled as part of a triumvirate and is held responsible for taking Turkey into the First World War on the German side.
>
> He fled in a German submarine just before the armistice in 1918. From Berlin he went to Moscow, where he failed to win Soviet support for a plot to overthrow the founder of the modern Turkish republic, Mustafa Kemal Atatürk. But Lenin allowed him to go to Turkestan to organise the Central Asian republics for the Communist cause. He soon changed sides, joining the revolt of the Muslim Basmachi guerrillas in 1921.
>
> He was pursuing his dream of a pan-Turkic state in the Caucasus and Central Asia when he was killed by the Red Anny in what is now Tajikistan

in 1922. Yesterday was the 74th anniversary of his death. Turkish scientists identified his remains earlier this year in a grave yard in Baldzhuan, 180 miles south-east of Dushanbe. A distinctive gold-capped tooth was found along with a surviving witness to the interment.

President Demirel said Enver Pasha had led a whirlwind life. "He was a nationalist, an idealist and an honest soldier who loved his country," he said. "He is a hero in the eyes of the Turkish nation, his exile has ended."

The ceremony also marked his rehabilitation. He has always been in the shadow of Ataturk, whose portrait still adorns every government office, but his record in Central Asia appeals to Turkey's ambition to extend its influence over the Turkic-speaking countries there.

President Demirel thanked his Tajik counterpart, Emomali Rakhmonov, for his help in returning the remains. Turkey provided 10 tons of Turkish Red Crescent humanitarian aid for Baldzhuan.

Mustafa Kemal Atatürk (1881-1938)

Although modern Turkey claims that the today's Turkey has nothing to do with the Turkey of the Young Turks who were found guilty of the Armenian Genocide, this claim is 100% false. In fact, Mustafa Kemal Pasha, who would later be known as Mustafa Kemal Atatürk, was also one of the Turks who after World War One was sentenced to death by a military tribunal along with a number of others who would later rise to power and form what is known today as modern day Turkey.

The Times of Greater London, on Saturday, May 19, 1920, page 12, ran a story titled, "KEMAL 'CONDEMNED' TO DEATH: NEW ARMENIAN CABINET.":

> A *communiqué* to the Press from the Court Martial announces that the following Nationalist chiefs have been condemned to death by default for high treason, rebellion, and instigation of a long list of crimes, ranging from massacres to the confiscation of funds belonging to orphanages:—
>
> Mustapha Kemal "Effendi," of Salonika, ex-inspector General of the Third Army; Kara Vassif Bey; Ari Fuad Pasha, ex-Commander of the 20th Army Corps; the convert to Islam, Ahmed Rustem, formerly known as Alfred Rustem Bilinski, ex-Ambassador at Washington; Dr. Adnan Bey and his wife, Halida Edib Hanum. With the exception of Kara Vassif, who is in Malta, and Ahmed Rustem, who is believed to be in Italy, all the above are in Anatolia.
>
> Much anxiety is felt in Armenian circles on account of the withdrawal of the greater part of the American Relief Commission and there is a tendency in some quarters to suggest that the commission was withdrawn from Tiflis and Erivan much more hastily than the situation warranted. On the other hand, it may be pointed out that the Commission, being a semi-military body, could not remain in Trans-Caucasia in the event of a Bolshevist occupation of that region.

Mustapha Kemal Pasha - 1918

The *Jagadamard,* an Armenian newspaper often well-informed concerning Trans-Caucasian affairs, learned that two Maximalist Socialists are in the new Armenian Cabinet, the rest of which is composed of Dashnakists, who are described as Radicals with strong Socialist bias.

It is reported here that Eshref Bey, a notorious band leader, was killed near Ada Bazar in the fight with Ahmed Anzavur's volunteers. The anti-Nationalist *Alemdar* learns from an eyewitness that four persons professing to be Nationalist delegates of Trebizond with one of their armed guards have been lynched by an anti-Nationalist vigilance committee formed at Samsun within an hour's distance of the town.

No confirmation of the reports that Tiflis has been occupied by Bolshevists has been received here, though according to eye-witnesses a small outbreak occurred at the beginning of the month, and resulted in the lynching of some local Reds and the execution of others.

It should be made clear that Atatürk was supported in every possible way (as noted throughout this book) by the United States during and after the Armenian Genocide. The son of Rear Admiral Colby M. Chester, Arthur T. Chester, had been in Turkey and was in direct contact with Mustapha Kemal, working with him on the formation and development of "Modern" Turkey.

Chapter 7:

Turks and Russians Vying for Armenian Support

In 1908, after the sultan was deposed and the Ottoman Constitution was proclaimed, Hagop returned home to Husenik, under a new name, Shahan Natalie. He was able to stay there for barely a year. The 1909 massacres of Armenians in Cilicia drove him back into exile in America. From 1910 to 1912, he attended Boston University, where he studied literature, philosophy (particularly Plato), and theater (particularly Shakespeare).

In 1912, he decided to return home once again and boarded a ship headed for Turkey. However, during that period war had erupted in the Balkans, and the Turkish passport-bearing Shahan Natalie was ejected from the ship by Greek authorities as a citizen of an enemy nation. His Armenian identity was ignored. He was put aboard another ship, leaving for the United States and was deported from the country.

During Shahan's absence in Turkey, in the beginning of this world conflagration, in 1914, both the Russian and the Turkish governments officially appealed to various Armenian national organizations with many promises in order to secure the active participation of the Armenians in military operations against each other. The principal stage of war would be Armenia itself. Both Turkey and Russia were very anxious to win the co-operation of the Armenians, because, judging from their past experience, they were convinced that without such co-operation they would not be able to accomplish the much desired military successes in the Armenian Highland.

With such aims in view, Russia, through Count Varantzoff Dashkoff, informed the Armenian National Council (then in existence at Tiflis) that should the Armenians pledge unreserved support for the Russian armies in the course of the war, Russia would grant autonomy to the six Armenian vilayets. The Russian Armenians, however, through bitter experience, knew very well what little practical value could be attached to the promises of the Russian Czar. Throughout the 19th century, at three different times, the Russians had made similar promises to the Armenians when waging war against Turkey and Persia, and, although the self-sacrificing co-operation of the Russian Armenians enabled the Russians to occupy the districts of Elizavetpol, Erivan and Kars in 1806, 1828, and, again, in 1878, their promises to the Armenians were promptly forgotten at the end of these wars. But this time the Armenians knew that Russia was not alone. The two great liberal nations of the West, France and England, were her Allies. After long and weighty consultation, with their hopes pinned on France and England, the Armenians resolved to aid the Russian armies in every possible way.

While Russian diplomacy was in the midst of these negotiations in Tiflis, during the last days of August 1914, a Turkish mission of twenty-eight members left Constantinople for Western Armenia with the intention of organizing a Pan-Islamic and a Pan-Turanian movement among all the races of the Near East, effectively against Russia and her Allies. The leaders of that mission were Omar Nadji Bey, Dr. Bahaeddin Shakir, and Lieutenant Hilmy—all of them very influential members of the Committee of Union and Progress. The mission also included representatives of all the Eastern races, such as the Kurds, Persians, Georgians, Chechens, Lezgines, Circassians, and the Caucasian Tartars, but not the Armenians. During those same days, the annual Congress of the Armenian National Organization was in session at Erzeroum. In the name of the Turkish government, the above mentioned mission appealed to the Armenian Organization with the following proposition:

> If the Armenians,—the Turkish as well as the Russian Armenians,— would give active co-operation to the Turkish armies, the Turkish government under a German guarantee would promise to create after the war an autonomous Armenia (made up of Russian Armenia and the three Turkish vilayets of Erzerom, Van, and Bitlis) under the suzerainty of the Ottoman empire.[38]

In an attempt to talk the Armenians into accepting the proposal, the Turkish delegates informed them also that they their mission had already garnered the cooperation of the Georgians, the Tartars, as well as the mountaineers of the northern Caucasus. Non-compliance of the Armenians under such circumstances would be foolish and fraught with danger on both sides of the border between Turkey and Russia. In spite of these promises and threats, the executive committee of the ARF, Dashnaktsutiun, informed the Turkish mission that the Armenians could not accept the proposal, advising that the Turks should not to participate in the impending war, as it would be disastrous for the Turks themselves. The Armenian members of this parley were the well-known publicist, E. Aknouni, the representative of Van, A. Vramian, the director of the Armenian schools in the district of Erzeroum and Rostom (Stepan Zorian). This audacious refusal of the Turkish proposals cost Aknouni and Vramian their lives a few months later. Rostom had the luck to escape the murderous plots against his life.

The Armenians' bold retort to the Turkish proposal exasperated the Turks, justifying the Turkish government's determination to exterminate the Armenians. And in reality, arrests and persecutions within the Armenian vilayets began in the early part of September, 1914, a month and a half before the commencement of the Russo-Turkish war. The persecutions gained a momentum as the months rolled by and tens of villages in different parts of Armenia were subjected to fire and sword. In the district of Van alone, in February and March of 1915, twenty-four villages were razed to the ground and their populations put to the sword. In early April of the same year, they

---

38 Garo Pasdermadjian (Armen Garo), *Why Armenia Should Be Free Armenia's Role In The Present War*, BOSTON
Hairenik Publishing Company, 1918.

attempted the massacre of the inhabitants of the city of Van as well, but the Armenians took up arms, and, guided by their brave leader, Aram Manoogian, defended themselves and their property for a whole month, until the Armenian volunteers from Erivan with Russian soldiers came to their rescue, saving them from the impending doom. This resistance on the part of the inhabitants of Van gave the Turkish government a pretext to initiate the deportation of the entire Armenian population of Turkish Armenia in June and July of 1915, under the pretense of relocating them to Mesopotamia, but, in fact, organizing what came to be known as death march.

Out of the million and a half of Armenians deported, scarcely 400,000 to 500,000 reached the deserts of Syria and Mesopotamia, and most of them were women, elderly people, and children, famished, raped, tortured and doomed to death. More than a million defenseless Armenians were murdered at the hands of Turkish soldiers and Turkish mobs. The gang of robbers, headed by Talaat and Enver, resorted to this fiendish means to eliminate the Armenian question once and for all, because the Armenians had had the courage to oppose to their Pan-Turanian policies. The barbarities of Jenghiz Khan and Tamerlane pale in comparison with the savageries perpetrated upon the Turkish Armenians in the summer of 1915 during this wholesale massacre organized by the Turkish government. Henry Morgenthau Sr., the U.S. ambassador to the Ottoman Empire, in Constantinople, during those frightful months, documented these atrocities with his authentic compassionate pen for the civilized nations and generations to come. This was the price the Armenian people paid in the Ottoman Empire for being in the way of Turco-German policies.

In the meantime, an unwilling returnee to the U.S., Shahan Natalie undertook responsible work within the Armenian Revolutionary Federation's U.S. district. He became a member of the editorial staff of the party's *Hairenik* monthly. He served as its editor-in-chief from 1912 to 1915. He was also elected a member of the party's United States Central Committee, as an officer of its Executive Body.

Receiving the news of the Great Atrocity, like all exiles, Shahan Natalie experienced nightmarish moments of anguish and rage. And the vengeful youth renewed the oath of the orphaned boy that he was, vowing to do his utmost to punish the Genocide perpetrators, even if the world chooses to ignore their crime against humanity.

Shahan Natalie's doubts that they will dodge punishment became reality after World War One. The Ottoman military tribunal convened in Constantinople condemned to death the principal perpetrators who had been extradited to Malta by the British authorities. However, the British placed no value whatsoever on the sentence and secretly released the enemies of humanity.

Chapter 8

Turkish Resistance to the Young Turks

A popular belief among Armenians is that all the Turks of the Ottoman Empire supported the Armenian Genocide. Although most historical accounts may trigger such an assumption, the facts of what actually happened as documented by the news of that time period indicate otherwise.

The articles below document not only that there were Turks trying to prevent the Armenian Genocide long before it happened, but that they had been warning the Armenian political leaders of what was to come if they continued to side with Talaat and the CUP. This is only a small sample of articles from the archive.

New York Times, Sunday, October 15, 1915 – Page 19

TURKISH STATESMAN
DENOUNCES ATROCITIES

Cherif Pasha Says Young Turks Long Planned to Exterminate the Armenians.

An arraignment of the Young Turks, or the Committee of Union and Progress, as having for years plotted the extermination of the Armenian people, is contained in a letter recently addressed by Maimed Cherif Pasha to the editor of the Journal de Genève. The views of this eminent exile should doubtless be considered in the light of the fact that he was obliged to fly from his native land because of his secession from the party now in power in Turkey, but even from his enemies, and the fact that he has formidable ones is evidenced by the nearly successful attempt made upon his life by Turkish police agents in Paris about two years ago must imply that he has had excellent opportunities for observation of the Young Turks' policy, since he was prominent in their councils when they first obtained power with the overthrow of the Abdul Hamid regime, and left their ranks to build up the Liberal opposition party only when he became convinced that their leaders had no intention of carrying out the program of reform to which they were pledged. He is the son of the late Saʻīd Pasha, who was one of the chief advisers of Abdul Hamid and the first Grand Vizier under the new Constitutions. His wife is Princess Emanate, the daughter of Prince Halim and he is the brother-in-law of Prince Saʻīd Halim the present Grand Vizier. He, himself, was at one time Turkish Minster to Sweden.

After branding the Armenian atrocities perpetrated under the present regime as surpassing the savagery of Genghis Khan and Tamerlane, Cherif Pasha continues:

"To be sure, the state of mind of the Unionists was not revealed to the civilized world until they had openly taken sides with Germany; but for more than six years I have been exposing them in the *Mecheroutiette* (his newspaper, published first in Constantinople and then in Paris) and in different journals and reviews, warning France and England of the plot against them and against certain nationalities within the Ottoman borders, notably the Armenians, that was being hatched.

"If there is a race which has been closely connected with the Turks by its fidelity, by its services to the country, by the statesmen and functionaries of talent it has furnished, by the intelligence which it has manifested in all domains—commerce, industry, science, and the arts—it is certainly the Armenians."

Cherif Pasha then enumerates some of the contributions which Armenians have made to Turkish civilization, including the introduction of printing and the drama, and gives credit to an Armenian, Odian Effendi, for having collaborated with Midhat Pasha in framing the Ottoman Constitution, and he lays stress upon their fine qualities as agitators against the despotisms of Turkey and Persia—qualities, one suspects, which have not highly recommended them to the autocratic «reformers» of the Young Turk regime. And he continues:

«Alas, at the thought that a people so gifted, which has served as the fructifying soil for the renovation of the Ottoman Empire, is on the point of disappearing from history—not enslaved, as were the Jews by the Assyrians, but annihilated—even the most hardened heart must bleed; and I desire, through the medium of your estimable journal, to express to this race which is being assassinated my anger toward the butchers and my immense pity for the victims.

"Having fulfilled this pious duty, let me make some exceptions relating not to the unhappy Armenian nation but to certain individual Armenians and some propagandist groups who have for the last six years so maladroitly constipated themselves the defenders and apologists of this Committee of Union and Progress, the author of all their present sufferings. How often have I warned them against the bad faith of the Unionists, the perversity of whose black souls I knew only too well! Besides, the massacres of Adana, provoked by the Union's orders ought to have brought them to a sense of the real state of affairs. Some of them by a wrong appreciation of their interests, others influenced by political alliances of an evil sort like that poor Constantinople Deputy, Zohrab Effendi, who has expiated his errors on the scaffold—all the Armenian political leaders; or almost all, by identifying themselves with the political fortune of the Union, have compromised instead of serving their national cause.

«If instead of enrolling themselves under the banner of that baneful and treacherous association, they had arranged themselves openly beside the true liberals who had long been pointing out the danger of their course, even at peril of their lives, they would not only have remained true to their principles, but they would also have spared their unfortunate brethren the persecutions they suffered before the war and their whole nation the prospect of an extermination unique in the annals of history.»

Next is an article from December 22, 1915, about prominent Turks opposing Talaat and the CUP, some at the cost of their lives. This article was quite difficult to find as Talaat had done his best to have it destroyed.

Many Turks appear to have understood the value of the Armenians and the dangers of the Germans, who would be the ones to replace the Armenians.

Hickory Daily Record - Wednesday December 22, 1915 – Page 4

DECLARES TURKISH EMPIRE MENACED WITH DESTRUCTION

Special correspondence of the New York World.

Constantinople, Nov. 10.—The empire of the Turks never was threatened with danger of destruction as it is today. Financially, socially and politically, Turkey already is in ruins. There are cities entirely depopulated; commerce, and traffic in the whole country is stopped; more than 250,000 men have fallen in the battlefield or died of disease; not less than 300,000 wounded soldiers are crowded in the hospitals, and surely more than 3,000,000 families are on the verge of starvation. Yet it is astonishing to say that there never has, been recorded in the history of the Ottoman Turk such a spirit of resistance and determination as a small group of Young Turks, who have taken the destinies of the realm in their hands, are demonstrating.

The writer has resided for a long period in Constantinople. He visited different parts of Turkey recently, and can bear witness, with a clear conscience and impartiality, to the awe and terror in which Turkey is submerged today.

A few weeks ago, at the opening of the Ottoman Parliament, an incident occurred in the Senate which afforded the most accurate demonstration of the miserable situation of the country. Senator Ahmed Riza Bey, the leader of the Young Turk revolution in 1908 and ex-president of the first Parliament, was the sole person among the members of the chamber and of the Senate who dared to take the stand to interpellate the government. The act of Riza Bey is more worthy of admiration in that a preceding act of the same kind had cost him and his friends very dearly. A few months ago Senator Ahmed Riza Bey, Gen. Galib Pasha, Ahmed Mouktar Pasha (former Grand Vizier) and Abdurahman Sherif Bey, ex-minister of education and historian of the empire, handed in a written interpellation, but when the Senate met, Ahmet Riza and Galib Pasha took the stand and criticized the government vehemently, while Sherif Bey voted with them and Ahmed Montkar Pasha remined silent. The very same night Gen. Galib Pasha was found dead, killed.

Ahmed Riza Bey, notwithstanding the fate of his colleague, this time stood alone and spoke for hours, denouncing the government and using still stronger terms, when Enver Pasha and Talaat Bey were hurriedly summoned to the senate by the Committee of Union and Progress to frighten them. Ahmed Riza Bey emphasized three main points on which he demanded immediate explanation. His interpellation was published in the official organ *"Takrimi Veki,"* but its distribution was suppressed by the police.

Fears Conquest of Germany

"First of all," said Ahmed, "the government led the country into this disastrous war solely to please the Germans. After the war, instead of our armies conquering the Caucasus, instead of marching into the deserts of Africa, taking Egypt and all the northern coast of the Mediterranean, as our government promised so confidently at the opening of hostilities. today the English army is approaching the gates of Bagdad. Our offensive against the Russians on the Caucasian front failed where, under the command of our war minister, we lost three army corps. We are not on Russian territory, while we have lost a part of eastern Anatolia. While the operations on Gallipoli have been a deadlock for the English, it has been a graveyard for us. To put the year's history in a nutshell, more than half of our population is starving to death; our reserves are exhausted and we are ruined. What are our gains? Death and starvation.

"You say that a German army is marching over the corps of Serbia to come to our help. You are building up an arch of triumph to welcome the soldiers of the Kaiser. Yes, they may come, but tell me what guarantee you have that they ever will go back from here? Have the Germans guaranteed our independence, and what are those guarantees? I demand that the government shall answer to what end is sacrificed the life and existence of the empire. I fear, and with good reason, that the way is already paved to build a German colony over the relic of the great Ottoman empire."

Will be Enslaved

"Second—Has the government any knowledge that Ottoman subjects namely, the Armenians—have been subject to outrage? Do you know that all the Armenians inhabiting Anatolia have been driven out of their homes, their property confiscated and, after separating men and women, the criminals have been let loose from the prisons to rob and massacre them on their way to their unknown destinations? The Armenians have been one of the most useful elements of our country. They have largely contributed to the material and intellectual welfare of the empire. To what avail are they to be exterminated? Who, what element will you bring to the valleys and mountains of Anatolia to take the place of the deported Armenians? The Germans, you will say, I know; but are you aware that the Turkish peasant and the Turkish merchant will be enslaved by the German colonists within a score of years? With their thrift, with their intelligence, with the protection by the German government, the German immigrants will become the masters of the country, while we have to be their servants. Does the government take the repressibility for this outrage?

Graft in Name of Patriotism

"Third—Who are these irresponsible persons who call themselves 'Mousdafai Millel' (the committee of natioal defense), who are boldly robbing everybody in the country, poor as well as rich? No merchant has escaped their notice; goods have been taken from the stores in Stamboul and Pera amounting to millions. They have taken goods which have no military value—articles of luxury, rugs, caviar, silk stockings, ladies' shoes, costumes a la mode. All these sorts of things are of no use to our soldiers in Gallipoli; but they have gone into the houses of the members of this committee or they have been turned into cash to fill the pockets of private individuals who are playing a great role in the doom of Osmanli.

"I want a straightforward answer from the government. I want the government to come forward, take the responsibility and explain its attitude."

To these questions Talaat Bey, the Minister of the Interior and the man in power in Turkey, made but a short reply:

"The interpellations made could not be answered by the government. All those are external affairs, therefore they could not be discussed here without injuring the interests of our great and victorious empire."

The answer of Talaat epitomizes most accurately the attitude of the few who are now in power today in Turkey. It is a wrong idea to suppose that there is another government in the country than that of Enver, Talaat & Co. Sultan Mehmed Richad has as much influence in the politics of Stamboul as any Pasha living somewhere in Asia Minor.

Sultan a Nonentity

The Sultan himself is a harmless. though useless person. Personally he is kindly inclined, but unfortunately he lacks mentality, intelligence, energy and determination. During the reign of his elder brother, Abdul Hamid, being for thirty-three years kept in solitude and having acquired the habit of drinking *mastika* (alcohol), he has lost his health and his mind. I am assured from authentic sources that the Sultan does not know that his country is in a state of war with the English. He has only a vague idea that the Russians are attacking the straits in order to open a route for their wheat exportation, and that the Ahmans (Germans) have come to his assistance to beat the Muscovites.

One authentic story told about Sultan Mehmed V. is illuminating. After the first Balkan war the opponents of the committee killed Mahmoud Shevket Pasha, then Grand Vizier and Minister of War. The very next day, an imperial irade was issued appointing Said Halim Pasha as grand vizier. A few months later, Halim Pasha went to the palace to seek an audience of the sultan. The master of ceremonies notified His Majesty of the wish of the

Grand Vizier. Evidently, the Sultan had forgotten that he had a new Grand Vizier whom he had received already many times, and excalimed: "What! Grand Vizier! Wasn't he shot some time ago?"

With such a man at the head of the Empire, Enver and Talaat have no fear about drawing up new temporary laws every morning and making the Sultan sign them without knowing or understanding their contents. Perhaps the Sultan could have been aided by the heir apparent, Prince Yussouf-Izzeddin Bey, but he's very closely watched, virtually a prisoner, and is only allowed an automobile ride every afternoon at 4 o'clock from the palace through the Grand Rue of Pera to the Sultan Bajazid and back.

The Real Masters of Turkey

The real masters of Turkey are sitting neither at Yildiz Kiosk nor at the Sublime Porte, neither at the Parliament nor at the Senate. They must be sought among a few influential members of the Committee of Union and Progress. The political organization of the government is absolutely nominal. It is true there is a Sultan in Turkey, a Grand Vizier with its cabinet, ministers, a Parliament with all its legislative formalities and working commissions, a Senate with all its venerable gray-haired old Pashas and Beys — but all this means nothing. They do nothing except bow down and say *"evet effendem"* (yes, sir) to the commands of the mysterious power of Enver, Talaat & Co., who with a finger-point can make peace or war, can order massacres and hang scores of notables on the Galata bridge, and make laws in a minute to make millions of people — men, women and children homeless, wretched and miserable.

Chapter 9

German and Ottoman Genocidal Cooperation

On August 2, 1914, after the outbreak of World War I, the Ottoman-German Alliance was ratified between the German and Ottoman Empires. This was a union of two countries with similar genocidal tendencies.

Although the first genocide of the 20th century is often claimed to be that of the Armenians from 1915-1923, there was a small, less known genocide carried out in German South West Africa (modern-day Namibia). The victims of this racial extermination were the indigenous Herero and Namaqua peoples.

General Arnold von Winckler (11th Army) talking to İsmail Enver Paşa, Ottoman minister of war.

The colonial Germans had been exploiting them and their native lands since 1885, following a fraudulent purchase carried out by Franz Adolf Eduard Lüderitz (1834-1886), a German tobacco merchant.

The land purchase scheme was between Lüderitz and the local tribal chief, Captain Josef Frederiks II of Bethanie. The unit of land measurement in the agreement was the German geographical mile, which is almost five times greater than the English mile. Lüderitz and the signing witness, Johannes Bam, a German Missionary, knew that Chief Frederiks had no understanding of what a German geographical mile was. Frederiks thought he was selling the useless coastal lands found on the Atlantic Ocean. Little did he know, what he had in fact comprised almost his entire tribal area for only £600 in gold and 260 rifles.

Following the purchase, when Chief Frederiks became aware of the actual land mass he had sold including the fertile lands his tribe needed for survival, he complained to the German Imperial Government to no avail.

On August 7, 1884, and with no objections from the other colonial power in Africa, Great Britain, German South West Africa was officially declared.

After the formation of German South West Africa, Lüderitz went on to purchase from other chiefs the entire coastal strip from South Africa to Angola, an area totaling 220,000 square miles. In April 1885, a year before his untimely death, Lüderitz sold his land holdings to the German Colonial Society.

On January 5, 2017, a Class Action Complaint was filed in United States District Court, Southern District of New York, Civ. No. 17-0062. The case was filed against the Federal Republic of Germany on behalf of the Ovaherero and Nama indigenous peoples. The summary of the complaint best describes what lead up to and resulted in the first genocide of the 20th century.

SUMMARY OF THE COMPLAINT

1. Plaintiffs bring this action on behalf of all the Ovaherero and Nama peoples for damages resulting from the horrific genocide and unlawful taking of property in violation of international law by the German colonial authorities during the 1885 to 1909 period in what was formerly known as South West Africa, and is now Namibia. Plaintiffs also bring this action to, among other things, enjoin and restrain the Federal Republic of Germany from continuing to exclude plaintiffs and other lawful representatives of the Ovaherero and Nama people from participation in discussions and negotiations regarding the subject matter of this Complaint, in violation of plaintiffs' rights under international law, including the U.N. Declaration on the Rights of Indigenous People to self-determination for all indigenous peoples and their right to participate and speak for themselves regarding all matters relating to the losses that they have suffered.

2. From 1885 to 1903, over a quarter of Ovaherero and Nama lands (originally over 50,000 square miles) and countless cattle had been seized without compensation by German colonists with the explicit consent of the German colonial authorities. Since cattle grazing was the primary economic base for their survival, the Ovaherero and Nama communities suffered from these terrible losses. German colonial authorities also turned a blind eye to the widespread and systematic rape of Ovaherero and Nama women and girls, as well as the indiscriminate use of Ovaherero and Nama peoples as forced laborers without compensation.

3. After learning that they were going to be forced into concentration camps, and that the remainder of their lands and property were going to be confiscated, the Ovaherero rose up in early 1904, followed by the Nama in 1905, The uprising was crushed by German Imperial troops under the command of General Lothar von Trotha, who announced that his goal was to annihilate the Ovaherero people. His orders were effectively carried out, resulting in the deaths of over 100,000 Ovaherero and Nama, with the remainder thrown into concentration camps under atrocious and sub-human conditions, where there was an extraordinarily high death toll, and the survivors who were well enough to stand were forced to work as forced/slave laborer. The surviving women were subjected to systematic rape and other abuses.

4. After decades of denying that the near destruction and eradication of the Ovaherero peoples by the German Imperial authorities was, in fact, a genocide, and refusing to even consider the issue of reparations or compensation, Defendant The Federal Republic of Germany

("Germany") recently entered into negotiations with the Republic of Namibia ("Namibia") regarding these issues. However, Germany has refused to include representatives of the Ovaherero and Nama peoples in these discussions, even though they were the primary victims of the atrocities perpetrated by the German colonial authorities. Germany has also refused to explicitly admit that what it did constitutes a genocide under international law, even though it has been quick to pass resolutions and declarations blaming Turkey for the allegedly genocide of the Armenians by the Ottoman Empire during World War I.

The first Genocide of the 20th century, the systematic eradication of the Ovaherero and Nama peoples, has striking similarities with what befell the Armenian people less than a decade later. In both genocides, the common denominator was Germany.

Victims of the Namibian Genocide (Photo via Zed.fr)

Germany's military cooperation with the Ottoman Empire didn't start with the Ottoman-German Alliance of 1914. The history of Germany's influence over the Ottoman Empire's military stated as far back as 1835 with Prussian Captain, Helmuth Moltke. Moltke became a military instructor of the Ottoman army. Over the decades that followed, Moltke was joined by other officers and military personnel charged with promoting the Europeanization of Ottoman forces.[39]

Wilhelm Leopold Colmar Freiherr von der Goltz

After defeat in the Russo-Turkish War (1877–1878), Sultan Hamid of the Ottoman Empire, asked for German aid in reorganizing the Ottoman Army, so that they would be able to resist the advance of the Russian Empire. In response to the Sultan's request, Baron von der Goltz (1843-1916) was sent to Constantinople. Von der Goltz spent twelve years on this work, which provided the material for several of his books. Goltz Pasha, a name of honor which was bestowed on him by the Ottomans, paved the way for Germany to gain an economic, political, and military foothold in the Ottoman Empire.[40]

From 1883 to 1885, Goltz trained the so-called Goltz generation of Ottoman officers, many of whom would go to play prominent roles in

---

39 Professor Oliver Janz, *German Soldiers in the Ottoman Empire, 1835-1918* (Freie Universität Berlin, 2016)

40 Vahakn N Dadrian, German Responsibility in the Armenian Genocide: A Review of the Historical Evidence of German Complicity (Watertown, Mass: Blue Crane Books, 1996), 7.

Ottoman military and political life.[41]

In *Absolute Destruction*, touching on the Armenian Genocide in the context of German military culture, Isabel V. Hull asks if it was "institutional extremism," which created the culture of and willingness to resort to, "terrific violence and destruction in excess" to a degree that it even endangered "Germany's own security" and harmed its "political goals." All these, Hull notes, were "in contravention of international norms, and even contrary to ultimate military effectiveness."[42]

Goltz encouraged the Ottomans to concentrate on eastward expansion. This adopted policy would directly endanger the indigenous Armenian population found in the path of Goltz ambitious plan. But given the culture of military practices in Germany and in the Ottoman Empire, the former factor became the solution to the latter.[43]

The Ottoman leaders, namely Talaat, Jemal and Enver, followed the recommendation of Ewald Banse (1883-1953), a German geographer who studied the racial composition of the Ottoman Empire and concluded that, "to get the Armenian Question out of the world, one had to get the Armenians out of the world."[44]

As part of the modernization of the Ottoman military, Captain Erich Serno was sent to expand the Ottoman air force, which had existed since 1911. Thus, Serno became the creator of the new Turkish air force, which was based on the German model.

During the first year of World War One, transportation of ammunition for the Ottoman army from the Central Powers was blocked in the Balkans. To remedy this, Germany built ammunition factories in Constantinople. Heinrich Frank, a military operational manager of the Navy arsenals' bullet factory, passed on his knowledge to the Ottomans for this purpose.[45]

The Allied powers had accused German military personnel "having instigated" the Armenian massacres. They also accused the German military of having "supported" the Young Turks in their policy of the extermination of the Armenians.[46]

Harry Stürmer, correspondent of the *Kölnische Zeitung* in Constantinople, leveled similar charges against German officers, claiming they had "coolly [taken] the initiatives of aiding the mass extermination of Armenians." He asserted that "Germans 'of all ranks right up to the highest levels'" who were

---

41 Akmeşe, Handan Nezir The Birth of Modern Turkey The Ottoman Military and the March to World I, London: I.B. Tauris page 24

42 Isabel Hull, Absolute Destruction: Military Culture and the Practices of War in Imperial Germany (Ithaca, NY [u.a.]: Cornell Univ. Press, 2006), 1.

43 Vahakn N Dadrian, German Responsibility in the Armenian Genocide: A Review of the Historical Evidence of German Complicity (Watertown, Mass: Blue Crane Books, 1996), 124.

44 Cited in Hilmar Kaiser, Imperialsim, Racism, and Development Theories (Ann Arbor: Gomidas Institute, 1997), 19.

45 Oliver Stein, German Soldiers in the Ottoman Empire, 1835-1918 (Freie Universität Berlin, 2016)

46 Dinkel, Christoph. "German Officers and the Armenian Genocide." Armenian Review 44 no. 1 (Spring 1991): 78

stationed in the Ottoman Empire uttered "venomous expressions, shortsighted condemnations of Armenians based on no awareness of the facts," which were based on, "mindless recitations of official Turkish reports."[47]

Ernst von Kwiatkowski, the Austro-Hungarian consul of Trabzon, in eastern Turkey, dispatched a telegram dated October 22, 1915, stating: "I learn from usually reliable German sources that the first suggestions towards Armenian neutralization, though not the methods actually implemented, have come from the German side."[48]

(left to right) Kaiser Wilhelm II, Enver Pasha, Sultan Mehmed V. - October 15, 1917

A letter to Matthias Erzberger, a German politician, sent by P. Liebl, a Franciscan priest from Vienna, dated March 26, 1916, accused Wangenheim, the German ambassador to Constantinople, of "having suggested" the deportations of Armenians.[49]

There were also "accusations made by British and American newspapers: That Otto Liman von Sanders was the main culprit of the Armenian persecution; that the Foreign Office files would incriminate the emperor" and other German high officials in office at the time of war.[50]

Such "open secrets," known "in domestic political and military circles" in Germany, together with a plethora of evidence in German archives, could confirm the Allied powers' accusations about German military involvement in the massacres.[51]

Global Net — Stop the Arms Trade (GN-STAT) published a report in April, 2018, in which Germany is implicated in providing arms, training and

---

47 Harry Stürmer, Zwei Kriegsjahre in Konstantinopel (Lausanne, 1917), p. 59-60. Cited in Dinkel, 78-79.
48 Cited in Dinkel, 79.
49 Cited in Dinkel, 123.
50 Dinkel, 82.
51 Dinkel, 80, 84.

assistance to the Turks during the Armenian Genocide. Their report echoes much of what has been stated above, but digs in deeper as to what extent German officers took part in the murders by actually picking up rifles and firing them themselves?

In his "New report details Germany's role in Armenian genocide," an article published online on the German based *Deutsche Welle* (www.dw.com) on April 5, 2018, Ben Knight writes:

> Many of the firsthand German accounts in the report come from letters by Major Graf Eberhard Wolffskehl, who was stationed in the southeastern Turkish city of Urfa in October 1915. Urfa was home to a substantial population of Armenians, who barricaded themselves inside houses against Turkish infantry. Wolffskehl was serving as chief of staff to Fahri Pasha, deputy commander of the Ottoman 4th Army, which had been called in as reinforcement.
>
> "They (the Armenians) had occupied the houses south of the church in numbers," the German officer wrote to his wife. "When our artillery fire struck the houses and killed many people inside, the others tried to retreat into the church itself. But ... they had to go around the church across the open church courtyard. Our infantry had already reached the houses to the left of the courtyard and shot down the people fleeing across the church courtyard in piles. All in all the infantry, which I used in the main attack ... acquitted itself very well and advanced very dashingly."

In "Ideological support," a chapter of the article in question, Ben Knight shares some more examples of the German military forces' direct participation in the killing of Armenians:

> While German companies provided the guns, and German soldiers the expert advice on how to use them, German officers also laid what Landgraeber calls the "ideological foundations" for the genocide.
>
> That the German Reich shared the Ottomans' mistrust of the Armenians was no secret — both feared they were colluding with mutual enemy Russia, while Gottschlich's book quotes navy attaché Hans Humann, a member of the German-Turkish officer corps and close friend of the Ottoman Empire's war minister, Enver Pasha, as saying: "The Armenians — because of their conspiracy with the Russians — will be more or less exterminated. That is hard, but useful."
>
> Another figure the report focuses on is the Prussian major general Colmar Freiherr von der Goltz, a key figure who became a vital military adviser to the Ottoman court in 1883 and saw himself as a lobbyist for the German arms industry and supported both Mauser and Krupp in their efforts to secure Turkish commissions. (He once boasted in his diary, "I can claim that without me the rearmament of the army with German models would not have happened.")
>
> "Not publicly, but among his friends and relatives, von der Goltz would show himself an Armenia-phobe," said Landgraeber. "Several witnesses

heard him describing them as 'a greasy trader people.' He helped persuade the Sultan to try and end the Armenian question once and for all."

Landgraeber also considers von der Goltz a source for later Nazi ideology. The Prussian officer published a military book in 1883 titled *"Das Volk in Waffen" ("The People Armed")*, in which, as Landgraeber puts it: "He adopts positions that Hitler would take up later — for example, the aim of a military campaign should be to destroy the enemy totally, not just to fight and force a capitulation. He believed in total war. That was also the ideological foundation that he gave the Ottomans, and which they used in the Armenian issue."

Landgraeber is keen to underline that the new research does not absolve the Ottoman Empire of its guilt — but simply fills in the gaps in the historical record. "It happened as we have researched it, and nothing should be sugarcoated — but the entire picture should be more complete."[52]

In 2015, the German president, Joachim Gauck, recognized the genocide, during a speech he gave at a nondenominational religious service in Berlin Cathedral on the eve of the 100th anniversary of the Armenian Genocide.

Gauck stated: "In this case, we Germans collectively still have to come to terms with the past, namely when it comes to shared responsibility and perhaps even complicity in the genocide of the Armenians."[53]

A couple of weeks before Soghomon Tehlirian assassinated Talaat Pasha on a Berlin street, Talaat had a secret meeting with British spy, Aubrey Herbert. In Herbert's memoirs titled *"Ben Kendim: A Record of Eastern Travel,"* Talaat Pasha stated the following in regards to Germany and her involvement in the Armenian Genocide:

He [Talaat Pasha] himself had always been against the attempted extermination of the Armenians; it was, in any case, impossible, and a country that adopted such methods cut itself off from civilisation. He had twice protested against this policy, but had been overruled, he said, by the Germans. "In England you hear only one side of the case," he said.[54]

Even if Germany was the driving force of the Armenian Genocide as Talaat Pasha implies in his claims made to Aubrey Herbert, the Ottoman Empire participated in carrying out the actual crime, thus are in no way absolved of their guilt and responsibility.

It is also noteworthy to consider the dates of German influence on Ottoman military reforms and the Armenian Genocides of 1894-1896 as well as the Adana massacres of 1909. Were these killings also a result of the Germans?

---

52 http://www.dw.com/en/new-report-details-germanys-role-in-armenian-genocide/a-43268266
53 http://www.dw.com/en/german-president-gauck-labels-ottoman-massacre-of-armenians-genocide/a-18404147
54 Aubrey Herbert "BEN KENDIM: A Record of Eastern Travel, (London, Hutchinson & Co. Paternoster Row, 1925): 309.

German soldiers holding bones of Armenians killed near the village of Hekim Khan, Armenia - November 10, 1918 (Tsolak Dildilian collection)

Chapter 10

Russians Turned Bolshevik

In 1914, after the Armenian revolutionaries sided with Tsarist Russia, effectively turning down the Turks' call for support of the Ottoman Empire against the Russians, a campaign to massacre the Armenians began. The historically Armenian city of Van with a sizeable Armenian population became one of the first Armenian regions to come under attack by the 5,000-strong Ottoman Army led by Djevdet Bey, Halil Bey (1881-1957), Köprülü Kâzım Bey (1880-1968), and Rafael de Nogales (1879-1936), a Venezuelan soldier.

Armenian volunteers of the Caucasus taking the oath of allegiance administered by the church dignitaries before leaving of the battlefield in October, 1914.

According to the news from the Russian consul at Urumiah, Persia, dated the 15 May, 1915, 6,000 Armenians were massacred in and around Van. The Armenians were defending themselves against the attacks from the Turks and Kurds, but needed urgent help.

My paternal grandmother, Nargis Manoogian (1889-1942), a native of Van, witnessed the Armenian self-defense forces repel the well-equipped albeit less motivated Ottoman Army, on the 17 May, 1915. This victory can be largely credited to the leadership of Sargis Hovannisian, a.k.a. Aram Manoogian (1879-1919). The Armenians had set up a provisional government which did its best to create some form of normalcy for the inhabitants of Van and, more importantly, to coordinate the defense efforts.

After the dust had settled from the battle, and the threat of the Turkish army had been neutralized, the Russian army arrived to find peace restored and the Armenians in control of Van. This victory, however, did not last long. By the middle of July, after heavy fighting between the reinforced Ottoman Army, backed by the Germans, the Russian forces, who had become the driving force of defense, were ordered to evacuate. The Armenians, who did not have the means to overcome the now much larger Ottoman army, had no choice but to evacuate along with the retreating Russians. The last Armenians left Van, bound to Persia, on August 4, 1915. And their exit marked the fall of Van. But the Ottoman victory, too, was short-lived.

On 29 September, 1915, following their defeat on the Caucasus front, the Ottoman Army left the city of Van. Taking advantage of the Turks' departure, some Armenians, including my grandmother, who had escaped to Transcaucasia (now referred to as South Caucasus) returned to their homes.

With the Turkish defeat at the Battle of Koprukoy, on 19 January, 1916, Russian forces once again advanced into the Ottoman Empire, eventually making their way to Van. With their presence, they were viewed as guarantors of the Armenians's safe return. This time, however, the Russians did not allow the repatriated Armenians to set up a provisional government as they had done before.

Just as things were beginning to level out in Van, the Armenians were once again handed a devastating blow. The Russian forces, who had been following the Tsar's orders, found themselves taking orders from the Bolshevik government thanks to two revolutions which took place in March and October of 1917. The Russian army began to disintegrate, as more and more soldiers deserted. To make matters worse, on March 3, 1918, the new 'democratic' Russian government signed the Treaty of Brest-Litovsk with the Ottoman Empire. Signed by Germany, Austria-Hungary, Bulgaria, Ottoman Empire, and Russian SFRS (Soviet Federative Socialist Republic), this treaty put an end to Russia's involvement in the war. The treaty stipulated pulling the borders back to prewar areas, effectively ceding the cities of Batum, Kars, and Ardahan to the Ottoman Empire.

The first two pages of the Treaty of Brest-Litovsk, in (from left to right) German, Hungarian, Bulgarian, Ottoman Turkish, and Russian.

In early 1918, the Ottoman Third Army began an offensive against the Armenians. Having been likewise targeted by the Turks, Assyrians joined the Armenians of Van, who attempted to resist. During these heavy battles my paternal grandmother's husband was killed, leaving her with their two young sons, Antranig (1909-1990), my eldest uncle, and Hamazasp (1917-2012). They were in the last caravans to evacuate Van, led by my paternal grandfather Vahan Ivan Manoogian (1889-1953), an officer of the Tsar's army and a native of Dilijan, Armenia. They made their way to Persia and eventually settled in Baghdad, Iraq.

Central Powers' delegates at Brest-Litovsk (1917-1918): German General, Max Hoffmann (1869-1927); Austrohungarian Foreign Minister, Ottokar Czernin (1872-1932); Grand Vizier of Ottoman Empire, Talaat Pasha (1874-1921); and German Foreign Minister, Richard von Kühlman (1873-1948).

The loss of the Armenian territories because of the Bolshevik revolution also led to the loss of tens of thousands of Armenian lives until 1923 and under the direct orders of the founder of modern Turkey, Mustapha Kemal.

While curating Shahan Natalie's archive, clues about people who had been backing the Young Turks and the leaders of the Bolshevik movement surfaced. Further digging uncovered a treasure-trove of documents that link powerful people in the United States to the origins of the Bolshevik movement, particularly a New York banker named Jacob H. Schiff, a key sponsor.

Seven months after the bloodless Russian revolution of March 1917, Bolsheviks overthrew the Provisional Government in October and signed the Treaty of Brest-Litovsk to exit the war. Following a bloody civil war, the Bolsheviks eventually established the Union of Soviet Socialist Republics Russia (U.S.S.R.) in 1922, including the territories of Eastern Armenia. Coming to power with the financial support of people like the New York, German born Jewish banker, Jacob H. Schiff, the Bolshevik government's purges resulted in the deaths of about 60 million Soviet citizens, including thousands of Armenians. As a consequence of the Bolshevik Revolution, not only the Western Armenian territories were abandoned by the Russian troops that had functioned as guarantors of the survival of the Armenian population, but also the lands of Eastern Armenia, making it vulnerable to the Turkish invasion.

(Left) Jacob H. Schiff (1847-1920). (Right) Vladimir Ilyich Lenin (1870-1924) addressing Russian soldiers about to fight the Polish Army, Petrograd, Russia, 1920.

The article below shows how Schiff sponsored some of the initial endeavors of the Bolshevik movement that would end up putting an end to the first independent Armenian republic in 1920.

NEW YORK TIMES – Saturday, March 24, 1917

PACIFIST PESTER TILL MAYOR CALLS THEM TRAITORS

Socialists at Carnegie hall Fail to Make Russian Celebration a Peace Meeting.

RABBI WISE READY FOR WAR

Sorry We Cannot Fight with the German People to Overthrow Hohenzollernism.

KENNAN RETELLS HISTORY

Russians Turned Bolshevik
Relates How Jacob H. Schiff Financed Revolution Propaganda in Czar's Army.

The most violent clash between patriots and pacifists that has occurred in New York City since relations were broken with Germany marked the celebration of the Russian revolution held last night in Carnegie Hall. It was precipitated by Mayor Mitchel, whose declaration that we were about to go to war in behalf of the same kind of democracy that had freed Russia was met with a determined demonstration by pacifists, evidently previously organized, which threatened for a time to break up the meeting.

After the uproar had lasted for fifteen minutes, the Mayor, white with anger, stepped to the edge of the stage and shouted: "This country is on the verge of war—" A loud chorus of "No" made his voice heard with: "And I say to you in the galleries that tonight we are divided into only two classes—Americans and traitors!"

"I hope they put you in the first ranks," shouted a leader of the pacifists.

"You do me a great honor," replied the Mayor, and the applause which followed, coupled with the ejection of some of the trouble makers, gave the Mayor's supporters the majority.

The meeting started in orderly fashion. The century old fight of Russian revolutionists was pictured in glowing words, matched by the promise of the Russia to be.

On the front of the speaker's stand hung a pair of leg irons, from a Siberian prison. They were unlocked. An authority on Russian affairs, George Kennan, told of how the movement by the Society of the Friends of Russian Freedom, financed by Jacob H. Schiff, had at the time of the Russo-Japanese war spread among 50,000 Russian officers and men in Japanese prison camps the gospel of the Russian revolutionist. "And," said Mr. Kennan, "we know how the army helped the Duma in the bloodless revolution that made the new Russia last week."

The galleries were largely filled with Socialists, downstairs an admission fee had been charged and the crowd was more orderly until awakened by the protestations of the pacifists.

Mayor Mitchel was introduced by Herbert Parsons, President of the Society of Friends of Russian Freedom, as a "man of a race that has also struggled freedom." There were rumblings of trouble when a few voices in the galleries started to hoot the Mayor.

"We are gathered here," the Mayor began, "to celebrate the greatest triumph of democracy since the fall of the Bastile." There where some cheers. "America rejoices," he said. "How could she do otherwise when she sees power in Russia transferred from the few to the many, and in the country where there seemed the least hope of the cause of democracy triumphing.

"America, the greatest democracy, is proud tonight because democracy in Russia has supplanted the greatest oligarchy that remained on the face of the earth." Then the Mayor stepped back and said:

"But I submit we have another reason to be proud. It is now inevitable, so far as human foresight can make a prediction, that the United States is to be projected into this world war and—"

"No! No!" rolled the chorus from the galleries.

There was quiet for an instant. Then the audience downstairs and in the boxes began to rise and shout of "Yes! Yes!" answered the galleries.

"The United States if for peace!" a voice from the gallery cried, and the tumult started anew. The ushers escorted some of the leaders of the disturbance out of the arena, and when the Mayor got partial order he said:

"We are to be projected into the war through no fault of ours, but because of conditions which have been thrusted upon us—"

"No! No! No!" the galleries started again. Some one shouted an epithet at the Mayor, which brought, even from the galleries, shouts of "Put him out! Choke him!"

"And when America does enter the contest," shouted the Mayor, "it will be to vindicate certain ideas and fundamentals as those on which the Republic was built, and among them will be the cause of democracy throughout the world. Let us be glad that, instead of fighting side by side with autocratle Russia, we shall be fighting side by side with democratic Russia."

It was at this point that the galleries became so demonstrative that Mr. Mitchel told them they must be Americans or traitors.

"You are for America or you are against her," he said, and here the Mayor made reference to the accusation he made against Senator Wagner, "You are for America or against her, whether in private life or in legislative halls," he said.

The Mayor then left the hall, followed by shouts of condemnation and of praise.

When the tumult had died down Rabbi S. S. Wise, a worker for world peace but not an extreme pacifist, was introduced.

"I feel it is my duty to say a word in support [hisses] and in reply to the Mayor. I would have this great audience know that I believe the Mayor was right—[This brought shouts of "no. You're as bad as he is"]

"I am here to talk, and I'm going to talk," shouted the Rabbi. "If you don't like what I say, go. I am going to say. The Mayor is right when he says we are on the verge of war. I pray God it may not come, but if it does the blame will not rest upon us but upon that German militarism, which may it be given to the German people to overthrow as the Romanoffs have been forever overthrown.

Russians Turned Bolshevik

"God knows we want peace. No man ever fought and stood for peace as has Woodrow Wilson. [Cheers.] I do not believe that war is absolutely inevitable, but I thank God I am a citizen of a republic that has been patient.

"I am for peace. I say, but I would to God it were possible for us to fight side by side with the German people for the overthrow of Hohenzollernism."

Then the rabbi praised the Russian revolution, but he ran into opposition when he said:

"At the risk of incurring the displeasure of those of you who have such bitter memories I hope that amnesty will be extended to the Czar himself. May God forgive the Czar." [Shouts of "No, never!"] "May God forgive the monarch who never knew what mercy was."

This was followed by shouts by a man in the gallery.

"I cannot forget," continued the Rabbi, "that I am a member and a teacher of race which half has lived in the domain of the Czar and as a few, I believe that of all the achievements of my people, none have been nobler than that part of sons and daughter of Israel have taken in the great movement which has culminated in the free Russia."

It was after a review of the struggle of the Russian revolutionists, of whom he has been the leading American writer, that Mr. Kennan told of the work of the Friends of Russian Freedom in the revolution.

He said that during the Japanese-Russian war he was in Tokyo, and that he was permitted to make visits among the 12,00 Russian prisoners in Japanese hands at the end of the first year of war. He told how they had asked him to give them something to read, and he had convinced the idea of putting revolutionary propaganda into the Russian Army.

The Japanese authorities favored it and gave him permission. Later he sent to America for all the Russian revolutionary literature to be had. He said that one day Dr. Nicholas Russel came to him in Tokyo, unannounced, and said that he had been sent to help the work.

"The movement was financed by a New York banker you all know and love," he said, referring to Mr. Schiff, "and soon we received a ton and a half of Russian revolutionary propaganda. At the end of the war 50,000 Russian officers and men went back to their country as ardent revolutionists. The Friends of Russian Freedom had sowed 50,000 seeds of liberty in 100 Russian regiments. I do not know how many of those officers and men were in the Petrograd fortress last week, but we do know what part the army took in the revolution."

Mr. Parsons then arose and said:

"I will now read a message from White Sulphur Springs sent by the gentleman to whom Mr. Mennan referred."

This was the message:

"Will you say for me to those present at tonight's meeting how deeply I regret my inability to celebrate with the Friends of Russian Freedom the actual reward of what we had hoped and striven for these long years! I do not for a moment feel that if the Russian people have under their present leaders shown such commendable moderation in this moment of crisis they will fail to give Russia proper government and a constitution which shall permanently assure to the Russian people the happiness and prosperity of which a financial autocracy has so long deprived them. JACOB H. SCHIFF."

This message from President Wilson was read:

"The American Ambassador in Petrograd, acting under instructions from this Government, formally recognized the new Government of Russia. By this act, the United States has expressed its confidence in the success of and its natural sympathy with a popular government. WOODROW WILSON."

Vladimir Resnikoff, the blind Russian baritone, sang a number of folk songs and the Symphony Orchestra, directed by Nikolai Sokoloff played Tchaikovsky's Symphony No. 4 in F minor and other selections. Miss Lillian D. Wald delivered a eulogy of Mme. Catherine Breshkovskaya, the Russian revolutionist, who had visited this country and who is now in Siberia, to be brought back at the age of 70 years to see in Petrograd the triumph of the cause for which she worked and suffered.

The following resolution was unanimously adopted:

Resolved, That the Mayor of the City of New York be requested to transmit the following cable to Professor Paul N. Milyoukoff, Minister of Foreign Affairs in the new Russian Government:

"Citizens of New York having at the call of the Society of the Friends of Russian Freedom assemble in mass meeting at Carnegie Hall on this 23rd day of March, 1917, extend their congratulations to the Russian people upon the success of the revolution in Russia, and express their admiration for those who in the years gone by and those who in recent days have fought so bravely for liberty. They convey their earnest wishes for Russia's complete realization of self-Government, and declare their conviction that it will mean enduring friendship and co-operation between the Governments and peoples of Russia and the United States of America."

At the close of the meeting the pictures of the revolutionary leaders were shown upon a screen, together with a picture of George Grey Barnard's statue of Lincoln which is to be placed in Petrograd.

This act by Jacob H. Schiff is only one of many that is documented in this book. Obviously, with his support of the Bolshevik movement, he made an indirect contribution to the execution of the Armenian Genocide for reasons never before presented to the general public and will be presented in some of the chapters that follow.

Chapter 11

Secret Treaty

Lev Davidovich Bronstein, aka Leon Trotsky (1879-1940)

When the hostilities against the Armenians began in 1914, the revolutionary Armenians, a minority among the Ottoman Armenians, had taken sides in the great war with Russia. Although in the past Russia had betrayed Armenia and never kept her promise to help Armenia gain independence, the Armenian revolutionary leaders believed that Russia allied with Europe might behave differently and be compelled to make good on their promise of the formation of an independent Armenia. Little did the Armenians know that the Russian Empire had no intentions of helping Armenia, much like its allies. Russia had planned to divide the spoils of the war with France and England, after the Turks' defeat.

Following the Russian Revolutions of 1917, secret documents of the Russian Foreign Office were made public by the new leaders of Russia. These documents were eventually printed in the newspapers of the time and are presented below in the order in which they appeared.

THE MANCHESTER GUARDIAN OF LONDON

DECEMBER 17, 1917 – PAGE 4

THE RUSSIAN "SECRET DOCUMENTS": FULL TEXT.

TSAR'S STIPULATIONS AS TO PERSIA AND THE RHINE.

Telegraphic summaries have recently appeared in the British press for a number of secret documents of the Russian Foreign Office, which related to agreements with the Allies under the regime of the late Tsar and have been published by M. Trotsky. The full text of these documents has not hitherto been available, but as they have been printed in the Petrograd newspapers they cannot but be common knowledge to Germany or any other country interested. The *"Isvestia"* (the organ of the Soviet) and the *"Pravda"* (the organ of the Bolsheviks) of November 23 have just reached this country. They contain the first instalment of the secret documents as made public by M. Trotsky. Below we give a translation of these according to the Russian version.

With reference to the Russo-French agreement as to the left bank of the Rhine, negotiated in the middle of last winter by the Briand Government, it must be remembered that as far back as the secret session of the French Chamber at the beginning of June the policy of M. Briand was repudiated by his successor in the French Premiership, M. Ribot; that this repudiation was registered in the resolution of the Chamber after the secret session, which limited the territorial claims of France strictly to Alsace-Lorraine; and that this limitation was since been reaffirmed by French Ministers.

Constantinople and Persia.

The following relate to Constantinople, the Straits, and Persia:—

I.

A confidential telegram of the Minister of Foreign Affairs to the Ambassador in Paris, March 5, 1915. No. 1,226:—

On February 23 (March 8) the French Ambassador, on behalf of his Government, announced to me that France was prepared to take up a most favourable attitude in the matter of realization of our desires as set out in my telegram to you, No. 937, in respect of the Straits and Constantinople, for which I charged you to tender Deleassé my gratitude.

In his conversations with you, Deleassé had previously more than once given his assurance that we could rely on the sympathy of France, and only referred to the need of elucidating the question of the attitude of England, from whom he feared some objections, before he could give us a more definite assurance in the above sense. Now the British Government has given its complete consent in writing to the annexation by Russia of the Straits and Constantinople within the limits indicated by us, and only demanded security for its economic interests and a similar benevolent attitude on our part towards the political aspirations of England in other parts.

For me, personally, filled as I am with most complete confidence in Deleassé, the assurance received from him is quite sufficient, but the Imperial Government would desire a more definite pronouncement of France's assent to the complete satisfaction of our desires, similar to that made by the British Government.

(Signed) SAZONOFF.

II.

Confidential telegram of the Minister of Foreign Affairs to the

Secret Treaty

Ambassador in Paris (?London), March 7, 1915. No. 1,285:—

Referring to the memorandum of the British Government (?Embassy) here of March 12, will you please express to Grey the profound gratitude of the Imperial Government for the complete and final assent of Great Britain to the solution of the question of the Straits and Constantinople, in accordance with Russia's desires. The Imperial Government fully appreciates the sentiments of the British Government and feels certain that a sincere recognition of mutual interests will secure for ever the firm friendship between Russia and Great Britain.

Having already given its promise respecting the conditions of trade in the Straits and Constantinople, the Imperial Government sees no objections to confirming its assent to the establishment (1) of free transit through Constantinople for all goods not proceeding from or proceeding to Russia, and (2) free passage through the Straits for merchant vessels.

In order to facilitate the breaking through of the Dardanelles undertaken by the Allies, the Imperial Government is prepared to co-operate in inducing those States whose help is considered useful by Great Britain and France to join in the undertaking of reasonable terms.

The Imperial Government completely shares the view of the British Government that the holy Moslem places must also in future remain under an independent Moslem rule. It is desirable to elucidate at once whether it is contemplated to leave those places under the rule of Turkey, the Sultan retaining the title of Caliph, or to create a new independent State, since the Imperial Government would only be able to formulate its desires in accordance with one or the other of these assumptions. On the separation of the Caliphate from Turkey as very desirable. Of course the freedom of pilgrimage must be completely secured.

The Imperial Government confirms its assent to the inclusion of the neutral zone of Persia in the British sphere of influence. At the same time, however, it regards it as just to stipulate that the districts adjoining the cities of Ispahan and Yezd, forming with them one inseparable whole, should be secured for Russian interests which have arisen there. The neutral zone now forms a wedge between the Russian and Afghan frontiers, and comes up to the very frontier line of Russia at Sulfaer. Hence a portion of this wedge will have to be annexed to the Russian sphere of influence. Of essential importance to the Imperial Government is the question of railway construction in the neutral zone, which will require further amicable discussion.

The Imperial Government expects that in future its full liberty of action will be recognized in the sphere of influence allotted to it, coupled in particular with the right of preferentially developing in that sphere its financial and economic policies.

Lastly, the Imperial Government considers it desirable simultaneously to solve also the problems of Northern Afghanistan adjoining Russia in the same sense of the wishes expressed on the subject by the Imperial Ministry in the course of the negotiations last year.

(Signed) SAZONOFF.

Frontiers East and West.

The following refers to the redrawing of the Germanic frontiers east and west and to the questions of Scandinavia, Poland, Rumania and China:—

A confidential telegram to the Ambassador in Paris:—

Petrograd, February 24. 1916. No. 948.

Please refer to my telegram No. 6063, 1915. At the forthcoming Conference you may be guided by the following general principals:—

The political agreements concluded between the Allies during the war must remain intact, and are not subject to revision. They include the agreement with France and England on Constantinople, the Straits, Syria, and Asia Minor, and also the London Treaty with Italy. All suggestions for the future delimitation of Central Europe are at present premature but in general one must bear in mind that we are prepared to allow France and England complete freedom in drawing up the western frontiers of Germany, in the expectation they the Allies on their part would all us equal freedom in drawing up our frontiers with Germany to insist on the exclusion of the Polish question from the subjects of international cussion and on the elimination of all attempts to place the future of Poland under the guarantee and the control of the Powers.

With regards to the Scandinavian States, as is necessary to endeavor to keep back Sweden from any action hostile to us, and at the same time to examine betimes measures for attracting Norway on our side in case it should prove impossible to prevent war with Sweden.

Rumania has already been offered all the pollical advantages which could induce her to take up arms, and therefore it would be perfectly futile to search for new baits in this respect.

The question of pushing out Germans from the Chinese market is of very great importance, but its solution is impossible without the participation of Japan. In it preferable to examine it at the Economic Conference, where the representatives of Japan will be present. This does not exclude the desirability of a preliminary exchange of views on the subject between Russia and England by diplomatic means. (Signed) SAZONOFF.

France and the Rhine.

The following relate to the proposals by a former French Government regarding Alsace-Lorraine and the left bank of the Rhine:—

Petrograd, January 330, 1917. No. 502.

Copy to London confidentially. At an audience with the Most High N. Doumergue submitted to the Emperor the desire of France to secure for herself at the end of the present war the restoration of Alsace-Lorraine and the special position in the valley of the River Saal as well as to attain the political separation from Germany of her trans-Rhenish districts and their organization on a separate basis in order that the future of River Rhine might form a permanent strategical frontier against Germanic invasion. Doumergue expressed the hope that the Imperial Government would not refuse immediately to draw up its assent to these suggestions in a formal manner.

His Imperial Majesty was pleased to agree to this in principle, in consequence of which I requested Doumergue, after communicating with his Government, to let me have the draft of an agreement, which would then be given a formal sanction by the exchange of Notes between the French Ambassador and myself.

Proceeding us to meet with wishes of our ally, I nevertheless consider it my duty to recall the standpoint put forward by the Imperial Government in the telegram of February 24, 1916, No. 948, to the effect that, "while allowing France and England complete liberty in delimiting the western frontiers of Germany, we expect that the Allies on their part will give us equal liberty in delimiting our frontiers with Germany and Austro-Hungary." Hence the impending exchange of Notes on the question raised by Doumergue will justify us in asking the French Government simultaneously to confirm its assent to allowing Russia freedom of action in drawing up her future frontiers in the west. Exact data on the question will be supplied by us in due course to the French Cabinet.

In addition we deem it necessary to stipulate for the assent of France to the removal at the termination of the war of the disqualifications resting on the Aland Islands. Please explain the above to Briand and wire results.

(Singed) POKROVSKY.

II.

A telegram from the Ambassador in Paris:—

January 31 (February 12), 1917. No. 88.

Copy to London. Referring to your telegram No. 507 confidentially, I immediately communicated in writing its contents to Briand, who told me that he would not fail to give me an official reply of the French Government, but that he could at once declare, on his own behalf, that the satisfaction of the wishes contained in your telegram will meet with no difficulties.

(Signed) ISVOLSKY.

III.

Copy of Note of the Minister of Foreign Affairs of February 1 (14), 1917, No. 26, addressed to the French Ambassador in Petrogrand:—

In your Note of today's date your Excellency was good enough to inform the Imperial Government that the Government of the Republic was contemplating the inclusion in the terms of peace to be offered to Germany the following demands and guarantees of a territorial nature:—

1. Alsace-Lorraine to be restored to France.
2. The frontiers are to be extended at least up to the limits of the former principality of Lorraine, and are to be drawn up at the discretion of the French Government so as to provide for the strategical needs and for the inclusion of French territory of the entire iron district of Lorraine and of the entire coal district of the Saar valley.
3. The rest of the territories situation on the left bank of the Rhine which now form part of the German Empire are to be entirely separated from Germany and freed from all political and economic dependence upon her.
4. The Territories of the left bank of the Rhine outside of French territory are to be constituted an autonomous and neutral State, and are to be occupied by French troops until such time as the enemy State have completely satisfied all the conditions and guarantees indicated in the treaty of peace.

Your Excellency stated that the Government of the Republic would be happy to be able to rely upon the support of the Imperial Government for the carrying out of its plans. By order of his Imperial Majesty, my most august Russian Government, to inform your Excellency by the present Note that the Government for the carrying out of its plans as set out above.

IV.

A telegram from the Ambassador in Paris, February 26 (March 11), 1917, No. 168:—

See my reply to telegram No. 167, No. 2. The Government of the French Republic, anxious to confirm the importance of the treaties concluded with the Russian Government in 1916 for the settlement on the termination of the war of the question of Constantinople and the Straits in accordance with Russia's aspirations, anxious, on the hand, to secure for its ally in military and industrial respects all the guarantees desirable for the safety and the economic development of the Empire, recognizes Russia's complete liberty in establishing her western fronts.

(Signed) ISVOLSKY.

THE MANCHESTER GUARDIAN OF LONDON
JANUARY 19, 1918 – PAGE 5

ASIATIC TURKEY: FULL TEXT OF ALLIES' AGREEMENT WITH EX-TSAR.

Below is the full text, as published in the "Isvestia" of November 24, of the memorandum of an agreement arrived at between Britain, France, and Russia during the regime of the ex-Tsar with regards to zones of influence and territorial acquisitions in Asiatic Turkey. The memorandum was made public by M. Trotsky as having been found among the secret papers of the Russian Foreign Office. The summary telegraphed by our correspondent in Petrograd appeared in the *"Manchester Guardian"* of November 28. The memorandum is dated March 6, 1917, and the following is a full translation:—

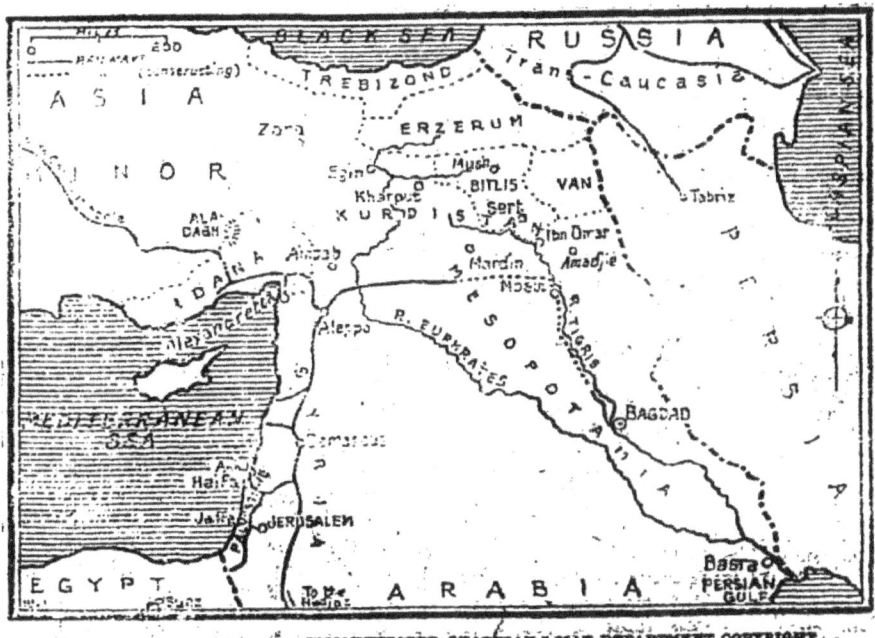

As a result of negotiations which took place in London and Petrograd in the spring of 1916, the allied British, French, and Russian Governments came to an agreement as regards the future delimitation of their respective zones of influence and territorial acquisitions in Asiatic Turkey, as well as the formation of Arabia of an independent Arab State, or a federation of Arab States. The general principles of the agreement are as follows:—

Russia obtains the provinces of Erzerum, Trebizond, Van and Bitlis, as well as territory of the southern part of Kurdistan along the line Mush-Sert-Ibn-Omar-Amadjie-Persian frontier. The limit of Russian acquisition on the Black Sea Coast would be fixed later on at a point lying west of Trebizond.

France obtains the coastal strip of Syria, the vilayet of Adana, and the territory bounded on the south by a line Aintab-Mardin to the future Russian frontier, and on the North by a line Ala-Degh-Zara-Egin-Kharput.

Great Britain obtains the southern part of Mesopotamia, with Bagdad, and stripulates for herself in Syria the ports of Haifa and Akka.

By agreement between France and England the zone between French and British territories forms a confederation of Arab States, or one independent Arab State, the zones of influence in which are determined at the same time.

Alexandretta is proclaimed a free port.

With a view to secure religious interests of the Entente Powers, Palestine, with the holy places, is separated from Turkish territory and subjected to a special regime to be determined by agreement between Russia, France and England.

As a general rule to contracting Powers undertake mutually to recognize the confessions and privileges existing in the territories now acquired by them which have existed before the war.

They agree to assume such portions of the Ottoman Debt as corresponds to their respective acquisitions.

THE MANCHESTER GUARDIAN OF LONDON
FEBRUARY 22, 1918 – PAGE 5

PETROGRAD DOCUMENTS
THE WAR AIMS OF TSARIST RUSSIA.

II.

RUSSIA'S CLAIMS.

Memorandum of the Russian Foreign Office.

On February 19 (March 4), 1919, the Minister of Foreign Affairs handed to the French and British Ambassadors a memorandum setting forth Russia's wish for the annexation of the following territories at the end of the present war:—The city of Constantinople; the western coast of the Bosphorus, of the Sea of Marmara, and of the Dardanelles; the coast of Southern Thrace up to the line Enos-Midia; the coast of Asia Minor between the Bosphorus, the River Sakaria, and the point on the Gulf of Ismie to be determined later on; the islands of the Sea of Marmara and the islands Imbros and Tenedos. The special rights of France and England in the territories outlined above would remain intact.

Both the French and the British Government have expressed their assent to the satisfaction of our wishes provided the war is successfully terminated and the demands of France and England, both within the confines of the Ottoman Empire and in other places, are satisfied. These demands, so far as they concern Turkey, amount to the following:— Constantinople is to be proclaimed a free port to the transit of goods not proceeding from or to Russia, and the passage of merchant vessels through the Straits is to be free. Further, France's and England's rights in Asiatic Turkey are to be recognized and to be defined by means of a special agreement between France, England, and Russia. The holy Moslem places are Arabia are to be left under an independent Moslem rule. They neutral zone of Persia established by the Convention of 1907 between England and Russia is to be included in the British sphere of influence.

The Russian Government, while on the whole agreeing to these demands, nevertheless made certain stipulations for the sake of defining exactly our own wishes with regard to the holly Moslem places. It is necessary, without delay, to establish whether these places are to remain under the rule of Turkey, with the Sultan as Caliph, or it is contemplated to form new independent States. In our opinion it would be desirable to separate the Caliphate from Turkey. In any case complete freedom of pilgrimage must be secured.

Likewise, while agreeing to the inclusion of the neutral zone of Persia in the sphere of British influence, the Russian Government nevertheless deems it just to stipulate that the districts of the cities of Ispahan and Yezd should be secured for Russia, and also that a part of the neutral zone which forms a wedge between the Russian and Afghan frontier, and which approaches the Russian frontier at Zulfagar, should be included in the Russian sphere of influence. The Russian Government deems if desirable at the same time to settle the question of Northern Afghanistan, adjoining Russia on the lines of the wishes expressed by it in course of the conversations of 1914.

On Italy's intervention in the war our wishes were communicated also to the Italian Government, which on its part gave its assent on the condition that the war terminate successfully, that the Italian claim in general and her claims in the east in particular are realized, and that we allow Italy the same rights in the territories conceded to us as we allow to France and England.

Chapter 12

Arming the Enemy

"Armenia suffered at the hands of the Turks. Now she suffers because of the greed of the nations, that are more eager for Armenian oil than they are to save the lives of the Armenian. In fact they have put guns into the hands of Armenia's enemies. What will be the verdict in the day of reckoning? Christianity, so far as it applies to Armenia, or any other weak nation, is figured in dollars and cents. To the world Armenian oil is of more consequence than Armenian blood."
 – *The Garden Island Newspaper (Lihue, Hawaii), July 5, 1921, page 4.*

On October 18, 1915, *The New York Times* reported that thousands protested the murder of Armenian people in the Ottoman Empire. The headline stated that the Turks had killed 500,000 Armenians and that, according to evidence taken from the U.S. State Department, 250,000 Armenian women had been violated. Protestors packed into the Century Theater at Central Park West and 62nd Street.

A resolution that was presented and adopted read as follows:

Whereas, The civilized world has been shocked by a series of massacres and deportations of Armenians in the Turkish Empire; and

Whereas, These crimes and outrages committed upon an industrious, thrifty, and peace loving people, find no justification, viewed either in the light of law or humanity; and

Whereas, Those Armenians who survive are in great need of succor and relief, be it hereby

Resolved, That as American citizens, we make our most solemn protest against these cruel and inhuman practices and implore all officials and others having influence in the Turkish Empire, to put an end to these wrongs and to render every aid to the American Ambassador and other who would rescue and repatriate a people, who, by their history and achievements have been a credit to the empire.

Resolved, Further, That war, wherever and by whatsoever nation waged, affords no warrant for inhumanity towards innocent persons. The slaughter of noncombatant men, the tortures, mutilations, and outrages committed upon women and children wherever committed have given to the fairest places upon the earth the semblance of hell. In the name of God, of Nations and our common humanity, we call upon the nations at war to cease these crimes against civilization and morality.[55]

At this time, the United States had not entered into World War I. Nor had it officially taken sides. Thus, the U.S. representative was safely present in the Ottoman Empire, protected by the 1830 Commerce and Navigation Treaty. And U.S. Ambassador Henry Morgenthau was in contact with the Turkish leaders who were behind the crimes against the Armenian people.

Later that month, on October 31, 1915, *The Pacific Commercial Advertiser* newspaper in Honolulu, HI, reported on the killing of Armenians and stated that "the Turkish government assured Ambassador Morgenthau the intention was to obliterate the Armenian race, following that by the destruction of the Greeks and all other foreigners." When Ambassador Morgenthau's wife, Josephine Sykes, personally appealed to Talaat Pasha, then minister of the interior, on behalf of the Armenian women and girls who were being sent to death or a worse fate, Pasha replied, "This amuses us."[56]

In James W. Colt's archive which is housed at University of Rochester's River Campus Libraries, folder number 3, titled "Spanish Rifles, 1915," reveals that, in fact, Americans had taken sides in the war, albeit secretly.

According to Colt's file, the Spanish Rifles Deal of 1915 began on July 24, when Colt met with Grand Duke Michael Alexandrovich of Russia, the younger brother of Nicholas II, the Emperor of Russia. The meeting took place at 3 Whitehall Court, London, England at 12 p.m. During the meeting, the Grand Duke agreed to help Colt with the transportation of the weapons.

According to a report of the meeting signed by Colt, 200,000 Spanish Mauser Rifles with bayonets and 400 million rounds of ammunition would be sold to a neutral government (Russia) and, at a given time, delivered to the Turks. At this early stage of the deal, it not only involved Grand Duke Michael, but also General Yerurouino, Colonel Belaieff, and General Ruben of Russian Commission, India House.[57]

The documents are not clear as to the final outcome of the deal, but they do indicate that among those backing the arms deal, there there were very influential Americans, as well as British subjects, including the war correspondent for the Daily Mail, G. Ward Price.

Interestingly, the American representatives in this deal were the owners of a mineral concession in the Ottoman Empire, that included crude oil found on Armenian-inhabited lands. At the time, 1/6th of the world's oil reserves were believed to be in these territories.

In an article dated May 4, 1923, "Chester Says He Had a Chance To Avert World War," retired Rear Admiral, Colby M. Chester, founder of the Chester Concessions, stated in an interview that his refusal to meet with an American capitalist in Rome, in 1911, to arrange with him the development of

---

55 New York Times, *THOUSANDS PROTEST ARMENIAN MURDERS*, (New York, NY, New York times, October 18, 1915) 3.

56 The Honolulu Advertiser, *SATURNALIA OF SLAUGHTER AND RAPE REPORTED*, (Honolulu, HI, October 31, 1915) 1.

57 James Wood Colt, *INTERVIEW BETWEEN J.W. COLT & THE GRANDE DUKE MICHAEL*, (University of Rochester's River Campus Libraries, folder number 3, titled "Spanish Rifles, 1915", July 24, 1915)

the Tripolitan Sulphur concessions, which belonged to Chester, was the prime cause of the Tialian-Tripolitan war. This led immediately to the first Balkan war, then the second, and, ultimately, it caused the First World War.

Chester went on to explain how he might have prevented America's entrance into the world war. In 1914, with the onset of WWI, America had interned 100 German ships which Chester had attempted to purchase for the Turkish navy. This purchase was prevented by the United States government. "I feel that it was a mistake, for I am sure if I had been permitted to buy these ships the United States would have been kept out of the war," Chester said.[58]

Had Chester been successful in purchasing the 100 German ships, not only would these weapons of war have fallen back into the hands of the Germans, with whom Turkey had allied during World War I, but Talaat would be likely to have succeed in carrying out his plan to obliterate the Armenians, as well as Greeks, Assyrians, and other non-Muslim minority groups.

Chester and those who had mineral concessions in the Armenian-populated areas were physically arming the Turks, thereby contributing to the Armenian Genocide. They had also embarked on a propaganda campaign to paint a benevolent image of Talaat Pasha and the Young Turks, while, at the same time, defaming the Armenian people, the rightful owners of the lands that Chester had been granted the right to exploit.

To inaugurate their propaganda campaign of whitewashing the image of the ruling regime, a lengthy article, "The Young Turks, written by Chester himself," was published in the *National Geographic Magazine*, January 1912, Volume XXIII.[59]

The article starts out with Chester qualifying himself as a witness to what had really happened in the Ottoman Empire, telling how he knows everyone of importance thanks to his close friendship with the Turkish leaders of the past and present.

With the subtitle of "The 'Unspeakable Turk' No Longer Exists," Chester tells the reader that the Turkey of 1912 was not the same Turkey of 3 years earlier, which had given rise to the slur 'unspeakable Turk,' This title was spread because of the Adana Massacres of some 30,000 Armenians. It was later proven that this slaughter was organized by the Young Turks and not the Sultan Abdul Hamid, as reported by Chester. He claimed the new Turkey was populated by men of "sterling character and unswerving integrity—men well fitted to lead their country through crises similar to those through which our own nation [United States of America] passed in its struggle of birth."

On September 18, 1922, *The Santa Cruz Evening News* published an article on page 3, titled "It Is Certainly Confusing," in which Colby M. Chester once again paints a positive image of the Turks. In this case, he also takes the opportunity to smear the image of the Armenians.

IT IS CERTAINLY CONFUSING

There are many Americans disposed to discount the tales of horror that come out of the Near East.

---

58 The Evening times, *CHESTER SAYS HE HAD A CHANCE TO AVERT WORLD WAR*, (Sayre, PA, The Evening Times, May 4, 1923) 1.
59 see Appendix IV

The Armenians have been pictured for years as the victims of Turkish butcheries; for years and years the collection plate has been passed around in the churches for their relief; and every once in a while some Armenian girl--always a good look one—takes the platform under clever management and coins money out of tales of the sufferings her people are alleged to have undergone at the hands of the unspeakable Turk.

And yet travelers, men and women of our acquaintance, come back from that eastern country with reports that the stories broadcasted about Armenian massacres are not so; that the Armenians are for the most part a lazy lot that cannot be driven from their country by promise of better times elsewhere; that they are unreliable, and that they prey upon the Turks, quite as much as the Turks prey upon them.[60]

In any event, it is certainly confusing to anyone who reads the often repeated accounts of the sorrows of the downtrodden Armenians to read this statement from Rear Admiral Colby M. Chester, of the United States Navy, in the September 1922 issue of *Current History* magazine:

> The harem has vanished out of Turkey, and there are fewer men with plural wives than there are married men with mistresses in the United States.
>
> There is more honesty to the square inch in Turkey than there is to the square yard in most other countries of the world.
>
> There are no prejudices against Christians in Turkey, let alone killing of Christians. Massacres of the past were enormously exaggerated by prejudiced writers and speakers.
>
> Armenian massacres by the Turks have been almost entirely unknown since constitutional government was proclaimed in 1908. The wholesale deportations of 1915 were brought by Turkish fear that Armenian agitators would get into trouble, * * * so the Armenians were moved from the inhospitable regions where they were not welcome and could not prosper, to the most delightful and fertile part of Syria. In due course of time the deportees, entirely unmassacred and fat and prosperous, returned—if they wished to do so.
>
> There are few men in the American navy alive today with as fine a record as that of Rear Admiral Colby Mitchell Chester. It dates from the civil war, when he participated in battle of Mobile Bay and the capture of Fort Morgan. He is a man known as a man of scientific trend, one careful in the use of words, whose work while in charge of hydrographic inspection in the coast survey service won him distinction; a commandant of navy yards, and once commander-in-chief of the south Atlantic squadron; and a man stationed for years in European waters, where he studied conditions in the Near East. Now when such a man speaks as he does in a reputable magazine concerning the Turks and the Armenians, it is certainly hard for a newspaper reader to say where the truth lies in some of the stories that come out of the Near East.

---

60 Santa Cruz Evening News, *IT IS CERTAINLY CONFUSING,* (Santa Cruz, CA, Santa Cruse Evening News, September 18, 1922) 3.

Clearly these lies of Chester could not go unchallenged and a reader of the paper, Fannie E. Laybourn, took the time to write a letter to refute what the newspaper had considered a highly credible source. It was published on September 22, 1922, on page 8, under "Letters From the People" section with the title "An Interesting Letter On Near East Atrocities."

    To the Editor of The News:

    Sir—Many of your readers were surprised and pained to note in the issue of Sept. 18, the prominence given to reprint of the statement of Rear Admiral Chester, from *Current History* magazine, together with editorial comment far from encouraging and helpful to those who have made great effort, and often great sacrifice of time and strength and money, to respond to a mighty call for help.

I know not Rear Admiral Colby M. Chester, and will not ask for space to discuss him, but I do know that volumes have been written by the noblest and best of American manhood and womanhood who have in person witnessed in the lands of the Near East, of which Armenia is but a part, things far more horrible than our imagination can picture. Christian missionaries have labored and prayed and pleaded for help for decades, and since the more awful tragedies of the past eight years, scores of helpers have gone to administer the relief that America has so wonderfully provided. Some have lost reason at the sight of the suffering, and the hopelessness of relieving even a small per cent of the sufferers, and many have laid down their lives in service there. I count among these latter, those whom I knew well and loved.

Is the witness of this large number true, or has it been "the story of some good-looking Armenian girl, under clever management, coining money out of tales of the suffering of her people are alleged to have undergone at the hands of the unspeakable Turk," that led to the organization of the Near East relief? Did she deceive James L. Barton, Wm. H. Taft, Chas. Evans Hughes, Elihu Root, John R. Mott, Robert E. Speer, John H. Finley, Henry Morgenthau, and some other 40 men most prominent in America's political, educational and religious affairs, to allow themselves to be named by Congress in an act of incorporation approved by the president on August 6, 1919, to serve as trustees and committees?

Did her smile and story unloose the purse strings of the hardheaded business man like Cleveland H. Dodge and persuade him to pour out the vast portion of his wealth that has gone not only direct to the work, but has paid all overhead expense of the organization?

Did this beautiful girl and clever management so fascinate that it led into splendid action our own state chairman, Judge Curtis D. Wilbur, whose beloved sister, Mrs. W. A. Shedd, gave her life in Persia? When E. Guy Talbot of Los Angeles, regional director for the Pacific coast, returned last fall from a survey of the field, did he report the whole terrible story as false, and the "deportees, entirely unmassacred, and fat and prosperous?" If so, where did he find his "cast" for this wonderful, awful, but encouraging "movie," "Alice in Hungerland"?

Did her story—but she didn't get to Santa Cruz; and we had only strong men who were no better looking than our fellow citizens, but who brought to us facts and inspiration, which, together with the information that we all are interested may gain, stirred into local action those who stand high in business life, together with the pastors of the churches, the leader in our schools, and the goodly company of men and women who have labored long and hard to see that Santa Cruz held to her fair name of extending the hand of mercy to the needy.

If the story of suffering is not so, I wonder why my beloved niece, a bright college girl in her twenties, marched 400 miles over the mountains in the dead of winter, two years ago, from Teheran to Hamadau, Persia, with 275 children orphaned through Turkish atrocity, and has cared for them since, aided only by a little native help, in old buildings left by the British army.

I might continue to ask Why? Why? Why? But only ask permission now to quote two or three extracts from the voluminous reports of Henry Morganthau, a Jew by race and religion, the former American ambassador to Turkey, printed in World's Work during 1918-1919:

"It is absurd for the Turkish government to assert that it ever seriously intended to 'deport the Armenians to new homes.' The treatment which was given the convoys clearly shows that extermination was the real purpose of Enver and Talaat. How many exiled to the south under these revolting conditions ever reached their destination? The experiences of a single caravan shows how completely this plan of deportation developed into annihilation. The details were furnished directly by American consul at Aleppo, and are now on file in the state department at Washington."

Mr. Morgenthau recites the facts and horrors of this one of many such deportations—the victims robbed of their money, the few men remaining brutally murdered, womanhood left to the passion and lust of the gendarmes who had been represented as their protectors, while helpless little children were left to wander and perish of hunger unless picked up and cared for by our orphanages, established by Christian America, and where hundreds of thousands of lives have been saved, and must still be cared for.

Again Mr. Morganthau says, after long investigation, "The general purpose of all these first had reports was that the utter depravity and fiendishness of the Turkish nature, already sufficiently celebrated through the centuries, had now surpassed themselves. There was only one hope of saving nearly two million people from massacre, starvation and worse, I was told—that was the moral power of the United States."

And there was deep pathos in our ambassador's words upon his return to this land of freedom and plenty, when he said, "My failure to stop the destruction of the Armenians had made Turkey for me a place of horror, and I found intolerable my further daily association with men who, however, accommodating and good natured they might have been to the American ambassador, were still reeking with the blood of nearly a million human beings. Could I have done anything more, either for Americans, enemy aliens, or the persecuted peoples of the empire, I would willingly have stayed."

Respectfully yours,
FANNIE E. LAYBOURN,
Santa Cruz, Sept. 21.[61]

Fannie E. Laybourn's letter to *The Santa Cruse Evening News* was a powerful testimony, painting a picture of the former American ambassador as a defender of the Armenians. Although this is true in print, I think it is important to see that Morgenthau might have also fed into arming Talaat and company in a similar way as Colby M. Chester, before he penned his memoirs in 1918.

On May 21, 1916, *The Cincinnati Enquirer* ran a story on page 2, titled

---

[61] Fannie E. Laybourn, *LETTERS FROM THE PEOPLE: An Interesting Letter On Near east Atrocities,* (Santa Curz, CA, Santa Cruz Evening News, September 22, 1922) 8.

"Turkey; Jackpot of Nations," in which Morgenthau is reported to have spoken at a luncheon given in his honor at the Hotel Gibson by the Chamber of Commerce City Club and Armenian Relief Committee. He was presenting "American Opportunities in the Orient" to 450 business and professionals in attendance. Morgenthau stated:

> "Turkey at peace will redeem herself. Let us think internationally. Do not let our country try to intervene to stop the war until the nations are though battling. If you business men were engaged in fierce competition would you listen to your minister or doctor who tried to settle matters. America can help adjust the differences if we keep aloof.
>
> "I do not want to talk about politics. Half of you, if not all, could have done what I did. Russia, notwithstanding what my religion was insisted that I represent her. It was a compliment not to me, but to the United States. I was able, as representative of all the warring nations, to protect all their citizens. Unfortunately Armenia had no nation. The only thing Turkey refused to listen to was concerning the Armenians."

He spoke of the confidence Turkey had in the United States:

> "The United States had no desire for their territory and they knew it," said the diplomat. "They are jealously guarding what they have left. The missionaries have 785 schools in Turkey for Armenians. I believe the missionaries are the bearers of a second civilization and I wanted them to feel that the American Embassy was their second home.
>
> "The missionaries stood by the Armenians when the trouble arose. I will not harry you with details. There are four or five thousand Armenians scattered that need clothing, food and shelter. They are in a pitiful condition.
>
> "We ought to show ourselves equal to the emergency and he a big brother to the stricken land. Do not let us stand before the world only for money making. We should give aid in every stricken land."

Morgenthau added what was possibly the real reason why America should stay "aloof" and not "try to intervene to stop the war." He stated to the business men and professionals:

> "We could raise enough money and have a federation of all relief, under one large committee. No one would be missed. If the country helps now, we will be given the preference commercially when the war Is over. It is commercial charity."[62]

It would seem that both Chester and Morgenthau, as representatives of the United States, were ready to do that which is necessary to help Turkey so that when the war did end and the dust did settle, commercial preference would be given to those who helped rather than hindered Turkey's war effort, as well as their intentions to annihilate the Armenian people who potentially could stand between the jackpot (oil and minerals) and the international investors.

---

62 The Enquire, *TURKEY: Jackpot of Nations,* (Cincinnati, OH, The Enquire, May 21, 1916) 2.

Chapter 13

Morgenthau

"[My grandfather] took it upon himself to go completely outside the bounds of diplomacy and perhaps legality and to use his influence and what he thought of as the moral authority of the United States to try to intervene directly in the policy of the Turkish government in exterminating the Armenian people."
- Henry Morgenthau III

Henry Morgenthau (1856–1946) was an American lawyer, businessman, and, most notably, the American ambassador to the Ottoman Empire during the First World War.[63]

One of the most celebrated non-Armenian heroes of the tragedy which befell on the Armenian people, Morgenthau is credited for personally saving the lives of thousands of Armenians and securing millions of dollars in donations for the Committee on Armenian Atrocities (later named the Near East Relief) which provided humanitarian aid to survivors of the Armenian Genocide.

Born into an Ashkenazi Jewish family on April 26, 1856, Morgenthau was the ninth of 11 children to Lazarus and Babette (Guggenheim) Morgenthau.[64] His formative years were spent in his native Mannheim, Baden, Germany. His family emigrated to the United States in 1866 and settled in New York.

Henry's father, Lazarus, who had been a successful cigar manufacturer in Germany with three factories employing as many as 1,000 people, attempted to reestablish himself in business in the United States, but was unable to do so. In order to provide financial support for his family, he became a fundraiser for Jewish houses of worship.

Henry attended City College of New York, where he received a BA and later graduated from Columbia Law School. He began his career as a lawyer, but made a substantial fortune in real estate investments.[65] He married

---

63 Balakian, Peter (2003). The Burning Tigris: The Armenian Genocide and America's Response. New York: HarperCollins. pp. 219–221.
64 http://findingaids.cjh.org/?pID=480672
65 Balakian. The Burning Tigris, p. 219.

Josephine Sykes in 1882 and had four children: Helen, Alma, Henry Jr. and Ruth.[66] Morgenthau built a successful career as a lawyer and served as the leader of the Reform Jewish community in New York.[67]

In 1912, Morgenthau, who had become a millionaire, contributed generously and supported the candidacy of Woodrow Wilson for his bid to become President of the United States. He had first met Wilson in 1911 at a dinner celebrating the fourth anniversary of the founding of the Free Synagogue society and the two "seem to have bonded", marking the "turning point in Morgenthau's political career".[68]

Morgenthau's participation in the American government began after the election of Wilson who offered Morgenthau the position of ambassador to the Ottoman Empire. Morgenthau's desire to be designated the financial chairman of the campaign finance committee went unfulfilled, nor was he offered a cabinet post as he had hoped. Wilson believed that having a Jewish Ambassador in the Ottoman Empire, as there had been with other prominent German born Jewish Americans Oscar Straus (United States Minister to the Ottoman Empire from 1887-1889; 1898-1899 and United States Ambassador to the Ottoman Empire 1909-1910) and Solomon Hirsch (1889–1892)[69], served as a bridge between Muslim Turks and Christian Armenians.

On October 31, 1913, *The New York Times* reported on the farewell dinner in honor of Morgenthau and the start of his ambassadorship in the Ottoman Empire:

WISH MORGENTHAU SUCCESS IN EMBASSY
Many Friends of New Ambassador to Turkey Entertain Him at Farewell Dinner.
WILSON A BIT OF RADIUM
President's High Ideals Praised by Guest of Evening— Encyclopedia Britannica Given to Him.

Two hundred friends and business associates of Henry Morgenthau gathered last night at dinner at the Hotel Astor to bid him good-bye on the eve of his departure on his mission as Ambassador to Turkey and to testify to their appreciation of him. They lauded his qualities as a New Yorker, as an American, as a philanthropist, and as a financier and lawyer.

The heard praise of him from a predecessor at the Porte, Oscar S. Straus, and a benediction by his pastor, the Rev. Stephen S. Wise. They toasted Mrs. Morgenthau, who sat in a balcony, and united with Morgan J. O'Brien, the toastmaster, in wishing him godspeed.

Judging by the guests at the speakers' table, politics and profession have played no part in Mr. Morgenthau's friendships. Mr. Straus represented

---

66 About Henry Morgenthau. henrymorgenthaupreserve.com

67 Oren, Michael B (2007). Power, Faith, and Fantasy: America in the Middle East 1776 to the Present. New York: W. W. Norton & Co. pp. 332–333.

68 Balakian. The Burning Tigris, p. 220.

69 http://www.shapell.org/manuscript/president-benjamin-harrison-appoints-third-jewish-minister-to-turkey-1889

the Roosevelt Cabinet and Henry L. Stimson the advisers of President Taft, and near them was Col. E. M. House, the intimate friend of President Wilson. Others at the table were **Jacob H. Schiff**, Abraham Goldsmith, A. Barton Hepburn, I. N. Seligman, and James Speyer.

In the course of the evening Mr. O'Brien announced that the committee had bought a set of the Encyclopedia Britannica for Mr. Morgenthau and forwarded it to the embassy at Constantinople. Mr. Morgenthau in accepting it said that he had finished his course of instruction for his ambassadorial post and felt that the encyclopedia capped it.

"But I do not promise to absorb all of it." He concluded.

Mr. Morgenthau was the last speaker of the evening. After he had been introduced by Mr. O'Brien he said:

"We have heard much about the Melting Pot of America. I am the amalgam of that melting pot. I am just a composite picture of the men in this room and other that I have come in contact with in America. I would like to say a word about our President, Woodrow Wilson.

"I believe and believed in the start that we have been fortunate in discovering a bit of human radium. His justice and his eternal fight against snobbishness in one of America's greatest institutions of learning first attracted me to him. It was his fight for democracy at Princeton that first cause me to know him. He is a wise man, and the country will come to know him and to believe in him as justice personified."

Mr. Morgenthau highly praised Robert Fulton Cutting, who sat near him, and then made Oscar S. Straus blush by alluding to him as the "good Ocar, who is pointed out to me as a man I must be like."

"I am going to be as good as I can be," said Mr. Morgenthau. "I feel that I'm going on my mission as the representative of all people. I feel delighted at getting away and having a real reincarnation. I have been listening to my own funeral orations and enjoyed them.

"I am going to devote the rest of my life on the altar of public service," he said amid applause. "And in parting let me express a thought. I feel that I have been fully compensated for the work I have tried to do philanthropy by the gratitude and thanks that the 1,500 mothers and children in the Bronx House have given me.

"Before I go I will express a wish. I wish that we could get together in the good things we do. Twenty years ago a dinner like this would have been impossible. If we have done so much here in New York, why cannot we by a united effort do still more and wipe out that class hatred which is growing in the rest of the country against what it believes is capitalistic New York?"

Mr. O'Brien in beginning the speeches of the evening said in part: "This is a unique gathering of med from every calling and profession, to do honor to a friend, who had been signally honored by the President of the United States. Away from the busy marts of finance and business, apart from the turbulence of factional politics, friends are met to honor a friend.

Mr. O'Brien then sketched Mr. Morgenthau's career in this city, and dwelt especially on his philanthropic activities. Among them were his establishment and maintenance of the Bronx House, this directorship in Mount Sinai Hospital, his Presidency of the Free Synagogue and his generous contributions to charity.

Mr. Morgenthau's interest in public affairs, Mr. O'Brien said, was seen in his Chairmanship of the Safety Commission, which established rules for fire prevention, in his investigation of educational commissions and, finally in his service with the Democratic Nation Committee as Chairman of its Finance Committee.

"While we recall with pleasure his professional victories," said Mr. O'Brien in conclusion, "and his business success; while we admire his devotion to charity and religion, we more than all love his gentle and kindly nature. So to-night we united in extending this simple tribute of our affection and from our hearts we express our sincere wishes for the long life and happiness of our friend, Henry Morgenthau, the American Ambassador to Turkey."

Oscar S. Straus in his speech gave Mr. Morgenthau the benefit of his own experience in Turkey.

"Your mission to Turkey is more human than material," he said. "Let your diplomacy be human diplomacy, not dollar diplomacy."

R. Fulton Cutting had much to say in praise of Mr. Morgenthau, and described the high places he would occupy in the world's affairs from this time on, and then Dr. Edward T. Devin, Professor of Philanthropy at Columbia, spoke of the Ambassador's philanthropies. Rabbi Wise and Frank R. Lawrence, an associate in the law, also spoke eloquently of their friend.

Among those who were present at the dinner were W. C. Brown, George Gordon Battle, William N. Cohen, William H. Chesebrough, John D. Crimmins, Justice Victor J. Dowling, J. Clarence Davies, W. A. Day, Robert W. De Forest, Joseph P. Day, Robert E. Dowling, Justice P. H. Dugro, Abram I. Elkus, Daniel Frohman, Dr. John H. Finley, Dr. Lee K. Frankel, Isaac Gimbel, Sol R. Guggenheim, Capt. J. B. Greenhut, Murray Guggenheim, Justice Greenbaum, and Daniel P. Hays.

Dr. John Haynes Holmes, Darwin P. Kingsley, Clarence H. Helsey, ex-Justice Leventritt, Prof. Samuel ChCune Lindsay, Adolph Lewisohn, Dudley Field Malone, Louis Marshall, Marcus M. Marks, Dr. Henry Moskovitz, J. Van Vechten Olcott, William Church Osborn, Ralph Pulitzer, George W. Perkins, Herman Ridder, John D. Rockefeller, Jr., Charles N. Sherrili, Cyrus I. Sulzberger, Jesse I Straus, Nathan Straus, John T. Underwood, Sarmrel Untermeyer, Martin Vogel, Felix M. Warburg, and Henry Wollman.

Shy of finishing his first year as U.S. Ambassador to the Ottoman Empire, Morgenthau reported to the State Department on possible massacres of Christians. This was done after the government had begun massacring the Armenians who had refused to support the Central Powers against Russia, should Turkey ally with Germany in the war. *The Evening Sun* newspaper, in Baltimore, MD, reported on August 26, 1914, page 2:

CHRISTIAN MASSACRE IN TURKEY FEARED
Reported Mussulmen Plan To Take Advantage Of European War
CRUISERS MAY BE SENT
Believed Appearance Of Tennessee And North Carolina Might Prevent Serious Outbreak.

Washington, Aug. 26. – Grave anxiety is felt by the Administration because of the prospects of a general massacre of Christians in Turkey, the danger of which has been communicated to the Department of State by Henry Morgenthau, Ambassador to Turkey.

Mr. Morgenthau has taken the matter up with the Sublime Porte and with the Sultan himself, but, according to his advices to his Government, the only assurance he has been able to obtain has been that the Sultan will do all in his power to protect American citizens.

To Visit Wrath on Christians.

According to the information acquired by the American Ambassador, the Mahommedans in Turkey are determined to avail themselves of the disturbed conditions in Europe, to visit their wrath on all Christians and Jews in both Turkey in Europe and Turkey in Asia.

The Sultan, in response to the urgent representation of the American Ambassador, has promised to do what he can to protect citizens of the United States. Mr. Morgenthau pointed out that the United States is not engaged in war and that this country would not hesitate to undertake reprisals for outrages perpetrated on its citizens.

Serious consideration is being given to the advisability of sending to Turkish waters the Tennessee and the North Caroline, the "gold ships" which are now in European waters, the former at Falmouth and the latter at Cherbourg, according to the latest reports, as soon as they have discharged their mission of relief to American refugees stranded in the belligerent countries without funds.

Cruisers Might Cool Their Ardor.

It is believed that the appearance of these two cruisers in Turkish waters would have a deterrent effect on the excited and hostile Mussulmen and might serve to curb their spleen toward American, although the Administration would gladly do something to afford protection to Christians and Jews of other nations if it could devise a method of achieving that end.

Exact figures are lacking, but the number of foreign missionaries in the Ottoman Empire is probably under 1,000. This total is increased greatly by the number of communicants of their missions and the native workers in substation and the like.

The Turkish Government recognizes the adherents of nine non-Mahommedan creeds. In Constantinople itself, only about one-half the population is Mussulman. In the Turkish islands of the Aegean Sea the population is almost entirely Christian. Only when the figures of the Asiatic Turkey are reckoned do the totals appear overwhelmingly Mussulman. The proportion averages will be about five to one.

The following day, August 27, 1914, *The Hartford Caurant,* in Hartford, CT, reported, on page 3, more details of the overall situation in the Ottoman Empire. The U.S. Secretary of State Bryan, who had met with the Turkish Ambassador to the United States, was also quoted. Bryan reported that the claims made of Morgenthau predicting a massacre of Christians was untrue:

TURKISH CABINET IS WAVERING
Diplomats Fear Country May Be Drawn Into War.
TENSION ACUTE IN CONSTANTINOPLE
England and Russia Trying to Keep Turkey Neutral.

Washington, Aug. 26. – Tension is so acute in Constantinople that diplomats there fear Turkey may at any moment be drawn into the general European war on the side of Germany and Austria.

A strict censorship has been put on the newspapers in Turkey, which are now controlled by the military and are being used, according to diplomatic dispatches here, to create a strong pro-German feeling. The Turkish cabinet is wavering between a declaration of war and the preservation of neutrality. The diplomatic representatives of the various powers are in constant conference with the government officials, Great Britain and Russia endeavoring to keep Turkey neutral. The German ambassador, it is understood, has intimated that while Germany wishes Turkey to remain neutral, he believed the Ottoman empire should mobilize to prevent an invasion by Russia.

Feeling is most acute over the entry into the Dardanelles of the German Cruisers, Goeben and Breslau. Great Britain, Russia and France not only

The U.S.S. North Carolina, Mediterranean Sea, c. 1914, Library of Congress, LC-D4-22805.

requested ten days ago that if these ships were bought by Turkey, the crews be sent to either Germany or Austria, but promised safe conduct. Today many of the German sailors are still on board and 150 or more are said to have been distributed among Turkish torpedo boats.

The British government is observing these incidents with much disfavor and the situation has been aggravated by the inability of several English merchant ships to pass through the Dardanelles, even after the grand vizier had given the requisite permission. Subordinate officials disobeyed the instructions.

Great Britain has let it be known that if the Goeben and Bresalu enter the Mediterranean with German crews aboard, they will be fired on by the English fleet.

Neither Great Britain nor Russia, however, has assumed a threatening attitude diplomatically, hoping to persuade Turkey to remain neutral. A few days ago the Russian ambassador was requested to cease using the wireless on a Russian vessel in the harbor. He acquiesced rather than bring on an issue with his government.

Developments in Turkey were generally discussed today in official circles. The Turkish Ambassador had a long conference with Secretary Bryan, chiefly concerning an alleged statement with which American Ambassador Morgenthau had been credited in some published reports. Later Mr. Bryan issued a statement, saying the story that Mr. Morgenthau had predicted a massacre of Christians was untrue.

Secretary Bryan said: "While Americans are anxious to leave Turkey, as they are to leave other parts of Europe in which war has broken out, or may break out, there is nothing in Ambassador Morgenthau's telegram to justify the reports as published."

Mr. Morgenthau's recent telegrams, it is understood, recorded conditions as much relieved now, though a week ago there was some apprehension over the position in which Americans might be placed if the war were extended to Turkey.

The cruiser North Carolina will go to Constantinople with gold for Americans. Many of the Jews in Palestine are destitute, and an appeal for funds has been made to Jewish charities in America. Temporary relief for Americans has been provided personally by Mr. Morgenthau, who has advanced several thousand dollars to meet the immediate wants of those in need.

Mr. Morgenthau has raised a total of $75,000 by subscription but has advised the state department that additional funds are necessary.

The Hutchinson Gazette, in Hutchinson, KS, was more specific about Secretary Bryan's denial on August 27, 1914, page 1, and named Armenia as the area where Morgenthau had reported the dangers to Christians:

Turkish Uprising is Denied in Washington

Bryan Denies That Morgenthau Cabled of Danger to Christians in Armenia.

Washington, Aug. 26.—Reports that Ambassador Morgenthau had informed the state department of an uprising against Christians in Armenia, were denied today by Secretary Bryan, who deplored the reports as calculated to stir public sentiment in this country.

It is understood, however, that Morgenthau has informed the state department that he has cabled Jacob Schiff and Nathan Strauss that the Jews in Palestine are in urgent need of assistance.

Whether the Palestine Jews are in danger from the Mohammedans or whether Morgenthau had referenced to financial assistance was not made clear.

The fear that there might be an anti-Christian uprising in the Moslem countries has been to some extent allayed by the report from India that the Mohammedans there have notified the Turkish Moslems that they will remain loyal to Great Britain in the present crisis.

Winfield Courier, in Winfield, KS, on page 6, reported, on November 26, 1914, that Turkey was refusing to transmit coded dispatches between Ambassador Morgenthau and the State Department:

U. S. QUESTIONS TURKEY
MUSSULMAN EMPIRE AGAIN IN BAD WITH WASHINGTON.

It is Reported the Porte Refuses to Transport Diplomatic Dispatches in Code.

By Associated Press.

Washington, Nov. 25. – The United States is inquiring of Turkey about the reported action of the Porte, in refusing transmission to code dispatches between neutral diplomats in Constantinople their home offices. Such an action would prevent Ambassador Morgenthau from communication from Washington and the State Department.

News of Turley is reputed actions come through the Cable company and so far there has been no official notice served on the State Department by any authorized agent of the Turkish government. The United States will insist on its right of free communication with its diplomatic representatives as long as telegraph and cable lines are open to general use, or in fact workable. There is always an implied understanding that such messages shall be strictly neutral and not to the means conveying information of military value.

The Daily Journal, in New Bern, NC, called the atrocious events in the Ottoman Empire a holy war on its front page, on December 6, 1914:

TO GIVE AID TO CHRISTIANS
STATE DEPARTMENT SENDS URGENT ORDERS
TO U. S. AMBASSADOR IN TURKEY

Washington, D. C., Dec. 5. – The State Department today cabled to Ambassador Morgenthau who is at Constantinople, instructions to spare no expense or efforts in providing for the needs of Christian refugees who have been driven out of the interior towns by the moslems and have to seek safety on the seacoast.

Reports from Constantinople are to the effect that the holy war which is in progress in Turley is becoming more critical each day and no Christian is safe.

On December 8, 1914, *The Decatur Daily*, in Decatur, AL, ran an article on page 2 quoting a 'well-informed Turk' denying that a holy war against the Christians was underway. The story outlined what amounted to a holy war, claiming the last one took place in 1492.

"HOLY WAR" HAS NOT BEEN PROCLAIMED
SAYS DISPATCH RECEIVED FROM LONDON

Sacred Flag Has Not Yet Been Hoisted in Turkey

(By Herbert Temple.)

(International News Service.)

London, Dec. 8. – I am informed by an intelligent and well-informed Turk now in this city that no holy war has been proclaimed to the Mussulman world nor is one likely to be. "Holy war" is a term much abused in westers parlance; and "holy wars" are much rarer than one would think from reading British and American newspapers.

"The holy war can only be started by the raising of the sacred flag of Mohammed by the Sheik-ul-Islam, or the chief of the Islamic faith," said my informant. "This has not been done up to the present time, I can give you positive assurance. I understand the Sheik-ul-Islam was urged by the pro-Germans to raise the sacred flag, but wisely refused to do so. This is a political war.

"Since before the conquest of Constantinople by the Turks in 1452 the sacred flag has never been raised but once. This was when the Sulton

Mahmoud Ali, grandfather of the present ruler, resolved to be rid of his vicious Janizaries, or household guards. He sent messages to this body declaring that the sacred flag had been unfurled at the Court of Sultas Ahmed. The Janizaries promptly answered the call. They entered the gate singly or in small groups and were promptly and without mishap killed by a select corps of executioners stationed there by Mahmoud Ali.

"But it is a point of Mohammedan law that the sacred flag (once unfurled, cannot be furled until 70,000 heads are forfeit. There were but 49,000 Janizaries. To carry out the letter of the law the Sultan had 21,000 headstones broken down from Mussulmans' graves. This famous incident in Turkish history is known as 'Vakai Hayrie.'

"Since then a holy war has twice threatened but never really been declared. The present Emperor of Germany after his second visit to Sultan Bbdul Hamid went to Palestine, visiting first and with some ostestation the tomb of the celebrated Sultan Saladin, the opponent of Richard the Lion Hearted of England. The Kaiser was roundly scolded in the European press and a holy war was talked of.

"Soon after the European war started this summer Turkey called the Mussulmans to the flag, fearing trouble, and also esjoined light military service on the Christian solders, of whom, since the young Turk regime, there are numbers in the Turkish army. At the request of the Sultan the Ameer of Afghanistan sent 130,000 men, under command of Crown Prince Mehmed Bahadour, to attack British India, and 80,000 under Bahadour Jenk to attack Russia. The chief Sheik of the Arabs also joined the movement. The sacred flag has not yet been hoisted. Even if it is Christians or foreigners residing in Turkey need have no fear, except of such violence from lower elements as might occur in any hostile country. The law of Mohammed strictly enjoins that care be taken not to injure non-combatants, especially women and children, in the wars of the Crescent."

Printed directly below this article was news from the well-informed Turk, there was a contradictory report that, in fact, Christians were fleeing for their lives:

CHRISTIANS FLEE TO CITIES ALONG TURKISH COAST

Washington, Dec. 8. – Christian refugees are fleeing in large numbers from the interior of Turkey to coast cities since the proclamation of a holy war by the Sheik-ul-Islam, head of the Moslem church. Ambassador Morgenthau cable this information to the state department form Constantinople Friday.

Calling from Bucharest under a later date, he informed the department that he learned through the Serbian minister to Rumania of a proclamation by the Turkish government of a holy war against Serbia and all her allies. The Serbian government has made reply to the proclamation by declaring that all treaties between her and Turkey have ceased to exist. Mr. Morgenthau did not express any alarm for the safety of Americans in Turkey. Assurances have repeatedly been given by the Turkish government that Americans and their property would be fully protected.

Long after the official start of the Armenian Genocide of April 24, 1915, Ambassador Morgenthau sent a communication to the State Department to inform them of the Armenian massacres in Turkey. This communication refers to earlier messages, though this particular communication is claimed by historians to be that which is the first communication from Morgenthau to inform the State Deparment of the Armenian Genocide:

```
Secretary of State,
    Washington.

            858, July 16, 1 p m.

            Confidential.  Have you received my
841?   / Deportation of and excesses against
peaceful Armenians is increasing and from har-
rowing reports of eye witnesses it appears that
a campaign of race extermination is in progress
under a pretext of reprisal against rebellion.
        Protests as well as threats are una-
vailing and probably incite the Ottoman govern-
ment to more drastic measures as they are deter-
mined to disclaim responsibility for their
absolute disregard of capitulations and I be-
lieve nothing short of actual force which obvi-
ously United States are not in a position to
exert would adequately meet the situation. / Sug-
gest you inform belligerent nations and mission
boards of this.
                    AMERICAN AMBASSADOR,
                        Constantinople
```

In an attempt to save the Armenians from wholesale slaughter, Ambassador Morgenthau negotiated a deal with the Turkish government to allow all the Armenians to leave Turkey and emigrate to the United Sates. On September 14, 1915, *The Gazette*, Montreal, Quebec, Canada, ran a front-page news story to announce the deal:

BETRAYAL: The Promise Never Kept
Morgenthau Approached Turkish Gov't
to Have Them Transported to America
(Special to The Gazette.)

Chicago, September 13.—The Chicago Daily News prints this dispatch from Sofia, the capital of Bulgaria:

"Henry Morgenthau, American ambassador to Turkey, recently made an offer to the Turkish Government to raise $1,000,000 to transport to America the Armenians who have thus far escaped the general massacres. Enver Pasha, the minister of war, and Talaat Bey, minister of the interior, accepted the offer, and on September 3 the ambassador asked the Government in Washington to appoint a committee of five Americans, whom he recommended, to take charge of the great undertaking. Mr. Morgenthau declined, however, to give me their names when I saw him recently in Constantinople.

"Since May," says the ambassador, "350,000 Armenians have been slaughtered or have died of starvation. There are 550,000 Armenians who could now be sent to America, and we need help to save them. One million dollars is too little for the propose of transporting them, as it takes $100 to equip, feed and transport one man. Perhaps $5,000,000 will be necessary. I should like to see each of the western states raise a fund to equip a ship and bring the number of settlers it wants. The Armenians are a moral, hard-working race, and would make good citizens to settle the less-thickly populated parts of the western states.'

"Turks admit that the Armenian prosecution is the first step in a plan to get rid of Christians, and that Greeks will come next. Jews are also marked for slaughter or expulsion. American missionaries must also be driven out, for Turkey hence-forth is to be for Turks alone. The Shek-ul-Islam, on being questioned, said that the deportation of the Armenians was contrary to Moslem law, but that he was powerless in the face of military despotism.

"Foreigners in Constantinople hold the Germans, in part at least, responsible for the prosecution of the Armenians, for they are doing nothing to prevent the distribution of inflammatory literature among the savage tribes inciting them to attack Christians."

By September 24, 1915, as the situation for the Armenians went from bad to worse, *The Salt Lake Tribune,* in Salt Lake City, UT, ran a story on page 2, appealing to the general public to provide aid to the Armenian people:

APPEAL TO BE MADE FOR THE ARMENIANS
Plan Will Be Carried Out Without Participation by U.S.
Government

WASHINGTON, Sept. 23.—Information from Embassador (sic) Morgenthau at Constantinople to the American Board of commissioners for foreign missions concerning the plight of Armenians in Turkey, banished to isolated towns for alleged hostility to the Turkish government, will be the basis of an appeal to the American people for assistance similar to that made for homeless Belgians.

This appeal, it was learned tonight, will be issued from New York after the report of Charles R. Crane and James L. Briton, representing the commission, who conferred today with state department officials, is made public.

The plan for sending help to the Armenians will be carried out without any official participation by the United States government, for it is understood that the Turkish foreign office has let it be known that it will brook no interference with this policy from any foreign power.

The joint committee interested in launching the appeal is composed of members of the foreign missions commission and representative American and English colleges in Turkey.

It was revealed at the state department today that since Embassador (sic) Morgenthau's protest to the foreign office in Constantinople against reported ill-treatment of Armenians, nothing further has been done by this government. Minor concessions from the Turkish government resulted from Embassador (sic) Morgenthau's action, which was taken under general instructions from the state department. The Turkish officials claim that the steps which they have taken against the Armenians were necessary as a war measure to prevent rebellion and plotting against the government.

Acting Secretary of State Polk would not disclose the exact nature of the Turkish reply to the American inquiry regarding the Armenian policy, but he said no further action was contemplated at this time.

Morgenthau's plan to transport the Armenians to the United States continued to move forward. *The Honolulu Advertiser,* in Honolulu, HI, reported the following as front-page news, on October 3, 1915:

PLAN TO RESCUE ARMENIANS NOW MAKING PROGRESS

(Associated Press by Federal Wireless.)

WASHINGTON, October 3—The efforts being made by Ambassador Morgenthau to secure official sanction to a plan to transport the remnants of the Armenian people to the United States, to enable them to survive, and to devise ways and means whereby at least two to three hundred thousand of the persecuted race may be transported to a new land, is making progress. Yesterday it was announced that the Turkish government has agreed to permit the migration of as many Armenians as Ambassador Morgenthau can secure transportation for, provided these emigrants become naturalized Americans.

Since April it is estimated that at least half a million Armenians have perished from massacres, starvation and disease. So acute is the distress that the American ambassador felt obliged to interfere and to offer this good services in transporting the entire Armenian people to America. The ambassador cabled to Washington asking that five prominent Americans be appointed on a commission to raise the million dollars for the first part of the big plan.

The starving Armenians are principally old people and children. The men have been slain and the young women subjected to a worse fate.

From Ambassador Morgenthau's 1918 memoirs titled "Ambassador Morgenthau's Story", he wrote in chapter 27 of his conversation with German officials regarding his plan to save the Armenians:

> I then made another plea in behalf of the persecuted Christians. Again we discussed this subject at length.
>
> "The Armenians,'" said Wangenheim, "have shown themselves in this war to be enemies of the Turks. It is quite apparent that the two peoples can never live together in the same country. <u>The Americans should move some of them to the United States, and we Germans will send some to Poland and in their place send Jewish Poles to the Armenian provinces</u>---that is, if they will promise to drop their Zionist schemes."
>
> Again, although I spoke with unusual earnestness, the Ambassador refused to help the Armenians.
>
> Still, on July 4th, Wangenheim did present a formal note of protest. He did not talk to Talaat or Enver, the only men who had any authority, but to the Grand Vizier, who was merely a shadow. The incident had precisely the same character as his pro forma protest against sending the French and British civilians down to Gallipoli, to serve as targets for the Allied fleet. Its only purpose was to put Germans officially on record. Probably the hypocrisy of this protest was more apparent to me than to others, for, at the very moment when Wangenheim presented this so-called protest, he was giving me the reasons why Germany could not take really effective steps to end the massacres. Soon after this interview, Wangenheim received his leave and went to Germany.
>
> Callous as Wangenheim showed himself to be, he was not quite so implacable toward the Armenians as the German naval attaché in Constantinople, Humann. This person was generally regarded as a man of great influence; his position in Constantinople corresponded to that of Boy-Ed in the United States. A German diplomat once told me that Humann was more of a Turk than Enver or Talaat. Despite this reputation I attempted to enlist his influence. I appealed to him particularly because he was a friend of Enver, and was generally looked upon as an important connecting link between the German Embassy and the Turkish military authorities.
>
> Humann was a personal emissary of the Kaiser, in constant communication with Berlin and undoubtedly he reflected the attitude of the ruling powers in Germany. He discussed the Armenian problem with the utmost frankness and brutality.
>
> «I have lived in Turkey the larger part of my life,» he told me, «and I know the Armenians. I also know that both Armenians and Turks cannot live together in this country. One of these races has got to go. And I don't blame the Turks for what they are doing to the Armenians. I think that they are entirely justified. The weaker nation must succumb. The Armenians desire to dismember Turkey; they are against the Turks and the Germans

in this war, and they therefore have no right to exist here. I also think that Wangenheim went altogether too far in making a protest; at least I would not have done so.»

I expressed my horror at such sentiments, but Humann went on abusing the Armenian people and absolving the Turks from all blame.

"It is a matter of safety," he replied; "the Turks have got to protect themselves, and, from this point of view, they are entirely justified in what they are doing. Why, we found 7,000 guns at Kadikeuy which belonged to the Armenians. At first Enver wanted to treat the Armenians with the utmost moderation, and four months ago he insisted that they be given another opportunity to demonstrate their loyalty. But after what they did at Van, he had to yield to the army, which had been insisting all along that it should protect its rear. The Committee decided upon the deportations and Enver reluctantly agreed. All Armenians are working for the destruction of Turkey's

power and the only thing to do is to deport them. Enver is really a very kind-hearted man; he is incapable personally of hurting a fly! But when it comes to defending an idea in which he believes, he will do it fearlessly and recklessly. Moreover, the Young Turks have to get rid of the Armenians merely as a matter of self-protection. The Committee is strong only in Constantinople and a few other large cities. Everywhere else the people are strongly 'Old Turk'. And these old Turks are all fanatics. These Old Turks are not in favour of the present government, and so the Committee has to do everything in their power to protect themselves. But don't think that any harm will come to other Christians. Any Turk can easily pick out three Armenians among a thousand Turks!"

Ambassador Morgenthau's plan to bring the Armenians didn't go unnoticed, nor was it welcomed by everyone. *The Evening Public Ledger,* in Philadelphia, PA, published a letter on October 2, 1915, on page 4, from a prominent Armenian religious leader:

OPPOSED TO BRINGING ARMENIANS TO U.S.
Rev. H. Y. Yardumian Believes Misery of Exiles Would be Increased

The transporting to America of all Armenians now being driven from their homes by the Turks would be to impose additional misery on a persecuted people, in the opinion of the Rev. Haig Y. Yardumian, vice president of the Armenian National Defense Union and moderator of the Evangelical Alliance of America.

In his home at 724 South 60th street the Rev. Mr. Yardumian discussed today the plan advocated by Henry Morgenthau, United States Ambassador to Turkey, who has signified his willingness to contribute $1,000,000 in this country for that purpose.

"The project seems humane on the surface," the Rev. Mr. Yardumian said, "but there is evidently a diplomatic handicap that hinders Mr. Morgenthau from doing something better than importing a dependent group of women, old men, children, diseased persons ad cripples to the

United States.

WOULD ADD TO MISSERY.

"I do not wish to say anything further on the political significance of the matter at the present time, but I can say that the bringing of these people to America would add to the misery of an already unhappy race. Such a sudden change would in itself be a sudden and crushing blow, but one which would please the Young Turks mightily, as it would further their desire to remove every Christian element from their Mohammedan country.

The Rev. Mr. Yardumian them explained that the Turks have practically destroyed all of the young-able-bodied Armenians by putting them in the first ranks of battle, where they have been killed, and shooting as traitors those who objected to this manifestly unfair persecution. In addition to this he asserts that the exiled Armenian families have been split up, the children under 10 years of age being taken in hand by Turks to be converted to Mohammedan faith, and the women sent to the most remote and pestilent parts of the empire.

"DEPLOMACY AND SWORD."

"To induce these people to come to America and throw away every possibility of reassembling their families would not only be difficult, but cruel," he said. "Here is the only feasible plan which can be brought to the rescue of these people:

"Diplomatic pressure, backed by the sward of the neutral countries, should be brought on the Turks to make them give the Armenians free passage to a place of safety on the western coast of Asia Minor, a neutral zone, which could be under the protection of the Red Cross of the United States, Holland and Switzerland. At the conclusion of the war it would be a simple matter to decide the future habitat of the exiles."

Ten days after Rev. Haig Y. Yardumian raised his concerns about Morgenthau's plan, *The Independence Daily Reporter*, in Independence, KS ran a story, on page 7, in which the Morgenthau plan is reported to have failed:

TURKEY BREAKS PROMISES
RESCINDED ARMENIAN PROMISE A DAY AFTER MAKING IT.
Massacres Are Renewed Now Worse Than Ever—No Protection for Christians.

Washington, Oct. 12.—Armenian massacres in Asiatic Turkey have been renewed with vigor since Bulgaria's entrance into the war as Turkey's ally. This information reached the state department from Ambassador Morgenthau, who stated that the majority of the Armenians in Asiatic Turkey have been killed.

Although representations were made by this government some time ago warning Turkey that further atrocities against the Armenians would eliminate the sympathies of the American people, no answer has been received. Earlier representations were promising that Armenians desiring to leave the country would be permitted to do so without harm and that Christians would be spared. Information reaching this country indicates that these conditions were not adhered to but were rescinded the next day.

How is it that the Turks' offer could have been rescinded the day after it was accepted? How did Morgenthau not know this? Although Morgenthau had made a public announcement in September of his deal with Talaat, his memoirs indicate that he had been considering such a plan as early as July when he had met with German officials who suggested Armenians be taken to America and also exchanged with Polish Jews. Was this but just another political game on the part of the Turks to give them enough time to kill off all the Armenians, or was this plan less humanitarian as suggested by Rev. Haig Y. Yardumian and part of a bigger plan that Morgenthau was a part of?

Besides Morgenthau's aid to the Armenians, there were other minority groups in the Ottoman Empire that were facing persecution that needed the Americans' help, namely the Jews. On March 6, 1916, the New York Times reported on a humanitarian mission to help those Jews in danger:

U.S. WARSHHIPS' AID TO JEWS IN TURKEY
Ambassador Morgenthau Says They Helped Diplomat's Work for Humanity.
SHOWED NATION'S INTEREST
Tells Educational Alliance Our Position in the War is Like That of Noah and His Ark.

How diplomacy had been aided in the work in behalf of humanity by the prompt arrival of two American warships in the harbor of the Turkish capital, was told by Ambassador Henry Morgenthau, in a brief address last night at the annual meeting of the Educational Alliance, East Broadway and Jefferson Street. Although these war vessels were merely on a peaceful errand, the good impression thus created by this practical display of friendship and protection by the United States Government for the Jewish inhabitants threatened with expulsion, resulted in improving the relations between the people and the official representatives of the Turkish Government, he said.

"You here cannot know how much cause the Jewish people of Turkey had to show their appreciation to the American Government for the aid given so timely," said the Ambassador. "And when these warships came, bringing to them the gold which some of you gentlemen here contributed for their relief, their sentiments of appreciation was expressed in no ordinary words of thanks. The Jewish people and the Turkish inhabitants had been living in amity, but the incident of this friendly act of another nation immediately improved these conditions.

"It showed that the Jewish people were not forsaken; that they had sympathy and the friendship of a powerful nation back of them in the hours of their distress. I want to say that the Turkish officials have the kindest feelings for the Jews. These have been no expulsions of the inhabitants of the Jewish faith. Some were forced to depart from Jaffa when the Turkish Government began preparations to intern the subjects of nations with which it was at war. The Jewish aliens were given their choice of three methods of procedure: To accept the Mohammedan faith, to be interned, or to leave the country. For this latter purpose the American Government permitted me to use two warships.

"There were no more deportations except of those of belligerent countries affected by the military laws. Now those who remain in Turkey are living in peace, attending their affairs and affected by no other causes than the economic conditions brought about by the war.

"These economic conditions are felt severely among some sections of the Jewish population. A great many of the men have enlisted, many of them the earners and breadwinners of the families left behind. I look for a great deal of trouble and suffering; I fear it will be almost a famine if this war continues much longer. In Saloniki, too, which has a population almost entirely of Jews, they are going to have a lot of trouble."

The Ambassador referred to the experimental colonization plan in Palestine as a desirable thing for the good of all Jews throughout the world. If the people there succeeded in establishing model colonies and made them self-sustaining it would be a great step forward in a great movement, he said. He said that while Palestine could never provide for many millions of Jewish people, nevertheless it could be made a center of highly developed industry, forming a national sphere of Jewish influence everywhere, and under this movement Jewish art and literature would be developed and retained in their highest form.

Suggesting that the United States should continue its policy of peace and neutrality, and by all means keep out of the world conflict, the Ambassador said:

"Sometimes it seems to me our position is something like Noah in the ark. We have sent out the dove of peace, and it has returned. This great flood of war is still rising. Let us continue to keep out of it upon dry land, and when the flood goes down we will not go with it."

Justice Samuel Greenbaum of the Supreme Court, President of the alliance, reviewing educational work of the organization, which had accomplished so much for good citizenship in its thirty years of existence, beginning when the Russian persecutions had started so many emigrants from that country, said the future called upon it for even greater work in all its departments. At the end of the European war, he predicted, there would be larger immigration than ever before to this country.

Jacob H. Schiff said in part:

"What makes a nation is the common language that the people of that nation speak. Those who do not want to speak common language cannot be a part of the nation. The Morgenthaus and the Greenbaums are the true leaders of Israel, for they are teaching the strange people the common language of the country—they are the leaders of Israel; and the men who tell you you are a separate nation and try and make you look at the American problem from a Jewish viewpoint are like the men who made the golden calf."

Although Morgenthau was an ambassador, one has to remember that he was also a wealthy and powerful businessman who was tightly connected to some of the most powerful men in the world. And with most politicians at that time (as it is believed to also be the case today), special interests of wealthy and powerful supporters came with certain expectations. In the case of Morgenthau, he was not an exception to the rule, but rather he seemed to play by the rules of watching out for those who buttered his bread, like Jacob H. Schiff, who had also deemed Morgenthau a leader of Israel.

After Morgenthau had resigned from his post as U.S. Ambassador to Turkey, some of the deals he had negotiated during his service in the capacity of the U.S. Ambassador to the Ottoman Empire were reported in the newspapers. One particular deal, which would one day become one of the most controversial land grabs, starting more than 30 years after Morgenthau, was the formation of Israel, in 1948. On May 22, 1916, *The Harrisburg Daily Independent*, Harrisburg, PA, ran a story, on page 3, claiming that Morgenthau was negotiating a deal to purchase Palestine:

TURKS MAY SELL PALESTINE
Former Ambassador Morgenthau Says He Discussed
Matter With Officials—Might Be a Republic
By Associated Press.

Cincinnati, O., May 22.—Henry Morgenthau, who recently resigned as Ambassador to Turkey, spoke before the Wise Center Forum here yesterday and told his listener that the sale of Palestine after the War, so that the Ottoman empire might secure money, had been discussed by him. He told of how he broached the matter to the Turkish Ministry and how eagerly it was discussed.

"We even got do to figures," said Mr. Morgenthau. "They argued as to whether it should be an international state or a republic."

Mr. Morgenthau said that is to whether Russian or German Christians would allow the Jews to possess Palestine was thoroughly discussed. "I told the ministry that if the harbor was built at Jaffa, Jerusalem would yearly attract 500,000 visitors who spend at least $100 each. Seeing that there was a way for the Jews to pay for Palestine, the Ottoman government wanted to make concessions immediately and asked that the building of the harbor and hotels be started," he said.

Although this particular deal never came to fruition, the plan to make Palestine the homeland of the Jewish people had been perused by Morgenthau and his backers as the Ottoman Army began weakening.

The front-page news of *The Des Moines Register*, Des Moines, IA, on June 23, 1917, was about a group led by Morgenthau to secure Palestine for the Jewish people. They also revealed the amount of support the plan had from the United States:

JEWISH REPUBLIC IN PALESTINE MAY BE RESULT OF WAR

President Considering Including Zionist Recommendation When Peace Comes.

MISSION IS NOW EN ROUTE

Party Instructed to Investigate Conditions of Palestine Jews on Trip.

TO REALIZE DREAM OF AGES

Reclamation of Holy Land From Unspeakable Turk Seems Near at Hand.

BY JOHN CALLEN O'LAUGHLIN.

(Special to Chicago Heald and The Des Moines Register).

WASHINGTON, D. C., June 22.—President Wilson is giving serious consideration to the Zionist recommendation that one of the war acts of the United States shall be the establishment of a Jewish republic with Jerusalem as the capital.

Ostensibly the commission, consisting of Henry Morgenthau, former ambassador to Turkey; Maj. Felix Frankfurter, U. S. A., and E. W. Lewin-Epstein, connected with the Zionist movement, is en route to Egypt and Palestine for the purpose of aiding suffering Jews and especially those, numbering about 1,000 who are naturalized American citizens.

Mission Is Instructed.

This, however, will be only a small part of the duty of Mr. Morgenthau and his associates.

As a matter of fact they have been instructed to make a thorough investigation of the situation of the Jews in Palestine and neighboring sections of Turkey and to follow carefully the campaign against the Turks and Germans which the British are conducting.

The reports the commission will make will be of the utmost value to the president in guiding him as to the character of terms he will fix as conditions for the settlement of the war.

Every Nation Concerned.

Every nation is concerned about the Jewish question and is anxious once and for all to free Jerusalem from Turkish misrule. The British military expedition now is operating towards the city where Christ suffered and it is expected that within a comparatively short time it will be rescued from Turkish control.

Two British expeditions are moving against Turkey from the east, one passing through Mesopotamia and the other from Egypt along the eastern shore of the Mediterranean. Eventually, if they compass it, those expeditions will meet, but that is along tome in the future, in view of the desperate resistance the Turks, aided by the Germans, are making.

It is important, of course, that the military campaign which the British from the south and the Russians from the North are carrying on, shall have success, since that would have a tremendous bearing upon the end of the war.

Business to Aid Jews.

With this ultimate result, however, the Morgenthau commission will have no concern. It will be it's business to aid the Jews in every way it can; to see that those who are suffering shall get the supplies which American men of war were forced to unload at Alexendria, Egypt and enjoy the benefit of the $10,000,000 relief fund which has been collected in the United States, and finally, to ascertain the desire of the Jewish people reference to their future political conditions.

It is apparent to the president and others in Washington that a Jewish state could not stand alone. It will have to possess the moral and perhaps political support of a strong nation or nations if it is to live.

Control May Be in U. S.

It was suggested recently from London that control of Palestine, once it has been wrested from the Turks, shall be turned over to the United States. This nation, it was pointed out, is free from any entanglements in the near east and that it could be depended upon to pursue a thoroughly unselfish policy in connection with the administration of the territory.

The President and this cabinet from all reports have no intention of taking possession of territory so far from the new world. I n view of this determination, the plan has been advanced that the Jews be permitted to form a republic, the independence and territorial integrity of which shall be guaranteed by the United States and Great Britain an if Russia, France and Italy so desire by them also.

It is a reflection upon the paucity of human ideas that this guarantee proposal should be advocated; for Belgium enjoyed similar guarantees and they were ruthlessly violated by Germany.

I this case, however, attention is drawn to the fact that the signers of the agreement will be nations who are fighting to uphold the principle of the sanctity of treaties and that there is no likelihood that they would have violated their pledged word, however great might be the temptation.

Freedom is demanded.

It is important for the world from every point of view that Jerusalem should be free. Religion, race, economics, all demand it. It has been a century-old dream of Christian nations. It inspired the crusades, it always had uplifted men and women professing the religion of Christ.

Repeatedly President Wilson has pronounced himself in favor of the independence of the small nations. This pronouncement has met with the hearty approval of the Jews who have consistently labored in the uplifting of the land in which they originate. Imperial Russia sought to solve the Jewish question by endeavoring to induce her subjects of that race to emigrate to Palestine.

Philanthropic Jews have established colonies of their down trodden co-religionists in Palestine and elsewhere.

Near Jaffa there were, a few years ago twenty-six colonies, consisting of mainly Russian Jews. Some were maintained by private enterprise, others by the Chovawe-Zion association, and others again by the Jewish Colonization association, which was founded by Baron E. de Rothschild.

Chance Is at Hand.

What particularly has been desired by the philanthropic Jew is that their co-religionists should be given the same opportunity that they have had.

Now the chance has come to the Christian nations. They are fighting Turkey which is responsible for the suffering of humiliation of a people who have persisted in spite of the terrible burdens and hardships thrust upon them.

It is apparent that the sentiment of the allied peoples will not consent to a continuance of Turkish control of Palestine. This is certainly true of Britain as well as the United States. It likewise will be true of the Russian democracy in which the Jews is bound to assert himself as he has done in other lands.

The British government, which had been notified of the departure of the Morgenthau commission has promised to facilitate its work and investigation in every possible way. That government, too, is considering the disposition to be made of Palestine, once it has been freed.

It will be necessary first of all to establish a military government which will be administered by British army officers, but it is expected that the military will be able to turn control of civil affairs over to the Jews within a reasonable time, and that during the period of the war those people will enjoy more or less self-government.

I the meantime, the reports of the Morgenthau commission will reach Washington, and the president will be able to determine exactly what kind of demands he will make upon the central powers. But it seems certain at this moment that one result of the war will be freedom for the Jews.

Buffalo Evening News, in Buffalo, NY, reported, on August 15, 1917, on page 3, of a delay in Morgenthau's mission and shed some light on the plan he was carrying out:

**President's Envoy Cannot Proceed
Until British Advance at Gaza.**

Special To the NEWS.

WASHINGTON, Aug. 15—Henry Morgenthau, former ambassador to Turkey, before leaving for Europe, ostensibly as the head of a mission to investigate possibilities for ameliorating the condition of war sufferers in Palestine, took his instructions, it was learned, direct from President Wilson.

Mr. Morgenthau is now in France and it is understood that his visit to Palestine has been postponed owing to the check of the British expeditionary forces at Gaza by the Turkish troops. It had been expected that the British advance would swiftly penetrate deep into Palestine, as was promised by the success of their initial operations along the Egypto-Palestine border.

The Morgenthau mission has not been abandoned, however, and it is possible for the envoy to fulfill a part of it before proceeding to Egypt and Palestine. It was declared by a high authority that the special purpose of this visit to Europe and Asia is to study, especially in its political details, the entire Jewish problem, and particularly with relation to the proposed creation of an independent Palestine.

There is a strong belief, also, that Mr. Morgenthau, who knows personally the influential statesmen and military chieftains in Turkey, intended upon reaching the British lines in Palestine to seek conferences with Turkish officials and to discuss with them the possibilities of separate peace for Turkey.

The Messenger-Inquirer, Owensboro, KY, reported, on January 20, 1918, on page 15, further details of the plan. In the article, they characterized Morgenthau's work in Turkey as 'secret service' and claimed: "Upon Mr. Morgenthau's return to the United States he was promptly dispatched to France and Spain on a secret mission."

WHAT THE NEW ERA MEANS TO HEBREWS

In an editorial on the president's latest address to congress the American Jewish Chronicle says:

"We Jews are doubly interested in the president's great peace message—because of its reference to the small and oppressed nationalities and Palestine. The plan to establish a national Jewish homeland has the full sympathy of the president.

"President Wilson does not insist on the dismemberment of the Turkish Empire; all America asks of Turkey is an assurance of 'an absolutely unmolested opportunity of autonomous development for its foreign nationalities."

Interviews with the foremost statesmen of the allied national elicits the depressing information that there is little or no intention of returning the Jerusalem district to the Jews for an sort of homeland. The present character of the British operations all point to a permanent occupation by France and England of Palestine. If the English armies retire, it is believed in Paris there will be an autonomous government set up with the beneficent influence of the British-French entente predominating for commercial and territorial reasons.

The situation is not a tempting one for discussion, as the complexion undergoes kaledoscopical changes—the peace conference only will dispose of the question in a permanent manner. One thing only is certain, that Turkish pogroms have ended once and for all. The Jews of Palestine will henceforth enjoy unrestricted racial and political development under the government assigned by the Great Peace conference.

In Russia the Jews today are subjected to greater and more bitter indignities than before the revolution. The Russian proletariat, long educated to a hatred of the Hebrews, have suddenly been released from all government restraint, and the Ghetto has acted as a buffer for angry masses of the canaille, incensed against anything that offers either active or static resistance.

In the combat zone of Central Europe it is estimated the Hebrews have perished by millions. The Polish pogroms are as naught compared to the situation the Jews found themselves in with the opening of hostilities. Even now, despite the heroic efforts of the American Jews to alleviate the situation, all Central Europe rings with the protest and anguish of the Jews.

Emigration After the War

While the general emigration after the war to the United States will be comparatively insignificant, it is certain there will be a great Jewish immigration.

Europe will need all of her own nationals for the work of reconstruction. There will even be an emigration from the United States of commercial and technical quality, but this will be offset by the counter immigration of Jews from Europe who expect little improvement in their political and social status there. More than half of the entire population of Jews was situated in the present war zone.

When the first Jews came to what is now New York, 216 years ago, they were permitted to remain on the condition "that the poor among them shall not become a burden to the community but be supported by their won nation."

The condition has been faithfully lived up to. Even today all the city departments interlock to inform the Jewish relief centers of Jewish sufferers. The unfortunates are promptly and well taken care of by a series of Jewish relief institutions.

The United States today is a real haven for Zionism. There is a glittering circle of Jewish intellectuals who command the attention of the whole nation. Jewish—but Americans of the first water.

Mr. Henry Morgenthau, one of the most distinguished of our diplomatic corps, performed secret service in Turkey while Ambassador that was sufficient to materially temper certain views held in Washington in regards to Kaiserlich. Upon Mr. Morgenthau's return to the United States he was promptly dispatched to France and Spain on a secret mission. His wife wears the cross of the Legion of Honor for distinguished service to the French republic. Both today head various relief movements, not of Gentiles and for Hebrews. (Ed.: bolded and *underlined by Ara K. Manoogian)*

Nathan Strauss, of New York, is one of the most prominent Jews in New York today. The lives of millions of babies are said to have been saved as a direct result of the work of the milk reform which Mr. Strauss started in New York City in 1892, and which has now spread throughout this country and Europe.

In New York City alone during the first 22 years of the work, his milk depots distributed 35,000,000 bottles and 18,000,000 glasses of milk at the rate of one cent each. He cut the death rate of children under five years in

New York City from 126 in every thousand to only 64.

Outside of these home philanthropies his greatest interest lay in heling the inhabitants of Holy Land. He spent a quarter of a million dollars establishing soup kitchens, an anti-rabies institute, a public health board, and other benefactions in Jerusalem, and planned the thorough modernization of that city.

The Rev. Dr. Stephen S. Wise, rabbi of the Free Synagogue, is a rigid iconoclast for political purity. In every campaign in New York for any office Dr. Wise performs political and social research and publishes his opinion which affect a great portion of the electorate.

A year and a day later, *The Messenger-Inquirer*, in Owensboro, KY, reported, on January 21, 1919, on page 4, of what Morgenthau thought was the only solution to the ongoing problem with the Turks and their failure to govern:

CARVE UP TURKEY

Henry Morgenthau, former American ambassador of Turkey, and who has made an exhaustive study of the Turkish subject, is an stating that "Turkey is not reformable. Her vitality is exhausted. She is not sick; she has just disintegrated and passed away. The skeleton may still make some motions, but it is only the wind that is moving the limbs. There is no heart left through which the red blood of humanity can flow."

The Turkish empire has for centuries been the menace of the East. It has never made a forward step in the matter of amelioration of the condition of the subjects or of the outside assistance under the mistaken idea of forming a balance of power. The century, under his scheme, would be partitioned into smaller homogeneous districts, so that the people could govern themselves. Of this matter of Mohammedan rule over Christians, he says:

"Turkish Mohammedan rule over Christian people must cease. These old nations now under Turkish misrule, must have their rights restored."

Likewise he is equally emphatic about the freedom of the Dardanelles: "The Dardanelles must remain open and unfortified," he said. "they are the great waterway between Asia and Africa and are as vital to commerce as the mouth of the Mississippi."

This will be one of the important questions that will engage the attention of the to-be-formed league of nations.

As stated in the beginning of this chapter, Henry Morgenthau played a very big role in the successful election of President Woodrow Wilson. Those whose support Morgenthau had secured for this task were wealthy bankers. Quite possibly, the bankers had secured the help of Morgenthau. Two of these bankers were not members or supporters of the party that Woodrow Wilson represented. They were supported the party of the popular incumbent Republican President, William Howard Taft. Those two bankers were from the firm of Kuhn, Loeb & Co., namely, Paul Warburg and Jacob H. Schiff. On the flip side and in support of the incumbent, also from Kuhn, Loeb & Co., was Felix Warburg. In order to secure Wilson's victory, a plan was implemented where the Republican ex-president Theodore Roosevelt 'threw his hat into the ring.' He ran as a third-party candidate, the "Bull Moose." Roosevelt was financed by Otto Hermann Kahn of Kuhn, Loeb & Co. The end the result was that the Republican vote was split and the weaker candidate won the election.[70]

As a thank you, President Wilson signed into law the Federal Reserve Act, that which Taft refused to support. In the end, Wilson signed the Federal Reserve Act, on December 23, 1913, as an early Christmas gift to the bankers of Kuhn, Loeb & Co. Henry Morgenthau appears to have been a part of this deception. On March 15, 1914, *The Messenger-Inquirer*, Owensboro, KY, had a front-page news announcing:

"Henry Morgenthau, who was secretary of the National Democratic committee, and who, it is said, is to be recalled from his present post of United States ambassador to Turkey to accept a place on the Federal reserve board or the appointment as chairman of the board of control of the reserve bank at New York. Either of these positions will be considered one of high honors."

Although Morgenthau would never realize these posistions of high honor, his son, Henry Morgenthau Jr., would serve secretary of the Treasury from January 1, 1934, to July 22, 1945. Under the provisions of the original Federal Reserve Act, the Treasury Secretary was also ex-officio chairman of the Federal Reserve Board. This ex-officio membership ended on February 1, 1936, as a result of the Banking Act of 1935, which changed the makeup of the Board.[71]

---

70 Mullins, Eustace (2014) The Secrets of the Federal Reserve, pp. 28-29
71 https://www.federalreservehistory.org/people/henry_morgenthau_jr

Chapter 14

Presenting the Armenian Case

After World War I ended in 1918, in which the Turks were defeated, the peace talks were in progress. Having declared independence on May 28, 1918, as a result of the fall of the Russian Empire, the Democratic Republic of Armenia was in a vulnerable state. The new government dominated by the ARF had failed to build a properly equipped military force with the 150,000 Armenian officers and soldiers that had been serving in the Russian Empire. Before the October Revolution of 1917, Russia had agreed to unofficially send these troops home in such a way as to hide that fact from other newly independent countries that might demand the return of their own citizens. However, at one point the flow of Armenian military from Russia stopped, because of the new Bolshevik leadership. By that time, only 35,000 had made it to Armenia.

Besides the regular army, Armenia also had a 10,000-strong volunteer force. For the territory controlled by Armenia, 45,000 troops were far too few to repel the Turkish army, whom the Allies had failed to disarm. With every passing day, the Turks were organizing and planning their return to power. With this impending threat, the Armenians turned to the U.S. with a request for needed protection in the interim, until a final peace agreement could be signed.

On September 27, 1919, the United States Senate Subcommittee on Foreign Relations began a two-week long hearing to discuss Senate Joint Resolution 106 for the maintenance of peace in Armenia.

[S. J. Res. 106, Sixty-sixth Congress, first session.]

JOINT RESOLUTION For the maintenance of peace in Armenia.

Whereas the withdrawal of the British troops from the Caucasus and Armenia will leave the Armenian people helpless against the

attacks of the Kurds and the Turks, and whereas the American people are deeply and sincerely sympathetic with the aspirations

of the Armenian people for liberty and peace and progress: Therefore be it

Resolved by the Senate and House of Representatives of the United States of America in Congress assembled, That in the opinion of the Senate, Armenia (including the six vilayets of Turkish Armenia and Cilicia), Russian Armenia, and the northern part of the Province of Azerbaijan and Trebizond, should be independent, and that it is the hope of the Senate that the peace conference will make arrangements for helping Armenia to establish an independent republic.

Sec. 2. That the President of the United States is hereby authorized to use such military and naval forces of the United States as in his opinion may seem expedient for the maintenance of peace and tranquility in Armenia until the settlement of the affairs of that country has been completed by treaty between the nations.

Sec. 3. That the President is hereby authorized to suspend the foreign enlistment act to the extent necessary to enable Armenians in the United States to raise money and arm and equip themselves as an armed force to go to the aid of their countrymen in Asia Minor.

Sec. 4. There is hereby appropriated out of any moneys in the Treasury not other-wise appropriated the sum of $---to enable the President to execute the foregoing resolution.

The first witness to testify was Miran Sevasly (1864-1935), a practicing lawyer and Chairman of the Armenian National Union in the United States. He was born in Smyrna, on July 10, 1864, and immigrated to the United States in May of 1908 after receiving his legal education at the University of Aix, France.

Sevasly was credited for his role in raising 10,000 Armenian residents in the United States to fight on the Turkish front in the Armenian Legion of the allied army. In 1922, King George II of Greece made him a Knight of the Golden Cross for saving refugees from the Smyrna conflagration.

Mr. Sevasly presented the Armenian case and answered questions, which was recorded by the stenographer as follows:

Miran Sevasly

Mr. SEVASLY. Mr. Chairman and gentlemen, will you permit me to thank you for the opportunity you have given the Armenians, or the American citizens of Armenian birth, to appear before you and state briefly their case on behalf of the Armenian people, toward whom we know this great Republic entertains much genuine sympathy.

I should not care, perhaps, to go into any detail on the political aspects of the Armenian question. I shall not speak, except by referring to it, of the question of the mandate which I know is exercising the minds of many American citizens. I shall not even refer at any length to the future status of Armenia, or to the political frontiers of Armenia, because these I consider matters that will have to be disposed of by the peace conference. I will only refer just by way of parenthesis to the service the Armenians have rendered during this last war which entitle them to be considered as belligerents. They have contributed more than 100,000 men to the Russian army, and that army has been sent to the front in Poland, where it fought with the Russians against the Central Powers.

Senator WILLIAMS. Those were Russian Armenians?

Mr. SEVASLY. Russian Armenians. In the second place, the Armenians. have held the Caucasian front against the Russians for more than a year, and thus helped England to bring about their success in their Mesopotamian campaign against Turkey. Were it not for the fact that the Armenians have held the Caucasian front, England would not so easily have brought that campaign to such a successful conclusion.

Senator WILLIAMS. Or the Mesopotamian campaign?

Mr. SEVASLY. Yes.

Senator WILLIAMS. Or the Palestine campaign, either?

Mr. SEVASLY. Or the Palestine campaign. Lord Cecil testified to that in an official document which he sent some time ago to the president of the Armenian delegation in Paris.

Senator WILLIAMS. Gen. Allenby also recognizes that fact.

Mr. SEVASLY. Yes, sir. The Armenians have not only done that, but they have contributed to the forces that have fought in the Holy Land and in Syria against Turkey. Also from this country about 2,000 volunteers went to the front, thanks to the labors of the Armenian National Union; 2,000 volunteers went from here to fight in Palestine, and they did fight valiantly, and they decided the battle in favor of the Allies against the Turks, and it was the result of that battle that enabled the Allies to conquer Syria and to take Jerusalem, and opened the way to Armenia and Cilicia. But they have done more. One thousand Armenian volunteers went to the French front and fought gallantly on the plains of Picardy and Champagne, and of those 1,000 men hardly 50 have survived. To say after all this that the Armenians should not be considered as belligerents and should not be entitled to the same consideration as the Arabs or the King of Hedjaz is, I respectfully submit, a misnomer.

Senator WILLIAMS. Who. has been contending for that?

Mr. SEVASLY. Well

Senator WILLIAMS. Go ahead with your own statement.

Mr. SEVASLY. It is not only that, gentlemen, but the Armenians have lost 1,000,000 men because they have refused to side with the Turkish barbarian. An alliance was offered to them. They were told that if they sided with the Turks they would be given everything, but they refused it completely, and at a convention held at Erzeroum on the eve of this war, in 1914, the Armenians refused to side with the Turks. These considerations are so well known to you, as the distinguished Senator opposite has so well testified, that I thought it was un-necessary to dilate upon this situation.

Now, another situation, which it was thought was very unfair to the Armenians, was the terms of the armistice with Turkey. Turkey was allowed practically to be in control of the Armenian provinces.

Senator WILLIAMS. Well, upon that, let it be stated that the United States was not a party to that armistice, because she was not at war with Turkey.

Mr. SEVASLY. Well, the situation now is this, that in this part of the country, in Cilicia, the Armenians have gone in there, there has been a gradual influx of Armenians into that country, and as the English and French have some troops there, and as the country is contiguous to the sea, there is more safety there, and I am glad to say there are some 200,000 Armenians now who are inhabiting that country, and normal conditions are being restored.

Senator WILLIAMS. That is southwestern Armenia.

Mr. SEVASLY. Yes, sir.

Senator WILLIAMS. On the Mediterranean litoral; Alexandretta and neighboring towns. A sufficient force of French and other Allies are there at this time to maintain order and to protect the inhabitants, that is what you mean?

Mr. SEVASLY. Yes. Normal conditions are being restored, the stores are being opened, and after this troubled situation, and the deportation of Armenians and massacres, now they are gradually picking up; and they have two daily papers in the city of Adana, and that shows their recuperative powers.

Now, the country between Cilicia and the Caucasus here [indicating on map] has been very much depleted. There has been a very large depletion of the Armenian population by reason of deportations and massacres. That is the part of the country that has suffered most, I think. I do not like to exaggerate numbers, but I think about 750,000 Armenians have actually disappeared—have died from deportations or massacres.

Senator WILLIAMS. You mean the country between the Black Sea and the Caspian Sea in northeastern Armenia That is what you are referring to now?

Mr. SEVASLY. Yes; from here to this part [indicating on map].

Senator WILLIAMS. Up along southeast of the Black Sea, you indicate?

Mr. SEVASLY. Yes.

Senator HARDING. You say 750,000 Armenians have disappeared?

Mr. SEVASLY. At least that many.

Senator HARDING. Do you know relatively the number massacred?

Mr. MALCOM. By the number massacred, do you mean those who have died by massacre, or those who have died from deportations and everything else

Presenting the Armenian Case

Senator HARDING. Suppose we use the term that covers both.

Mr. MALCOM. According to the last report—

Senator WILLIAMS. To get this plain, I would like to ask a few questions.

Senator HARDING. Well, Senator, I have asked Mr. Sevasly a question and he has not answered it.

Senator WILLIAMS. I did not hear it. Excuse me.

Senator HARDING. I want to know the number of those who have suffered through the mistreatment of the Turks.

Mr. SEVASLY. The reports that we have from there, through travelers who have come from there, and from our ambassador, Mr. Morgenthau, and others, is that at least 800,000 Armenians have disappeared, either by massacre or by famine, and being deported across the desert, and it is a question whether in that part of the country there are—I do not know, but I do not think that the number is more than 100,000 of Armenians left in central Armenia.

Senator HARDING. Let us clear that a little bit. You say there have disappeared 800,000 from a section in which only 80,000 are left. Do I understand you aright?

Mr. SEVASLY. No; I say all told, whether you take Cilicia or whether you take all Armenia, the total number of Armenians who have died from massacres or deportation or from famine is not less than 800,000.

Senator WILLIAMS. Or from being sent out into the desert?

Mr. SEVASLY. We have reports from the missions and from our State Department, the consular reports, and all of these reports corroborate the statement I am giving you. It would be a long detail to give it to you.

Senator WILLIAMS. I am afraid you and the chairman do not understand one another. Let me ask you a few questions. How many Armenians have been killed during the war on the Flanders front, in the Caucasus, in Palestine, and everywhere else, as far as you know?

Mr. SEVASLY. Fighting men?

Senator WILLIAMS. Yes; fighting men.

Mr. SEVASLY. The fighting men killed in France are about 950. I do not know exactly what the numbers are in Palestine; but I will state that they are about 2,000.

Senator WILLIAMS. In Mesopotamia were there any?

Mr. SEVASLY. No.

Senator WILLIAMS. How many were killed in the Caucasus fighting against the Turks, either of Russian Armenians or Turkish Armenians?

Mr. SEVASLY. I would say not less than 35,000.

Senator WILLIAMS. How many Armenians were massacred, deported into the desert, or elsewhere, during the war?

Mr. SEVASLY. During the war I may say that two-thirds or three-fourths of the population of central Armenia, of the six provinces and Cilicia, have been deported, and not only from there but from parts of Turkish territory that do not come within the so-called provinces of Armenia.

Senator WILLIAMS. I understand. In the seaport. towns, upon the littoral, there was a population mainly Greek or Turkish, but containing many Armenians; and there were some of them in Constantinople. Now, all of these men, women, and children who were subjected to what is called "the white death," who were stripped and despoiled and turned loose in the desert without food—upon the desert or else where—what figures have you go that you can give the committee in regard to that?

Mr. SEVASLY. I thought that was a question which had already been thrashed out, and practically the consensus of opinion had been made. I have not got any details here, but there is a memorial of the delegation of integral Armenia which refers to them. I shall leave a copy of that with you.

Senator WILLIAMS. Find the place, so that the stenographer can copy it in his report.

Senator HARDING. Is this information covered in the documents you want to file?

Mr. MALCOM. No.

Senator WILLIAMS. I want to get those things separate from one another.

Mr. MALCOM. We can furnish memoranda on that, if you wish it.

Mr. SEVASLY. I can furnish you a memorandum at any time you like.

Senator WILLIAMS. Very well; give it to the stenographer. Now, let me ask this question: Give us a historical and chronological narrative as well as you can of what has happened since the armistice in the way of actual warfare and the destruction of life and property in Turkish Armenia.

Mr. SEVASLY. Well, I would like to say that of the population of Armenia, about half a million took refuge in the Caucasus. I would like to refer to that because it is very important. Half a million of those Armenians escaped these massacres and deportations, and went into the adjoining country and took refuge in the Caucasus, where they are now, and one of the great problems we have is to enable these people to come back to their country and settle, and they will not go there to settle now because there is no security, because the Turks have organized a large army of 30,000 or 40,000 men at Erzeroum, and are bent upon attacking those immigrants who left Armenia and who should come back there for the purpose of reconstructing the country, with the Armenians in the Trans-Caucasus.

Senator WILLIAMS. I understand that. I understand that the Georgians to some extent, as well as the Turks, have been attacking the Armenians lately. My question is this: I wish you would state now—and if you can not, give subsequently to the stenographer a statement—as accurately as you can concerning the history of the attacks upon the Armenians since the armistice was signed, and give the number of lives destroyed, of men, women and children, and the amount of property destroyed. If you can not give it now

Mr. SEVASLY. I do not think I can supply a detailed report now, but the situation is this, that the Turks have not disbanded their army that the Turks are all armed and the Armenians are not armed; that the Turks have got an army of about 30,000 or 40,000 men, which is against the very stipulations of the armistice terms, and that they are bent upon attacking, and in fact they have started to attack, according to the telegrams which were published yesterday, the Armenians who have migrated from Turkish Armenia into Russian Armenia, and whose repatriation is necessary for the reconstruction of the country. That is a very important fact. And there have been partial massacres at a place in Russian Armenia, called Karabagh, against which the Armenians protested, there being a protest by the Catholicos, the primate of the Armenians, to the English general who was in the Caucasus, a formal protest, corroborated by the protest of the Armenian Patriarch at Constantinople, and of the Armenian Government of Erivan. There were partial massacres at Aleppo a few months ago, and we had daily reports in the Armenian papers in Constantinople of the state of unrest and want of security throughout this country.

Senator WILLIAMS. That is not the point I am trying to get. The British have withdrawn their forces?

Mr. SEVASLY. They are withdrawing them.

Senator WILLIAMS. And I am informed that there has been a new massacre of Armenians, many of them retreating across into Persia, together with the British and American citizens or subjects that happened to be there. But the object of my last question is to find out, if you know—or if you do not just say that you do not— the number of Armenians, according to the best information you have, who have been massacred in the late attacks of the Turks, Georgians and Kurds since the British troops have been withdrawn, or during the re-treat of the British troops.

Mr. SEVASLY. The reports are that about 600 Armenians have been massacred in the district of Karabagh. Now, I do not know whether the British troops have already withdrawn, but I am perfectly sure that they are withdrawing, and that they are withdrawing from Batoum. They had troops along the railroad line from Batoum to Tiflis and along the railroad line to Bakou, down in the large oil center.

Senator WILLIAMS. As a matter of fact, they have withdrawn except for a garrison at Batoum and a garrison at Bakou, to protect the future withdrawal which has not yet been completed. They have withdrawn the protection from the line of railroad between the two places.

Mr. SEVASLY. We say this, that it would be necessary to keep that line, because it is the only line through which relief can go into Armenia, and we have that relief work there. Col. Haskins has gone there, and before Col. Haskins, Mr. Hoover sent men under Capt. Abraham Tulin, and he came back a month ago, and I have had frequent conversations with him on the situation of the country, and what he says refers to the future management or protectorate by America. He says that if America will accept the protectorate it would not be necessary to have more than 10,000 to 20,000 troops for the protection of the country; that all those bugaboos about that part of the country being a sort of Mexico in disguise are ill founded; that it is not so; that the prestige of America, with a few troops there, would be ample to keep the peace, to see that Armenia is safeguarded or protected during the reconstruction period.

Senator WILLIAMS. I would like to ask you this question: Suppose America should send a small force there and invite the principal allied and associated powers to join her; is it your opinion or not that an international force could be organized, with such reinforcement as the native Armenians could give, that could enforce peace in the territory?

Mr. SEVASLY. I think so, Senator.

Senator WILLIAMS. You are not an expert, of course, on military affairs, so that you are no judge of how many troops would be necessary.

Mr. SEVASLY. No, sir; I am simply repeating what this captain told me. I am not a military man, at all.

Senator WILLIAMS. If the United States Senate passed a resolution similar to this, what in your opinion would be the moral effect upon Turkey and upon these people who are now trying to exterminate the Armenian race in order to put an end to the Armenian question?

Mr. SEVASLY. Among English-speaking men it is said it would act like magic on the whole of the East, upon the whole of the eastern world. Once they know out there that the eagle is soaring around Ararat there will be no trouble whatever.

Senator WILLIAMS. You think, then, that the moral effect of the passage of the resolution, even if not a soldier or marine was ever sent, would be great; that the prestige would be very valuable in the preservation of the Armenian race?

Mr. SEVASLY. The moral effect will be great; but a few soldiers would—

Senator HARDING. Would add to the moral effect?

Mr. SEVASLY. Yes; I mean it would be the outer sign that this thing, that this paper, is not printed matter alone, but that it has—

Senator HARDING. Punch to it?

Mr. SEVASLY. Yes; punch to it. I do not know that I am putting my case properly.

Senator WILLIAMS. Go ahead with your statement.

Mr. SEVASLY. Now, there is the question of relief which is very important out here. If no troops came there, the relief work would be very difficult. I believe Col. Haskins was at Erivan, which is a small Armenian republic. The Armenians there organized a small republic there, having their seat at Erivan. That is in Russian Armenia.

Senator HARDING. I wanted to ask you this: Suppose the Armenians were free from the menace of massacre and warfare, have they food and supplies sufficient to undertake the work of reconstruction?

Mr. SEVASLY. They need help just like the populations of other states, of Serbia and other countries, need the help of others.

Senator WILLIAMS. In that connection, Mr. Chairman, Batoum is upon the Black Sea?

Mr. SEVASLY. Yes.

Senator WILLIAMS. That is held by the entente, by the allied forces?

Mr. SEVASLY. England has possession there.

Senator WILLIAMS. That is a seaport?

Mr. SEVASLY. Yes.

Senator WILLIAMS. That is also one of the termini of the railroad that runs from the Black Sea to the Caspian?

Mr. SEVASLY. Yes.

Senator WILLIAMS. So that if that country was to be supplied it would have to be supplied through Batoum?

Mr. SEVASLY. Yes, sir.

Senator WILLIAMS. It could not be well supplied through the Mediterranean over the railroad?

Mr. SEVASLY. The railroad is not completed through there, and the country there is mountainous and rugged.

Senator WILLIAMS. Yes. I am talking about the trans-Caucasian Armenia Russian and Turkish Armenia. That country could not be supplied except through Batoum? It could not be supplied through the Mediterranean from Alexandretta or another port, because of lack of railroad facilities?

Mr. SEVASLY. Yes, sir.

Senator WILLIAMS. There is a railroad there to the Caspian at Bakou. Wherever it runs, it does run across there?

Mr. MALCOLM. Yes.

Senator WILLIAMS. So that the entrepot or the depot for the distribution of supplies now is through the Black Sea?

Mr. SEVASLY. Yes.

Senator WILLIAMS. And the Bosphorus and the Dardanelles, and from Russia?

Mr. SEVASLY. Yes.

Senator WILLIAMS. So that the French occupation of Alexandretta and the Mediterranean littoral does not relieve this situation?

Mr. SEVASLY. No, sir.

Senator WILLIAMS. That is what I wanted to get at.

Mr. SEVASLY. No, sir. In the first place we were told that the French had sent an army of 10,000 or 12,000 men. In fact, I made representations to the State Department on the subject, and I was told about a fortnight ago that the French had sent 12,000 men, and it made a wrong impression on me, as I understood that the 12,000 men sent by France were to replace the Britishers who were going to withdraw from the Caucasus.

Senator HARDING. Yes.

Mr. SEVASLY. Now, we had some reason to believe that that information was not altogether correct—I mean, the way I put it to you. It seems the French are sending soldiers, but they are not sending them to the Caucasus. They are sending them to cover the territory—

Senator HARDING. Which is French?

Mr. SEVASLY. No; to cover the territory which comes within the pale of the secret treaties of 1916 [SEE APENDIX ##].

Senator HARDING. Within the French sphere of influence?

Mr. SEVASLY. Yes.

Senator WILLIAMS. Can you tell me the distance, approximately or accurately, or if you can get it, put it in the record later, from Alexandretta to Batoum?

Mr. SEVASLY. I have not got it handy now.

Senator WILLIAMS. And also the distance from Alexandretta to Bakou. My object is to show that if the French troops had Alexandretta it could not be of any preventive force in connection with the massacres that have been going on.

Mr. SEVASLY. The papers and telegrams say that the French intend to cover the territory as far as Mardin; that is south of Armenia. There is a straight line from Alexandretta to Mardine [indicating on map]. Well, it will have this effect, that the people will think that the French are coming up that way. But it is a far cry from Mardine to the trans-Caucasus.

Senator HARDING. Proceed. Our time is slipping by.

Mr. SEVASLY. Yes. I beg the committee to take into consideration the pressing need of protecting the Armenians in the trans-Caucasus. If the British troops are withdrawing, there is an army that the Turks have organized, the north. The stock of ammunitions the Armenians the is being exhausted, of and after such a protracted war and ordeals, these people need to be protected. Supposing this league of nations goes through tomorrow, unless some one of the great powers accepts the responsibility to constitute the. Armenian State, there will be no Armenians left to make it.

Senator WILLIAMS. The Armenian question will be settled by the extermination of their race?

Mr. SEVASLY. Yes. There has been great evidence of progressive tendencies of this historic race; but I am not going to dilate on their past history, which is known to you. The Armenians have appealed to the country long ago. I remember presenting a memorial to the State Department long before the league of nations was on the tapis, and America accepted 75 years ago the moral mandate by sending your missionaries and educational workers, and opening up schools and colleges. We are not going to close this way, now.

Senator WILLIAMS. That is not involved in this. This is merely to maintain peace until the treaty.

Senator HARDING. You would hardly argue that that is ground for assuming a mandatory? Because under those circumstances we would be mandatories over all the earth. We have our missionaries everywhere.

Mr. SEVASLY. I would not say that it is ground, alone, but it is an issue that is of moral value.

Senator HARDING. I wanted to ask you a specific question. In his resolution, Senator Williams has a provision authorizing the President to suspend the foreign enlistment act, as to enable the Armenians in this country to raise and arm and equip troops here.

Mr. SEVASLY. I fully endorse that.

Senator HARDING. How much of a military force do you think that. the Americans of Armenian origin, or the nonnaturalized Armenians, in this country, could raise?

Mr. SEVASLY. Well, I am not a good statistician.

Mr. GULESIAN. Eight or ten thousand.

Mr. SEVASLY. I should say from seven to ten thousand men, we could get. I know many Americans who have said they were perfectly willing to go out there and serve. I think if you passed the resolution it would be a very good thing to pass. They will be able to get these quarters and organize a unit in this country, and that would prevent America from having to send her own soldiers there later on.

Senator NEW. Would the force of Armenians be sufficient—Armenians, I mean, that you could raise in this country; would that force be sufficient—to meet the military needs of this situation?

Mr. GULESIAN. Practically, altogether.

Mr. SEVASLY. If we raise a unit here it will take some months before this unit is prepared: We have in this country an Armenian general, and there is another of the greatest Armenian generals, Gen. Antranik, who is coming here for this purpose, in order to give effect to section 3 of the resolution. We have a man who has been trained at the military school in Paris, who I believe is here, in Washington to-day, and he will submit the plans. He and the other generals who are coming over will submit the plans to the State Department showing how this plan can be carried out.

Senator NEW. Have you any idea how much of a military, force would be necessary there? I know you said you were not a military man, and that you were not qualified to speak definitely on that subject, but have you any kind of an estimate? Would it take 15,000 or 30,000 or 50,000?

Mr. SEVASLY. I will say what this American captain told me, the gentleman who was sent by Mr. Hoover to Armenia in charge of relief work—

Mr. SEVASLY. He told me he did not think more than 20,000 were needed for it. Of course, I can not speak with authority of that.

Senator WILLIAMS. Let me ask you this question. Whatever might be the force the Armenians could raise in the United States, would there not be a pretty large force now in the French and British Armies and in our own Army that would be very glad, if released, to cooperate with the force raised here to go to Armenia, in behalf of their own people?

Mr. SEVASLY. I think that meets the situation, too. But we applied some months ago—in April last I sent this memorandum to the State Department on this very subject—and I made a suggestion in the way that the honorable Senator spoke of, that the Armenians who are now in the American Army should be engaged in this.

Senator HARDING. There are a lot of them in the French and British Armies, too, as separate units.

Mr. SEVASLY. Yes; as separate units. We think that if we can send from here an organized body of 10,000 to 15,000 men, it may be that there would be a conjunction of Americans; and there is already in Silesia an Armenian legion, to which I referred in the beginning of my address. With this Armenian legion and the nucleus of the Armenian Army in the Caucasus, which is now ill supplied with munitions, we could very easily form within a comparatively short period the nucleus of an Armenian Army in whose hands will be placed the duty of the protection of the State against all intruders.

Senator HARDING. Have you anything else?

Mr. SEVASLY. No, sir.

The next to testify was Moses H. Gulesian (1863-1951), a native of Armenia, born on February 18, 1863, to Serkes and Margaret Gulesian of Maresh, Armenia. At the age of 18, the young Gulesian, a trained coppersmith who worked for himself had saved 18 Turkish pounds (about $75), left home without telling his parents who he knew would object to his departure to the United States. Arriving in Alexandretta the port he was to sail from, he wrote home telling his parents of his plan. His father attempted to stop him by telegraphing the authorities to have him detained in Smyrna, money taken from him, and ordered to return home. Fortunately for him, his negotiating skills helped him talk his father into returning his money and his freedom. On May 4, 1883, with one Turkish pound, (which no one would exchange for food) and not knowing a single word in English he sailed into New York harbor. His first home when he arrived was the Bowery Mission at 227 Bowery, New York, NY. The young immigrant, like many Armenians given a chance to prosper, in a short period of time established himself as a model American. With hard work, determination and going to night school to learn English, he soon became a millionaire thanks to his dealings in manufacturing and real estate. During the Armenian massacres of 1894 to 1896, because of his wealth, he was able to bring his entire extended family of 23 people who escaped with just the clothes on their backs to the United States. He turned the top floor of his 6-story factory into a refuge for Armenians fleeing to the U.S., sometimes having as many as 200 people at a time living there. He provided them with language classes, vocational training, and guidance to adapt to their new country.

Moses H. Gulesian

He was credited for saving the American naval frigate Constitution, a.k.a. Old Ironside, in 1905.[72] This act of patriotism won him an invitation to be the first immigrant to join The Sons of Liberty (est. 1765).

His wealth was also well known to Armenian Revolutionaries, from whom Gulesian had received a postcard, sent from New York, in July of 1907. It stated: "My Brother, we today have killed H. S. Tavashanjian [Hoannes S. Tavashanjian was a New York rug importer] and next Monday will kill you. You are a millionaire and you give nothing to our party. Believe me you die." It was signed Committee on Revolution.[73]

In December of 1913, one of Gulesian's buildings that housed a hotel caught fire and 28 men lost their lives. Since Mr. Gulesian had ignored orders

---

72 "Saving 'Old Ironside'" (Traverse City Record Eagle; Traverse City, MI, January 10, 1952), p. 4

73 "Boston Merchant Threatened." (The Washington Post; Washington, D.C., July 25, 1907), p. 1

to erect fire escapes, Mr. Gulesian stated that he had not done so as he thought his building was one of the safest in Boston. And besides, had been equipped, he claimed, many of the victims, who 'went there at all hours, most of them intoxicated and many carrying whisky bottles,' would not have been able to escape anyway.[74]

In Mr. Gulesian's testimony, he proposed that the United States grant American-Armenians the right to volunteer and form a military force that could defend Armenia. He went on to describe Armenia as a virgin country in need of becoming modernized and could be a profitable market for Americans to sell farming equipment and machinery of all kinds. He added that modernization was lacking because the Turks did not allow it. He said: "You will see hundreds of men and women in the wheat fields today taking the sickle in the hand and reaping, just the same as you will see a man in this country clean up the edge of a lawn." When asked about the mineral deposits, he agreed with Senator Williams that Armenia had iron, coal, copper and petroleum. He also told of copper and gold mines at the foot of Mount Ararat which has never been developed in any way, which with moral support from the U.S., Armenia 'will gain a great deal financially, and have the everlasting blessing and prayers of the poor, suffering Armenians.' He added: "I do not believe that you gentlemen, or the United States Senate, will turn your backs. There are many good men in it. I trust them."

The next witness was M. Vartan Malcom, born September 12, 1883, in Siva, Armenia, by the name of Melcom V. Melconian. He immigrated to the United States on September 23, 1896, becoming a citizen on October 8, 1906. There is no record of his parents coming to the United States, nor is there any mention of them or their names in any public records. It is possible that he came to the United States after becoming orphaned in the 1894-1896 Armenian massacres. He attended public school in Chicopee, Mass., then Amherst College, and finally Harvard Law School. Malcom was general counsel in New York City of a well-known liability insurance company and of many of the leading Armenian merchants. At the time of testifying to the Subcommittee on Foreign Relations, Mr. Malcom had just published a book titled "The Armenians in America."

Vartan Malcom

Mr. Melcom started his testimony with a question regarding the Armenian territories that were believed to be a part of Azerbaijan. These issues had been discussed between Senator Williams and Mr. Gulesian.

---

74 "Ignored Order to Erect Fire Escape" (Trenton Evening Times (Trenton, NJ, December 5, 1913) p. 12

Presenting the Armenian Case 147

[Mr. MALCOM] Mr. Chairman and gentlemen: A question was asked about Azerbaijan. The northern part of this Province is inhabited wholly by Armenians (indicating on map). The southern portion, which is now a part of Persia, is inhabited by some Armenians and also other races, including Tartars. The Armenians claim this northern section only (indicating on map) because the principal race there is Armenian.

[Senator WILLIAMS] Then this ought to be amended to include— no; Senator Lodge has got it right. He says, "the northern part of. the Province of Azerbaijan," and so forth.

[Mr. MALCOM] Yes.

Malcom went on to present his findings from his research for his book about Armenians in America to show how the Armenian immigrants in America had contributed far more than other ethnic immigrant groups. He presented charts to the committee showing that Armenians arrived in the U.S with more money and useful talents than any other race. He showed that Armenians before the war were the top wage earners in the Ottoman Empire, with the most professional and skilled laborers and the least non-skilled laborers. As for immigrants to the United States, Armenians topped the list of those who could read and write (92.1%) vs. the Portuguese, who ranked the lowest (47.5%). And then in terms of those immigrants in industries able to speak English, Armenians once again topped the list at 82.9 vs. Polish at 50.6%. In Mr. Malcom's study on the number of immigrant children in the public schools (which in those day was not common among immigrants who were busy scrapping out a living), the Armenians once again topped the list at 4% of those examined. The Greeks at .046%, with the Ruthenians at .035% and coming in last were the Croatians at .015%. As for housing, the Armenians were the ones living in the largest homes and paying the highest rent with the least number of occupants. The Serbians had houses just a little larger than the Armenians, but were paying less rent and had almost twice as many people living in them. As for those races who become American citizens, when measuring the number of immigrants in the manufacturing and mining industries, once again Armenians topped the list. The study showed 58.2% of Armenians vs. 3.7% of Greeks at the other end of the scale.

Malcon then spoke of the possible investment opportunities in the field of mining in Armenia:

[Mr. MALCOM] Now, with regard to the mines, there are some valuable mines, and I might add that about 1909 **Kuhn, Loeb & Co., of New York [Jacob H. Schiff],** sent a special commission to study these mines in Armenia. I happened to be in Constantinople at that time, and **Mr. Chester**, who was the representative of this concern, proposed to the Turks to build certain lines of railroad throughout Armenia—I am referring to Turkish Armenia—provided this company would be permitted to use the mines on each side of the railroad for a number of years, at the end of which the railroad would be returned to the Government. I am referring to this as an important fact, for the reason that a great concern like **Kuhn, Loeb & Co.,** which are interested in investing its money, made a special study of the mines and natural resources of Armenia and they were willing to invest a large sum of money to develop the country if the Turkish Government would let them do it. In connection with this subject I will read some extracts from a memorandum pre-pared by G. H. Paelian, secretary of the Armenian Engineers Association, in regard to the natural resources, etc., of Armenia. [Reading:]

There are many forests in the country, mainly in the northwest of Mersina, Hajin, Dersim, Arghana-Maden, and the Taurus and Amanus Mountains.

As regards mineral resources, according to Consul General Cr. Bie Ravendal, of Constantinople, "It may be truthfully asserted that Turkey is exceedingly rich in valuable minerals, and that its mineral wealth has hardly yet been touched." This has also been the testimony of English and German explorers. Its chief mineral products are:

Coal, found mainly in the region of Kharpout, Palu, Sivas, Keumur Khan (coal region), Chemeshgazak, in the mountains of Armenia, and at the foothills of the Taurus Mountains.

Copper mines at Arghana-Maden, near Diarbeldr, are regarded to be some of the largest and most produc-tive in the world. The production is limited to black copper, which amounts to approximately 1,500 tons during the last few years, containing 70 to 75 per cent pure copper. Copper ore is also found at the hinterland of Trebizond (Gumish Khanah, Herasund, Karahissar, etc.), all in the districts of Kharpout and Adana.

Iron ore is found near Van and in the Adana region (the output of which is 40,000 tons per year); also in Bigghar Dagh and Beirut Dagh, in the vicinity of Zeitoun.

Chrome mines are near Mersina, the output of which was 1,800 tons in 1900. There are others near Alexandretta, etc.

Silver mines at Bulghar Maden produce annually 57,200 lab of silver and 400 tons of silver lead. Silver is also found near Adana and Kharpout (Kebban Maden), near Gumush Khanah, etc.

The estimated output of zinc in 1911 from mines of an Anglo-French concern operating in the Mersina region was 2,000 tons.

Salt is abundant in Armenia. The mines at Sivas, Erzeroum, and Van yield a large output annually.

Other mineral products are emery, found in Adana; asphalt, on the Euphrates; gold at Bulghar Dagh, near Kharpout, and Van.

Lead at Bulghar Dash; platinum on the shores of the Choruk River and in Sasoun; petroleum near Trebizond and east of Lake of Van, etc.

For industrial development Armenia possesses all the requisites—raw material and power. It has large area of mineral wells, coal, and a considerable amount of water power (the power for the electric lighting of Tarsus is secured from the Cydnus River); but in the hands of the Turks the country still remains practically un-exploited.

Armenia is a wheat-growing country and old-fashioned flour mills are common everywhere, although modern hydraulic power mills equipped with modern machinery—two in Mertina, three in Tarsus, several in Sivas, etc.—have been installed.

Cicilia is the center of the cotton industry. In 1913 there were 35 cotton ginning plants and four cotton spin-ning and weaving mills in Adana and Mersina, one in Tarsus, one in Trebizond, and one in Arabkir for the manufacture of "manousa" (home-spun dress goods).

The rug industry is being carried on in Caesaria, Sivas (500 looms, 1,500 operatives), Adana and Kharpout (170 looms, 500 operatives).

There are five ice factories in Adana, two in Mersina, two in Tarsus, and one in Trebizond.

There are tanneries in Aintab, Marash, Sivas, and many other cities, also soap factories.

Besides the above, silk and wool weaving, hand embroidery, making of ornamental weapons, copper vessels, leather goods, shawls, silver and gold thread laces, wine, olive oil, etc., are common industries in Armenia.

Armenia, or in fact the whole of the prewar Turkish Empire, has been considered a field with great potentialities for the European and American manufacturers. Many capitalists saw great possibilities for commercial and industrial enterprises, and had applied for numerous concessions for the construction of railways, electric plants, telephones docks, warehouses, etc. But in spite of all their efforts progress was exceedingly slow. The principal causes for this were the rivalry of the powers to secure control of Turkey and the corrupt Turkish Government

In Mr. Malcom's testimony, he added the importance of recognizing Armenia's independence because of a possible threat from France and Great Britain, with their desires to take control of parts of Armenia:

[Mr. MALCOM] It seems to me, further, that the recognition of Armenia as an independent State by the United States may help to prevent the distribution of the integral Armenia among the powers. It is quite apparent to me at least, that under the secret treaties of 1916, to which England, France and Russia were parties, they are going to divide up Armenia unless we keep it intact by recognizing its independence, and furthermore

[Senator WILLIAMS] By the way, that treaty has been canceled by the defection of Russia.

[Mr. MALCOM] Is it, or will France and England—

[Senator WILLIAMS] And also canceled by France. France, in the conference at Paris, waived and surrendered its rights under that convention.

[Mr. MALCOM] Was that put in writing, or was it simply an oral statement?

[Senator WILLIAMS] I do not remember—I never did know, rather, go that I can not say I do not remember; but I am perfectly sure that France has waived that right. Whether she did it in writing or in the conference, or whether she did that by Clemanceau's waiver before the conference, I do not know; but it has been waived.

[Mr. MALCOM] We Armenians—

[Senator WILLIAMS You are talking about a convention whereby Alexanderetta and the littoral there—

[Mr. MALCOM] The littoral was given to France.

[Senator WILLIAMS] (continuing). Were to go to France; yes.

Mr. MALCOM. Yes.

[Senator WILLIAMS] That has all been set aside.

[Mr. MALCOM] Russian Armenia to Russia?

[Senator WILLIAMS] Yes.

[Mr. MALCOM] And Armenia bordering on Mesopotamia, to England.

[Senator WILLIAMS] Russia's part of it was vacated by her defection to the enemy, and France's part was voluntarily waived. France may be seeking a mandate, but not anything else.

[Mr. MALCOM] The point I desire to call to the attention of the committee is this, that even if that is so—that is, if there is some understanding that France and England have given up their rights under this treaty, even if that is so—it seems to me that the recognition of integral Armenia as an independent state would—

[Senator WILLIAMS] That would strengthen it?

[Mr. MALCOM] It would strengthen the understanding. Moreover, an independent, free State of Armenia in this section of the world will be a safeguard, it seems to me, to the future peace of the world. The Armenians have for centuries fought for political liberty and independence. They want to be free. Now, if something turns up and parts of Armenia are under different mandates or under "spheres of influence" between Russia, Italy, Greece, or England, or France, there will be a division of Armenian territory and population, which is unnatural. This division will never satisfy the Armenians. By recognizing the independence of Armenia as a whole the United States will certainly bring about a united Armenia, and at least help to prevent future troubles.

[Senator WILLIAMS] I quite agree with you about that; but so far as the division of Armenia itself into separate mandates is concerned, it is my opinion, and I suppose it is yours, that France and England and Italy and Greece are all very anxious that the United States should take over the mandate—they are more than willing to have her do it—until Armenia is put upon her feet. However, that question is not involved in these resolutions at all.

[Senator HARDING] You are speaking of the aspirations of Armenia. In view of that fact, I want to ask you, would the people of Armenia, prefer recognition as an integral State under their own policies of self-determination to any mandatory as proposed in the treaty?

[Mr. MALCOM] No; I would say, speaking for myself, that the Armenians would prefer a mandatory, under the present circumstances.

[Senator WILLIAMS] For a limited period?

[Mr. MALCOM] For a limited period.

Mr. Malcom then gave what he might have thought was a strong argument for the United States to take the mandate over Armenia, which knowing what we know now about the U.S. and their interests in the Armenian territories, most especially the $1/6^{th}$ of the accessible world's oil resources, this claim of statement of Mr. Malcom might have helped decide the fate of taking or not taking the mandate:

[Mr. MALCOM] I think, from all our information on this side, England and France and Italy and Greece all want the United States to take the mandate of Armenia, because it is best for the Armenians and because it will prevent any of these European powers getting it and thereby gaining an advantage over the others.

Senator NEW. Suppose a mandatory was accepted either by France or Italy, would it not work out the same results to Armenia that would be brought about by the acceptance of a mandate by the United States?

[Mr. MALCOM] No.

[Senator NEW] Why not? That is what I want to know.

[Mr. MALCOM] In the first place, neither Italy nor France is financially and economically able to help the Armenians. They have not got sufficient for themselves.

The second reason is that England and France and Italy—in fact all these European powers—have for years made a football out of Armenia. For these reasons the mandate of the United States is the best mandate for Armenia. America is wealthier; it is disinterested. By taking it over it will wipe out a cause for intrigues between the powers at the expense of the Armenians. Moreover, **under American protection or care many Armenians will go back to Armenia with their American experience and their wealth.**

[Senator NEW] Mr. Chairman, I think that this is a very important phase of this question, and I would like very much indeed to pursue it myself, further, but I have got to ask to be excused now. I must be on the floor at 12 o'clock.

[Senator WILLIAMS] So far as this resolution is concerned, all of this recent testimony and discussion is irrelevant. There is no question involved here of a mandatory.

[Senator NEW] Yes, but for general reasons I would like to pursue this inquiry if I could; but I must go now.

[Senator WILLIAMS] Is not the chief reason why the Armenians would prefer a mandate of the United States, rather than of any of the others, because the United States would be the only altruistic power that would consider solely the interests of the Armenians?

[Mr. MALCOM] That is what I wanted to say; but I have said it in a different way.

[Senator HARDING] Now, to revert to the inquiry. You have just spoken, probably because of your native interest in Armenia-

[Mr. MALCOM] Yes.

[Senator HARDING] (continuing). Of the desirability of an American mandatory from the Armenian view-point. You are an American citizen?

[Mr. MALCOM] I am.

[Senator HARDING] I want to ask you what you think of the mandatory from the viewpoint of an American?

[Mr. MALCOM] I will give you a very frank answer, Senator Harding.

[Senator HARDING] Very well.

[Mr. MALCOM] I should say that the United States is in honor bound to help Armenia to get on her feet, whether it assumes that obligation under the word "mandate" or something else, because the war is not at an end yet; the treaties have not been signed and ratified; and the Armenians being belligerents in fact and having sacrificed much blood to defeat Germany and her associate, Turkey, are entitled to help. I feel that legally the United States is bound to send some help to them and to do something for them until the status of Armenia is finally settled. Other than that I have no opinion as to whether or not the United States should take any mandatory. But speaking for myself, and as an American citizen—and not having in view the service of the Armenians in the war and their present plight—I believe the United States should respond with some help. I came to the United States in my youth. I received all my education here and I feel just as much an American as anyone. As an American I feel in my heart that the United States should at this crisis give the Armenians a hand. America is in honor bound to do it. And I say this because I have talked with native Americans who for the last two or three years have been working in Armenia. I have met there Americans of the Yankee type; I have heard many of them say to me that they feel that America should do something for Armenia. And there is a legal as well as a moral justification for this. The war is not at an end; the treaties have not been signed; the Armenians are still fighting and we should take some step to protect them with the British and the French.

[Senator WILLIAMS] Until their status is settled?

[Mr. MALCOM] Until their status is settled.

Mr. Malcom ended his testimony and submitted a memorandum of support to be added to the record which read:

(The memorandum referred to is here printed in full in the record as follows:)

MEMORANDUM BY THE ARMENIAN NATIONAL UNION OF AMERICA.

Armenian National Union of America,
Washington, D. C., September 27, 1919

Hon. HENRY CABOT LODGE,
Chairman Senate Foreign Relations Committee.

DEAR SIR: On behalf of the Armenian National Union of America, which represents Armenians and American citizens of Armenian origin now residing in the United States, I beg to submit herewith a memorandum in support of Senate resolution 38, of which you are the author, and of Senate joint resolution 106, of which Senator John Sharp Williams is the author.

Cordially, yours,

M. Vartan Malcom.

I.

There is established precedent in support of Senator Lodge's resolution favoring the recognition of integral Armenia as an independent state. Poland, Ukrainia, Finland, Czecho Slovak Republic, and the Kingdom of Hedjaz, which, before the war, were under the domination of other Governments, have been officially and semiofficially recognized as independent states. In the case of Finland, Poland, and Ukrainia no objection was raised against the formation of these new countries, although they previously formed a part of the Russian Empire, one of the Allies. The example of the Kingdom of Hedjaz is even more pertinent. Here was a piece of territory that belonged to Turkey, against which the United States was not at war, and yet the United States has virtually recognized the independence of this Arab kingdom by permitting its representatives to sign the treaty of peace with Germany upon equal basis with that of the United States and other allied and associated nations.

II.

The recognition of integral Armenia as an independent state by the United States will prevent the division of Armenia among European powers. It is apparent that under the secret treaty of 1916, to which England, France, and Russia are parties, Armenia was to have been divided between these powers, without, of course, consulting the wishes of the Armenians. The provisions of this treaty violates the principle enunciated by the

President and incorporated into the treaty. with Germany, viz: "Certain communities formerly belonging to the Turkish Empire have reached the stage of development where their existence as independent nations can be provisionally recognized subject to the rendering of administrative advice and assistance by a mandatory until such times as they are able to stand alone. The wishes of these communities must be a principal consideration in the selection of the mandatory." Senator Lodge's resolution, therefore, carries out the provisions of the quoted paragraph and at the same time gives notice to the world that this country will not acquiesce in bartering the rights and liberties of smaller nations to satisfy the imperialistic ambitions of European powers.

III.

The independence of integral Armenia is a necessary safeguard for the future peace of the world. The Armenians will never be satisfied until they have regained the independence of their country as a whole. No people can live happily and in peace if their population and country is divided up against their will. It is a foregone conclusion that the divisions of Armenia into "spheres of influence" will be a sure cause for war. Thus in recognizing the independence and territorial boundaries of Armenia the United States will help to create a united Armenia and materially aid to prevent future wars.

Moreover, the peace of the Near East necessitates the creation of a state which shall perform the part that Switzerland is now playing in the heart of Europe. Armenia will be an element of order and equilibrium in that part of the world. The Armenians will check the spread of Pan-Turananism from Constantinople to India, and will arrest the spread of Bolshevism from Russia to the Mediterranean. They will serve the highest interests of civilization and peace and progress in the Near East. America, therefore, by espousing the Armenian cause will be laying the foundation of a permanent peace throughout the world.

IV.

Armenia's contributions in the present war entitle her to independence. From the beginning of the war these people refused offers from the enemy and threw in their lot on the side of the Allies. Over 150,000 of them served on the eastern front with Russia. After the Russian collapse the Armenians, single handed, resisted the Turko-German advance towards Baku in the Caucasus. By keeping Turks fighting in the Caucasus region, according to Lord Cecil, they helped the success of the British campaign in Mesopotamia and Syria. In France only one-tenth of the Armenians who joined the "Légion étrangère," returned alive. Over 8,000 Armenians, mostly volunteers from the United States, fought in Palestine under Gen. Allenby, who has credited them with valor and glory. When the United States entered the war, hundreds of Armenians in this country volunteered and thousands were drafted and many of these died on the field of battle. "The Armenians have therefore been belligerents. Their losses due to the war, which exceed a million (out of a nation of four and a half million souls) are proportionately much heavier than those of any other belligerent."

V.

The Armenians need immediate assistance or else over two million of them now concentrated within a small area in the northern part of Armenia are in danger of annihilation. Senator Williams's resolution which authorizes the use of the naval and military forces of the United States to help protect the Armenians is urgent, and the United States, as well as France, England and Italy are duty bound to give her assistance. The war is not ended. None of the treaties have been fully ratified, and this small assistance should be given to the Armenians as a part and continuation of war work. In the hour of need Armenia did her utmost for the Allies, and the United States with her allies is now honor bound to send help to her until the war has been actually settled, and her status and rights determined.

VI.

Whatever troops or warships the President may deem sufficient to send will not be for fighting purposes, but merely for a steadying effect. The United States need not contribute over 10,000 soldiers to assist England and France, whose troops are already on the spot, to protect the Armenians. Americans are not going there to fight. They are going there merely for effect. It is impossible to depict with words the great influence the United States exercises in the Near East. All the natives—both Turks and Christians—regard Americans with a certain reverential awe and respect which is difficult to describe. During the last four years hundreds of Americans have traversed the length and breadth of Armenia to help the refugees and not one has ever been molested. Small detachments of British and French troops (both at war with Turkey) have quietly occupied parts of Turkey, and no attempt has ever been made to oust them. The fact is that the Turks themselves have lost and suffered so terribly during the war that they will welcome allied occupation. The United States is regarded as absolutely disinterested and altruistic and her presence will be the guiding factor to calm the fears of the natives and keep peace. Moreover, it must be borne in mind that the military power of Turkey is practically null, although sufficiently strong enough to do harm to the defenseless Armenians. Constantinople, the seat of the Ottoman Government, is occupied by the Allies; Smyrna is in the hands of the Greeks; Cilicia is protected by British and French troops. All the territories lying south of the Armenian border, that is, Mesopotamia, Arabia and Persia, are under British control. Thus the whole of Asia Minor is practically in the hands of the Allies of the United States. This is a fact which strongly refutes the possibility of any fighting and loss of life in this region.

Respectfully submitted on behalf of the Armenian National Union of

America.

M. VARTAN MALCOM.

Washington, D. C., September 27, 1919.

Over the 2 weeks that followed, there were 3 more days of hearings ending on October 10, 1919. The case for the Armenians was very well presented with some of the top leaders of the Armenian community in America and Armenia itself testifying. In addition to this, letters of support to the Armenian case were presented and added to the record. The whole transcript can be found in Appendix V of this book.

After waiting for 7 months and the conditions in Armenia going from bad to worse, the United States Senate passed Senate Resolution 359 which read as follows:

U.S. Senate Resolution 359

May 11, 1920

66th Congress

2nd Session

S. RES. 359. [Senate Resolution 359]

In the Senate of the United States

May 11, 1920

Mr. Harding, from the Committee on Foreign Relations, reported the following resolution; which was ordered to be placed on the calendar.

May 11 (calendar day, May 13), 1920.

Considered and agreed to.

Resolution

Whereas the testimony adduced at the hearings conducted by the subcommittee of the Senate Committee on Foreign Relations have clearly established the truth of the reported massacres and other atrocities form which the Armenian people have suffered; and

Whereas the people of the United States are deeply impressed by the deplorable conditions insecurity, starvation, and misery now prevalent in Armenia; and

Whereas the independence of the Republic of Armenia has been duly recognized by the supreme council of the peace conference and by the Government of the United States of America: Therefore be it

Resolved, That a sincere congratulations of the Senate of the United States are hereby extended to the people of Armenia on the recognition of the independence of the Republic of Armenia, without prejudice respecting the territorial boundaries involved; and be it further

Resolved, That the Senate of the United States hereby expresses the hope that stable government, proper protection of individual liberties and rights, and the full realization of nationalistic aspirations may soon be attained by the Armenian people; and be it further

Resolved, That in order to afford necessary protection for the lives and property of citizens of the United States at the Port of Batum and along the

Presenting the Armenian Case 157

line of the railroad leading to Baku, the President hereby requests, if not incompatible with the public interest, to cause a United States warship and a force of marines to be dispatched to such port with instruction to marines to disembark and protect American lives and property.

May 11 (calendar day, May 13), 1920. — Considered and agreed to.

In the end, the U.S not only failed to take the mandate over Armenia, but also to allow Armenians gather up a volunteer force from among Armenians living in the U.S., which would have perhaps been the tipping point between Armenia defending its independence over what has been recorded in history as the loss of Wilsonian Armenia to the Turks, while the rest of Armenia fell into the hands of the Bolsheviks.

Senate, Committee on Foreign Relations - 1919: John Sharp Williams (1854-1932); Claude A. Swanson (1862-1939); Gilbert M. Hitchcock (1859-1934); Henry Cabot Lodge, Chairman (1850-1924); Porter J. McCumber (1858-1933); Key Pittman (1872-1940); Frank B. Brandegee (1864-1924); Warren G. Harding (1865-1923).

Chapter 15

One Man Armenian Lobby

One of the prominent champions of the Armenian Question was Vahan Cardashian (1883-1934). Born in Caesarea (modern-day Kayseri), he moved to the United States in 1902 and attended Yale Universality Law School from 1904 to 1908.

Cardashian wrote six lectures regarding the Armenian Question and presented them to the Brooklyn Institute of Arts and Sciences in 1908. *The Brooklyn Daily Eagle* newspaper wrote about it on September 5, 1908:

> **The Ottoman Empire.**
>
> Under this title Vahan Cardashian, an Armenian, discussed The Ottoman Empire and the Eastern Question, Armenia and its people. It is a little book on a big subject, and a substantial part of the volume is made up of six lectures the author prepared to deliver before he Brooklyn Institute of Arts and Sciences.
>
> At the outset, Mr. Cardashian disclaims any ulterior motive in the execution of his little work. He does not speak as a representative of any society or association, disbelieving in any movement which conflicts with the public peace and morals. "I have probably departed from the usual policy of a foreign writer on the subject, in that I have spared no nation or person in praise or condemnation as deserved, and have not yielded to the temptation of justifying this or that cabinet or party." The inherent barbarity of the Turk, as well as his good qualities, are discussed with equal frankness, and the author attempts to show the perfidious and Chauvinistic character of the diplomacy of Europe in dealing with the Eastern Question.
>
> Turkey, he believes, can never be reformed from within, but only by application of foreign force, and points to the fact that no Mohammedan ruler has ever established a civilized system of government. "Do you want to reform Turkey? Take her away from the Turks."
>
> This little work will help many to a brief understanding of Turkish history, and of conditions in that country to-day, and presents in condensed form all that the average reader need know of the Eastern Question. (J. B. Lyon Company, Albany)

In 1911, at the outbreak of the Italo-Turkish War (1911-1912), Cardashian left his private practice as a New York City lawyer to become the consul of the Turkish Embassy and consulate general to the United States.

Cardashian's crowning achievement for his service to Turkey was the

160 BETRAYAL: The Promise Never Kept

Panama-Pacific International Exposition in San Francisco, which opened on April 30, 1915. Cardashian was responsible for building a pavilion, which housed one million-dollar worth of Turkish rugs, rare paintings, and beautiful brass works.[74]

On October 13, 1915, *The San Francisco Chronicle* ran a story about Cardashian facing death should he return to Turkey.

San Francisco Chronicle – October 13, 1915 – page 1

Adjutant Commissioner of Turkey Not Safe in Own Country

Director of Exhibits Says Cardashian Would be Hanged by Leaders in the War

If Vahan Cardashian, Turkish exposition adjutant high commissioner, returned to Constantinople now his friends, Talaat Bey and Enver Pasha, the ringleaders of the war, would hang him at the head of Galata bridge, George Atiyah, director of Turkish exhibits, said last night at a dinner in Cardashian's honor.

The event was given in the Turkish pavilion by exhibitors and attaches. Cardashian was presented with an engraved gold watch. Maurice A. Hall, Turkish Consul-General, and Director Frank L. Brown of the exposition attended.

Cardashian, he said spent $75,000 of his own money on the exhibit when the conditional appropriation of $150,000 made by the Turkish Prime Minister was withheld after the war broke out.

Atiyeh explained his reference to Cardashian's danger by saying that Turkish leaders were executing intelligent men now as part of the war programme.

San Francisco Chronicle – December 14, 1915 – page 1

Turkish Exhibit of Rugs Being Sold

Commissioner Cardashian Issues a Formal Statement in Matter

Vahan Cardashian, Adjutant High Commissioner of Turkey to the exposition, yesterday issues the following statement:

---

74 TURKEY TO OPEN UNIQUE PAVILION (San Francisco Chronicle, San Francisco, CA, February 12, 1914) p.6

"The high commission of Turkey to the Panama-Pacific International Exposition was nominated by the Cabinet and confirmed by an imperial decree. The direction of al the affairs of the high commission was entrusted absolutely to the adjutant high commissioner. The collection of the exhibits, consisting largely of rugs, was a purely official act, and enjoyed the unqualified sanction and approval of the imperial Government.

"This collection constituted the official exhibits of the Turkish Government. During the entire life of the exposition it was exhibited in the pavilion of Turkey and was awarded a grand prize, the highest award, as the official exhibits of Turkey. Now, at my direction, as the Adjutant High Commissioner of Turkey to the exposition, this collection is being sold at public auction at St. Francis Hotel."

The Wilkes Barre Record newspaper Saturday Decmber 15, 1917

At the end of the war, Cardashian founded the American Committee for the Independence of Armenia (ACIA). Thanks to his diplomatic connections he made while representing Turkey in the United States, he was able to gain the support of many prominent politicians, community leaders, and famous personalities who joined the board of the ACIA.

The main mission of the ACIA was to bring official recognition of the newly independent Armenian republic and to gain much needed support from the United States. This came in the form described in the previous chapter. The Committee was also responsible for a number of forums, in which the board members presented evidence to gain support from the public at large in order to put pressure on Washington to help Armenia in every possible way.

Cardashian also authored many articles to keep the Armenian Question alive in the United States. His articles were usually a response to pro-Turkish propaganda and misinformation. Some of his articles, he pointed at people behind the Armenian Genocide, be they Turks or non-Turkish supporters. In later articles, when it became clear that the United States not only refused to support the Armenian cause, but also worked against it, Cardashian became very critical of the government. The following are news articles reflecting the activities of Cardashian and the ACIA.

Norwich Bulletin (Norwich, Conn.) – June 3, 1919 – Page 1

PROTESTS U.S. MANDATE FOR CONSTANTINOPLE

New York, June 2.—Vahan Cardashian, spokesman, in America for the determination of integral Armenia, issued a statement today protesting against the proposal that the United States accepts a joint mandate for Armenia, Anatolia and Constantinople. Mr. Cardashian characterized such a plan as a proposal that the butcher and sheep should be asked to lie down together.

Grand Forks Herald (Grand Forks, M.D.) – June 24, 1920 – page 1

ARMENIANS CLAIM RIGHT TO PROVINCE

New York, June 24.—Vahan Cardashian of the American committee for the independence of Armenia takes issue with the recent statement of Damad Ferid Pasha, premier of Turkey and brother-in-law of the sultan, as cabled from Constantinople. The Turkish premier stated that the provinces of Van, Bitlis and Mosul, said to be claimed by the Armenians, have only 5 per cent of Armenians and that the leaders of the Turkish nationalist movement were not really Turks, but adventurers from other countries. Concerning this, Mr. Cardashian says:

"We do not claim Mosul. That is part of Mesopotamia. In the provinces of Van, Bitlis and Erzerum there was in 1914, a Turk and Kurd population of 551,000 as against 581,000 Armenians. Today, there is a Turk and Kurd population of only 96,000 in those three provinces and possibly 4,000 to 5,000 Armenians. But there are 286,000 Armenians from these provinces who have taken refuge within the boundaries of the Armenian republic. And also over 75,000 Armenians from these provinces are to be found in other contiguous regions.

"Mustafa Kemal (Turkish nationalist leader) whom the Grand Vizier presents as a Jew, was born a Turk and his parents were from Saloniko and were Deunmes, what is converts, as were the parents of Talat and Djavid. Rustem, whom he presents as a Pole, is of Polish extraction as Enver. He is Moslem, was the Turkish ambassador in Washington in 1913 and was the director of Turkish propaganda during the great war. Fuad, I do not know who he is. But the majority of the Turks are of foreign extraction. Of the 33 Grand Viziers up to 1909 seventeen were of foreign extraction.

The Hartford Courant Sun – February 23, 1921 – Page 10

AN ARMENIAN VIEW.

Vahan Cardashian of New York, whose name suggest Armenian birth or parentage, has distributed a pamphlet entitled, "Wilson—Wrecker of Armenia," in which he holds that the outgoing president of this country is largely responsible for Armenia's present plight and he describes Armenia as ranking next (at least) to the most distressful country.

Mr. Cardashian says that when the Sèvres treaty gave Smyrna and Thrace to Greece France and Italy, became aroused at the expansion of Greek and British influence in Constantinople and near Asia and set themselves to the work of bringing about a revision of the treaty at any cost. With the knowledge of their respective governments French and Italian nationalist kept the Turkish nationalist movement alive and lrance, as a means of destroying the rise of Armenian claims to Cilicia, withheld from the Armenians arms and munition for self defense and forcibly demobilized their fighting armies, as a result of which 20,000 Armenians were slaughtered in Marash and Hadjin.

France and Italy stopped the Greeks from conducting further hostilities against Kemal which gave him a chance to turn his attention to the Armenians while Italian ships took his troops to the Armenian front. In September of last year, Turkish troops were able to attack the Armenian republic over a 500 mile front and not a word of encouragement came to Armenia from the Allies.

Armenia soon lay prostrate and at this juncture the league in session at Geneva—we quote from the pamphlet— "as a remains of relieving Armenian from the disaster which had overwhelmed her, with incredible naïveté addresses itself to the President of the United States and asked him to mediate between Turks and the Armenians to ascertain from Kemal how much and what kind of bribe he would accept to clear out of Armenia."

Mr. Cardashian writes:—

Yet it is clear as one studies the situation which has arisen during the past year and a half that even with the omissions and commissions of the Allied governments and of the Soviet government of Russia—the ugly greeds, the secret intrigues, the hypocritical pretensions – still Armenia could have been saved from destruction had the United States government frankly and unequivocally shouldered the full measure of the moral responsibility in respect of Armenia. Why did it not do so? What lies at the bottom of the tergiversation of the American policy towards Armenia? There is a sinister element here that is not clear. It is time that it was brought to light.

Mr. Cardashian goes on to say that the pro-Armenian element in this country is centered in the churches and, for information and guidance, depends upon the missionaries and the misfortunes of the Armenian s have furnished the missionaries with an opportunity to collect for the recent and the "evangelization" of the Armenians who have been Christians for 17 centuries. Then he adds this—

It is evident that form the point of view of missionary interest, it is essential that the Armenians remain rather a suffering Christian people under Ottoman persecution than that an independent, Christian Armenian state be established which would, of necessity require no further relief or "evangelization" by American missionaries.

If one asks where Mr. Wilson comes in he is answered as follows:—

It is this missionary element that has been the chief adviser and counsellor of President Wilson and which he guided his American policy. It was this element which prevented the declaration of war against Turkey by the United States, a situation which has so tied the hands of Washington in the dealings with the Allied Powers touching the Near East. IT was this element which pushed the President to demand firs the acceptance of the American mandate for the whole of Turkey and second for an Armenian to consist largely of Turkish Armenia, even against the overwhelming sentiments of the American people against a mandate for Armenia, and of the Armenian people against a separation of Armenia into two sections. They are not advocating the abandonment of the Armenian Republic and it's 2,000,000 Armenian inhabitants and the setting up of a makeshift government in four provinces of Turkish Armenia, where there are now less than 50,000 Armenians, and where no more than 1,000,000 Armenians can be brought together. Under such an arrangement, the Armenians would, of course, be in the power of the Turks and the missionaries; they would be easy to proselyte, and always poor, and more or less depended upon American relief organizations for life itself.

The President, Mr. Cardashian writes, had the opportunity to help Armenia but he did not and declined to adopt any remedial measure, except in connection with and as a means of promoting his own pet project, the league of nations. He made the Armenian case a football of politics. The President, he writes, never told the Armenians nor the Powers that Armenia should no longer look to America for relief but led them to believe that he would do something. Everybody waited on him and he let things drag until Armenia succumbed to the criminal negligence, duplicity and hate of six civilized and uncivilized nations.

This is the indictment which Mr. Cardashian brings against Mr. Wilson and he closes by expressing the hope that the American people, under the leadership of the new President will not fail to respond to the call of Armenia.

One Man Armenian Lobby

Hartford Courant Sun – April 6, 1924 – Page 10

REJECTS LAUSANNE PACT, SAYS GERARD
Armenia and U.S. Rights
Sold for Chester Grant He Asserts
KEMALISTS DECLARED TO BE ON LAST LEGS
Treaty Wrongly Assumes Turks Are Civilized, Declares Prof. Hart.

New York, April 5.—Calling upon the Senate to reject the Lausanne treaty, James W. Gerard, former ambassador to Germany, declared before the foreign policy association today that the state department had sold the cause of Armenia and American rights in Turkey for the Chester oil concessions.

"I will put to Secretary Hughes two pertinent question," Mr. Gerard said.

"Why did he take so active and vigorous a part in behalf of the Chester oil concessions, even at the risk of forcing resumption of hostilities, and why does he now deny that he has had anything to do with it?"

Why did he request General Goethals to accept the presidency of the Chester Company, and in what capacity did he direct the reorganization of that company?"

Retreat alleged.

"Secretary Hughes made a hurried and inglorious retreat from the position which he took in December, 1922. He acccpted the Turkish views on the capitulations and upon the Armenian case. In other words, in surrendered to the Turks the rights which he claimed for American nationals and for Armenia before the granting of that concession. Obviously he went to Lausanne fully prepared to make any and all sacrifices to cinch this oil concession, and he betrayed Christian Armenia and his own country to attain his purpose."

Referring to the Kemalist government, Mr. Gerard said:

"The Kemalist regime is on its last legs. Fractional armed conflicts, widespread banditry and hopeless economic chaos seriously threatened Kemal's regime. The establishment of the 'republic' and abolition of the Caliphate in a country of illiterate, primitive and fanatical peasants are eloquent proofs of the instability of Kemal's government. Kemal is not removing, as is alleged by some superficial observers, hindrances from the path of progress, but he is in reality resorting to desperate measures to get rid of his opponents."

Sees Kemal's Downfall.

America stands to gain nothing by resuming relations with Turkey in this state, Mr. Gerard asserted. "The downfall of Kemal is inevitable and imminent. By now surrendering our rights to him we shall find it difficult to reassert them against any regime which may overthrow and succeed him. We can well afford to wait."

Professor Albert Bushnell Hart of Harvard, in a letter sent to the meeting, said the fundamental trouble with Lausanne treaty was that it assumed that "the so-called republic of Turkey is a modern civilized nation."

No Faith In Turkey.

"There is no assurance that the Turks who authorized the signature of the treaty will carry out any provision that hereafter may seem inconvenient," Professor Hart's letter continued. "The Turks have been making the same kind of promises of good behavior and protection to the foreigner and recognition of the rights of minorities for more than a hundred years and they have never observed one of those pledges."

Albert W. Staub, American director of the near east colleges, favored the ratification of treaty and maintained that the Turks had made sufficient progress during recent years to justify the confidence of the United States.

The Detroit Free Press – April 13, 1928 – Page 6

ARMENIAN AND MR. CARDASHIAN

The activities of Vashian Cardashian, an Armenian propagandist operating from New York city, are not unfamiliar to readers of these columns. From him the executives of the so-called American Committee Opposed to the Lausanne Treaty have been wont to take their inspiration in attacks on the Turkish policy of the American government.

But Mr. Cardashian isn't content to direct the anti-administration effort of men like Bishop Manning and former Ambassador Gerard. The other day he wrote a letter to Senator Borah, chairman of the senate foreign relations committee, in which he says that "two members of the President's cabinet" and their confederates in the state department "bartered the Armenian case" at the Lausanne conference. The price, we are told, was a share of Mosul oil.

It is seldom that a foreign agitator displays such impudence, but in Mr. Cardashian's case it is unfortunately true that well-meaning, though misguided Americans, were partly responsible. They emboldened him to make baseless charges against their own government in a spirit and in a language which no other country would tolerate for a moment. Mr. Borah has an opportunity to bring the fellow to account by forcing him to come across with names and facts. Meanwhile Mr. Cardashian seems to be too stupid to realize that the Armenian case never was an American cause—also, that with sponsors of his type to uphold it in this country it can only win popular hostility. The best friends of Armenia ought to see what they can do to silence his crusade of insults and invective.

With the failures of the United State government, Cardashian continued his one man crusade to keep the Armenian Question and the crimes committed by Turkey in the public eye. In 1929, Cardashian sues Turkey.

> The Brooklyn Daily Eagle – July 10, 1929 – Page 5
>
> New York Man Sues Turkey for $20,000
>
> Washington, July 10.—Vahan Cardashian of New York City instituted suit yesterday in the District Supreme Court for $20,000 damages against the Turkish Government. He alleged that he had not been paid for legal services rendered from 1909 to 1914.
>
> In asking the court to inquire into his claim and determine the amount due him, Cardaskhian declared that when the Senate declined to agree to ratification of the Lausanne Treaty he had been deprived of his rights to make his claim within the jurisdiction of Turkish tribunals.

On July 12, 1934, at the age of 51, Vahan Cardashian, the one man Armenian lobbying organization that sounded the alarm, fought for the rights of the Armenian people, and pointed out those who betrayed the Armenian people, had a heart attack and died.

> The Brooklyn Daily Eagle – July 13, 1929 – Page 13
>
> **Vahan Cardashian**
>
> Vahan Cardashain, lawyer and prominent for many years as the champion of Armenian liberty in this country, died of heart disease yesterday at his home, 359 W. 129th St., Manhattan. He served as counselor and statistician of the Ottoman Chamber of Commerce in America from 1910 to 1914 and was counsel to the Turkish Consulate General in New York. In 1913 he was Turkey's fiscal agent in this country and in 1914 was Adjutant High Commissioner of Turkey to the Panama-Pacific Exposition. As a lecturer he had spoken before the Brooklyn Institute of Arts and Sciences, Yale University and the American Academy of Political and Social Science. He was the author of a number of books on the Near East Question. His mother, a sister and a brother survive him.

Vahan Cardashian had devoted the last 20 years of his life to the Armenian people and their fight for justice. Prior to this struggle for justice, Cardashian was a successful attorney.

In 1913, one of Cardashian's clients was none other than Colby M. Chester and the newly formed Ottoman-American Exploration Company (OAEC). Cardashian was hired to represent the OAEC in negotiating with the Ottoman government for the Chester Concessions.

James W. Colt, Chester's man on the ground in the Ottoman Empire, who had been working towards obtaining the concessions since 1908 for the recently dissolved Ottoman-American Development Company, wrote letters to J.V. MacMurray and Secretary of State, William Jennings Bryan, telling them of the newly formed OAEC and asking that the Department instruct the American Embassy to assure the Ottoman Government of the Department's favorable attitude towards the OAEC and its individual members. The OAEC's representative, Mr. Cardashian, was in Turkey conducting negotiations with Turkish officials and an assurance from the American Embassy as to the legitimacy of the OAEC, would be helpful in securing the concessions.[75]

---

75 Colt to MacMurray and to Bryan, July 1, 1913; Philips to Bryan, August 14, 1913, DS 867.602 Ot 81/183 and 155.

Chapter 16

British Spies

Prior to the Armenian Genocide of 1915-1923, the British had planted, in the Ottoman Empire, a number of spies who lived adventurous but short lives.

Three of these spies not only witnessed the Armenian Genocide but, to a certain extent, they helped the Young Turks carry out their sinister intentions.

They are: Thomas Edward Lawrence (1888-1935). Aubrey Nigel Henry Herbert (1880-1923), a.k.a. Ben Kendim; G. Ward Price (1886-1961), war correspondent of the Daily Mail.

Thomas Edward Lawrence (1888-1935)

One of the most famous and well-known of the British spies was Thomas Edward Lawrence (1888-1935). He was an archaeologist, military officer, diplomat, and writer. His work, based on his wartime activities was made into a 1962 Hollywood movie titled *Lawrence of Arabia*.

Lawrence was present at the Paris Peace Conference that began on January 18, 1919. Lincoln Steffens (1866-1936), a New York-based reporter, sought him out for an interview, which he described as 'the queerest' he had ever had in all his interviewing life. As a prominent diplomat, his opinions expressed in this interview do reflect the general inclinations of British foreign policy, as far as the Near East is concerned.

I discovered this interview in the October 14, 1931, issue of *Outlook and Independent* magazine, which I was able to obtain and share the entire interview in this chapter:

Armenians Are Impossible

An Interview with Lawrence of Arabia

By Lincoln Steffens

(OUTLOOK AND INDEPENDENT – October 14, 1931)

Lincoln Steffens describes his interview with Lawrence of Arabia as "the queerest I ever had in all my interviewing life." Apparently the man who helped create the Kingdom of Irak remained as mysterious in intimate conversation as he did in the press reports of his political activities. "I offer the curiosity," writes Mr. Steffens, "as I wrote it at the time [in Paris during the Peace Conference in 1919] and I'll have to leave it to those who read it to guess what it's all about, if anything"

It was in his room, at his hotel, but I had asked for it, and my purpose was to learn from this Imperial pioneer something about the practical politics of Asia Minor and the Near East. And I thought I was directing the course of the conversation. It only occurred to me afterwards, with some shock, that he also had had a purpose, and that his purpose was to load me up with British propaganda for the American mandate over the Armenians. That was what I found I had. Other things, too, but I was amazed and not a little humiliated to discover that I had chiefly reasons—reason which appealed to me, a self-determinist in theory—why we Americans should go halfway around the world to take charge of the Armenians and not only save them from the Turks, Greeks, French, Italians, British and themselves, but, somehow, to save ourselves from ourselves and them.

He said, for example, that the Armenians were "the last word in human impossibility." They correspond, as a race, with "the last man" in academic debate. To an underdog fancier like me, the undermost dog among nations had, and it has, an irresistible fascination. And I said so.

English humor is not like ours. It's the opposite. American humor consists, in part, at least, in what is said; the British in what a Britisher doesn't say. This Briton obviously liked heartily what I said. I thought he was going to laugh with joy or something; he swelled up till he looked like the British Empire; as if about to burst. But he didn't burst; he didn't laugh; he didn't say anything that showed the slightest sign of humor. All he said, after a long pause, was:

"Righto."

And then, after another pause, when he had recovered his self-determination, he spoke seriously, rather dully, in fact, of our American idealism. He thought it fine; I thought he thought it a bit too fine. We Americans were too idealistic.

And he thought the Armenians too practical. We were correctives, the one on the other, therefore; we were a cure for them, they for us; both desperate cases, especially the Armenians.

I gathered that he had some inexpressible sympathy or—let me rather say—some knowledge or experience of the Armenians that gave him a human understanding for the Turks (and all the other near neighbors of the Armenians), who are forever trying to kill off this orphan race. He seemed to think that was the only thing to do to the Armenians. He didn't say so. You may observe that I do not quote this authority very freely. The reason is that his method was, apparently, not to say anything himself, but to get me to say the things he wished to have printed in such a form that he could, if necessary, deny them. So he did not say that the Armenians should all be killed off. He only gave me the impression, at the time, that that was the sole solution of the Armenian problem; and that that was his reason for desiring us Americans to take on the job.

He felt, or he made me feel, that the Turks shouldn't do it; they were too rough and ready—and not Christians. Nor the Greeks; they enjoyed it too much and were inefficient; they never finish anything, and when their aesthetic pleasure in the killing of Armenians was sated they quit. And so with all the other old, rival races. They stopped work before all the Armenians were dead. Even when they all went at the task together, they invariably left a couple here and a couple there: Adams and Eves who, the moment one's back was turned, bred and bred and bred so that the next time one visited Armenia there were the Armenians as before, millions and millions of them, all meek and lowly, but busy by day at business and at night secretly breeding and slyly spreading and spreading and—

He spread all over me his Malthusian despair and such a dread of the Armenians that I was about to swallow whole his whole scheme for the American Armenian mandate when my saving American humor gave me pause.

"But why should not the British do this job also?" I asked, and, to warn his sense of humor that I was striving to be not altogether final but funny withal, I smiled. In vain. He had no sense of American humor—I think. He waited for my genial grin to go away and then, when he saw I was alone again and quite serious, he answered me seriously.

A perfect massacre of the Armenians, he reasoned, might make a scandal, if the British did it, and, he explained, though the Empire had withstood some such shocks and must, of course, withstand others, too many more just now might jar it. And the Empire should not be jarred, unnecessarily, just now. The British Empire is the beginning of world government. All our great troubles—wars, revolutions, strikes, plagues, etc.—all came from the fact that the earth as a whole was not governed as a whole. The British will end this anarchism some day. But the Empire is young as yet, comparatively small, weak and over burdened. Think of the islands, colonies, strategic points, seas and trade routes—all the new burdens and responsibilities thrown upon the British Empire by the defeat of German Imperialism! No. The Empire must be spared for the present. Later, when the freedom of the seas is put ashore, so to speak; when British rule is extended from the wave to the land, all lands, then Great Britain could, and it would, go forth gladly to meet a shock like the one I—he said I—was proposing in Armenia; but not yet, not now; not in the infancy of the Empire.

Moreover, he conveyed, British Imperialism, at this stage, was interested rather in natural resources than in peoples as such. The English are a practical folk; not idealistic, you understand. They realize that a world government must be founded, not like "your" League of Nations, upon ideas and ideals, principles and peoples, but upon solid things—oil, ore, air, the sea.

"But," I argued (and you can see how far he was carrying me on: I argued for his country against my own). "But," I said, "there are rich lands and fat deposits in Armenia."

He was still. He was so still so long that I thought I had floored him; that he had not known about the wealth of Armenia. But I noticed again that tendency to swell and go to pieces. And how I did wish he would laugh! It would have relieved me and him, too, I think. But no, he didn't laugh; he didn't even smile. He just waited till he could and then he reminded me that I had heard, as he said he had, that Armenia was to be divided. The back country, where the natural wealth is, was to be cut off from the front, where there is nothing but Armenians. The American mandate was to be over the Armenians; some other ally—not the British, but another equally practical power—was to get Armenia.

"But," I objected; "what is the use of the natural wealth of a country without the people to work it? Mines, oil deposits, fat lands—natural resources," I explained patiently to him, "are no good to Capital without Labor to dig and develop them. And the natives of a country are the natural labor thereof; the cheapest, the most obedient, the least organized, the best."

He was bored, I could see, but he was polite; he listened, so I gave him examples, one after the other, from the American as well as from the British colonies, to show him that it was a mistake to separate the people of a country from the resources of that country. They must be worked together, developed together, and—they were usually. There was no other way. I pictured to him the helplessness of the Turks or the French bankers, or any nonworking people, trying to get out the riches of Armenia without the Armenians. And I wound up with what struck me as a very good line.

"I am crying," I cried, "not idealistically, not 'Armenia for the Armenians' but practically 'the Armenians for Armenia.

He looked me up and down with interest, I thought; as if he were getting some new view of us Americans. I had told him he didn't know us, and he had declared that he did.

"Any conscious Englishman," I remember he said, "can understand any unconscious American."

Just what he meant by that I don't quite see, but it was remarks like that which gave me the uneasy impression that he had got us all wrong, and I had made up my mind to show him before he was through with me that we Americans are not all such sheer idealists as he and most Europeans seemed to have inferred from the one example of President Wilson and the 14. But he was too long and too silent in his study of me. I began to feel that he was finding some fault in me or us. Perhaps I had leaned too far toward the practical side; I recalled how he disapproved of the Armenians for that. I hedged, therefore. I spoke more idealistically again and, I trust, patriotically.

"If we Americans took over the Armenians," I declared, "we would do it for their good. We should govern them always with the idea of making them fit to govern themselves."

"Yes, yes, we understand all that," he said. But I felt that he didn't, so I went right on with my syllogism.

"Well, then," I said tactfully, "you must see also that to that end: to make the Armenians fit to govern themselves, we should have to make them work. And since you cannot work a people without something to work them on, we should need the mines and the land of Armenia; not to get the riches out of them, but as a training ground whereon to teach the people industry, thrift and—all the Christian virtues which go into the making of good men and good citizens."

He looked puzzled, swollen. I didn't know what was the matter with him till he decided at last to express himself.

"There's no lack of thrift in the Armenians," he said dryly, "and, of course, you know that they are Christians, arch Christians?"

Of course I knew that. I had merely, in my enthusiasm, forgotten it for the moment. He had me there, however, so I backed up on work and I stuck—and I stick—to work.

"But," I said, "the Armenians must work. That is the secret of success, whether for an individual or a nation—work, hard work. And the Armenians must have Armenia to work on."

"Armenians won't work," he said. "That is the trouble with your plan and that is the trouble with the Armenians. That is the trouble, really, with all these old races that have been civilized, learned the game and, having once dominated the world and worked it, have lost control, gone back, as you say; or, as I say, carried on. They have gone forward logically, psychologically, physiologically. They do not care for hard labor. It is that which distinguishes them from the childlike, truly backward nations you Americans have had to do with. Primitive peoples are merely lazy. They can be forced forward, worked, developed, exploited, if you please. There is some hope for them; some use. But these forward peoples, the excivilized nations—they are not lazy. They are too intelligent to work for others. They are exploiters themselves, instinctive, inbred, incorrigible, hopeless.

"All nations are breeding men. They talk about developing their countries, but it's the other way around: their countries are developing them. And the old nations show the kind of men the new nations are making. These old peoples are the result of evolution. You can see on the shores of the Mediterranean what you are selecting, breeding, evolving at home, now. The living among the old races here are the survivors of a civilization, commercial in character, like yours."

"Ours," I corrected, to get the English into it. He drove right over me.

"You new nations have got to learn from the old peoples," he repeated, "that the modern representatives of the exgreat and exfamous nations are the inevitable, the natural products of the artificial selection of an order of society which imprisons the courageous, deports the original, depresses the mass, discourages any sort of variation from the average of the species and preserves the meek, mean, sly, shrewd and thrifty. For these are the commercially fit. The modern Greeks are the direct heirs and their unpleasant characteristics are the enduring traits descended from the ancient Greek culture—as the old Greeks actually practised it; not as the great, exceptional Greeks talked and sang and carved it, but as the average Greeks practised it in business—the Greeks, I mean, who sentenced Socrates to death. The Egyptians, as. we British inherit them, are the greatgreat-great little grandchildren of Egyptian culture, the belated answer to the riddle of the Sphinx which their great-grand-fathers raised up so beautifully out of their childlike labor. The Arab of today is the dust of the desert dried by the arts, the custom, the business of ancient, glorious Arabia"

He stopped another protest of mine, anticipating it: "The Greeks of old, and the Egyptians, the Syrians, the Turks and the rest, they had their geniuses too—their poets and artists, their generals who conquered backward peoples and captains of industry who gave them employment, and they had their own Labor also. But the picked breeds, the aristocracies, plutocracies did not last. Their descendants did not descend, they didn't even survive. The children of the successful, of the rich, of the powerful, the privileged, went to the dogs, and they will with you. And the succeeding generations of Labor, overworked, underfed, dispirited and disciplined, reduced to dull slaves, died or were killed off. It was the middle class that proved and proves fit to survive in that sort of organization of society, the lower middle class. So you have all the ancient world peopled now with practically nothing but business men, little business men —merchants, traders, shopkeepers, moneylenders, peddlers, nonproducers. They will buy and sell, and, descended from buyers and sellers, selected through many generations of commercial competition, they buy and sell well. They can and they do go anywhere in the world to trade; not to create, not to organize, build, plan and labor. Their brothers who did those things are the childless dead. No, only the merest, shrewdest traders live and them we find everywhere beating their way. I have met Arabs in the Straits Colonies, South America,—peddling, trading, getting rich. And as for the Syrians, Greeks, Armenians—

"And Jews," I suggested. He ignored me.

"My old peoples," he said, "will go anywhere where there are workers to work, venturing slyly, suffering meekly, saving money, working. Yes, they work. They work as a laborer won't work. They work as only a business man will work—long, hard, close upon a narrow margin of profit. But," he distinguished, "they will not labor. They can't. They cannot see 'work for wages.' It is an instinct with them, a trait, an intelligence developed as we develop pointing in a pointer dog and setting in a setter, by successful selection. They know in their blood that it is no use working for wages, even high wages, if you want to get on and be rich. There is nothing, there can be nothing but a bare living in any possible wagescale—no interest, no capital, no compound progress. They don't say this; it's too obvious to them; they live it. They are wise as only an old race can be wise—to the game. They see from the moment they open their puppy eyes that it is absurd to labor to produce wealth. The thing to do is to watch and wait till the wealth is produced and then, somehow, to get it from the producers. And they know how to do this as an animal knows the animal business and a plant knows the vegetable business—by instinct. So they will practise medicine, law—any profession which, like a business, gets a variable share of the finished, final, coined form of the commonwealth after the common people have made it. But to go out and by the sweat of the brow to dig up and manufacture the raw stuffs of the earth into marketable commodities—no. The old peoples hate to do that and, as for your Armenians—they simply won't."

He rested, watching me and, seeing that I wasn't watching him, he slipped me some more of his propaganda. "The Armenians," he said, "are the most intelligent, the most perfectly selected, the most highly developed race in the world—from the civilized point of view."

I named my candidate again.

"The Jews?" he echoed. "You spoke of them before, and I was gratified. It showed that you were getting an inkling of what I was trying to say about old races. The Jews are the most familiar example to an untraveled person of an old, shrewd, intelligent people, and, yes, they are instinctive exploiters. They drive at secondhand wealth. But they will work. They hate to, but they can be made to work. And worse still, they are creative, inventive, sentimental. There are artists, philosophers, prophets among them still. They are imperfect. They are an unfinished product of civilization, about half-done. I understand why they are feared and hated; they have some of the mental superiority of race-age. But, to mention Jews in the same breath with the old peoples I am talking about is absurd. Why, my old races drove or traded your Jews out of their own country. They can't live on the Arabs, Syrians, Egyptians. They do well in England, they get rich in France and Germany, and, of course, in the United States, they yes, yes. But the Chinese, for example, the Chinese absorb Jews as a whale does little fishes; our own Scotch skin them alive; so do the Arabs, Turks, Greeks and, as for the Armenians—

"Jews," he said, taking breath, "the Jews themselves feel about Armenians the way the antiSemitic Europeans feel about the Jews; and so do the Greeks, Turks—all the other races that have ever had them on them. They feel that the Armenians would put them all to work. And they would. The Armenians are all that the Jews are, plus all that all the other races are—and they are Christians besides!"

He halted, not for words, I take it—an educated Englishman has plenty of English. It was more as if he were balking at the conclusion which he preferred to have me jump at rather than to have it to quote from him. And when I didn't jump, he went on, dully, to give me another chance.

"The Armenians," he said, "must not have Armenia, not the back lands. They would not work them themselves, not even for themselves. They want them, yes, but only to own. They would not even do the work of organizing the work of development. They would let them out as concessions to others to manage. They want to live on the coast, in cities, on rent, interest, dividends and the profits of trading in the shares and the actual money earned by capital and labor."

"There are lots of people like that," I said. "The Armenians aren't the only ones."

"I see you still do not grasp my point," he said. "There are indeed others who would like to do that. The French bourgeoisie is moving in that direction, and our own English are coming to it, especially our Little Englanders of the so-called upper-class. They have that as their ideal. They would like to do nothing, but they can't. They are harmless. They are willing to do nothing but spend. But they do spend, you see. Even your Jews are spenders, great spenders. But your Armenians will do nothing and they won't spend. They get and they save; they sell, but only to buy again and so get more and more. It takes evolution to develop such perfection of the true commercial spirit, and evolution is a matter of degree. And the Armenians are the nth degree. I tell you that if ever the Armenians are given a fair start in the world, if they get a free hold on any corner of the earth, they will own the whole planet and work all the rest of mankind. That's what the Turks know and dread and the Greeks and—all of us who know them. And so—".

He was drawing upon me for his conclusion again—I didn't want to say it. And so I urged him on. "And so—" I said.

"And so," he sidestepped, as we Americans say crudely, "and so we must divide them up, Armenia to one mandatory, the Armenians to another."

"And so," I sparred, "you are for Armenia for some ally, some partner of the British capitalist and the Armenians for us Americans. All right. Two questions occur: What can your ally do in Armenia without labor? And what in the world can we Americans do with the Armenians without Armenia?"

"Oh," he said, "there are other peoples in the Balkans, in Asia Minor, India and Africa—backward nations, really backward, nations that would labor. These can be brought to Armenia and put to work. There is no lack of labor."

"So that solves the British, the practical problem," I said. "Now for the idealistic, the American problem. What are we to do with the Armenians?"

He would not say. His British humor or his diplomatic caution or—something wouldn't let him. He shied off upon the danger to Asiatic labor and European capital of having the Armenians anywhere near where the mines and lands were being worked.

"And so," I said, not without some (American) humor. "And so—"

A shadow crossed his eyes, but not his voice. He spoke sunnily again of "American idealism." I was tired of hearing it, awfully bored, but he liked to talk about it. And this time he changed the key of the song a little. He called us young, said we were inexperienced as yet in the management of other, older races and, therefore no doubt, prone to judge harshly the colonial conduct of the British and other practical rulers whose most conscientious agent sometimes found it necessary to kill and otherwise put the fear of God into the minority of a subject people in the common interest of the majority and the security of invested capital.

"You don't realize," he concluded, "how difficult and delicate a task it is to govern a strange, a foreign people."

"You're wrong," I said, exasperated, and I repeated my charge that he didn't know us. "You are as ill-informed about my people," I declared, "as you say we are about the Europeans, Turks, Armenians and the rest." I cited the Philippines, Cuba, the Sandwich Islands—all foreign countries which we were governing successfully. And I reminded him that we had all sorts of foreigners in our very midst. The United States was not called the melting pot without reason. We had all sorts of foreigners there. We made even his Armenians labor. We did our hard job, I asserted, as well as any government on the face of the earth, not excepting the British, and to convince him that we were practical I related what I had seen done to foreign labor in New England, down South, out West and all over. But I happened to mention also our own natives, the American Indians.

He fairly leaped at that. "That's it," he cried. "That's what I have had in mind all along. Your policy with your Indians is the one for the Armenians." I was taken aback, astonished. I asked him what he thought our Indian policy had been and he said he understood that we had killed them all off all; had we not?

I looked him over the way he had me several times. I enjoyed doing it too.

"And so," I said, after a long pause, "so you think that that is what we ought to come over here and do to the Armenians—kill 'em all off; all."

"No, no, no," he corrected. "How you pressmen do misunderstand and misquote."

He didn't mean at all to say that we should adopt massacre as a policy. He knew we would not, could not do that. Well then, what did he mean? What should we do? He would not say. He wheeled round and round like a couple of whirling dervishes; it was wearisome. But I got it at last. I had to say it my self, but it was right—I think. He didn't correct me.

He definitely and distinctly did not mean that we should set out consciously and deliberately to wipe out the Armenians. Not at all. He merely trusted or believed that after trying everything else, we would end by doing That; and doing it well, too; leaving no Adam and Eve to go on raising Cain—

"But wouldn't that be a scandal?" I asked.

He thought not. He reminded me that we were so idealistic and enjoyed such repute for philanthropy that we seemed to be able to do anything within reason without losing either our idealism or our good name.

"There was no scandal, was there, over your Indian policy?" he asked. "And you never ceased to think that what you did was right? You have conquered part of Mexico, you have occupied Hawaii, taken the Philippines and Porto Rico by force of arms from Spain; freed Cuba and kept a mortgage on it; you have bought the Danish Islands; and you have put your Marines ashore in Central America and forgotten them. You will soon be forced to restore order in the rest of Mexico. And yet," he said, with admiration, I thought, "you are still for self-determination for small nations. You are a small empire, and you have warned us in your Monroe Doctrine that you are going when you get ready to be a great empire. And yet you are antiimperialists. You have just fought a war against German Imperialism, and—"

"So did you," I shot in.

"Oh, that is different," he fired back. "We are Imperialists. We frankly call ourselves an Empire and we fought honestly for our Empire against the German's Empire. But you—you fought against empire for—self-determination."

There was a point there, and he waited maliciously, I felt, for me to meet it. And when I didn't—I couldn't right off in a second like that—when I didn't answer, he went on.

"I believe that you Americans can do anything whatever and not be doubted, either by the world or by yourselves. There is something great, very great about that, something useful to the world. It suggests that you Americans could, and you surely would, do in Armenia proper that which has to be done there, with thoroughness; gradually, but completely, without missing a single or, rather, a married Armenian, and all without a scandal, without disturbing in the least your belief that you are—How shall I say?—well, not like us English or the French, Germans, Turks and, I am afraid, not a bit like the Armenians."

"And," he hastened to add, "somebody has to solve the Armenian problem. It seems to me to be poetic justice, good politics and sound business to let the most idealistic people in the world take over the most practical people in the world." What was he giving me? Was this British humor? I looked at him, hard. He didn't blink. He had that puffed-up appearance I had noticed before—but, no—not a twitch. It's a strain to interview an Englishman, and a risk. I remembered that he would repudiate the interview if there were the slightest "comeback." I decided to put him to the test right away.

"As I understand it," I said, "we Americans are a commercial culture, as the Armenians, as all these old nations were that ought to be killed off." He nodded. "They thought they were developing business when they were really developing a certain variety of the human species—a race of business men dependent upon the productive labor of other people whom they do not now govern and who hate them because they can beat anybody at trade and live without working—liars, profiteers, parasites—the most practical brains with the most Christian ideals and manners."

"You Americans talk well," he said. "No Englishman could be found to state anything like that as clearly as that."

"If now we Americans could, in our present, the early state of the development of this sort of man—if we could, by governing the Armenians, see close up the practical workings of our culture; if we could understand that what we were looking at and dealing with in the Armenian of today is the American of the future—"

"Of tomorrow," he corrected.

"Then," I went on, "we might fail with the Armenians, we might, in exasperation, kill them all—"

"Hear, hear."

"We might kill all the Armenians, but, we would go home—"

"Cable," he suggested, "it's quicker."

"Cable home," I accepted tentatively, "cable a warning to look out: 'Look out for the crossing of practical business with Christian idealism. 'Too much business and too much idealism might injure both these good things and us also, as a people."

"Hear, hear!" he exclaimed.

"It might make of great, rich America an Armenia which the British and the Russians (of the future) would find it 'necessary' to take over as a mandatory divided into two parts: one, the United States proper for England; the other, the people themselves, for Russia."

He was silent. I waited to see whether he had any sense of American humor. He waited, too, for a while and then, seeing that I expected something, he spoke.

"Your idea" he began.

"My idea!" I exploded.

"Yes," he said. "That's an idea. It's a good idea, good in theory, but—It's characteristically idealistic. I am considering it practically. Do you believe really that any American governors of the Armenians would be conscious enough to see their likeness to the Americans?"

"You English do," I retorted cuttingly.

"True," he agreed thoughtfully. "We see the meaning of the Armenians to the Americans, we Imperial English do. But I doubt, I am wondering whether our Little Englanders could be brought to foresee their fate in the fate of the old nations they govern."

I was beaten, helpless, flabbergasted. Fortunately he didn't see that. His eyes were down. He rose, but he was thinking deeply, as he led me to the door. There he looked up.

"Goodbye," he said, "I like your theory. I am afraid it won't work out in practice, but write it. It's suggestive. Write it carefully; not too clearly, and, by the way, don't quote me. I have said nothing, nothing."

Aubrey Nigel Henry Herbert (1880-1923)

Aubrey Herbert was the second son of the 4th Earl of Carnarvon, who was Colonial Secretary in the ministries of Lord Derby and Disraeli, and afterwards Lord-Lieutenant of Ireland.

A year after leaving Balliol, an appointment at the British Embassy at Constantinople gave him opportunities for travel in the Near East.

Herbert chronicled his adventurous life as a spy in his book *BEN KENDIN: A Record of Eastern Travels*, which was published after his death in 1924.

Herbert's memoirs are filled with clues as to what lead up to the Armenian Genocide and who had their hands in it. He also had the opportunity to meet with Talaat Pasha just weeks before he was assassinated in 1921. The chapter from Herbert's book titled *Interview With Talaat Pasha* can be found in Appendix VI.

180 BETRAYAL: The Promise Never Kept

G. [George] Ward Price (1886-1961)

G. Ward Price began his professional journalistic carrier in 1909 as a special correspondent of the London based *Daily Mail*.

During the Balkan war of 1912, he accompanied the Ottoman army as a Correspondent of the *Daily Mail*. During the First World War, as the Official Correspondent with the Allied Forces, he reported on events in the theater of war in the Middle East, in particular the Dardanelles and the Salonika front. In 1918, a book written by Price titled "The Story of the Salonica Army" was published in New York.

The reason I added Price to the British spy list was my discovery of unpublished letters and telegrams between him and James W. Colt of Jaocb H. Schiff and the Chester concessions, regarding a secret arms deal. That deal appears to have concluded in December of 1915. And, according to the documents found in Colt's file, Price appears to have helped find the financial means in London, to carry out the purchase of 200,000 Spanish Mouser rifles with bayonets and 400 million bullets at a time when almost no one wanted to get involved in a deal that would arm Germany's most powerful ally in the war, Turkey. In fact, judging by a letter from Price to Colt on August 21, 1915, Colt had possibly lost interest in the deal. Price wrote: "I understand from him [Whiting] that you had ceased to be interested in the affair."

G. Ward Price

Chapter 17

ARF 9th General Assembly

Coincidentally, on the day that the United States Senate Subcommittee on Foreign Relations began discussing Senate Joint Resolution 106 for the maintenance of peace in Armenia, on September 27, 1919, the Armenian Revolutionary Federation's 9th General Congress was convened in Yerevan, the capital of newly independent Republic of Armenia. It concluded at the end of October 1919.

Shahan Natalie participated in ARF's Congress as the United States District delegate. On the Congress agenda was placed the issue of retribution against those Turks principally responsible for the Great Atrocity. Here, Shahan Natalie experienced the first serious embitterment of his political life, when some of the delegates deemed this policy wrong.

Armenian Revolutionary Federation 9th General Assembly; Yerevan, Armenian, 1919; Shahan Natalie 3rd row from front in the center.

The following document was written by my Shahan Natalie in 1919 during his return to the United States from Armenia.

Shahan's notes on the ARF 9th General Assembly

The General Assembly lasted nearly seven weeks. The gravity of an assembly, unfortunately, within the Federation, is measured by its duration. It has been taught to the ranks to swell with as much pride as a meeting drags on. Among them, there is an implicit satisfaction for all their questions and desires, when it is said that a meeting has lasted forty days. Neither is the administration exempt from that mind-set. And because of that, particularly the concept of the General Assembly will not have been fulfilled, if it does not drag on for forty days.

The evidence of forty days is sufficient to certify that it is not the gravity and seriousness of issues, but the inexorable right of each and every delegate to show off his oratorial "talent" -- not to miss the sought-after opportunity --, proving that not even forty days are sufficient to cover the agenda.

And indeed, never has a General Assembly been adjourned, with its agenda completely covered. A committee has always been selected (with General Assembly plenipotentiaries) assigned to resolve the remaining issues (almost always, the most important ones), as well as those other assignments to be dealt with.

The 9th General Assembly did not form an exception from that rank.

To take detailed notes would signify to record the spoken orations verbatim.

For me, however, as a delegate who would go to Yerevan, there was one leading voice. -- the voice of my father's blood, mingled with the voice of blood from millions of Armenian martyrs.

This voice is also, I am certain, the leader of more than a decade of delegates, who would set out by the same ship from Polis and disembark in Batumi.

The evidence is that Polis Representative Body had assembled with such precision the list of more than two hundred names of those Turk monsters, who had luxuriated up to their throats in the blood bath of the Armenians. We already had their names, official statuses, deeds accomplished, a complete life story linked to the bloodshed of a million Armenians.

We kept that list with us, to put it on the desk of the Federation's Supreme Court of Justice. A pro forma step, depicting party discipline. Because not one of us could imagine even a single word which did not translate into the most sanctified call of our soul.

With that list we also had that extra-ordinary official declaration of Turkish participation in the war of 1915, broadcast in *"Troshak"*, proclaiming all members of the Turkish Cabinet personally responsible for all the misdeeds, if on the occasion of war there were to have occurred horrors upon the heads of Armenians in Turkey. The Federation Upper Body believed in some way to propel the Turkish leadership of the day toward repentance.

This declaration was already an official verdict, previously given, which was entering into effect, given that its foundations had been contrived to unimaginable extents. Consequently, it had become an undertaking, a promise given to the Armenian people.

It remained for the General Assembly only one more time to reiterate that the Federation was the master of its word.

For me, that was the pivotal axis of the issues. And without this issue, the assembly could not be name revolutionary. It was a crime to allow from afar describing a revolutionary in any other way.

With that understanding and with the immeasurable respect among ourselves regarding the General Assembly, as well as clear confidence that I was setting foot inside the hall of Armenia's Parliament, which for more than forty days became our meeting site. It was the Super-Parliament, which had come to replace the Parliamentary Council.

I must say, that among myself and those like me, from the very first day, many things faltered from the viewpoint of decorum. It was not with a pleasant impression that we saw, that this assembly, through whose door we were entering with religious scruples, from Tiflis and Yerevan, in the name of student associations, school boys had come, and with such weak-minded arrogance. They were sitting side by side with those "big ones", which we had aggrandized from afar, surrounding them, and they were speaking with them on a first-name basis and in the familiar tense. -- ("Avetik", "Simon", et alii), when we could not forgive the dishonorable intimacy of stressing the word "comrade".

That image was the first tremor, which was going to open a rift, but I wanted not to look at that rift.

However, not wanting was insufficient.

Above the stage, completely overtaking façade, on a fiery red fabric, was the motto: "Proletariats of all countries, unite!" and beneath it, the opening of our trusted assembly, which had a force within it;, before the start of which it was revealed that my effort to defy was for nothing, and also revealing that the tremor raised the same emotions among all the Turco-Armenian delegates going from the Diaspora as well. There was only one (Bedrosian), who thought that he was demonstrating the debut of his intelligence, by proving that the mutiny of the other were "anti-revolutionary."

As unexpected as this revelation was for us, equally incomprehensible was our revolt, shown toward him for those, who have only noticed passivity in the spirit of Turco-Armenians. And to give the student representatives occasion to demonstrate their social talent and products from a diocesan school as food for lap dogs, and their super eminence above university outsiders.

The insincere caresses of the tempted, not expecting the unexpected, as an immediate convenient retort, "It's only because of the opening"; and those words were ineffective in forcing the rebellious spirit to retreat. That spirit had read more into those letters than what the actual words contained. And the students, when they were discovering that the formulas they had be forced to memorize were ineffective now, were not reluctant to force the rebels to retreat with their insulting comments.

This moment and event I will never be able to forget. Because that was the first honest confession, that the Federation is the name of two things; and of these, the one does not resemble the other.

The retreat would at last become the share of the students and the teachers. Because the rebels were refusing to yield even one letter from their threat. And the seconds were elapsing, and the moment of the congress's public opening was approaching.

And we remained standing, until that last nail was pried loose and the crimson banner was taken down, criticizing the orthodox socialites' scathing visual and oral comments hurled in our direction.

* * *

The second issue, on the days of adjournment, was the agenda item postponed until the last minute. That issue, which for us was the principal one -- the list of the perpetrators and the Assembly's message about them, as an echo of our martyrs' legacy.

As the days were elapsing and the need to bring the interminable to termination were showing the necessity to determine a date of adjournment, and moreover, impatience was beginning to take voice in me. The days were presenting numerous opportunities to eradicate indulgences and to exhaust patience. Many times a written request had been submitted for the presidency to place that issue on the next agenda. Many times, indications of exhausted patience had been expressed vocally. With an Eastern roguish smile, a veiled promised had always been the response. We were Easterners as well, and it was not difficult to quickly see that "doeshek alte:" was the intent of those smiles. Until the days of adjournment, a threat (similar to the threat on opening day) necessitated that the presidency place the issue on the table.

It was time for the issue to be discussed.

The General Assembly, in order at least not to curb the eagerness of the orators, more specifically of those, from whom going on stage and speaking at the podium would play the role of a forbidding force, had decided not only the time allocation for each speaker, but also the condition that each speaker was obliged to go on stage and express his opinion from the stage.

The first speakers about the issue were S. Vratsian, Ishkhan Arghoutian (members of the presidency) and Roupen Der Minasian. After their speeches, it was clear that I would be the fourth speaker. I know with certainty that many others were registered, but the issue was closed with my remarks, because an erupting revolution was becoming evident.

Here is what those three spoke, in summary and conclusion. --

It is true that the Turk annihilated the Turco-Armenians with a savagery not written in history. During the course of war, massacres can always occur, even if this one may not have had its equal. We were in battle against the Turk. And we must deem this our dues to that struggle, which has now given us our homeland and independence. Today, we are hence-forth a republic, and it is not acceptable, govern-mentally, to adopt that method, which we were employing yesterday. Therefore, we must remove that issue from this assembly's agenda.

Boldly and literally, they repeated the same things one after the other, of which every single word exploded a bomb in my being. I am certain also, in others. But the silence that pervaded the hall was of a different color.

Biting my tongue, I listened to their words, which as "governmental" as they may have been, were finding the doors to my brain closed tight. And their face henceforth was changing the traits familiar to me, and was making them irrecognizable. Once again I was realizing exactly what was the intent of their promises and delays.

When I was going up onstage to make my remarks, I know I was trembling and my teeth had pulverized all the fetters of my tongue.

Here is what I said, word for word. --

> You heard the three speakers, and you understood. I understood even more.
>
> I regret that they spoke. Would that they had not spoken. They should not have spoken. Because they are Caucasian-Armenians. And this issue is an exceptionally Turco-Armenian issue. The issue only of those, who have at least one martyr of their loved ones among the million.
>
> Listen well, then, that it is not in 1915 that I have given up martyrs. In 1895, I also gave up as a martyr my father, and I grew up orphaned. And it is the vengeance for my father's blood that has made me a revolutionary.
>
> I declare, therefore, that even if its name be DIVINE FEDERATION, yet severs its bond from those martyrs, my bond with this federation is also severed.
>
> I demand, that the right to speak about this issue be on condition of the speaker's having given up martyrs and that no single Caucasian-Armenian be allowed to speak. For forty days we have listened to you too much. Now, you listen to us for one day also.
>
> And to my Turco-Armenian comrades I also declare, that if they don't share my opinion, my demand from the Federation, let them know this very minute, that this issue for me, as a Turco-Armenian, I will not subject to their will. I consider this issue one between me and my father's assassin,

and an issue to be resolved. Nor do I recognize any assembly, or decision whatsoever which attempts to interfere, in the name of whatever it may be.

I conclude, asking, demanding all those speakers who have no martyrs, to resign from their right to speak.

The silence was more heavy and oppressive, when I was quietly leaving the stage.

That silence lasted for a while.

No one wanted to say a word. It was only decided. --

To consider the entire list presented to the Polis representative Body as sentenced to death. To duplicate that list and transmit it to the Central Committees. To call to responsibility any Central Committee, if one or the other name from that list is in its boundaries and does not implement the approved decision.

At the top of the list was the name of Talaat. (See Appendix VII for the list of 100 that were to be assassinated).

Shahan Natalie returning to United States from 9th General Assembly - 1920

Chapter 18

U.S. Mandate over Armenia

On April 26, 1920, the Supreme Council of the Principal Allied and Associated Powers in Paris, meeting at San Remo, requested that the United States assume a mandate over Armenia[76].

On May 25, 1920, *The Washington Post* announces the president to be the arbitrator for determining the borders between Turkey and Armenia in a front page article titled "Wilson Asks Congress for Power to Accept Mandate For Armenia." In it, doubt was expressed whether the Senators would approve Wilson's request.

Wilson's message to Congress on the mandate for the Armenian Nation reads:

> Gentlemen of the Congress:
>
> On the fourteenth day of May and official communication was received at the executive office from the secretary of the Senate of the United States, conveying the following preamble and resolutions:
>
> "Whereas, The testimony adduced at the hearings conducted by the subcommittee of the Senate committee on foreign relations have clearly established the truth of the reported massacres and other atrocities from which the Armenian people have suffered; and
>
> "Whereas, The independence of the republic of Armenia has been duly recognized by the supreme council of the peace conference and by the government of the United States of America; therefore, be it
>
> "Resolved, That the sincere congratulations of the Senate of the United States are herby extended to the people of Armenian on the recognition of the independence of the republic of Armenia, without prejudice respecting the territorial boundaries involved; and be it further
>
> "Resolved, That the Senate of the United States hereby expresses the hope that stable government, proper protection of individual liberties and rights, and the full realization of nationalistic aspirations may soon be attained by the Armenian people; and be further
>
> "Resolved, That in order to afford necessary protection for the lives and property of citizens of the United States at the port of Batum and along the line of the railroad leading to Baku, the President hereby requested, if no incompatible with the public interest, to cause United States warships

---

76 The United States recognized the independence of Armenia, but refused to recognize that of Georgia & Azerbaijan. (H. Lauterpacht, Recognition in International Law, Cambridge, 1947, p. 11. Papers Relating to Foreign Relations of the United States, 1920, vol. III, Washington, 1936, p. 778, hereinafter - FRUS).

and force of marines to be dispatched to such a port, with instructions to such marines to disembark and to protect American lives and property."

President Wilson went on to say:

"I know from unmistakable evidences given by responsible representatives of many peoples struggling towards independence and peaceful life again that the government of the United States is looked to with extraordinary trust and confidence, and I believe that it would do nothing less than arrest the hopeful processes of civilization if we were to refuse the request to become the helpful friends and advisers of such of these people as we may be authoritatively and formally requested to guide and assist.

"I am conscious that I am urging upon the Congress a very critical choice, but I make the suggestion in the confidence that I am speaking in the spirit and in accordance with the wishes of the greatest of the Christian peoples. The sympathy for Armenia among our people has sprung from untainted consciences, pure Christian faith and an earnest desire to see Christian people everywhere succored in their time of suffering, and lifted from the abject subjection and distress and enabled to stand upon their feet and take their place among the free nations of the world."

He concluded his message to Congress:

"Our recognition of the independence of Armenia will mean genuine liberty and assured happiness for her people, if we fearlessly undertake the duties of guidance and assistance involved in the functions of a mandatory.

"It is, therefore, with the most earnest hopefulness and with the feeling that I am giving advice from which the Congress will not willingly turn away that I urge acceptance of the invitation now formally and solemnly extend to us by the council at San Remo, into whose hands had passed the difficult task of composing the many complexities and difficulties of government in the one-time Ottoman empire and the maintenance of order and tolerable conditions of life in those portions of that empire which it is no longer possible in the interest of civilization to have under the government of the Turkish authorities themselves."

Even before the United States had been officially asked by the Supreme Council of the Principal Allied and Associated Powers in Paris to take the mandate, it was apparent that Congress would decline the offer. The mandate, had the U.S. accepted it, would have been governed under the authority of the League of Nations, an intergovernmental organization founded on January 10, 1920, as a result of the Paris Peace Conference that ended the First World War. It was the first international organization whose principal mission was to maintain world peace.

Accepting the mandate over Armenia would imply that the United States recognized the authority of the League of Nations, for America would have to make yearly reports to the League on the mandate and would be subject to the guidance and direction of the league. Under the treaty of Versailles, the

League was responsible for giving various mandates, but held a guiding and restraining hand on nations accepting them. Therefore, the Senate would be accepting America's allegiance to the League if it authorized the mandate, and the great majority in the Senate opposed the League, under which the mandate would be operative[77].

On March 25, 1920, the British Premier, Lloyd George addressed the House of Commons regarding the mandate of Armenia. He noted that France who had a mandate over Cilicia had been willing to hand Cilicia to the United States had the latter accepted the mandate.

"Up until the present we have only received requests from America to protect Armenia, without any offer to assume responsibility," Mr. Lloyd George said. "We hope France will undertake the responsibility but it is much to ask considering all the burdens France already has."

The premier contended that it was quite impossible for England to send armies to keep order in Armenia and Asia Minor. George stated that England would do her utmost to exert pressure in Constantinople to secure good treatment for Christians, but said that Briton was unable to accept a wider responsibility.

The Armenians are exceptionally intelligent people and must begin to depend on themselves for protection of their independence, Mr. Lloyd George said, adding that he understood that they could easily raise an army of 40,000 men. Great Britain would be willing to supply equipment and officers for their training. If that were done they could defend themselves against the Turks, the premier declared[78].

(San Fransisco Chronicle Newspaper, June 29, 1920)

---

77 The Washington Post, May 25, 1920 – page 1
78 GEORGE REFUSES TO OUTST SULTAN; The Charlotte Observer, Charlotte, N.C., March 26, 1920 – page 1

Chapter 19

The Treaty of Sèvres

Following the end of the WWI, the Treaty of Sèvres was one of six significant treaties resulting from the Paris Peace Conference, which commenced on January 19, 1919, and officially lasted until the end of 1923 when the Treaty of Lausanne was singed.

The Treaty of Sèvres, signed on August 10, 1920, was the only treaty that the internationally recognized independent Republic of Armenia signed. It was also the only legally recognized document that determined the borders of Armenia, which would later be known as Wilsonian Armenia. The treaty was signed by Mr. Avetis Aharonian, President of the Delegation of the Armenian Republic.

Signing of The Treaty of Sèvres - August 10, 1920

The Principal Allied Powers were the British Empire, France, Italy, and Japan. These world powers, by virtue of their signatures, would become the main guarantors that the terms of the peace treaty honored by Turkey.

Of the 433 articles in the treaty, eight of them were directly related to Armenia. Particularly, Article 88 and 89 were the most important articles for

Armenia. Article 88 recognized Armenia "as a free and independent State." Article 89 stated: "Turkey and Armenia as well as the other High Contracting Parties agree to submit to the arbitration of the President of the United States of America the question of the frontier to be fixed between Turkey and Armenia..."

The following is a text from the Treaty of Sèvres, which pertains to Armenia:

THE TREATY OF PEACE BETWEEN THE ALLIED AND ASSOCIATED POWERS

AND TURKEY

SIGNED AT SÈVRES

AUGUST 10, 1920

THE BRITISH EMPIRE, FRANCE, ITALY AND JAPAN,

These Powers being described in the present Treaty as the Principal Allied Powers;

ARMENIA, BELGIUM, GREECE, THE HEDJAZ, POLAND, PORTUGAL, ROUMANIA, THE SERB-CROAT-SLOVENE STATE AND CZECHO-SLOVAKIA,

These Powers constituting, with the Principal Powers mentioned above, the Allied Powers, of the one part;

AND TURKEY,

of the other part;

Whereas on the request of the Imperial Ottoman Government an Armistice was granted to Turkey on October 30, 1918, by the Principal Allied Powers in order that a Treaty of Peace might be concluded, and

Whereas the Allied Powers are equally desirous that the war in which certain among them were successively involved, directly or indirectly, against Turkey, and which originated in the declaration of war against Serbia on July 28, 1914, by the former Imperial and Royal Austro-Hungarian Government, and in the hostilities opened by Turkey against the Allied Powers on October 29, 1914, and conducted by Germany in alliance with Turkey, should be replaced by a firm, just and durable Peace,

For this purpose the HIGH CONTRACTING PARTIES have appointed as their Plenipotentiaries:

HIS MAJESTY THE KING OF THE UNITED KINGDOM OF GREAT BRITAIN AND IRELAND AND OF THE BRITISH DOMINIONS BEYOND THE SEAS, EMPEROR OF INDIA:

Sir George Dixon GRAHAME, K. C. V. O., Minister Plenipotentiary of His Britannic Majesty at Paris;

for the DOMINION of CANADA:

The Honourable Sir George Halsey PERLEY, K.C. M. G

High Commissioner for Canada in the United Kingdom;

for the COMMONWEALTH of AUSTRALIA:

The Right Honourable Andrew FISHER, High Commissioner for Australia in the United Kingdom;

for the DOMINION of NEW ZEALAND:

Sir George Dixon GRAHAME, K. C. V. O., Minister Plenipotentiary of His Britannic Majesty at Paris;

for the UNION of SOUTH AFRICA:

Mr. Reginald Andrew BLANKENBERG, O. B. E., Acting High Commissioner for the Union of South Africa in the United Kingdom;

for INDIA:

Sir Arthur HIRTZEL, K. C. B., Assistant Under Secretary of State for India;

THE PRESIDENT OF THE FRENCH REPUBLIC:

Mr. Alexandre MILLERAND, President of the Council, Minister for Foreign Affairs

Mr. Frederic FRANÇOIS-MARSAL, Minister of Finance

Mr. Auguste Paul-Louis ISAAC, Minister of Commerce and Industry;

Mr. Jules CAMBON, Ambassador of France

Mr. Georges Maurice PALÉOLOGUE, Ambassador of France, Secretary-General of the Ministry of Foreign Affairs;

His MAJESTY THE KING OF ITALY:

Count LELIO BONIN LONGARE, Senator of the Kingdom

Ambassador Extraordinary and Plenipotentiary of H. M. the King of Italy at Paris

General Giovanni MARIETTI, Italian Military Representative on the Supreme War Council;

His MAJESTY THE EMPEROR OF JAPAN:

Viscount CHINDA, Ambassador Extraordinary and Plenipotentiary of H. M. the Emperor of Japan at London;

Mr. K. MATSUI, Ambassador Extraordinary and Plenipotentiary of H. M. the Emperor of Japan at Paris;

ARMENIA:

Mr. Avetis AHARONIAN, President of the Delegation of the Armenian Republic;

HIS MAJESTY THE KING OF THE BELGIANS:

Mr. Jules VAN DEN HEUVEL, Envoy Extraordinary and Minister Plenipotentiary, Minister of State;

Mr. ROLIN JAEQUEMYNS, Member of the Institute of Private International Law, Secretary-General of the Belgian Delegation;

HIS MAJESTY THE KING OF THE HELLENES:

Mr. Eleftherios K. VENIZELOS, President of the Council of Ministers;

Mr. Athos ROMANOS, Envoy Extraordinary and Minister Plenipotentiary of H. M. the King of the Hellenes at Paris;

HIS MAJESTY THE KING OF THE HEDJAZ:

THE PRESIDENT OF THE POLISH REPUBLIC:

Count Maurice ZAMOYSKI, Envoy Extraordinary and Minister Plenipotentiary of the Polish Republic at Paris;

Mr. Erasme PILTZ;

THE PRESIDENT OF THE PORTUGUESE REPUBLIC:

Dr. Affonso da COSTA, formerly President of the Council of Ministers;

His MAJESTY THE KING OF ROUMANIA:

Mr. Nicolae TITULESCU, Minister of Finance;

Prince DIMITRIE GHIKA, Envoy Extraordinary and Minister Plenipotentiary of H. M. the King of Roumania at Paris;

HIs MAJESTY THE KING OF THE SERBS, THE CROATS AND THE SLOVENES:

Mr. Nicolas P. PACHITCH, formerly President of the Council of Ministers;

Mr. Ante TRUMBIC, Minister for Foreign Affairs;

THE PRESIDENT OF THE CZECHO-SLOVAK REPUBLIC:

Mr. Edward BENES, Minister for Foreign Affairs;

Mr. Stephen OSUSKY, Envoy Extraordinary and Minister Plenipotentiary of the Czecho-Slovak Republic at London;

TURKEY:

General HAADI Pasha, Senator;

RIZA TEVFIK Bey, Senator;

RECHAD HALISS Bey, Envoy Extraordinary and Minister Plenipotentiary of Turkey at Berne;

WHO, having communicated their full powers, found in good and due form, have AGREED AS FOLLOWS:

From the coming into force of the present Treaty the state of war will terminate.

From that moment and subject to the provisions of the present Treaty, official relations will exist between the Allied Powers and Turkey.

SECTION VI.

ARMENIA.

ARTICLE 88.

Turkey, in accordance with the action already taken by the Allied Powers, hereby recognises Armenia as a free and independent State.

ARTICLE 89.

Turkey and Armenia as well as the other High Contracting Parties agree to submit to the arbitration of the President of the United States of America the question of the frontier to be fixed between Turkey and Armenia in the vilayets of Erzerum, Trebizond, Van and Bitlis, and to accept his decision thereupon, as well as any stipulations he may prescribe as to access for Armenia to the sea, and as to the demilitarisation of any portion of Turkish territory adjacent to the said frontier.

ARTICLE 90.

In the event of the determination of the frontier under Article 89 involving the transfer of the whole or any part of the territory of the said Vilayets to Armenia, Turkey hereby renounces as from the date of such decision all rights and title over the territory so transferred. The provisions of the present Treaty applicable to territory detached from Turkey shall thereupon become applicable to the said territory.

The proportion and nature of the financial obligations of Turkey which Armenia will have to assume, or of the rights which will pass to her, on account of the transfer of the said territory will be determined in accordance with Articles 241 to 244, Part VIII (Financial Clauses) of the present Treaty.

Subsequent agreements will, if necessary, decide all questions which are not decided by the present Treaty and which may arise in consequence of the transfer of the said territory.

ARTICLE 91.

In the event of any portion of the territory referred to in Article 89 being transferred to Armenia, a Boundary Commission, whose composition will be determined subsequently, will be constituted within three months from the delivery of the decision referred to in the said Article to trace on the spot the frontier between Armenia and Turkey as established by such decision.

ARTICLE 92.

The frontiers between Armenia and Azerbaijan and Georgia respectively will be determined by direct agreement between the States concerned.

If in either case the States concerned have failed to determine the frontier by agreement at the date of the decision referred to in Article 89, the frontier line in question will be determined by the Principal Allied Powers, who will also provide for its being traced on the spot.

ARTICLE 93.

Armenia accepts and agrees to embody in a Treaty with the Principal Allied Powers such provisions as may be deemed necessary by these Powers to protect the interests of inhabitants of that State who differ from the majority of the population in race, language, or religion.

Armenia further accepts and agrees to embody in a Treaty with the Principal Allied Powers such provisions as these Powers may deem necessary to protect freedom of transit and equitable treatment for the commerce of other nations.

SECTION XII.

NATIONALITY.

ARTICLE 125.

Persons over eighteen years of age habitually resident in territory detached from Turkey in accordance with the present Treaty and differing in race from the majority of the population of such territory shall within one year from the coming into force of the present Treaty be entitled to opt for Armenia, Azerbaijan, Georgia, Greece, the Hedjaz, Mesopotamia, Syria, Bulgaria or Turkey, if the majority of the population of the State selected is of the same race as the person exercising the right to opt.

ARTICLE 351.

Free access to the Black Sea by the port of Batum is accorded to Georgia, Azerbaijan and Persia, as well as to Armenia. This right of access will be exercised in the conditions laid down in Article 349.

ARTICLE 352.

Subject to the decision provided for in Article 89, Part III (Political Clauses), free access to the Black Sea by the port of Trebizond is accorded to Armenia. This right of access will be exercised in the conditions laid down in Article 349.

In that event Armenia will be accorded a lease in perpetuity, subject to determination by the League of Nations, of an area in the said port which shall be placed under the general regime of free zones laid down in Articles 34x to 344, and shall be used for the direct transit of goods coming from or going to that State.

The delimitation of the area referred to in the preceding paragraph, its connection with existing railways, its equipment and exploitation, and in general all the conditions of its utilisation, including the amount of the rental, shall be decided by a Commission consisting of one delegate of Armenia, one delegate of Turkey, and one delegate appointed by the League of Nations. These conditions shall be susceptible of revision every ten years in the same manner.

The present Treaty, in French, in English, and in Italian, shall be ratified. In case of divergence the French text shall prevail, except in Parts I (Covenant of the League of Nations) and XII (Labour), where the French and English texts shall be of equal force.

The deposit of ratifications shall be made at Paris as soon as possible.

Powers of which the seat of the Government is outside Europe will be entitled merely to inform the Government of the French Republic through their diplomatic representative at Paris that their ratification has been given; in that case they must transmit the instrument of ratification as soon as possible.

A first procès-verbal of the deposit of ratifications will be drawn up as soon as the Treaty has been ratified by Turkey on the one hand, and by three of the Principal Allied Powers on the other hand.

From the date of this first procès-verbal the Treaty will come into force between the High Contracting Parties who have ratified it.

For the determination of all periods of time provided for in the present Treaty this date will be the date of the coming into force of the Treaty.

In all other respects the Treaty will enter into force for each Power at the date of the deposit of its ratification.

The French Government will transmit to all the signatory Powers a certified copy of the procès-verbaux of the deposit of ratifications.

IN FAITH WHEREOF the above-named Plenipotentiaries have signed the present Treaty.

Done at Sevrès, the tenth day of August one thousand nine hundred and twenty, in a single copy which will remain deposited in the archives of the French Republic, and of which authenticated copies will be transmitted to each of the Signatory Powers.

(L. S.) GEORGE GRAHAME.

(L. S.) GEORGE H. PERLEY.

(L. S.) ANDREW FISHER.

(L. S.) GEORGE GRAHAME.

(L. S.) R. A. BLANKENBERG.

(L. S.) ARTHUR HIRTZEL.

(L. S.) A. MILLERAND.

(L. S.) F. FRANÇOIS-MARSAL.

(L. S.) JULES CAMBON. (L. S.) PALÉOLOGUE.

(L. S.) BONIN.

(L. S.) MARIETTI.

(L. S.) K:. MATSUI.

(L. S.) A. AHARONIAN.

(L. S.) J. VAN DEN HEUVEL.

(L. S.) ROLIN JAEQUEMYNS,

(L. S.) E. K. VENIZELOS.

(L. S.) A. ROMANOS.

(L. S.) MAURICE ZAMOYSKI.

(L. S.) ERASME PILTZ

(L. S.) AFFONSO COSTA.

Chapter 20

Wilsonian Armenia

The Treaty of Sèvres, as mentioned in the previous chapters, was to establish peace between Armenia and Turkey. It also set the stage for the borders between the two states to be determined by the President of the United States, Woodrow Wilson.

On behalf of the Ottoman Empire, the Treaty of Sèvres was signed by the internationally recognized leader of post-World War I Ottoman Empire, Sultan Abdul Hamid. As the Supreme leader of the Ottoman Empire, the Sultan possessed ultimate power and did not need the consent of a representative body of the people to approve his decision. With that said, and to his credit, he did, nevertheless, consult with his senate and was given the approval of 48 out of 50.

The newly independent Armenia was recognized as a *de facto* government on January 19, 1920, by the Supreme Council of the Principal Allied and Associated Powers in Paris, namely Great Britain, France, and Italy on the condition that the recognition bestowed on them would not prejudge the question of the eventual frontier[79]. The United States recognized the *de facto* government of the Republic of Armenia on April 23, 1920[80], on the condition that the territorial frontiers should be left for a later determination[81]. Thus, the Republic of Armenia signed the Treaty of Sèvres as an internationally recognized body representing the Armenian people.

To date, the Treaty of Sèvres has been the only treaty between Turkey and Armenia, signed by a legitimate Armenian representation. There have been a number of treaties signed by persons or powers that were not internationally recognized as representing Armenia. The most noteworthy treaty that was NOT signed by a legitimate representative of the Armenian government was the Treaty of Lausanne, on July 24, 1923. This treaty illegally redrew the Turkish-Armenian borders as defined in the U.S. President Woodrow Wilson's Arbitral Award on Turkish-Armenian Boundary (November 22, 1920) and which said territories are under occupation by the country of Turkey today.

The following is the full text of the Arbitral Award on Turkish-Armenian Boundary by President of the United States Woodrow Wilson:

---

79 Hackworth G. H., Digest of International Law, Turkish-Armenian Boundary Question, vol. I, Washington, 1940, p. 715.

80 The United States recognized the independence of Armenia, but refused to recognize that of Georgia & Azerbaijan. (H. Lauterpacht, Recognition in International Law, Cambridge, 1947, p. 11. Papers Relating to Foreign Relations of the United States, 1920, vol. III, Washington, 1936, p. 778, hereinafter - FRUS).

81 Hackworth, op. cit., p. 715.

THE FRONTIER BETWEEN ARMENIA AND TURKEY

AS DECIDED BY

PRESIDENT WOODROW WILSON

NOVEMBER 22, 1920

Introductory Note

On April 26, 1920, the Supreme Council of the Allied Powers, in conference at San Remo, addressed to the President of the United States of America an invitation to act as arbitrator in the question of the boundary between Turkey and Armenia, to be fixed within the four vilayets of Erzerum, Trebizond, Van and Bitlis.

On May the 17th, 1920, President Wilson accepted the invitation of the Supreme Council.

On August 10, 1920, a Treaty of Peace was signed at Sevres by Plenipotentiary Representatives of the British Empire, France, Italy and Japan, and of Armenia, Belgium, Greece, Poland, Portugal, Roumania and Czecho-Slovakia, of the one part; and of Turkey, of the other part, which Treaty contained, among other provisions, the following:

ARTICLE 89: Turkey and Armenia, as well as the other High Contracting Powers, agree to submit to the arbitration of the President of the United States of America the question of the frontiers to be fixed between Turkey and Armenia in the Vilayets of Erzerum, Trebizond, Van and Bitlis, and to accept his decision thereupon, as well as any stipulations he may prescribe as to access for Armenia to the sea, and as to the demilitarization of any portion of Turkish territory adjacent to the said frontier.

On October 18, 1920, the Secretariat General of the Peace Conference, acting under the instructions of the Allied Powers, transmitted to President

Wilson an authenticated copy of the above mentioned Treaty.

On November 22, 1920, President Wilson affixed his seal to his decision delineating the boundaries between Turkey and Armenia.

This decision with a covering letter to the President of the Supreme Council was communicated under date of November 24, 1920, through the American Ambassador in Paris to the Secretariat General of the Peace Council.

President Wilson's letter and decision was as follows:

PRESIDENT WILSON'S LETTER

PRESIDENT WILSON
TO THE PRESIDENT OF THE SUPREME COUNCIL
OF THE ALLIED POWERS

MR. PRESIDENT:

By action of the Supreme Council taken on April 26th of this year an invitation was tendered to me to arbitrate the question of the boundaries between Turkey and the new state of Armenia. Representatives of the powers signatory on August 10th of this year to the Treaty of Sevres have acquiesced in conferring this honor upon me and have signified their intention of accepting the frontiers which are to be determined by my decision, as well as any stipulation which I may prescribe as to access for Armenia to the sea and any arrangement for the demilitarization of Turkish territory lying along the frontier thus established. According to the terms of the arbitral reference set forth in part III, Section 6, Article 89, of the Treaty of Sevres, the scope of the arbitral competence assigned to me is clearly limited to the determination of the frontiers of Turkey and Armenia in the Vilayets of Erzerum, Trebizond, Van and Bitlis. With full consciousness of the responsibility placed upon me by your request, I have approached this difficult task with eagerness to serve the best interests of the Armenian people as well as the remaining inhabitants, of whatever race or religious belief they may be, in this stricken country, attempting to exercise also the strictest possible justice toward the populations, whether Turkish, Kurdish, Greek or Armenian, living in the adjacent areas.

In approaching this problem it was obvious that the existing ethnic and religious distribution of the population in the four vilayets could not, as in other parts of the world, be regarded as the guiding element of the decision. The ethnic consideration, in the case of a population originally so complexly intermingled, is further beclouded by the terrible results of the massacres and deportations of the Armenians and Greeks, and by the dreadful losses also suffered by the moslem inhabitants through refugee movements and the scourge of typhus and other diseases. The limitation of the arbitral assignment to the four vilayets named in Article 89 of the Treaty made it seem a duty and an obligation that as large an area within these vilayets be granted to the Armenian state as could be done, while meeting the basic requirements of an adequate natural frontier and of geographic and economic unity for the new state. It was essential to keep in mind that the new state of Armenia, including as it will a large section of the former Armenian provinces of Transcaucasian Russia, will at the outset have a population about equally divided between

Moslem and Christian elements and of diverse racial and tribal relationship. The citizenship of the Armenian Republic will, by the tests of language and religion, be composed of Turks, Kurds, Greeks, Kizilbashis, Lazes and others, as well as Armenians. The conflicting territorial desires of Armenians, Turks, Kurds and Greeks along the boundaries assigned to my arbltral decision could not always be harmonized. In such cases it was my belief that consideration of healthy economic life for the future state of Armenia should he decisive. Where, however, the requirements of a correct geographic boundary permitted, all mountain and valley districts along the border which were predominantly Kurdish or Turkish have been left to Turkey rather than assigned to Armenia, unless trade relations with definite market towns threw them necessarily into the Armenian state. Wherever information upon tribal relations and seasonal migrations was obtainable, the attempt was made to respect the integrity of tribal groupings and nomad pastoral movements.

From the Persian border southwest of the town of Kotur the boundary line of Armenia is determined by a rugged natural barrier of great height, extending south of Lake Van and lying southwest of the Armenian cities of Bitlis and Mush. This boundary line leaves as a part of the Turkish state the entire Sandjak of Hakkiari, or about one-half of the Vilayet of Van, and almost the entire Sandjak of Sairt. The sound physiographic reason which seemed to justify this decision was further strengthened by the ethnographic consideration that Hakkiari and Sairt are predominantly Kurdish in population and economic relations. It did not seem to the best interest of the Armenian state to include in it the upper valley of the Great Zah River, largely Kurdish and Nestorian Christian in population and an essential element of the great Tigris river irrigation system of Turkish Kurdistan and Mesopotamia. The control of these headwaters should be kept, wherever possible, within the domain of the two interested states, Turkey and Mesopotamia. For these reasons the Armenian claim upon the upper valley of the Great Zah could not be satisfied.

The boundary upon the west from Bitlis and Mush northward to the vicinity of Erzingan lies well within Bitlis and Erzerum vilayets. It follows a natural geographic barrier, which furnishes Armenia with perfect security and leaves to the Turkish state an area which is strongly Kurdish. Armenian villages and village nucleon this section, such as Kighi and Temran, necessarily remain Turkish because of the strong commercial and church ties which connect them with Kharput rather (than?) with any Armenian market and religious centers which lie within Bitlis or Erzerum vilayets. This decision seemed an unavoidable consequence of the inclusion of the city and district of Kharput in the Turkish state as determined by Article 27 II (4) and Article 89 of the Treaty of Sevres.

From the northern border of the Dersim the nature and the direction of the frontier decision was primarily dependent upon the vital question of supplying an adequate access to the sea for the state of Armenia. Upon the correct solution of this problem depends, in my judgment, the future economic well-being of the entire population, Turkish, Kurdish, Greek, Armenian, or Yezidi, in those portions of the vilayets of Erzerum, Bitlis and Van which lie within the state of Armenia. I was not unmindful of the desire of the Pontic Greeks, submitted to me in a memorandum similar, no doubt, in argument and content to that presented to the Supreme Council last March at its London Conference, that the unity of the coastal area of the Black sea inhabited by them be preserved and that arrangement be made for an autonomous administration for the region stretching from Riza to a point west of Sinope. The arbitral jurisdiction assigned to me by Article 89 of the Treaty of Sevres does not include the possibility of decision or recommendation by me upon the question of their desire for independence, or failing that, for autonomy. Nor does it include the right to deal with the littoral of the independent Sandjak of Djanik or of the Vilayet of Kastamuni into which extends the region of the unity and autonomy desired by the Pontic Greeks.

Three possible courses lay open to me: to so delimit the boundary that the whole of Trebizond Vilayet would he within Turkey, to grant it in its entirety to Armenia, or to grant a part of it to Armenia and leave the remainder to Turkey. The majority of the population of Trebizond Vilayet is incontestably Moslem and the Armenian element, according to all pre-war estimates, was undeniably inferior numerically to the Greek portion of the Christian minority. Against a decision so clearly indicated on ethnographic grounds weighed heavily the future of Armenia. I could only regard the question in the light of the needs of a new political entity, Armenia, with mingled Moslem and Christian populations, rather than as a question of the future of the Armenians alone. It has been and is now increasingly my conviction that the arrangements providing for Armenia's access to the sea must be such as to offer every possibility for the development of this state as one capable of reassuming and maintaining that useful role in the commerce of the world which its geographic position, athwart a great historic trade route, assigned to it in the past. The civilization and the happiness of its mingled population will largely depend upon the building of railways and the increased accessibility of the hinterland of the three vilayets to European trade and cultural influences.

Eastward from the port of Treblzond along the coast of Lazistan no adequate harbor facilities are to be found and the rugged character of the Pontic range separating Lazistan Sandjak from the Vilayet of Erzerum is such as to isolate the hinterland from the coast so far as practicable railway construction is concerned. The existing caravan route from Persia across the plains of Bayazid and Erzerum, which passes through the towns of Baiburt and Gumush-khana and debouches upon the Black Sea at Trebizond, has behind it a long record of persistent usefulness.

These were the considerations which have forced me to revert to my original conviction that the town and harbor of Trebizond must become an integral part of Armenia. Because of the still greater adaptability of the route of the Karshut valley, ending at the town of Tireboli, for successful railway construction and operation I have deemed also essential to include this valley in Armenia, with enough territory lying west of it to insure its adequate protection. I am not unaware that the leaders of the Armenian delegations have expressed their willingness to renounce claim upon that portion of Trebizond Vilayet lying west of Surmena. Commendable as is their desire to avoid the assumption of authority over a territory so predominantly Moslem, I am confident that, in acquiescing in their eagerness to do justice to the Turks and Greeks in Trebizond I should be doing an irreparable injury to the future of the land of Armenia and its entire population, of which they will be a part. It was upon such a basis, Mr. President, that the boundaries were so drawn as to follow mountain ridges west of the city of Erzingan to the Pontic range and thence to the Black Sea, in such a way as to include in Armenia the indentation called Zephyr Bey. The decision to leave to Turkey the harbor towns and hinterland of Kerasun and Ordu in Trebizond Sandjak was dictated by the fact that the population of this region is strongly Moslem and Turkish and that these towns are the outlets for the easternmost sections of the Turkish vilayet of Sivas. The parts of Erzerum and Trebizond Vilayets which, by reason of t1ns delimitation, remain Turkish rather than become Armenian comprise approximately 12,120 square kilometers.

In the matter of demilitarization of Turkish territory adjacent to the Armenian border as it has been broadly described above, it seemed both impracticable and unnecessary to establish a demilitarized zone which would require elaborate prescriptions and complex agencies for their execution. Fortunately, Article 177 of the Treaty of Sevres prescribes the disarming of all existing forts throughout Turkey. Articles 159 and 196-200 provide in addition agencies entirely adequate to meet all the dangers of disorder which may arise along the borders, the former by the requirement that a proportion of the officers of the gendarmerie shall be supplied by the various Allied or neutral Powers, tile latter by the establishment of a Military Inter-Allied Commission of Control and Organization. In these circumstances the only additional prescriptions which seemed necessary and advisable were that the Military Inter-Allied Commission of Control and Organization should, in conformity with the powers bestowed upon it by Article 200 of the Treaty, select the superior officers of the gendarmerie to be stationed in the vilayets of Turkey lying contiguous to the frontiers of Armenia solely from those officers who will be detailed by the Allied or neutral Powers in accordance with Article 159 of the Treaty; and that these officers, under the supervision of the Military Inter-Allied Commission of Organization and Control, should be especially charged with the duty of preventing military preparations directed against the Armenian frontier.

It is my confident expectation that the Armenian refugees and their leaders, in the period of their return into the territory thus assigned to them, will by reframing from any and all form of reprisals give to the world an example of that high moral courage which must always be the foundation of national strength. The world expects of them that they give every encouragement and help within their power to those Turkish refugees who may desire to return to their former homes in the districts of Trebizond, Erzerum, Van and Bitlis remembering that these peoples, too, have suffered greatly. It is my further expectation that they will offer such considerate treatment to the Laz and the Greek inhabitants of the coastal region of the Black Sea, surpassing in the liberality of their administrative arrangements, if necessary, even the ample provisions for non-Armeman racial and religious groups embodied in the Minorities Treaty signed by them upon August 10th of this year, that these peoples will gladly and willingly work in completest harmony with the Armenians in laying firmly the foundation of the new Republic of Armenia.

I have the honor to submit herewith the text of my decision.

Accept (etc.).
WOODROW WILSON
Washington, November 22, 1920.

DECISION OF PRESIDENT WILSON

Respecting the Frontier Between Turkey and Armenia, Access for Armenia to the Sea, and the Demilitarization of Turkish Territory Adjacent to the Armenian Frontier.

WOODROW WILSON, President of the United States,
To Whom it shall Concern,
Greetings:

Whereas, on April 26, 1920, the Supreme Council of the Allied Powers, in conference at San Remo, addressed to the President of the United States of America an invitation to act as arbitrator in the question of the boundary between Turkey and Armenia, to be fixed within the four Vilayets of Erzerum, Trebizond, Van, and Bitlis;

And whereas, on May 17, 1920, my acceptance of this invitation was telegraphed to the American Ambassador in Paris, to he conveyed to the Powers represented on the Supreme Council;

And whereas, on August 10, 1920, a Treaty of Peace was Signed at Sevres by Plenipotentiary Representatives of the British Empire, France, Italy and Japan, and of Armenia, Belgium, Greece, Poland, Portugal, Roumarua, and CzechoSlovakia, of the one part; and of Turkey, of the other part, which Treaty contained, among other provisions, the following:

"*ARTICLE 89. Turkey and Armenia as well as the other High Contracting Parties agree to submit to the arbitration of the President of the United States of America the question of the frontier to be fixed between Turkey and Armenia in the Vilayets of Erzerum, Trebizond, Van and Bitlis, and to accept his decision thereupon, as well as any stipulations he may prescribe as to access for Armenia to the sea, and as to the demilitarization of any portion of Turkish territory adjacent to the said frontier*";

And whereas, on October 18, 1920, the Secretariat General of the Peace Conference, acting under the instructions of the Allied Powers, transmitted to me, through the Embassy of the United States of America in Pans, an authenticated copy of the above mentioned Treaty, drawing attention to the said Article 89,

Now, therefore, I, Woodrow Wilson. President of the United States of America, upon whom has thus been conferred the authority of arbitrator, having examined the question in the light of the most trustworthy information available, and with a mind to the highest interests of justice, do hereby declare the following decision:

I

The frontier between Turkey and Armenia in the Vilayets of Erzerum, Trebizond, Van, and Bitlis, shall be fixed as follows·

1. The initial point[82] shall be chosen on the ground at the Junction of

---

[82] It is my understanding that this initial point will lie upon the former Turkish-Peman frontier referred to in the Article 21 II (4) of the Treaty of Sevres; but 40 miles of the said frontier, within which the initial point of the Armenian frontier is included, were left undemarcated

the Tukish-Persian frontier with the eastern termination of the administrative boundary between the Sandjaks of Van and Hakluari, of the Vilayet of Van, as this administrative boundary appears upon the Bashkala sheet of the Turkish map, scale 1 200,000, editions published in the Turkish financial years 1330 and 1331 (1914-15). From this initial point the boundary shall extend southwestward to the western peak of Merkezer Dagh, situated about 6 kilometers westward from point 3350 (10,990 feet), about 2 kilometers southeastward from the village of Yokary Ahvalan, and approximately 76 kilometers southeastward from the city of Van.

the sandjak boundary specified above, then the admimstrative boundary between the Kazas of Mamuret-ul-Hamid and Elback, then the same sandjak boundary specified above, all modified, where necessary, to follow the main water-parting between the Zap Su (Great Zab River) and the Khoshah Su, and dividing equably the summits of the passes Krdes Gedik and Chokh Gedik;

then northwestward about 28 kilometers to Klesiry Dagh,

a line to be fixed on the ground, following the mam water-partings between the Khoshah Su and the streams flowing into the Shatak Su, and traversing the pass south of the village of Yokary Ahvalan, and passing through Shkolans Dagh (3100 meters or 10,170 feet) and the Belereshuk pass;

thence southwestward to the junction of an unnamed stream with the Shatak Su at a point about 10 kilometers southward from the village of Shatak,

a line to be fixed on the ground, following the main water-partings, and passing through Koh Kiran Daghlar, San Dagh (3150 meters or 10,335 feet), Kevmetala Tepe (3,500 meters or 11,480 feet, point 3,540 (11,615 feet), in such a way as to leave to Armenia the village of Eyreti, and to Turkey the village of Araz, and to cross the Shatak Su at least 2 kilometers southward from the village of Dir Mouem Kihsa,

thence westward to the point where the Biths•Van Vilayet boundary reaches the Moks Su from the west, situated about 18 kilometers southward from the village of Moks,

a line to be fixed on the ground, following the mam water-partings, leaving to Armenia the villages of Kachet, Smpass, and Ozim, passing through Kanisor Tepe (3,245 meters or 10,645 feet), an unnamed peak about 3 kilometers south ward from Arnus Dagh (3,550 meters or 11,645 feet), crossing an unnamed stream about 2 kilometers southward from the village of Smpass, passing through point 3,000 (9,840 feet), following the boundary between the Vilayets of Van and Bitlis for about 3 kilometers southwestward from this point and continuing southwestward on the same ridge to an unnamed peak about 2 kilometers eastward from Moks Su, and then descending to this stream;

thence northward to an unnamed peak on the boundary between the Vilayets of Van and Bitlis about 3 kilometers westward from the pass at Mata Gedtk,

by the Turko-Persian Frontier Commission in 1914. The initial point contemplated lies about 1 kilometer southward from the village of Kara Hissa and approximately 25 kilometers southwestward from the village of Kotur, and may be fixed on the ground as near this location as the Boundary Commission shall determine, provided **it lies** at the junction of the Van-Hakkian Sandjak boundary with the frontier of **Persia.**

the administrative boundary between the Vilayets of Van and Bitlis, modified south of Vankin Dagh (3,200 meters or 10,500 feet) to follow the main water-parting;

thence westward to the peak Meidan Chenidiani, situated on the boundary between the Sandjaks of Bitlis and Sairt about 29 kilometers south eastward from the city of Bitlis,

a line to be fixed on the ground, following the main water-partmgs, passing through Veberhan Dagh (3,110 meters or 10,200 feet), crossing the Kesan Dere about 2 kilometers southward from the village of Khoros, leavingg to Turkey the villages of Semhaj and Nevaleyn as well as the bridge or ford on the trail between them, and leaving to Armenia the village of Chopans and the trail leading to it from the northeast;

thence westward to the Guzel Dere Su at a point about 23 kilometers southward from the city of Bitlis and about 2 kilometers southward from Nuri Ser peak (2,150 meters or 7,050 feet),

the administrative boundary between the Sandjaks of Bitlis and Sairt, and then, a line to be fixed on the ground, following the main water-partings, and passing through points 2,750 and 2,700 of Kur Dagh (9,020 and 8,860 feet respectively), Biluki Dagh (2,230 meters or 7,315 feet), and Sihaser Tepe (2,250 meters or 7,380 feet);

thence westward to the junction of the Bitlis Su and the unnamed stream near the village of Deshtwni, about 30 kilometers southwestward from the city of Bitlis.

a line to be fixed on the ground, following the mam water-partings, leaving to Turkey the Villages of Lered and Daruni, and to Armenia the village of Enbu and all portions of the trail leading northeastward to the Bitlis Su from Mergelu peak (1,850 meters or 6,070 feet), and passing through Mergelu Tepe and Shikh Tabur ridge;

thence westward to the Zuk (Gharzan) Su at the point about 11 kilometers northeastward from the village of Hazo and approximately 1 kilometer upstream from the village of Zily,

a line to be fixed on the ground, following the mam water-partings, leaving to Armenia the village of Desbtumi, passing through the eastern peak of Kalmen Dagh (2 710 meters or 8,890 feet) and continuing in such a manner ae to leave to Armenia the upland dolina, or basin of interior drainage, to traverse the pass about 3 kilometers westward from the village of Avesipy, passing through Sbelasb Dagh (1,944 meters or 6,380 feet);

thence westward to the Sassun Dere at a point about 4 kilometers southwestward from the village of Kabil JeVJz and approximately 47 kilometers southward from the city of Mush,

a line to be fixed on the ground, following the main water-partings through Cheyardash peak (2,001 meters or 6,565 feet), Keupeka peak (1,931 meters or 6,335 feet), an unnamed peak on the Sasswi Dagh about 4 kilometers south westward from Malato Dagh (2,967 meters or 9,735 feet), point 2,229 (7,310 feet), and leaving to Turkey the village of Gundenu,

thence northwestward to the Talury Dere at a point about 2 kilometers upstream from the village of Kaeser and approximately 37 kilometers northeastward from the village of Seylevan (Farkm),

a line to be fixed on the ground, following the mam water-partings and passing through an unnamed peak about 2 kilometers eastward from the Village of Seyluk, and through point 2,073 (6,800 feet), leaving to Armenia the village of Heyshtirem;

thence northwestward to the western tributary of the Talury Dere at a point about 2 kilometers eastward from the village of Helin and approximately 42 kilometers southwestward from the city of Mush,

a line to be fixed on the ground, following the mam water-partings, and passing through point 2,251 (7,385 feet),

thence northwestward to the junction of the Kulp Boghazy (Kulp Su) and Aekar Dere, approximately 42 kilometers southwestward from city of Mush,

a line to be fixed on the ground, following the main water-partings leaving to Turkey the village of Helin and to Armenia the Village of Kehirvamk;

thence northwestward to a point on the administrative boundary between the Sandjaks of Gendj and Mush northeast of Mir Ismail Dagh, and situated about 5 kilometers westward from the village of Pelekoz and approximately 19 kilometers southward from the village of Ardushin,

a line to be fixed on the ground, following the main water-parting, and passing through the Komiss Dagh;

thence northwestward to the Frat Nehri (Murad Su, or Euphrates) at a point to be determined on the ground about 1 kilometer upstream from the village of Dome and approximately 56 kilometers westward from the city of Mush,

the administrative boundary between the Sandjaks of Gendj and Mush northward for about 2 kilometers, then a line to be fixed on the ground, following the main water-partings westward to an unnamed peak approximately 6 kilometers east of Chutela (Akche Kara) Dagh (2,940 meters or 9,645 feet), then northward passing through Hadije Tepe on Arahik Dagh, leaving to Turkey the village of Kulay and to Armenia the village of Kluhuran;

thence northwestward to the Gumk Su at a point about midway between two trails crossing this river about half way between the villages of Elmaly and Chenajki, and approximately 26 kilometers northeastward from the Village of Cholik (Chevelik),

a line to be fixed on the ground, following the main water-partings, passing through an unnamed peak about 2 kilometers westward from the village of Shanghar, along Solkhan Dagh, and through point 2,200 (7,220 feet), leaving to Turkey the villages of Shanghar and ChenaJky, and to Armenia the villages of Kumistan, Lichinak, and Elmaly;

thence northwestward to the boundary between the Vilayets of Erzerum and Bitlis at an unnamed peak near where a straight line between the villages of Erchek and Agha Keui would intersect said vilayet boundary,

a line to be fixed on the ground, following the main water-partings, passing through point 2,050 (6,725 feet),

thence northward to an unnamed peak on said vilayet boundary about 8 kilometers northwestward from Kartahk Tepe on the Choris Dagh,

the administrative boundary between the Vilayets of Erzerum and Bitlis;

thence westward to the Buyuk Su (Kighi Su) at a point about 2 kilometers upstream from the junction of the Ghabzu Dere with it, and approximately 11 kilometers northwestward from the village of Kighi,

a line to be fixed on the ground, following the main water-partings of the Sheitan Daghlar, passmg through points 2,610 (8565 feet), Sheitan Dagh (2,906 meters or 9,535 feet), Hakstun Dagh, and leaving to Armenia the village of Dinek and the ford or bridge southwest of this village;

thence westward to the Dar Boghaz (Kuttu Dere) at a point about 3 kilo meters southward from the village of Chardaklar (Palu.mor),

a line to be fixed on the ground, following the main water-partings, leaving to Armenia the villages of Shorakh and Ferhadin, passing through Ghabartl Dagh (2,550 meters or 8,365 feet), Sian Dagh (2,750 meters or 9,020 feet), the 2,150 meter pass on the Palum or-Kighi trail near Mustapha Bey Konaghy, Feziria Tepe (2,530 meters or 8,300 feet), point 2,244 (7,360 feet), and point 2,035 (6,675 feet);

thence westward to the point common to the boundaries of the Sandjaks of Erzingan and Erzerum and the Vilayet of Mamuret-ul-Aziz, situated at a sharp angle in the vilayet boundary, approximately 24 kilometers westward from the village of Palumor and 32 kilometers southeastward from the city of Erzingan,

a line to be fixed on the ground, following the mam water-partings, and passing northwestward through an unnamed peak about 2 kilometers south westward from Palumor, through Silos (Ker smod) Dagh (2,405 meters or 7,890 feet) to an unnamed peak on the southern boundary of the Sandjak of Erzingan, about 8 kilometers southwestward from the Palwnor-Erzingan pa88, then turning southwestward along said Sandjak boundary for nearly 13 kilometers, passing through Karaja Kaleh (3,100 meters or 10,170 feet);

thence westward to an unnamed peak on the boundary between the Vilayets of Erzerum and Mamuret-ul-Aziz about 3 kilometers northeastward from the pass on the trail across the Manzur Silsilesi between Kennakh on the Euphrates and Pelur in the Dersim, the peak being approxiniately 40 kilometers southwestward from the city of Erzingan,

the administrative boundary between the vilayets of Erzerurn and Mamuret ul-Aziz, modified[83], in case of a majority of the voting members of the Boundary Commission deem it wise, to follow the main water-parting along the ridge between an unnamed peak about 2 kilometer southwest of Merjan Daghlar (3,449 meters or 11,315 feet) and Katar Tepe (3,300 meters or 10,825 feet);

thence northward to the Frat Nehri (Kara Su, or Euphrates) at a point to be determined on the ground about 6 kilometers eastward from the village of Kemagh and approximately 35 kilometers southwestward from the city of Erzingan,

a line to be fixed on the ground, following the main water-partings, leaving to Turkey the trail from Pelur m the Dersim to Kemakh on the Euphrates, and

[83] At the locality named, the vilayet boundary (according to Khozat-Dersim sheet of the Turkish General Staff map, scale 1 200,000) descends the northern slope of the Monzur-Silsileri for about 7 kilometers. The junction of the boundary between the Kazas of Erzingan and Kemakh in Erzingan Sandjak of Erzerum

to Armenia the village of Koja Arbler,

thence, northward to the boundary between the vilayeta of Erzerum and Trebizond at a point to be determined about 1 kilometer west of peak 2,930 (2,630 or 8,625 feet) and about 4 kilometers southward from the village of Metkut, or approximately 39 kilometers northwestward from the city of Erzingan,

a line to be fixed on the ground, following the main water-partings, leaving to Turkey the villages of Chalghy Yady, Toms, and Alamlik, and to Armenia the village of Erkghan and the road and col south of the village of Metkut, passing through Utch Kardash Tepe, Kelek Kiran (Tekke Tash, 2,800 meters or 9,185 feet), Kehnam Dagh (or Kara Dagh, 3,030 meters or 9,940 feet), dividing equably between Armenia and Turkey the summit of the pass about 2 kilometers westward from the village of Zazker and, similarly, the summit of the pass of Kral Kham Boghazy near the village of Chardakh, passing through point 2760 on Kara Dagh (9,055 feet), point 2,740 (8,990 feet), and a point to be determined on the ground, situated near the Iky Sivry stream lcsa than 2 kilometers westward from the Chimen Dagh pass, and located in such a manner as to leave to Turkey the junction of the two roads leading westward to the villages of Kuchi Kem and Kara Yayrak, and to Annerua the junction of two other roads leading to the villages of Metkut and Kirmana; the Boundary Commission shall determine in the field the most equable disposition of the highway between points 2,760 and 2,740;[84]

thence northwestward to the Kelk.it Chai (Kelkit lrmak) at the point where the boundary between the Vilayets of Treblzond and Slvas reaches lt from the south,

the administrative boundary between the Vilayets of Trebizond and Erzerum, and then the administrative boundary between the Vilayets of Trebizond and Sivas,

thence northward to an unnamed peak on the boundary between the Vilayets of Trebizond and Sivas about 4 kilometers southwestward from Borgha Paya (2,995 meters or 9,825 feet) the latter being situated approximately 38 kilometers southwestward from the city of Gumush-Khana,

a line to be fixed on the ground, following the main water-partings, leaving to Armenia the villages of Halkit, Smanh, Kihktm, and Kirtanos, and to Turkey the villages of Kar Kishla, Sadik, Kara Kia, and Ara, crossing the pass between the western tributaries of the Shiran Chai and the eastern headwaters of the Barsak Dere (Kara Chai) about 43 kilometers eastward from the city of Karahissar Sharki (Shebm Karahissar);

---

84 Vilayet with the boundary of Dersim Sandlak of Mamuret-ul-Aziz Vilayet lies within 14 kilometers of the Euphrates River This leaves to Turkey a military bridgehead north of an 11,000 foot mountain range and only 20 kilo meters south of the city of Erzmgan. I am not empowered to change the administrative boundary at this point, and these 40 square kilometers of territory lie outside the four vilayets specified in Article 89 of the Treaty of Sevres.

However, I venture to call the attention of the Boundary Commission to the desirability of consulting the local inhabitants with a view to possible modification of the vilayet boundary at this point.

thence northeastward, northward, and westward to an unnamed peak on the boundary between the Vilayets of Trebizond and S1vas situated about 7 kilometers northwestward from Yerchi Tepe (2,690 meters or 8,825 feet) and approximately 47 kilometers south southeastward from the city of Kerasun,

the administrative boundary between the Vilayets of Trebizond and Sivas;

thence northward, from the point last mentioned, on the crest of the Pontic Range, to the Black Sea, at a point to be determined on the seacoast about l kilometer westward from the village of Kesbab, and approximately 9 kilometers eastward from the city of Kerasun,

a line to be fixed on the ground, following the mam water-partings, leaving to Turkey the fields, pastures, forests, and Villages within the drainage basin of the Komit Dere (Ak Su) and its tributaries; and to Armenia the fields, pastures, forest, and villages within the drainage basins of the Yaghaj Dere (Espiya Dere) and the Venazit Dere (Keshab Dere) and their tributaries, and drawn in such a manner as to utilize the boundary between the Kazas of Tripoli (Tireholi) and Kerasun in the 7 kilometers just south of Kara Tepe (1,696 meters or 5,565 feet), and to provide the most convenient relationships between the new frontier and the trails along the ridges, as these relationships may be determined by the Boundary Commission in the field after consultation with the local inhabitants.

2. In case of any discrepancies between the text of this Decision and the maps on the scales of 1 ·1,000,000 and 1 ·200,000 annexed, the text will be final.

The limits of the four vilayets specified in Article 89 of the Treaty of Sevres are taken as of October 29, 1914

The frontier, as described above, JS drawn in red on an authenticated map on the scale of 1:1,000,000 which is annexed to the present Frontier Decision The geographical names here mentioned appear upon the maps accompanying this text,

The chief authorities used for the names of Geographical features, and of elevations of mountains, and the location of vilayet, sandjak, and kaza boundaries, are the Turkish General Staff map, scale 1 200,000, and, in part, the British map, scale 1:1,000,000.

The maps on the scale of 1 200,000 are recommended to the Boundary Commission, provided m Article 91, for their use in tracing on the spot the portion of the frontiers of Armenia established by this Decision.

II

The frontier described above by assigning the harbor of Trebizond and the valley of Karshut Su to Armenia, precludes the necessity of further provision for access for Armenia to the sea.

III

In addition to the general provisions for the hmitatlon of armaments, embodied in the Military, Naval and Air Clauses, Part V of the Treaty of Sevres, the demilitarization of Turkish territory adjacent to the frontier of Armenia as above established shall be effected as follows:

The Military Inter-Allied Commission of Control and Organization provided for in Articles 196-200 of the Treaty of Sevres shall appoint the superior officers of the gendarmerie stationed in those vilayets of Turkey lying contiguous to the frontiers of the state of Armenia exclusively from the officers to be supplied by the various Allied or neutral Powers according to Article 159 of the said Treaty.

These officers shall, in addition to their other duties, be especially charged with the task of observing and reporting to the Military Inter-Allied Commission of Control and Organization upon any tendencies within these Turkish vilayets toward military aggression against the Armenian frontier, such as building strategic railways and highways, the establishment of depots of military supplies, the creation of military colonies, and the use of propaganda dangerous to the peace and quiet of the adjacent Armenian territory. The Military Inter-Allied Commission of Control and Organization shall thereupon take such action as is necessary to prevent the concentrations and other aggressive activities enumerated above.

In testimony whereof I have hereunto set my hand and caused the seal of the United States to be affixed.

Done in duplicate at the city of Washington on the twenty-second day of November, one thousand nine hundred and twenty, and of
(SEAL) *the independence of the United States the one hundred and forty-fifth*

By the President:
WOODROW WILSON
BAINBRIDGE COLBY

Secretary of State In the end, as history has been written, the United States did not take the mandate for Armenia and this would eventually lead to Armenia loosing control over Wilsonian Armenia, the Armenian territories which today are occupied illegally by the country of Turkey.

The denial of the mandate was believed to be tied into foul play by the State Department. These charges against the State Department and two unnamed Cabinet officers were detailed at length but without complete documentation by Mr. Vahan Cardashian, attorney for the Delegation of the Armenian Republic, in an application for a Senate hearing and investigation. In his letter of March 24, 1928, to Senator Borah, Cardashian said if the Foreign Relations Committee failed to act favorably on his application he would request President Coolidge to present the American-Armenian dispute to The Hague Tribunal for adjudication. Cardashian's appeal follows in part:

> "My dear Senator Borah: I have the honour to apply for a hearing before the Senate Committee on Foreign Relations, upon the Lausanne Treaty, and to submit herewith a partial brief in support of this petition: "I charge that two members of the President's Cabinet bartered the Armenian case at the Lausanne Conference and conspired to effect the expulsion of nearly 1,000,000 Armenians from their ancestral homes, for a share in Mosul oil, and that they are now scheming to seize possession of the oil deposits in the deserted homes of their victims.

"I charge that these men and their confederates in this outrage have used and are now using the Department of State as their willing tool to carry out their infamous design; and that the Department of State, in an effort to cover up the tracks of those who have dictated its policy in this respect, has resorted to misrepresentation, intrigue and even terrorism, and has flooded the land with shameless and irresponsible propaganda.

...

"Under these clear circumstances, what, then, is the motive, the purpose behind the Turkish policy of the Department of State?

"I charge that it is oil.

"An Administration which has surrendered legitimate American rights and then has had the impudence to fill the air with irrelevancies, wild insinuations and falsehoods to divert attention from its disgraceful policy; an Administration which has deliberately trampled upon the Constitution of the United States in its conduct of foreign relations—such an Administration, I charge, would not hesitate, and has not hesitated, to sell out the Armenian people and their homes for oil, in the interest of a privileged group. ...

"If for any reason the Senate Committee on Foreign Relations should be unable and unwilling to consider these wrongs inflicted upon a gallant people, I shall then request the President of the United States to submit the points at issue between the present Administration and Armenia, to the Permanent Tribunal of Arbitration at The Hague, for adjudication."[85]

---

85 Washington United States Daily, April 11, 1928.

BOUNDARY BETWEEN TURKEY AND ARMENIA
AS DETERMINED BY
WOODROW WILSON, PRESIDENT OF THE UNITED STATES
OF AMERICA

Chapter 21

Joining the League of Nations

When it became clear that the United States was not going to take the mandate for Armenia, and the Turkish Nationalist Movement led by Mustafa Kemal and, remotely, by convicted war criminals Talaat, Jemal, Enver, were working towards continuing the genocide, Armenia applied for membership to the newly formed League of Nations. This membership was hoped to grant Armenia military support. The Armenian armed forces were clearly too small to defend the territory they had, nor was it enough to take control of the territories that were to be awarded to them by the proposed mandate of the U.S. President Woodrow Wilson.

The following is the application by the Armenian Republic for admission to the League of Nations.

LEAGUE OF NATIONS
APPLICATION BY THE ARMENIAN REPUBLIC FOR ADMISSION TO THE LEAGUE.
Memorandum by the Secretary- General.

1. On May 13th, 1920, M. Aharonian, President of the Delegation of the Armenian Republic at the Peace Conference in Paris, sent a telegraphic message to the President of the Council of the League of Nations, then meeting in Rome, asking to accept Armenia as a member of the League.

The Council, in its meeting of May 15th, 1920, referred this telegram for action to the Secretary-General.

The Secretary-General, in his reply dated May 13th, 1920, drew M. Aharonian's attention to the fact that only the Assembly is competent to admit as members of the League countries not mentioned in the annex to the Covenant.

It was added that probably the Armenian Government would be desirous of making an official request which would be distributed to the members of the Assembly before its first meeting.

On September 25th M. Aharonian, in accordance with instructions received from his Government, addressed a Note to the President of the League of Nations. In this Note it was requested to admit Armenia as a member of the League, a copy of this Note, which was duly distributed to the Members of the League and to the

Members of the Council, is annexed to this document.

(Annex 1.)

2. On October 9th, 1920, the Secretary-General addressed a letter to the Armenian Government asking them to send authenticated copies of any acts by which Armenia might have been recognised *de facto* or *de jure* by other Powers.

On October 18th, 1920, M. Aharonian replied to this request while sending authentic copies of documents bearing on the recognition of Armenia by certain other States, he drew the Secretary-General's attention to the fact that the most solemn act in connection with the recognition of Armenia by the Allied Powers is the Treaty of Peace between these Powers and Turkey, signed at Sèvres on August 10th, 1920. In the preamble to this treaty Armenia is mentioned as one of the Allied Powers.

It seems, therefrom, that Armenia has been recognised de jure by the other Allied Powers, viz., the British Empire, France, Italy, Japan, Belgium, Greece, Hedjaz, Poland, Portugal, Roumania, the Serb-Croate-Slovene State and Czecho-Slovakia. Besides, the Treaty signed at Sèvres on August 10th, 1920, between the Principal Allied Powers and Armenia in execution of Article 93 of the Treaty of Peace with Turkey (see Annex 2 to this Memorandum) states explicitly that Armenia has been recognised as a sovereign and independent State by the Principal Allied Powers (see for the text of this treaty Annex 3 to this Memorandum).

In Article 88 of the Peace Treaty of Sèvres, Turkey declares to recognize Armenia as a free and independent State, in accordance with the action already taken by the Allied Powers. The Section of the Treaty of Sèvres dealing with Armenia is annexed to the present Memorandum (Annex 2).

According to further information received from the Armenian Government, Armenia was recognised as a free and independent State by the Government of the Argentine Repnblic. This had already been notified to the Secretary General by M. Pueyrredon, Minister for Foreign Affairs of the Argentine Republic, in a telegram dated May 6th, 1920.

According to information which has reached the Secretariat unofficially, the Government of the United States of America have given recognition to the independence of Armenia.

At the Secretary General's request, M. Aharonian also sent an authenticated copy of Armenia's declaration of independence. The text of this document is annexed to the present Memorandum (Annex 3).

3. On March 12th, 1920, the Supreme Council of the Principal

Allied Powers enquired of the Council of the League of Nations as to whether they would be prepared to accept, on behalf of the League of Nations, the protection of the future independent State of Armenia.

On April 11th the Council of the League of Nations replied that it was of opinion that the constitution of a State of Armenia upon a free, secure and independent basis was an object which will receive, and which will deserve to receive, the sympathy and support of enlightened opinion throughout the civilised world.

They were of opinion that the best means to this end would be the acceptance of a Mandate for Armenia by a civilised State under the League of Nations, which solution, it was understood, would be welcome to the Armenians. The acceptance of such a responsibility would depend partly on the military measures which might be devised to liberate the territory and to protect the frontiers of the new State and partly on Finance.

The Council did not consider that the military situation of Armenia fell within its province.

With respect to Finance, it was of opinion that if a Mandatory State were relieved of financial liability such a State could probably be found by the League of Nations.

On April 26th the Supreme Council replied to the Council of the League of Nations that on April 25th they had appealed to President Wilson asking that the U.S.A. should accept a Mandate for Armenia and also that in any case the President of the United States should arbitrate on the boundaries of Armenia.

On May 31st, 1920, the Senate of the United States of America refused to accept a Mandate for Armenia. President Wilson accepted the post of Arbitrator of the frontiers of Armenia.

On September 20th, 1920, the Council of the League of Nations enquired of the Supreme Council whether it desired the question of Armenia to be submitted to the Assembly on November 15th, 1920, especially as regards the suggested financial guarantees.

In October, 1920, the Council of the League of Nations received appeals from the Armenian Government complaining of acts of aggression on the part of Turkish Nationalists and asking for the intervention of the League to ensure respect for the Treaty of Sèvres.

The Council in reply informed the Armenian Government that it was the duty of the Signatory Powers to the Treaty to secure its execution and promised to urge them to give Armenia all assistance possible.

In their communication to those of the Signatory Powers who are represented on the Supreme Council (France, Great Britain, Italy and Japan) on October 22nd, 1920, the Council reminded the four

Powers of the previous correspondence on the subject of Armenia and added that they would be glad if the frontiers of Armenia could be drawn without delay in view of the fact that the Armenian question might be discussed at the Assembly upon the occasion of the request for admission presented by Armenia.

As already stated, a treaty was signed at Sèvres on August 10th, 1920, by the Principal Allied Powers and Armenia, in execution of Article 93 of the Treaty of Peace with Turkey, In this treaty Armenia has agreed to certain provisions deemed necessary by the Principal Allied Powers to protect the interests of inhabitants of that State who differ from the majority of the population in race, language or religion. In addition to these provisions, and in accordance with Article 93 of the Peace Treaty with Turkey, there have been embodied in the treaty here under consideration provisions deemed necessary by the Principal Allied Powers to protect freedom of transit and equitable treatment for the commerce of other nations. The text of this treaty is annexed to the present Memorandum (Annex 3).

Article 1 of the Covenant of the League of Nations provides:—

"Any fully self-governing State, Dominion or Colony not named in the Annex may become a Member of the League if its admission is agreed to by two-thirds of the Assembly, provided that it shall-give effective guarantees of its sincere intention to observe its international obligations, and shall accept such regulations as may be prescribed by the League in regard to its military, naval and air forces, and armaments."

In this connection it may be recalled that when Armenia applied for membership of the League she declared "to accept the regulations established by the League of Nations" (Annex 1).

It may be also stated that the Permanent Advisory Commission for Military, Naval and Air questions has considered and drafted regulations in accordance with Article 1 of the Covenant, in regard to the military, naval and air forces and armaments of the Armenian Republic.

In their report to the Council on this subject the Commission stated that it had received from Armenia the following information regarding her army and navy:—

Army.—The military forces of this country consist at present of about 35,000 men.

The political and geographical situation of Armenia is such that its Government is unable to submit proposals relating to the future military status of the country. The Commission pronounced itself in favour of Armenia being allowed to keep her present military forces in view of the situation of the moment.

Navy.—As, at the present time, Armenia has no coastal frontiers it does not possess a navy.

As regard Armenia's aerial forces the Commission received the following information:—

"At the present time Armenia possesses five aeroplanes and repeats for her aerial forces the same considerations as she puts forward in the matter of her military forces in regard of possible demands at a later date."

The Commission also recommended that the proposed armaments should only be considered as having a provisional character and that, among other countries seeking admission, Armenia should agree to submit herself to a revision of the armaments, which, in the opinion of the Commission, can now be granted to her if this would be found necessary at a later date. The Commission suggested that a request for revision might be made by Armenia herself; it would have to be accompanied by a statement of the new conditions, on which the request would be based.

The report of the Commission has formed the subject of a resolution of the Council, placed before the Assembly.

In a letter dated October 18th, 1920, the Secretary-General suggested to the Armenian Government that the Assembly might wish to hear explanations regarding questions in connection with Armenia's application for admission to the League of Nations, and that in view thereof it might be desirable for the Armenian Government to send a representative to Geneva, when the Assembly would be meeting, or to give its agent in some capital the necessary instructions.

On October 24th, 1920, Avetis Aharonian, the head of the Armenian Delegation at the Paris Peace Conference, informed the Secretary-General that he would represent Armenia for the said purposes in Geneva.

Sadly, the internationally recognized Armenian Government, under attack on all fronts, was forced to surrender the remainder of its territories to the Red Army of the Bolshevik Russia, on December 2, 1920. And Armenia never joined the League of Nations that might offer the protection she needed and save her independece.

ANNEX 1.
LETTER FEOM THE PRESIDENT OF THE DELEGATION
OF THE ARMENIAN REPUBLIC.

27, Avenue Marceau,

Paris.

September 25th, 1920.

Ey. Docs. 7094/4395/4395

Sir,

In view of the signature of the Treaty of Sevres, finally formulating the recognition of the independence of the Armenian Republic by the Allied Powers, I have the honour, in accordance with instructions which I have just received from my Government, to apply for the admission of the Armenian State to the League of Nations.

Armenia declares that she accepts the régime established by the League of Nations.

I have the honour to be. Sir,

Your obedient servant,

(*Signed*) A. AHARINIAN,

President of the Delegation of the

Armenian republic to the Peace

Conference.

His Excellency, the President
 of the League of nations.

ANNEX 2.
PEACE TEEATY BETWEEN THE ALLIED AND ASSOCIATED POWEES AND TUEKEY, SIGNED AT SEVEES ON AUGUST 10th, 1920.

SECTION VI.

AEMENIA.

Article 88.

Turkey, in accordance with the action already taken by the Allied Powers, hereby recognises Armenia as a free and independent State.

Article 89.

Turkey and Armenia, as well as the other High Contracting Parties, agree to submit to the arbitration of the President of the United States of America the question of the frontier to be fixed between Turkey and Armenia in the Vilayets of Erzerum, Trebizond, Van and Bitlis, and to accept his decision thereupon, as well as any stipulations he may prescribe as to access for Armenia to the sea, and as to the demilitarisation of any portion of Turkish territory adjacent to the said frontier.

Article 90.

In the event of the determination of the frontier under Article 89 involving the transfer of the whole or any part of the territory of the said Vilayets to Armenia Turkey hereby renounces as from the date of such decision all rights and title over the territory so transferred. The provisions of the present Treaty applicable to territory detached from Turkey shall thereupon become applicable to the said territory.

The proportion and nature of the financial obligations of Turkey which Armenia will have to assume, or of the rights which will pass to her on account of the transfer of the said territory, will be determined in accordance with Articles 241 to 244, Part VIII (Financial Clauses) of the present Treaty.

Article 91.

In the event of any portion of the territory referred to in Article 89 being transferred to Armenia, a Boundary Commission, whose composition will be determined subsequently, will be constituted within three months from the delivery of the decision referred to in the said Article to trace on the spot the frontier between Armenia and Turkey as established by such decision.

Article 92.

The frontiers between Armenia and Azerbaijan and Georgia respectively will be determined by direct agreement between the States concerned.

If in either case the States concerned have failed to determine the frontier by agreement at the date of the decision referred to in Article 89, the frontier line in question will be determined by the Principal Allied Powers, who will also provide for its being traced on the spot.

Article 93.

Armenia accepts and agrees to embody in a Treaty with the Principal Allied Powers such provisions as may be deemed necessary by these Powers to protect the interests of inhabitants of that State who differ from the majority of the population in race, language or religion.

Armenia further accepts and agrees to embody in a Treaty with the Principal Allied Powers such provisions as these Powers may deem necessary to protect freedom of transit and equitable treatment for the commerce of other nations.

Translation:

ANNEX 3.

DECLARATION OF INDEPENDENCE OF UNITED AEMENIA,

MAY 28th, 1919.

In order to reconstitute Armenia in its entirety, and to assure the complete liberty and prosperity of the Armenian people, the Government of Armenia, faithfully interpreting the unanimous will of the Armenian people and of the desire it has expressed, hereby declares that, from to-day the different parts of Armenia, hitherto separated, are reunited for ever in one unified Independent State.

Exactly a year ago the National Armenian Council elected by the Conference of the Armenians of Russia, proclaimed itself the supreme power in the Armenian provinces of Transcaucasia. The Government created by the National Armenian Council after officially notifying this proclamation to the representatives of the Powers, has, during the last year, established its *de facto* power in the Armenian provinces of Transcaucasia.

The second Congress of the Armenians of Turkish Armenia, which met at Erivan in February, 1919, solemnly proclaimed that it recognised United and Independent Armenia alone.

To-day, in proclaiming the independence and unification of the Armenian territories of Transcaucasia and of the Ottoman Empire, the Armenian Government declares the form of Government of the unified State to be a democratic republic, and, moreover, it proclaims itself to be the Government of the United Armenian Republic.

Thus, the Armenian people is to-day supreme master of its reconstituted Fatherland, and the Parliament and the Government of Armenia are the legislative and executive power of the free and sovereign people.

The Armenian Government makes this proclamation by virtue of the resolution of Parliament of April 2nd, 1919, which conferred a special mandate upon it.

(Signed) AL. KHADISSIAN,

The Prime Minister and Minister for Foreign Affairs.

M. MANASSIAN,
Minister of the Interior.

GENEEAL K. AEAEATIAN,
Minister for War.

H. TCHIMICHKIAN,
Minister of Justice.

K. MELIK KAEAGUEUZIAN,
Minister of Education.

S. TOEOSSIAN,
Minister of Public Assistance.

K. VEEMICHIAN,
Minister of Food.

K. DJAKHETIAN,
Minister of Finance.

K. KHADISSIAN,
Chief Secretary to the Prime Minister.

Erivan, *May 28th*, 1919.

DOCUMENTS RELATING TO, OR CONNECTED WITH, THE REQUEST

FOR ADMISSION AS A MEMBER OF THE LEAGUE, MADE

BY THE ARMENIAN REPUBLIC.

These original documents, the first of which is reprinted as an annex to the present Memorandum, are available for inspection by delegates to the Assembly on application to the Secretariat.

1. First request for admission. (Telegram of the President of the Delegation of the Republic of Armenia at Paris, dated May 13th, 1920).
2. Telegraphic reply by the Secretary-General, dated May 13th, 1920.
3. Armenia's formal application for membership, dated September 25th, 1920. Printed as Annex 1 to this document.
4. Acknowledgment of receipt of this application.
5. Enquiry, dated March 12th, 1920, by the Supreme Council of the Principal Allied Powers addressed to the Council of the League of Nations as to whether they would be prepared to accept, on behalf of the League of Nations, the protection of Armenia.
6. Reply dated April 11th, 1920, from the Council of the League of Nations to the Supreme Council.

7. Resolution adopted by the Council of the League of Nations, in Paris on September 19th, 1920, instructing the Secretary-General to enquire from the Supreme Council whether it is desired that any of the proposals in the Memorandum to the Supreme Council and particularly that relative to the financial guarantee to be given to Armenia by the Members of the League, should be submitted for the consideration of the Assembly.

8. Reply of the Japanese Government, dated October 14th, 1920, stating that, if the other Great Powers see no objection, the Japanese Government agrees that the contents of the Note addressed by the Council of the League of Nations to the Supreme Council on April 11th be laid before the Assembly.

9. Reply of the Italian Government, dated October 12th, 1920, to the Council's inquiry dated September 19th, 1920, stating that M. Giolitti sees no objection to the Council's Note of April 11th being laid before the Assembly, but that the Italian Government has decided not to undertake any financial obligation besides those arising out of existing treaties.

10. First appeal from the Armenian Government, dated October 6th, 1920, for assistance against aggression from the side of Kemalist forces.

11. Second appeal from the Armenian Government dated October 12th, in the same matter.

12. Third appeal from the Armenian Government dated October 21st in the same matter.

13. Report by the Council on these appeals dated October 27th, 1920, and letters addressed to the Governments of States represented on the Supreme Council in pursuance to this Report, suggesting that the States signatories to the Treaty of Sèvres should give assistance to Armenia against her enemies and request from these States to continue, in collaboration with the Council of the Society and the Supreme Council, to examine the question of the protection of Armenia. This report declared equally that the Council would be happy to see the determination of Armenian boundaries without delay. Response to Armenian appeals.

14. Telegram from the Government of the Argentine Republic, dated 7 May 1920, announcing the recognition of Armenia as a free and independent State.

15. Accusation of reception of this telegram.

16. Letter from the Secretary General to the Prime Minister of Armenia, dated 9 October 1920, requesting:

1) Certified copy confirming the pieces by which Armenia has proclaimed her independence or by which full or total autonomy has been accorded to her, as well as all subsequent written communications.

2) Certified copy confirming declarations by which other Governments have recognized the Government of Armenia as a Government of fact or right.

17. Reply of M. Aharonian, President of the Armenian Delegation to the Peace Conference, containing copies of:

17) Declaration of independence of United Armenia.

18) Letter of the Peace Conference declaring the recognition of the act of the Armenian Government by France, Great-Britain, and Italy.

19) Letter of the Peace Conference declaring the recognition of the act of the Armenian Government by Japan.

20) Letter of the Peace Conference declaring the recognition of the act of the Armenian Government by the United States of America.

21) Extract of the Treaty of Sèvres recognizing the independence of Armenia.

22) Letter of His Eminence M. Hymans, declaring official recognition of the Republic of Armenia by the Belgian Government.

23) Letter of His Eminence M. Romanos, Minister of Greece in Paris, declaring the agreement of His Majesty the King of Greece for the appointment of an Extraordinary Envoy and Plenipotentiary Minister to the Armenian Republic in Athens.

24) Letter of His Eminence M. Leygues, authorizing the creation in Paris of a Consulate General of the Republic of Armenia.

25) Telegram of the representative of the Republic of Armenia at Rio de Janeiro, as part of the recognition of the Government of Armenia by Brazil.

OVERWEIGHTED.

President Wilson. "HERE'S YOUR OLIVE BRANCH. NOW GET BUSY."

Dove of Peace. "OF COURSE I WANT TO PLEASE EVERYBODY; BUT ISN'T THIS A BIT THICK?"

(Punch [magazine], London, U.K., Volume 156, 26 March 1919, p. 243)

Chapter 22

Operation Nemesis

After the Armenian Revolutionary Federation (ARF) Supreme Body refused to sanction the plan to carry out the capital punishment, to which the Young Turk leaders had been sentenced by the Turkish military tribunal in 1918, a secret group was formed in New England. Initially only three people were to know about the group's plan with the exception of those deemed capable of fulfilling the mission. These exceptions would be given only limited information. Sometimes they were misinformation if it was believed necessary, in order to get their assistance or financial support.

The primary organizers of the operation were Armen Garo, Arron Sachaklian, and Shahan Natalie, a.k.a. Nemesis. Armen Garo, Diplomatic Representative of Armenia to the United States, had been a Member of Parliament in the Ottoman Empire and had interacted with Talaat. Although Talaat had to be punished for what he had done to the Armenians, it appears that Armen Garo felt betrayed and had a personal score to settle with Talaat, which is more evident in the chapters to follow; Arron Sachaklian, a CPA and trusted friend of my grandfather's from their days they worked together on the newspaper, *Hayrenik*. Sachaklian's role was to manage the funds for the operation. My grandfather used Sachaklian also as a sort of archival depository,

Armen Garo (holding a fan) and Shahan Natalie - 1920

whom he frequently wrote, reporting his findings, as well as requesting needed funds.

Below are some excerpts from Shahan Natalie's notes on searching for Talaat.

> Talaat was in Berlin. We knew it.
>
> And Berlin, in the past, for a short period had been simply a center for the Revolutionary Student Association. And in 1920, except for a few individual students and some former ARF party members, there was no other political affiliation. It is true, there was an Armenian ghetto in those days. But it represented a part of that migratory Armenian population, who were seeking an affordable place to be able to eke out a living. And living in Germany at the time represented the most affordable place.
>
> America knew that the approved decision was sentenced to remain in words, if it did not take the task of implementing it in hand. And overlooking any formality whatsoever, it considered Germany as falling within its sphere.

On August 27, 1920, a sunny mid-day, from New York Harbor, my 35-year-old grandfather took his leave sailing East to embark on the difficult task of searching for a criminal convicted for his crimes against humanity, who had undergone plastic surgery to defy any detection.

Shahan had only heard that Talaat was in Berlin. And he had decided to confirm that report and deliver judgment with his own hand.

Fine-tuning his plans and with strong emotions, he crossed the Atlantic and, nine days later, was already in Paris, where he would determine his course of actions.

A known revolutionary in Berlin, Haig Der Ohanian, had been recommended to him.

On September 4, 1920, he arrived in Paris, where he decided to go to Geneva. Ten days later, he set out from Paris toward the shores of Leman, the historic city of revolutionary missions.

Shahan met Haig by chance in Paris – where he had come for personal business. He told his plan, and Haig promised to assist him in all his capabilities.

Shahan asked him to immediately go to Berlin, where Talaat was to be found, according to a received report. Shahan himself was going there from Geneva. Here, Shahan succeeded in securing a one-month visa to go to Germany by exception, because after the war the German government would only grant seven-day permission to foreigners to enter and live in Germany.

Haig was going to inform Geneva about his entering Berlin; and he kept Shahan waiting. Finally, having lost all hope, Shahan entered Berlin, on October 8.

Shahan's first two to three weeks in Berlin pass by waiting, because Haig didn't appear. Shahan wrote in his memoirs: "I cannot open my heart to anyone; I wander from café to café; I reconnoiter the streets; I search for traces; but for naught, because I am unfamiliar with the city and with the language. And my only acquaintance, who was going to help me, is in Paris."

In addition to these concerns, his frustration was growing as his stay was approaching its deadline. He was being consumed with rage every night, in his solitude.

And, finally, Haig arrives.

"I am embittered in a terrifying manner; I want to slap him. The realization of responsibility restrains my hand," Shahan writes.

"He smiles and in that smile I see the cynicism of mocking me and the task. I gnash my teeth and swallow a curse at him, who had recommended this character to me."

"But what's the use? I am a suppressed beast only, on whom they can easily laugh."

Haig doesn't show up for another week. He is a student—"a perennial student" – and he makes the excuse that he is obliged to go through the process of registering for university.

Shahan waits one more week.

His permission to stay in Berlin has already expired.

Finally, one day Haig deigns to make time for Shahan and talk with him. He suggests informing the other three revolutionaries in Berlin about the mission – Libarid, Vahan Zakariants, Hagop Zorian – and to have a consultation with them.

Shahan scheduled a consultation; He presented his plan and asked them to contribute to the cause to the extent possible. They all promised to help as much as they could. They also promised to help Shahan remain in Berlin. They recommended that Shahan stay in a hotel, where the police would not care to show up.

Based on this consultation and his brief familiarity over the previous days, Shahan concluded that Haig was someone who viewed the work as an opportunity to reap financial benefits. To succeed in his quest, Haig relied on Shahan's unfamiliarity with the place and the language. Shahan described the new recruits in his memoirs:

> "Libarid is that one from whom I can expect no benefit; sickly, distracted and nervous, who, even if he wanted, is of no use. The nature of his work in any case is far from corresponding to his distracted condition.
>
> Vahan is experienced in revolutionary activities, clever, knowledgeable about the place and language, but burdened with his business dealings, he promises me very little, on that premise that he promises little and strives to work little, so that I will be precisely aware of the reality of my strength.
>
> Zorian, a young student, although inexperienced but enthusiastic, yet a student with someone else's funding, he can barely promise me any great thing, contrary to all his willingness.
>
> Let's not forget that Haig is also a student, *"so called."*
>
> Fortunately, I had anticipated all of this until my corresponding from Geneva to America to send me Soghomon."

Before Soghomon's arrival in December, surveillance was conducted. Working with unwilling recruits who didn't put their heart in the mission was an impending train wreck. Very often the team members didn't show up to their assigned stations and, when Shahan was out of the country for two weeks to attend to work and renew his visa, no one showed up.

In January 1921, my grandfather learned that the Turks were holding a conference in Rome. The whereabouts of Talaat were still unknown then. My grandfather had hoped that he could learn of what Talaat looked like if he skied on the conference. If he happened to find Talaat in Rome and positively identified him, he was prepared to kill him himself.

The following is a transcript from the 1971 recording of Shahan telling what transpired. My father Khachig asked him questions:

SHAHAN: Now ... Now you know that Talaat is thus as we tell it. But how did we get to know Talaat?

Now I am going to Rome, because I feel that there are those coming from Malta, and that there is a conference there.

So, I must immediately go to Rome. Perhaps, there in Rome, fortune will allow me to have the opportunity to recognize the man. Because, as I said, after recognizing the man, there was nothing else because when you recognize him to some extent and you are certain it is Talaat, when you hit him, whether by day, by night, inside a store, next to a police officer, or in front of the police station ... wherever it may be, you must shoot and hit him. And you must hit him directly in the brain, so that you don't just injure him. And you must stand there so they come and arrest you. And for me, the only thing remaining that I am that man who knows he will be arrested. Should he flee, they won't even beat him. They arrest him, and take him. But even if he flees, so that they beat him for the benefit of the other. Do you understand?

And at that time I am also going from one consulate to the other, three or four consulates ... past which the train passes, you see, to go to Rome, I am after those visas. Now look ... I have always said, God's finger was in this – it was God himself leading us – in that task, you know? Because it was a Godly task that was being performed, we were persisting. I went to all the consulates to secure the visas.

He is in Berlin ... Now I am going to Italy. In order to go to Italy, I must pass through several countries. I am going with that thought that he is probably there, perhaps in a hotel lobby ... and there ... I cannot know which one is that so-called Talaat ... It is recognizing the man ... That is the most important thing. And I have secured all the visas. One visa is left, that I will secure. And there it is at three-thirty, or four, that they closed the consulates. If you succeeded in securing the visa, you have it.

And I, in Berlin, have acquaintance with a very old colleague. He knows all of Berlin. I took him with me by taxi from one end to another of the city where there is a consulate. I took him, and the last consulate where we went, and went in ... there is an office worker, who slammed the door shut ... as scheduled minute-to-minute.

Now the boy who is with me knows German very well, et cetera. He is very linguistic, a well-versed son of a dog. He is a Persian Armenian. And he was the only one still alive, in Berlin. The last time I went to Berlin, together with him, and I was there for a week in Berlin. I came from Berlin here.

KHACHIG: "Did you go there, in that place where he killed him?"

SHAHAN: Of course ... But in Berlin, all those places are so changed that, those places were exactly in ruins during the war ...

KHACHIG: The Second World War ...

SHAHAN: Yes ... They have rebuilt it now ... Berlin did not look like Berlin. America! High rises like America ... and

KHACHIG: What did the man do to you ... when he slammed the door?

SHAHAN: Now that boy talked everywhere so that the official would be convinced.

My soul is exhausted because of having to go immediately ... this door is also sealed. Therefore, tomorrow morning we must go to secure a visa. And when we go tomorrow morning, I get my visa, as arranged ... so you see, it becomes a two-day thing ... a delay ... But can you see it had to be so ... Although I absolutely did not recognize him ...

KHACHIG: What do you mean? ... So, you didn't get your visa? ... The door was closed ...

SHAHAN: It's over! The door is closed ... now therefore, I can't go the next day either ... I'm going to secure a visa the following day ... The train will already have left when they open the office. And the day after that, in the morning of the next day, I am going to get the visa ... That's the morning after that that I must take the train. Did you understand?

We went ... I secured the visa. Now, on the morning when I am going to leave ... I will be going to Rome. There, in the morning, now Solomon, that boy who was with me, and two other boys, who also were available for me for that kind of thing ... for certain tasks, I use those boys, like the Trabizon boy ... then, four of them are with me with me: Solomon, Zakar, Haig, Hagop.

With those four we take the taxi together, and we go to the railroad station. We go to the station, when we get there and go into the station, to the train which is waiting, as I said, some forty-five minutes before departure. We have to be sure, that, we cannot be late, you know ...

That's how we are. The train is waiting and next to that waiting train is a group of people ... a group that appears to be travelers on that thing. They are going, they are going there also ... But among them is that Trabizon Vali, whom you already recognize when you see him. The first Turk that I became acquainted with in Berlin was he. With a red beard – I think he used *henna* too. A typical Turk pasha, short of stature, toddling steps ... They are Turks. I already saw his face ... so if that man is there ... That is a group of Turks standing there, that group is behind ... So, that man's presence made me more cautious.

I said, now we will separate from each other. I will enter the *wagon*. I will go there. I already have my ticket. You, close by, as much as possible, so that their attention isn't piqued, as if blockaded, you know, and you watch those people. Because it is obvious, they are official. Jemal Pasha has come there. So, who is it that is going? It occurs to me that perhaps all of them ... so that is a good thing. They are going to Berlin [Rome] too. A good thing has happened. They will lead me so that I will be able, with ease, to go to whichever hotel they are going.

And I went. You look carefully at the faces. But specifically the faces. I will go up. The train is such that it is like a sleeping car. And those European sleeping cars have walking space. So that is the place from which I am watching, directly above his head. Because they are standing there and it is there, right in the sleeping car where is my compartment, and I have space. I have a seat. I am traveling second class, they are six people, three of them in second class, and upstairs I am in a coupée.

And ... I went, I boarded. Now, be careful, look at the faces, because it is from that place that we will have direction, as to which one, or what, etcetera. And I also watch from above. Now, in that group there is a group, of which three people are very eye-catching ... extremely. That's what it is, as soon as you see them, you say *they are somebody*. That one with the red beard is Jemal Pasha. You know that that one has been captured from the forest. And if you don't notice, the other two are more privileged, like fine Europeans ... He has boarded, and someone sees him, he will say that this one ... is a man ... there is something within him. Those two are there and around them four-five young ones, when I say young, I don't mean 15 to 20 years old. More like 30 years old, etcetera. The Turks want them.

Those also, then, have a traveler among them, for him, as I have my four boys, but who is the one to go close, we don't know. I boarded the *wagon*, and opened the window ... it comes down, right? ... And I am standing there ... and in no way so there will not be any doubt that those who are standing down below belong to me. ...

From that place, from above I watch them, and their faces. And because I have the pictures ... there are people who are of interest as Talaat. Which one looks like him? Is Talaat here ... The boys are watching also, and he comes, to board the train. The bell rings, the train gets underway. He is kissed, and three of them climb aboard, into the *wagon*. One of them, that eye-catching one, you know, is one of those characters. I later confirmed that ... later I confirmed it from the photographs. The *Bolis* chief of police, who handcuffed those intellectuals – *Bedri Bey* ... On that night, he was the *Bolis* chief of police, *Bedri Bey*, very well-known, blood-sucking, he was Talaat's cabinet thing ...

And ... That one, the eye-catching on, another 30-35 speakers ... one of them. The third one looked like a Jew, small, with short hair, chubby ... more so, he looked like a Jew ... slithering around everywhere ... Apparently that was his thin, from a spying point of view, that man you know, protecting *Bedri,* and his things ... because *Bedri* is also an eye-catching prominent person. Those three went up. I remained below. The time came. Good-bye ... They kissed each other, and so on. And ... The train went on its way.

And just to the right of the *coupée* window, is my place, next to me a German, three people, are on one side … We are face to face. On my side, then, three people, and those three are right across for me. They are sitting right across from me, in that *coupée*. I don't know who they are, you know. It is not Talaat. That is clear. They are not Talaat. But they are three Turks. So, they are going to Berlin, I surmise, since … it is a Berlin train… They are going to Berlin … I mean to say, Rome … So, those people can become leaders. You see, after whatever hotel they go, I will go to that hotel. I make plans for myself.

And … that notable face – *Bedri*– is sitting in the middle, that very … thing … talkative, that bluff talker, is sitting right across from me. On the other side also is *Bedri*, that other lizard, that creep … He is a hole-dweller type. … He irked me … so self-centered he was … pretentious … this one is a Jew, you know, more Jewish by his looks … jackass! … a moneyed English jackass. I have heard those adjectives a lot … that … that place also, where I would go … In that place where the Turks are … Because I have mingled inside Turkish circles … Thanks to that thing that they have not known I am Armenian. Yes, I repeat that situation so nobody will think that I am Armenian. I am everything, but I am not Armenian … Do you get it? …

And so … We went on, reach Milan … We alighted, to rest for a while, but the train is going to continue … in Milan, that little phony, you know, the Jewish character, and that notable man, disappeared. The other one remained. The one who was sitting directly across from me. Then … a short while later, I saw that from Milan to Berlin, by way of Trieste, past Engür, and from Engür they have gone to Enveri … Because Enver in Bokhara has already taken the Bokhara army … Et cetera, they were going there. Do you understand? But I don't know where he was killed … during battle … or by whom? … I don't have any information about his demise …

And … the train left that place … Now only that one was across from me … We are going … in the same manner … so that they will always think, well, I am either English or American …, those two are in doubt, partially that I am either wealthy, or American, or a man of the hill, and that way, he is going on…. Now, when we approached Rome, we are going into the Rome train station … Before that, where are they going to put this man … I still want to know, because this one boarded from Berlin, it is obvious. … He talks more than a little, giving himself value … you know, how half-directors give themselves more credit … He is one of those … This one, undoubtedly, is going some place, I said, someplace, a hotel, where those people will be gathered … since a conference …

And when we approached, I said, English … do you know English? I asked … *No*, he said … Do you know French? … mmmmm … I said, have you been to Rome? … *Yes!* … I said, It is my first time that I am going to Rome … let me ask you a question, which hotel do you frequent … so, where is it possible for me to go … And so, asking questions, I understood where he was going … I am going to such and such a hotel … Thank you very much, I said, because it is the very first time I am going and I don't know which hotel I should go to. Truly, I have not been … that was not a

Mikayel Varantian (1870-1934)

lie ...

When it stopped, I immediately went down and gave the name of the hotel to the taxi driver ... where the man is going to go ... the taxi drove there. It is a small hotel there ... that place wasn't spacious ... and it turned out that when I went into that hotel, in fact, it had a small lobby ... There are Turks there, and they are speaking Turkish ... This place doesn't look like a conference hotel ... By my estimation ... it turned out that that is the hotel in which they have room ... Varantian ... The ambassador of our days for the Republic of Armenia ... **Mikayel Varantian** ... That is the hotel ...

I went up to him ... I said, you are finished ... There, I said, do the Turks have a meeting? ... Tomorrow, I said, what is going on? I said, tomorrow ... In the hotel, they were speaking Turkish ... *Nothing!* ... He gave the impression that *he didn't have a clue* ... I want a hotel, I want a room in a hotel ... And at that time the Parliament had convened, and the hotels ... well, that conference thing, etcetera ... And the hotels ... no room ... I will be left on the street ... like that ...

Let me have a room, I said ... for a few days ... How is it possible? ... If there were one of the university students there ... students? ... they could possibly be using or can do something ... he did something ... he was a fine young man ... a Tashnak boy too ... **Mikayel Varantian**, from Armenia, correct? Khanamirian ... I took the boy by taxi. There I asked that place, in that hotel may I have a room ... NONE AVAILABLE! ... We must have gone to at least ten hotels ... TEN HOTELS! ... NO VACANCY ... They are all booked ...

The most famous hotel, *Excelsior Hotel* ... in Rome ... It had the largest place ... for meetings ... I went inside ... When they said there's no space, I started to yell... *What is the matter with you!* ... *Do you think I am going to be in the street?* ... I said, I am an American newspaper *Correspondent Journalist* ... In those days, I said a *Journalist* ... And now he repeated, a newspaper *journalist* ... They *wagon* them ... Already, spies follow him ... whichever office building you enter ... with a salute ... and especially let an American *journalist* be out on the street ... I said, I want a room ... And I will not leave!!! ...

I said, there's nothing to it at all, so they insist ... the thing is, when you get up ... you go through ... you shit there ... put something there ... I have come so far. I'm exhausted, really ... and the man can see that ... you know in my words still ... arrange it! If there's nothing like a 50-60 person conference hall ... He had a bed put in there. And I, in that room, went to bed ... I washed in the washroom ... And I have gotten up there ... put my satchel down ... and washed myself ... cleaned myself up ... rubbed a few things on my face to cool down ... I am tired ... I went down to the lobby right away. Because I saw that, this hotel is going to be a conference hotel. ... I went down, down there ...

So it was that the director ... the man explains that all rooms are taken ... There are outside conferences, things ... the rooms are full ... you are going to give them free ... where are you from? ... Armenian ... don't you have a hall? ... You schedule conferences, don't you? ... In there, I said, why don't you put a bed, a cot ... and I will sleep on it ... I WON'T GO!!! ... I will stay here!!! ... And the man, right away, said *okay, okay* ... And he arranged it. They have 50-60 person conference halls for such events ...

I went down to the lobby to see what there is from above ... I move my eyes around and about ... Next to some ... Whichever group ... I saw that they were standing up ... These are talking ... I look at their eyes ... They are Turks ... A little later, I saw that these are gradually dissipating. It became obvious that they have ended the conference ... and now the conference is over and now instead they are going to the flim-flam event ... That much for the plan ... Okay ...

But in those days, every day slips by ... I yet I cannot grab the real thing ... I can't ... I am so nervous ... I have such a spiritual issue ... I have heart palpitations ... It is overwhelming my entire life ... There is no sleep at night ... I am in such a state ... And one or two days later ... At least, I don't have anything ... My role as a prisoner, over Switzerland ... I went to Geneva ... Soghomon was there, in Geneva ...

Although Shahan didn't find Talaat in Rome, his discovery of the Armenian Ambassador Mikayel Varantian gave him a clue as to why the Armenian government led by the ARF was not interested in killing Talaat. As they stated at the 9th General Assembly in 1919, they were now a legitimate government, and the atrocities had been the price they had to pay for independence. However, the "legitimate" Armenian government was engaged in deals with the very Turks that continued massacring the Armenians. Finishing Talaat would impede their secret agenda and deals.

During my research I came across British secret reports that documented what happened in Rome. Shahan came, unfortunately, too late to see for himself.

E. 1809
FEB 10 1921
PARAPHRASE.   S E C R E T
From: War Office.
To: G.H.W. Constantinople.

Desp. 1730 7.2.21

87791 cipher M.I.2.

Reference report of Talaat's return to Germany given in Ambassador Rome's telegram No. 28 (D) dated 26th. A report from Geneva dated 31st January states Talaat believed to have left Rome on 11th or 12th January but it was uncertain whether destination was Anatolia or not.

10th FEB 1921

Movements of Talaat Pasha.

Copy of telegram dated 7th February to General Harington referring to Rome Telegram 28 of Jan.26th (E1243/1/44) and stating that according to a report from Geneva, Talaat is believed to have left Rome on January 11th or Jan.12th but it is uncertain whether destination was Anatolia or not.

No. 218.

Berlin,

February 8, 1921

My Lord:-

I have the honour to forward herewith copy of a Memorandum which I have received from a reliable source summarizing a conversation with Talaat Pasha.

I have the honour to be with the highest respect,

My Lord,
Your Lordship's most obedient, humble Servant,

Enclosure in dispatch No. 218 of February 6th 1921.

INTERVIEW WITH TALAAT PASHA.
February 4, 1921

Talaat Pasha left Berlin after Christmas and attended the conference which the Turkish Exiles in Rome had arranged for the purpose of drawing up the Memorandum to the Allied Powers requesting a conference.

He did not sign the Memorandum ostensibly because he was not furnished with the necessary authority by the Mohammedan Communities in Asia Minor, the Caucasus and Bokhara which he claims to represent.

It is more than likely that Mukhtar and the other signatories were not anxious that Talaat should be openly associated with them in their petition.

Talaat's position is more difficult than ever. Enver had returned to Moscow and Talaat was anxious to retain Russian support for Mustapha Kemal, so as to continue the pressure on the Greeks and the Allies. At the same time he recognizes the danger of compromising himself to such an extent that the Allies would refuse to recognize him when the time came to abandon Moscow and identify himself with Roman friends.

The promised London Conference does not fill him with much hope. The situation in Freece is still complicated. The Venizelists are in a minority but the Venizelist party is numerically the strongest unit in the Chamber. Mr. Lloyd George's invitation to Venizelos to discuss the situation is merely an act of courtesy which signifies nothing. The cardinal fact is the incapacity of the Greeks to fulfil the role assigned to them by the Serves Treaty. Constantine's return signified the inevitable intrusion of politics into the Greek army with obvious consequences.

Discussing the proposed conference Talaat stated that an envoy of Constantin en route to the United States on a private mission had visited him in Berlin early January to ascertain his views. Talaat informed him that the Enos Midia line represented the minimum Turkish demand. The withdrawal of the Greek troops from Asia Minor was self understood. Later in the conversation Talaat referred to a recent interview with the Greek General Metaxas, but it was not clear that the envoy referred to previously was Metaxas. He attached no importance to this interview as he had no confidence in Greek promises.

The position of the French was obviously untenable. The debates in the Chamber of Deputies displayed increasing impatience with the expensive military occupation of Asia Minor. He had been informed confidentially that France would grand considerable modifications of the Treaty to assure tranquility in Syria. Talaat foresaw a French offer to restore Smyrna to the Turks at the London Conference. France lacked funds to maintain a large force in Asia Minor. Any indemnity which Germany paid would not affect the question. This would probably take the form of payment in natura for the next few years.

The Conference gave England an opportunity to surrender Mesopotamia and all that its occupation entails, to the Turkish Nationalist, who would in return grant the necessary oil concessions to England and furnish a final answer to the Note of the United States Government of the 24th November. England would be in a position to say: "We are not getting the oil because we have a mandate in Mesopotamia. The owners of the land have given us concessions to exploit the local oil the right of way to the Russian fields." The recent article in the "Times" encouraged this view.

Incidentally Talaat mentioned that he was informed privately that discontent was rife in Serbia, especially in Albania and Novi Bazar. A rising of the mountaineers was expected in April. Greater Serbia was an unstable creation. Later on the conflicting interests of Serbia, Bulgaria, and Greece would have the Turks fresh possibilities in Eastern and Western Thrace.

A props of Enver's mission to Moscow Talaat stated that Enver would be in a somewhat embarrassing situation if Mustapha Kemal sent a plenipotentiary to the London Conference; nevertheless the Soviet Government were so disquieted about the state of feeling in Georgia, Azerbaijan and the other Mohammedan boundary States, that it could not afford to make Enver or Kemel definitely hostile. In the present conditions in Russia, failing support, neutrality was preferable to hostility.

Talaat expressed no surprise at the results of the Paris Conference. He did not profess to understand the significance of paper milliards. The Turks reckoned in gold. The gold wealth of Turkey when he was Financial Minister amounted to 120 millions of Turkish pounds. Some 12 million had been paid out during the war. The remainder of the gold was easy to bury in the sand.

Talaat mentioned that his compatriots in Rome were expecting an amnesty for the political prisoners in Malta. The wholesale arrest of this countrymen by the military authorities after the occupation of Constantinople showed a surprising lack of discretion on the part of Allied General responsible. For instance Rachmi Bey, the Governor of Smyrna, who had always favoured the British and incurred the odium of the Germans in consequence, was imprisoned with the others. In internment of the Midhat Schukri Bey and Salast Djimjoz (2) who had been opposed to the Central Powers prior to and (page damaged) similarly (page damaged)… of…injustice.

The British secret reports offered many clues that opened new paths for my research. The documents establish that the Turks were making deals with the United States and European powers over oil found in Turkey (most likely in Armenia) and Russia, which clearly the Turks via Enver Pasha and Mustapha Kemal (who would later establish modern day Turkey) had influence over. It also shows that there was a direct connection between the founder of modern Turkey and those responsible for the Armenian Genocide. These facts debunk modern Turkey's claims that they have no responsibility for what happened to the Armenians from 1915-1923, under the Ottoman government led by Talaat, Enver, and Jemal.

Chapter 23

Armen Garo

"Had we <u>chosen</u> to aid the Germans we would not have had any serious losses." – Garegin Pastermadjian, October 10, 1919, Washington, D.C.

Armen Garo, one of the coordinators of Operation Nemesis, was born Garegin Pastermadjian in the city of Erzurum, Erzurum Vilayet, Ottoman Emire on February 9, 1872.

Armen Garo has been hailed a hero of the Armenian people. And, as was the case with many of the Armenian revolutionary heroes, many of his selfless deeds aimed at the improvement of the Armenian people's condition, ended in disaster.

Armen Garo joined the Armenian Revolutionary Federation in 1895. His first notable act was his involvement in the takeover of the Bank Imperial Ottoman, on August 26, 1896, with the purpose of drawing the attention of the European powers to Sultan Hamid II's pogroms and massacres of the Armenian population in the Ottoman Empire. After the mastermind of the occupation, Papken Siuni (1873-1896) was killed during a long and bloody stand-off, Armen Garo took over as leader.

Dr. Garegin Pastermadjian - 1918

The occupation of the bank was chronicled in *Betrayed Armenia* by Diana Agabeg Apcar, published in 1910, in response to the April 1909 Cilicia massacres of 20,000 Armenians. Apcar wrote on page 15 to 18 :

> Further in answer to Ahmed Riza Bey's account of the Armenian "pretendus patriotards" in connection with the Ottoman Bank; I cannot do better than quote from Mr. Bryce's version of the story, and the massacre that followed: "In the following June serious trouble arose at Van, where some sort of insurrection is said to have been planned, though in the discrepancy of the accounts it is hard to arrive at the truth. Masses of

Kurds came down threatening to massacre the Christians, and a conflict in which many innocent persons perished, was with difficulty brought to an end by the intervention of the British Consul. A little later the Armenian revolutionary party, emboldened by the rising in Crete, where the Christians, being well armed and out numbering the Muslims, held their around successfully, issued appeals to the Embassies and to the Turkish Government to introduce reforms, threatening disturbances if the policy of repression and massacre was persisted in. These threats were repeated in August, and ultimately, on August 26, a band of about twenty Armenians, belonging the revolutionary party, made a sudden attack on the Imperial Ottoman Bank in Constantinople, declaring they were prepared to hold it and blow it up should the Sultan refuse their demand. They captured the building by a *coup de main*, but were persuaded by the Russian dragoman to withdraw upon a promise of safety. Meanwhile the Government, who through their spies knew of the project, had organized and armed a large mob of Kurds and Lazes—many of whom had recently been brought to the city—together with the lowest Turkish class. Using the occasion, they launched this mob upon the peaceful Armenian population. The onslaught began in various parts of the city so soon after the attack on the Bank that it had obviously been prearranged, and the precaution had been taken to employ the Turkish ruffians in different quarters from those in which they dwelt: so that they might less easily be recognized. Carts had moreover been prepared in which to carry off the dead. For two days an indiscriminate slaughter went on, in which not only Armenian merchants and traders of the cultivated class, not only the industrious and peaceable Armenians of the humbler class, clerks, domestic servants, porters employed on the quays and in the warehouses, but also women and children were butchered in the streets and hunted down all through the suburbs. On the afternoon of the 27th the British Charge d'Affaires (whose action throughout won

general approval) told the Sultan he would land British sailors, and the Ambassadors telegraphed to the Sultan. Then the general massacre was stopped, though sporadic slaughter went on round the city during the next few days. The Ambassadors, who did not hesitate to declare that the massacre had been organized by the Government, estimated the number of killed at from 6000 to 7000; the official report made to the Sultan is said to have put it at 8750.[86] Daring the whole time the army and the police had perfect control of the city—the police, and a certain number of the military officers and some high civil officials, joining in the slaughter. Of all the frightful scenes which Constantinople, a city of carnage, has seen since the great insurrection of A.D. 527 when 30,000 people perished in the hippodrome there has been none more horrible than this. For this was not the suppression of an insurrection in which contending factions fought. It was not the natural sequel to a capture by storm, as when the city was taken and sacked by the Crusaders in A.D. 1204, and by the Turks in A.D. 1453. It was slaughter in cold blood, when innocent men and women, going about their usual avocations in a time of apparent peace, were suddenly beaten to death with clubs, or hacked to pieces with knives, by ruffians who fell upon them in the streets before they could fly to any place of refuge."[87]

I would also like to quote from an article written by a Turkish Officer who signed his name as A. J. and published in the "Siper-i-Saika-i-Hurriet," a Turkish daily, on July 6, 1909.

> Every time that I hear the name Armenian I feel the bleeding of a moral wound within, me. It was the year I was sent into exile (1896). On a Thursday, before we had left the Military School for our vacation, a rumor flew through the school,—" They are massacring the Armenians." All my young patriotic companions turned pale from deep emotion. Every one tried to read in the sad faces of others the reason for this bad news. But each one avoided expressing his thought. After a time the details began to circulate to the effect that the Armenians had dared to destroy the Ottoman Bank and government buildings with bombs, and that this was the reason why they were massacred. At that time all of us trembled, because we also were enemies of that government, because we also wished to overthrow it, and although we were not convinced that the best service could be rendered by bombs, we were working quietly to spread our ideas. In our hearts a flame of enmity and indignation, no less terrible than bombs, was burning. The poor

---

86 In a recent publication "Fifty Years in Constantinople," the author Dr. George Washburn, ex-President of Robert College, estimates the number that were slaughtered in cold blood in the streets of the city as 10,000. Dr. Washburn adds the following: "The massacre of the Armenians came to an end on Friday, the day after the soldiers came to the College; but the persecution of them which went on for months was worse than the massacre. Their business was destroyed, they were plundered and blackmailed without mercy, they were hunted like wild beasts, they were imprisoned, tortured, killed, deported, fled the country, until the Armenian population of the city was reduced by some seventy-five thousand, mostly men, including those massacred."

87 "Transcaucasia and Ararat : Twenty Years of the Armenian Question."—JAMES Bryce.

Armenians were being massacred ruthlessly, because out of their number five or ten persons, resenting their Avrongs, had rebelled. But that which maddened these poor men, that drove them to rebellion and placed bombs in their hands was the stupidity of the people and the outrageous oppressions of the government. And now this inhuman government was killing with clubs a noble nation, under the pretext of putting down a rebellion produced by its own oppressions. Among the crimes committed by the former government the most unpardonable crime was the Armenian massacre. If there was a race up to that time among non-Moslem peoples which with sincere and deep feeling honored the Ottoman fatherland that race was the Armenian. It is the Armenians who wear most nearly the national dress, who speak and write Turkish best, and recognize the Ottoman country as their fatherland. Besides this it is the Armenians who engage in commerce and agriculture, and thus, by demonstrating its fruitfulness, increase the value of the Ottoman Empire. Because a few among them justly started an agitation, these our noble and industrious brethren were being massacred. What a terrible scene! When we left the school building we saw hundreds of the bodies of our Armenian compatriots being removed in manure carts; legs and arms were hanging down outside. This bloody scene will ever remain impressed on my mind.

"This shocking crime of Yildiz formed a deep lake of blood, and this lake, during the whole course of a cursed absolutism, up to the last moment, grew wider. Even during the past nine months of the Constitution, in spite of the brotherly feelings which had been shown, the awful events in Adana took place and the souls of all true Osmanlis melted into tears. Up to the present time the deep sorrow caused by this event has not disappeared, because this bloody wound in our social body cannot easily be cured. While we fill our stomachs with choice morsels, while we rest selfishly in our comfortable beds, these fatherless and brotherless orphans, widows hungry, naked, and barefoot wander hither and thither, and thousands of families are fleeing from the fatherland. We are convinced that the government is doing its work, but what has happened is so great a calamity that it can keep a government busy for years. However much sacrifice we may make, still it will be inadequate, because the happiness of the fatherland depends on healing such blood wounds as these as soon as possible. We are convinced that the government and all connected with it are persuaded of this as well as ourselves. We must now wipe out the traces of the misfortune brought by a cursed period. We must now comfort weeping hearts. We must understand and teach those who do not understand that patriotism and brotherhood do not differ from each other. The responsibility of the government for the Armenians is very great and very weighty. The whole Ottoman nation is under obligations to protect this suffering race, because the liberty we enjoy to-day is in large part due to the blood shed by the Armenians. We thought that these truths were so obvious that we preferred to keep silence, whereas to-day we understand that it is necessary from time to time to recall the greatness of our obligation. We must not forget that this unhappy people up to yesterday has endured only barbarism, and for twelve years has been constantly oppressed and ground to the earth, and has given thousands of victims. Hereafter we must work to assure them that the era of massacres has passed, and with all our strength of mind and soul we must quiet them. The obligation of the government to protect them is also very heavy, because our Armenian countrymen live among wandering tribes. We must all assist the government and point out its obligation. It must be declared in public and periodically that the one of the most important duties of the Ottoman nation is to protect, together with those of other races, the interests, the life, and property of the Armenians as well, since these are their sacred rights. Let investigations be made and let whatever is necessary be done in order to reach this aim."

This article by the Turkish officer, who, nevertheless, does not dare disclose his identity, together with James Bryce's account provide a far richer insight into the state of the affairs than the facile explanation of Ahmed Riza Bey who referred to the massacres as "les Massacres occasionnes par les aventuriers Armeniens" ("Occasional massacres by adventurous Armenians" – tr. author). Indeed, it held out little hope for the furtherance of liberty and justice in Turkey when the President of the Chamber of Deputies, in 1907, was trying to palliate the horrors of the Hamidian regime by misrepresentations.

The question must, what was the intended outcome of the Ottoman Bank takeover? What did the Armenians truly have to gain and who else might have been involved? To answer these questions, I would like to share newspaper articles of that time period, where Armen Garo turns to the newspapers to tell the backstory of how the taking of the bank was to be the start of a much bigger operation.

Daily News (London, Greater London, England), September 21, 1896, Page 5:

THE ARMENIAN REFUGEES

APPEAL BY LADY HENRY SOMERSET

RELEASE OF THE RAIDERS

INTERVIEW WITH THEIR LEADER

THE RELIEF WORK

TO THE EDITOR OF THE DAILY NEWS

MARSEILLES, Sept. 19.
Sir, - Impelled by the vivid accounts of your Special Correspondent here, Miss Willard and I came yesterday, and have been trying to help the Armenian refugees, who literally have not where to lay their heads. The Municipal authorities have been most considerate, and already a large

hospital, which happily is not in use, has been granted free of rent as a refuge. It will accommodate 300, but this is far below the needs, with ships constantly bringing in new groups. The Armenians here are doing all they can, but there are only about fifty families, and they are not well off. The hospital must be furnished and food provided. Nothing has impressed me more than seeing these crowded groups in the dreary shadows of workhouses, where they have been temporarily granted almost all that remains to them of former comforts of life. The great desire of these poor people is to go to America, whence came the educational impulse that opened a larger world to them. The passage money is five pounds. They cannot stay here unless supported by charity, for there is no work. Will not "The Daily News," through whose influence this refuge has been started, open its wide columns for subscriptions whereby this refuge may be temporarily maintained? We who came for the purpose will arrange for the honest distribution of any money that is received, and will send as many Armenians as we can to America, where Miss Willard has a plan for them to find friends and self support. Your correspondent has been our chief ally in what we have already accomplished, and if "The Daily News" stands by us, there is no fear of the outcome. We are profoundly impressed with a sense of duty and of our high responsibility. We feel that when these tortured children of the oldest Christian Church in the world touch Christian soil, they should find Christian welcome.

I am, yours faithfully,
ISABEL SOMERSET.

(FROM OUR SPECIAL CORRESPONDENT.)

MARSEILLES, Sunday.

Miss Willard has cabled a letter to America headed "Something practical to my sisters, officers, members of W.C.T.U., and to all good people of my native land." The following are extracts:

Why I came here? Because the awful massacres at Constantinople cast in this port hundreds of Armenians who took refuge from the Turks, in the ships lying in the Bosphorus, and have nothing but the clothes on their backs. More are coming continually, they lie on benches in the workhouse, and once in three or four days a few cents are given them for bread, by the French Government. Lady Henry Somerset and I read of all this in "The Daily News" as we set out on a brief bicycling tour in Normandy, hoping to get a little strength for the heavy work of autumn and winter. Lady Henry was very weary, and I have not been able to do anything this summer owing to almost utter failure of appetite; but when we read the accounts of these refugees we came here, and our hearts are deeply stirred. I wish I could put before you the sight of what we saw last night – a great, grey, barnlike room in workhouse, light so dim that nobody's face could be seen save in outline, in the corner a group of thirty Armenians of all grades, from a bank clerk, with his gold-corded cap to a wharf porter, with heavy shoulders. All these men were huddled together on the bare benches, penniless and forlorn, with bread and water only for food, and a board to sleep on in this deadly poisonous air.

Why were they here? Because their devoted nation has cherished the name of Christ and held to purity of the home through all the centuries since the Gospel came to man. We could nor speak a word to them, but we smiled and waved our hands, whereat good men rose, smiled, bowed, gave us a military salute with so much dignity, and the whole scene was one of such unspeakable pathos that we saw almost too dimly to make our way back to the streets. This morning we have bestirred ourselves. Lady Henry has gone out with the Correspondent of the London "Daily News," whose letters brought us here. They are to rent a warehouse, fit it up with sailors' beds, conveniences for washing, and to have supper ready to-night for the poor men. There are hundreds at Marseilles, and more constantly coming. I am going now to the American Consul to see if special arrangements cannot be made to send many to America. Their cry is, "Oh, send me to America." For forty years they have learned to love our land through the missionaries who taught them, lifted them up with so much of knowledge and refinement that they are hated for their acquirements by the Turk, who is determined on their extermination, and I believe that we, as Americans, have no right to hold ourselves aloof from helping England to protect them, since the horrors we have witnessed are largely the result of the work wrought in Armenian character and aspiration by some of our own best people. We ought to stand shoulder to shoulder with England for Armenian deliverance, and cannot but believe we shall be able to arrange to send the refugee to America to some Church or Society who will look after him or her, paying the passage to New York and agreeing to provide work for six months. By this means the undertaking needn't fall heavily upon any, and thousands might be cared for. They are strong, capable, and trusty. The police-court knows them not. They love God and keep his commandments. Their nation is being tortured and murdered for its Christian faith. There are tens of thousands of destitute women in Armenia, many young, whose coming to American might help to solve the hitherto insoluble servant question. All of them, as we know, are Christian women, industrious, skillful. I believe the machinery to work this plan may soon be provided, and with results that will mean loyalty to the people. God give us courage and tenderness in this hour of unequal contest.

FRANCIS WILLARD.

Armen Garo, or as we may now call him by his real name, Armenak Garabet was liberated last night with Haratobi and sent by the 11.30 express to Geneva after a heartrending separation from his companions. The governor of the prison called at the Prefecture in the morning and was directed by the prefect to stay up all night in expectation of something. At nine in the evening the governor received a telegraphic order what to do. He told the prisoners according to his instructions that two leaders would be sent immediately to Geneva, and the fifteen others would be embarked to-day for New York at half-past eleven. To-day, shortly before the appointed time, they were marched through the lonely streets with a strong escort. Strict orders were given not to allow communication with anybody, Armenian or otherwise. So strict were the orders that the passengers on board the Italie were kept from the forecastle where the prisoners were taken until the ship left her moorings. In the Rue de la Republique the police, who were still in possession of the prisoners' money, bought a complete outfit including hats and shoes. They remonstrated against this waste of money, when the official responsible for them said that unless they purchased clothes the Government had given him instructions to re-arrest them as rogues and vagabonds. Their funds amounted to 109 Turkish pounds. Out of this was deducted the outfits and the passage money of 85 francs each, being half the emigrants rate of French stream companies giving a special fare to persons sent by the Government. This did not include food. The police made arrangements with the steward, and paid in advance. The remaining funds, pitiably shrunk, were then handed to the refugees. Davidoff, a leading Armenian, notwithstanding his Russian name, was dismayed. He said they would write from new York to the French Government to tell how they were treated.

"If you talk any longer in that tone," said the official, whose instructions were evidently very strict, and whose temper was rising, "you go back to prison. Yes, you all go." Davidoff turned to a sailor, asking in how many days they would reach New York. The sailor looked curiously at him, and asked:

"Are you alright in your head? Don't you know this is the Italie of Compagnie Generale, and in ten minutes we are sailing to Buenos Ayres." The refugees, realising the situation, wept with rage at Garo and themselves being deceived. They entreated the Special Harbours Commissary to let them leave for New York. He replied that he was instructed to send them so far that they could never return to Europe.

For the last week I had been told daily by trustworthy informants that the release might take place at any moment, and confess the news took me rather by surprise, as I had become rather sceptical. However, in anticipation, I had secured the services of an intelligent quick Frenchman speaking Turkish, whose business is at the docks, and whom I could implicitly trust to watch out-going steamers. He was stopped in his endeavour to pass the gangway of the Italie, but went round to a steam launch and spoke to Davidoff over the taffrail. The latter declined at first to speak. "Why did you not blow up the bank?" "Because our chief Garo did not tell us." The answer to every other question was, "Mr. Garabet knows." They are evidently willing to live or die for Garabet. Davidoff gave my informer a message to the National Armenian Committee, probably asking for funds.

What does Garabet himself say? I must give no particulars about how the following interview was brought about, as to divulge it might injure innocent persons. Garo is about twenty-three and strikingly handsome. He is clean-shaven, and has a thin moustache and clear pal complexion, perhaps due to confinement, fair hair, brown eyes, and fascinating manner. He speaks with Irish fluency, scarcely pausing to take breath. The Greeks of Constantinople promised that if he attacked the Bank they would attack different parts of Stamboul. When he entered the directors' office at the Bank, Mr. Auboyneau first thought he was a burglar, and exclaimed, "Take all the money on this table, but spare our lives." "We haven't come for your money, but for the Armenian questyion," and picking up the stray money and bank notes, he placed them in the till, locked it, sealed it, and gave up the key to M. Auboyneau. To the Bank clerks, who were weeping, he said, "You did not weep over the 100,000 massacred." As regards the famous negotiation through the window, Garabet said the representatives of the Embassies first ordered him to leave the Bank and trust to the influence of the Embassies for lenient treatment. He replied "The Embassies might have stopped the massacres in Anatolia by one telegram. That telegram was never sent. If the Armenian nation cannot depend on their goodwill how can I? I will not leave without a safe conduct and hostages." Maximoff pedantically represented that the raiders' presence in the Bank was illegal. "So are the massacres in Armenia" was the quick retort. "Remember Berlin." He spoke five hours on and off to Maximoff, who was most anxious the Bank should not be blown up, as Russians were employed in it, and garabet was aware of this. In reply to the question whether he has available forces in Constantinople, Garabet says: "We have another organization quite ready, and enlisting the support of the Young Turks. In fact negotiations are going on between the Young Turks and ourselves." "Do you think at such a tremendous crisis as the present the Trochags and Armenian extremists should act together?" "Certainly, they are already bound by five articles." "Will you take active part in the next movement?" "Yes, and as long as one of us lives he will support every successive revolution with all his might until we get the rights of human beings. Personally we have no resources just at present. In fact, there were three plans to dynamite the Bank, the Embassies, and Yildiz Kiosk. I had no intention to blow up the Embassies, but did intend to blow up the Sublime Porte and the Seraskierat." "Why didn't you blow up the Bank?" "Because the Ambassadors gave their word of honour that the Armenian question would be settled immediately." "And Sir Edgar Vincent?" "Oh, he did all he could to get us saved." Garabet is thoroughly earnest, patriotic, and self-sacrificing, and is one of those extraordinary type of men that arise out of a revolutionary and desperate national situation/

Lady Henry Somerset is unequalled as an organizer, and worth all the officials of Marseilles put together. She works quietly and with a clear practical head that sees round difficulties, and how to turn them. We drove this morning to M. Bonnaud, the head of the Marseilles police, who obligingly walked with us across indescribably noisome and dilapidated alleys, over rough cobble stones, and through offal and nameless filth that obliged us to pick our steps. We had also to pick our steps across open drains to La Charite, and old disused hospital where Monsignor de Belzunce, in the reign of Louis XV., personally looked after plague stricken patients, and lost his life in setting this example of Christian charity. La Charite must be centuries old. Armenians were lying about in it like animals. Men, women, and children were all together. A frightful silence reigned among them. They awoke to life on hearing that the object of our visit was to keep them from perishing of starvation until they could leave France. The chief of the police gave Lady Henry and myself leave to go backwards and forwards, and even to set up a kitchen. Then came six hours of feverish activity. The Armenians were delighted to have something to do. They cleaned uninhabited rooms on the ground floor that were filled for 20 years with plaster and other rubbish. On our suggestion a boarded room was turned into a chapel, the authorities giving the fullest liberty to worship. A large room was called the refectory and another the kitchen. Lady Henry Somerset hired for 40 francs for a month, a stove, cauldrons, &c., and put down for the present 10l. to the Armenian fund. I bought out of "The Daily News" fund five dozen mugs, as many plates, and badly needed miscellaneous articles. The whole cost 31 francs. In the evening, to the inexpressible delight of all, the stove was in working order, and 150 Armenians each received a pound of bread, an onion, a capsicum, salt, and a few olives. A responsible manager was appointed out of the number, and a cook. Lady Henry bought herself all the provisions, and did her marketing. She spared herself no trouble. The food she gave seemed a miracle, and if it had come down straight from Heaven could not have given rise to more religious thankfulness. This and the other effects of her warm-hearted sympathy I can never forget. The deserted rooms abandoned to rats and scorpions awoke to life, and, what is more wonderful, to joy. Those Armenian witnesses of the most atrocious carnages the world has ever seen, those victims of vile diplomatic games and counter games; those exiles who, after a rough voyage in the steerage of ships, were friendless and unfriended on a foreign shore, with starvation facing them suddenly found relief and sympathy. The awful silence I have described was replaced by the buzz of conversation. The talk carried on in low tones was all about the miracle God had worked in sending the gracious English lady, who, by the way, is a fourth part French. How Lady Henry Somerset got through her work seemed to me well nigh miraculous. She and Miss Willard have been indefatigable. We get off two most deserving clerks to Paris tomorrow, and a man to America. General Booth is in telegraphic communication with Lady Henry, who is at the Hotel du Louvre with Miss Willard. One hundred and sixty more Armenians are due to-morrow.

A week later, on September 28, 1896, the Daily News (London, Greater London, England) on page 5, shared an excerpt of a follow up letter from Armen Garo:

THE ARMENIAN REFUGEES.

(FROM OUR SPECIAL CORRESPONDENT.)

MARSEILLES, Sunday.
    I have hopes that in two or three days or earlier the question of the refugees here will be satisfactorily dealt with. I am informed by a private telegram from Constantinople in reply to an inquiry that the probation forbidding Armenians to emigrate is not absolute. They will be allowed to embark on showing a passport. This passport, however, is not issued by the Turkish Government, but by any foreign consul. The Armenians we know too well are Turkish subjects. What can it mean? It will be interesting to see whether this regulation will stop further arrivals of Armenians here. I dread this possibility as much as people at Marseilles hope for it. The poor

Armenians received such a lukewarm welcome here that I felt justified in asking the other day whether the Government contemplated closing French ports to the survivors of Turkish bayonets and bludgeons. I was assured by high authority that such a step was impossible, as it would make any Government odious to the public of Paris, where a finer and more generous spirit prevails than at Marseilles. I am much afraid, however, that the new regulation is framed to save appearances, and will have the effect of keeping the poor Armenians in Turkey against their will.

I have received from Armen Garo a letter in which he returns to the story of the raiders' release. I mentioned the other day how Davidoff wept with rage on board the Italie. That Garo is in the same state of feeling may be gathered from some passages of his letter, which I must reluctantly regard as private. Having exercised these passages, which only express Garo's feelings regarding points upon which any reader of yours has enough information to form his own conclusions, I see no harm in publishing his letter:

We have just received the news of the departure of our fifteen comrades for Buenos Ayres, and they are almost destitute. Is it possible? They had promised to send our 15 comrades to New York. Passage and food were to be at the expense of the French Government. These promises were given to us over and over again by the official secretary of the Prefecture. We left at the office of St. Peter's Prison 120 Turkish pounds. This sum was given to us by the Russian Embassy and Sir Edgar Vincent as the price of the revolvers left by our comrades in the British yacht. Our passage and board from Constantinople to Marseilles was paid by the Embassies. Our comrades were to be free at Marseilles. But since they were illegally thrown into prison and were sent where they did not want to go, who was to meet the expense? Since they were to be free on French soil, by what right were they asked for money? But this money did not even belong to us. It was subscribed by our poor nation for the defence of our cause. A question, however, of more immediate importance is, Why do the authorities deceive us? They send our comrades to Buenos Ayres, where we have not a single countryman, while in the United States they would find thousands of Armenians.

(FROM OUR CORRESPONDENT.)

After Armen Garo left France, he found his way to Switzerland and studied natural science at the University of Geneva. In 1900, he received a doctoral degree in physical chemistry.[88]

From Geneva, Armen Garo traveled to Tiflis, where he founded a chemical research laboratory. Within a few years he secured the rights to develop a copper mine in the Armenian-populated territories of the Russian Empire. These commercial ambitions, however, were rendered futile after the Young Turk Revolution in 1908. Before that, Armen Garo was invited by the

---

88 Tasnapetean, Hrach (1990). History of the Armenian Revolutionary Federation, Dashnaktsutiun, 1890-1924

ARF and the residents of his native Erzerum to become their candidate in the upcoming elections for a Representative to the Ottoman Parliament following the Sultan's dethronement. He accepted the invitaiton and became a member of the Ottoman Parliament from the ARF.[89]

On June 11, 1912, Armen Garo, with his official letterhead, wrote a letter, in French, to James W. Colt, who together with Admiral Colby M. Chester, had worked on a railroad project connecting Constantinople with Baghdad, (see chapters 27 and 30). The English translation of the letter is as follows:

> *Constantinople, 11 June 1912*
> Mister James W. Colt
> In New York,
>
> My dear friend,
> Being very busy, I cannot write to you at length today; I will only summarize the result of the interviews that Mr. J. P. Carter and I myself have had with Djavid Bey individually.
> Yesterday, Djavid Bey made the following proposal to Mr. Carter:
> The Government would pay a total sum of 5,000,000 *Ltqs.* for the construction of a railway system of 1500 kilometers on a wide spread, be it 3333 *Ltqs.* per kilometer, while guaranteeing an interest rate of 5% and the amortization of capital, which makes an annuity of 169 *Ltqs.* per year and per kilometer, that is to say 3853 *francs* per kilometer.
> Outside of that Djavid Bey has proposed a formula to determine the exploitation of the line, to wit:
>
> $$F = 2300 \text{ Francs. } L +),20 \qquad R + 0, Fr. \qquad 60$$
> T
>
> In which, F = Cost of exploitation; 2300 *Francs* represent a fixed prepayment per kilometer; L = the length of the line; R = the total receipt of the line of which the 20% will be paid to the society of title for rent; T = kilometric train, which will be evaluated at 80 *centimes*.
> But all of these conditions in case the society would wish to take a firm deal, that is to say, without option.
> Mr. Carter left last evening, immediately after this interview, to London, to present the proposition to Mr. P. P. Morgan.
> Last evening, after Mr. Carter's departure, I had a very long interview with Djavid Bey and I succeeded in convincing him to grant the same conditions with right of option. I just wrote about that to Mr. Carter.
> – Thus, therefore, everything will depend now on the decision of Mr. P. P. Morgan.
> As soon as he gives his agreement, Mr. Carter must telegraph you to come here and elaborate the new convention. My personal impression is that Mr. Carter has been convinced that the affair is good, and that it will be done in the best conditions possible, thanks to the actual

---

[89] Derogy, Jacques. *Resistance and Revenge: The Armenian Assassination of the Turkish Leaders Responsible for the 1915 Massacres and Deportations*

circumstances that I have indicated in my previous letters.

I bid you farewell in the hope that I will have the opportunity to squeeze your hand soon,

Your devoted *Dr. G. Pasdermadjian*

(Translated from the French by Dr. Sylva Natalie Manoogian, PhD)

James W. Colt had been sent to the Ottoman Empire to search for mineral deposits by the investment banking firm Kuhn, Loeb & Co., which was run by Jacob H. Schiff. Colt was also working for J.P. Morgan of New York.

Armen Garo later wrote a detailed report titled "Project Of Railway System in Anatolia with Mining Concessions." (see Appendix VIII). This work of Armen Garo's became the formula for a viable project that attracted the interest of investors who fought over the valuable mineral deposits of the Ottoman Empire found mostly in Armenia. According to Chester, who held concessions there, these mineral deposits grew into an apple of discord, which eventually contributed to the outbreak of WWI and all the bloody conflicts that followed in the Middle East.

After the Armenian Congress in Erzurum of 1914, at which the Armenians declined an offer from the government controlled by Talaat Pasha to ally with the Turkish Government and the Germans against the Russians, Armen Garo went on a special mission to the Caucasus. There he joined the committee appointed by the Armenian National Council of the Caucasus to organize the Armenian volunteer units.[90]

On November 14, 1914, at the Bergmann Offensive, Armen Garo accompanied the second battalion of the Armenian volunteers, who engaged in battle for the first time, near Bayazid. During this battle, which lasted 24 hours,

The staff of Armenian volunteers of the 2nd Battalion in November 1914. Armen Garo are among those pictured.

Dro, the commander of the battalion, was seriously wounded, and Armen Garo was forced immediately to take his place.[91] From that day to March of the

[90] Derogy, Jacques. *Resistance and Revenge: The Armenian Assassination of the Turkish Leaders Responsible for the 1915 Massacres and Deportations*

[91] Chelebian, author, Antrang Chalabian; translated from Armenian by Jack (2009). Dro

following year, he remained at the head of that battalion and led it into eleven battles in the neighborhood of Alashkert, Toutakh, and Malashkert, until Dro recovered and returned to resume the command.

In the summer of 1915, Armen Garo went to Van during the Van Resistance becoming one of the first to enter the city after the Russians liberated it.

After the end of the WWI, Armen Garo was elected vice-President of the Armenian national delegation, which was sent to participate in the peace conference in Paris. He later on became the diplomatic representative of the Republic of Armenian to the United States in Washington D.C.

On October 10, 1919, Armen Garo testified to the United States Senate, Subcommittee on Foreign Relations in favor of SJR 106, for the maintenance of peace in Armenia (see full transcript and documents from the hearings in Appendix V). His testimony was as follows:

Statement of Dr. G. Pasdermadiian, Vice President of the Armenian National Delegation to the Peace Conference.

Dr. PASDERMADJIAN. I am vice president of the Armenian national delegation resident in Paris, but now I have come as the diplomatic representative of the Armenian Republic to the United States.

Senator HARDING. Originally you were sent to the peace conference in Paris?

Dr. PASDERMADJIAN. Yes; I was elected as vice president of the Armenian national delegation in Paris, and acted in that capacity during my stay there. I now come as the representative of the Armenian Government in America.

Senator HARDING. As the minister of the new Republic?

Dr. PASDERMADJIAN. Yes, sir; but not yet recognized.

Senator HARDING. Do you desire to make a statement or do you just wish to be questioned?

Dr. PASDERMADJIAN. If you will be kind enough to ask questions, I will try to answer.

Senator HARDING. Just tell what you know that you think would be useful to the committee.

(Drastamat Kanayan): Armenia's first defense minister of the modern era. Los Angeles, CA: Indo-European Pub. p. 46.

Dr. PASDERMADJIAN. I will explain our situation.

Senator HARDING. That is the best thing to do.

Dr. PASDERMADJIAN. You, of course, know that Armenia played a very important part in the Great War. We fought with the Russians and we refused to join the Turks. We fought with the Allies in many countries, and in doing so we lost many men. Had we chosen to aid the Germans we would not have had any serious losses. The fact is that we refused to cooperate with the Germans and the Turks, and we fought for the liberation of Armenia on the Allies' side, but since the armistice the situation in Paris was such that no allied help has been given us. We have received not a single rifle nor any ammunition to assist us in defending our people, and we are now surrounded by the hostile communities who, taking advantage of our known lack of means of self-defense, are continually her-asking us.

Senator HARDING. Now, before you get away from that with what armies did the greater part of the Armenians fight?

Dr. PASDERMADJIAN. With the Russian armies. We had 160,000 men in the Russian Army, besides over 10,000 volunteers. I myself fought as a volunteer. With the French Army in Syria we had 5,000 Armenians fighting under the French flag. We had 1,000 Armenian volunteers in the French Foreign Legion. Armenians everywhere fought with the Allies. We naturally expected that after the armistice we would get necessary relief from our Allies.

But, as I stated, we have received absolutely nothing from them, except certain food relief from America.

Now, what we ask of America is more of moral and economic character than physical only. We have a military force which lacks food, supplies and munitions. We need only a few thousand American soldiers for their moral effect. They will never have to fight, because the Turks will see that America is for Armenia and they will not fight. We want help for one or two years, until we are organized.

Senator HARDING. You have been an officer?

Dr. PASDERMADJIAN. Yes, sir.

Senator HARDING. Do you think that you could have 300,000 effective Armenians under arms if equipment and munitions were furnished for them?

Dr. PASDERMADJIAN. Very easily, sir. We could have 67,000; but we now need an army of 30,000 only.

Senator WILLIAMS. When you say you could have 67,000 you mean that you would have to rob the cradle and the grave to get them? You would have to take the young boys and the old men?

Dr. PASDERMADJIAN. Yes, sir.

Senator WILLIAMS. Like the Confederacy did; rob the cradle and the grave?

Dr. PASDERMADJIAN. Yes, sir.

Senator WILLIAMS. But you can raise 30,000 of military age?

Dr. PASDERMADJIAN. Yes.

Senator WILLIAMS. That is between 30 and 45?

Dr. PASDERMADJIAN. No; between 20 and 30 or 32.

Senator HARDING. Are they fairly trained in military tactics?

Dr. PASDERMADJIAN. Yes; and we have plenty of officers who fought for four years in the Russian armies.

Senator HARDING. So that you need only arms?

Dr. PASDERMADJIAN. Arms and munitions and some supplies, of course; and a few officers, if possible. We have officers, but we need, too, the Americans to cooperate with us in everything. We have thousands of soldiers who were in the Russian army, but we want some American officers to help reorganize our army, especially in the technical field.

Senator WILLIAMS. Of course the Armenians are an old European race, placed by migration in Asia. When I use the words "old European" in this connection, I am not reflecting upon the Armenians; but in addition to whatever force you want to use, do you not also want the prestige of some European flag?

Dr. PAADERMADJIAN. Yes.

Senator WILLIAMS. Of course, in saying "European" I am including the Americans, because we are all European.

Dr. PAADERMADJIAN. Yes.

Senator WILLIAMS. So that you do want the prestige of some European flag?

Dr. PASDERMADJIAN. Yes.

Senator WILLIAMS. You think you need but a very small force?

Dr. PASDERMADJIAN. Yes; to reorganize our own force.

Senator HARDING. I wanted to ask you, not as an intimation of our decision, but I am trying to arrive at what seems to be a possible thing to do: Do you think, if this country could provide arms and munitions and ammunition, and at the same time send a battleship to Batoum with a force of marines, that that would greatly relieve the situation there?

Dr. PASDERMADJIAN. That will relieve the situation throughout Caucasus; but until the American flag shall be in Erivan, the people who are living at Erivan will not know what is at Batoum. Our neighbors, the Orientals, are very impressionable.

Senator HARDING. We can send marines inland, for that matter.

Senator WILLIAMS. Senator Harding said with a force of marines in Batoum. Of course, he meant to send the marines farther inland, along the line of the railroad?

Senator HARDING. Yes; to Erivan. You think the moral effect of that would be great?

Dr. PASDERMADJIAN. Yes, sir; the moral effect.

Senator HARDING. Do you want to ask any other questions, Senator?

Senator WILLIAMS. No.

Senator HARDING. You do not care to have him dilate upon these details?

Mr. CARDASHIAN. No.

Chapter 24

Making deals with the Turks

We can only guess what deals Mikayel Varantian, Armenia's Ambassador to Italy, was discussing with the Turks during the Rome conference. Did those discussions eventually lead to the ARF's attempt to cooperate with the Turks with the purpose of retaking control of Armenia after the Bolsheviks' conquest on December 2, 1920?

Under the governance of the ARF leaders, survivors of the Armenian Genocide, the first Armenian republic lasted ony 18 months.

One day after surrendering Armenia to the Bolsheviks on December 2, 1920, the ARF leadership met with the Turks and signed the Treaty of Alexandrapol on behalf of a country that no longer existed, the first Republic of Armenia[92]. This treaty was intended to reconcile with the Turks, forgiving them their crime of killing the Armenians during the Genocide. But, in order for the treaty to go into effect, it would have to be ratified by the Armenian parliament. This gave the Turks an incentive to fight for the Armenians and bring the ARF leaders back into power. Fortunately, for the Armenian nation, the ARF return to power was never realized and the treaty of Alexandrapol only served as a reminder of who the leaders of the ARF were.

Shahan wrote two volumes on the treaty of Alexandrapol, one which was published and the other which is an unfinished work to one day be published.

On February 18, 1921, in a final effort to displace the Soviets, the ARF leadership staged a not so well-planned counter-revolt against the Bolsheviks. They soon found themselves in urgent need of help. Simon Vratzian, the last Prime Minister and symbol of ARF's failure and chicanery, sent the following desperate note to Behaeddin, the representative in Erivan of the Turkish high command.

> "Please forward the present request promptly to your high authorities, and as I have explained to you, urge them for an immediate answer.
>
> The fight of Armenia against the Bolsheviks, and for its own freedom and independence, serves, as we are convinced, not only Armenia itself, but also the interests of all the nations of the Near East.
>
> For this reason, Armenia hopes that during this fight she will receive help from her neighbors, and first of all the interests of the Turkish people also require that Armenia should come victorious out of this fight and remain independent.
>
> Relying on this conviction, the Armenian government requests the government of the Grand National Assembly of Turkey, that, in the name of the mutual interest of the two peoples and as speedily as possible it:
>
> 1. Return the Armenian war prisoners that are now on the war front of Erivan.

---

92 see Appendix XIV

2. Give the Armenian army some ammunition under certain conditions; first of all cartridges for Russian three-lined rifles and for Turkish Mausers; or else rifles of the Russian and Lepelsystem.

3. Communicate with us, if the government of the Grand National Assembly finds it possible to send military aid to Armenia, and if able to do so, to what extent and when?

In making this appeal, the Armenian government relies on the friendly relations that have been established with the treaty of Alexandropol, and which were disturbed during the Bolshevik rule.

Respectfully,
SIMON VRATZIAN
President of the Armenian Republic
Erivan, March 18, 1921.

Simon Vratzian (1882-1969)

This last attempt of the ARF to regain control of Armenia failed. When Vratzian wrote to the Turks for help, did he know that Soghomon had successfully handed down Talaat's death sentence three days earlier? Was he entrenched in a fight for his return to power and the news from Germany had not reached him? Needless to say, the Turks never assisted the deposed president of the first Armenian Republic, and the ARF was forced to retreat, never to fight again to take control of Armenia from the Bolsheviks.

Chapter 25

Soghomon

Soghomon Tehlirian was an engineering student in Berlin in 1921 when faith shone down kindly on him, putting him face to face with the architect of the Armenian Genocide, Talaat Pasha or so say the legends woven into the daring assassination scrupulously planned by the secret organization, Operation Nemesis.

When Shahan Natalie secured the needed funding for the Operation Nemesis, he put out a call for candidates that would be capable of assassinating someone responsible for the Armenian massacres. Yeranouhi Danielian answered the call nominating Soghomon Tehlirian as someone suited to do the job.

Soghomon Tehlirian (1896-1960)

My grandfather recalled the story of Soghomon's nomination, in a 1971 recording my father had made, with a chuckle in his voice. He had realized that Yeranouhi was in love with Soghomon and aspired to marry him. Why not let her chosen one be a hero? Little did Yeranouhi know then that Soghomon had committed himself to Anahit, his first love, who was waiting for his return from the mission.

Soghomon was in France when he was contacted to join the mission. He was asked to come to America to meet with my grandfather. By the time he arrived, however, my grandfather had already left the U.S. He was in Geneva, preparing to go to Germany to hunt down Talaat. Soghomon was introduced to report to Armen Garo, the diplomatic representative of Armenia to the United States.

By December, when the general whereabouts of Talaat were found, my grandfather called to have Soghomon sent. When he arrived in Germany, Soghomon would become the 7th, person officially involved in the operation and the one my grandfather would most depend on. This was due to the fact that three mostly unwilling recruits that my grandfather had enlisted on the ground in Berlin to help with surveillance were highly unreliable.

Most Armenians know Soghomon Tehlirian as the assassin of Talaat. He is revered like a true knight in shining armor who slayed the evil dragon that rained down terror on those who he found to be undesirable or in his way.

Armenian history claims that at the time of the assassination, Soghomon was a member of the Armenian Revolutionary Federation (ARF). At the time of the assassination, Soghomon was not a member of the ARF, nor was he even affiliated with them.

Soghomon was found not guilty of the murder of Talaat, but as Dr. Mansur Rifat stated so accurately in his article published on June 7, 1921 in the Deutsche Zeitung newspaper, "History reserves for itself the right eventually to proclaim the truth…"

Although Soghomon had lost his mother in the Armenian Genocide, Soghomon was not living with her at the time of her death, rather he was in Belgrade, Yugoslavia, with his father, who was a businessman and had a coffee import business.

After the genocide began, Soghomon joined the Armenian defense forces that was led by the Armenian national hero, General Antranik Ozanian.

In 1919, Soghomon made his way to Constantinople, where he frequented the home of General Antranik's family. The niece of General Antranik, Yeranouhi Danielian, had taken a liking to Soghomon.

Yeranouhi had told Soghomon of an Armenian traitor who had provided the black list of 250 of Armenians leaders and intellectuals to police chief Bedri. That list was promptly delivered to Talaat, who had those listed to be arrested on April 24, 1915 and eventually murdered.

Soghomon had decided that the Armenian traitor, who was living a privileged life in Constantinople, had to be punished for his crime. This would be the first assassination Soghomon carried out himself and without any direction of an organization.

Following the successful implementation of Operation Nemesis, the ARF leadership did everything in its power to prevent Shahan Natalie and Soghomon Tehlirian from face-to-face meetings. In fact, between 1956 and 1960, while both lived in the United States, they only exchanged a few letters. Shahan's opposition to the ARF's key policies had been making its leaders nervous.

The *Tashnags* had witnessed these two men's ability to forge a powerful alliance, which now could threaten their own safety. In view of these circumstances, it is not surprising that there is no mention of Shahan Natalie in either edition of *Soghomon Tehlirian's Memoirs* (1953 and 1956). In spite of this, however, Shahan spoke fondly of Soghomon in his recording in 1971. He was well aware what had been going on behind the scenes. Shahan's sympathizer's

Shahan Natalie and Soghomon Tehlirian - 1921

inside the ARF had information of the party's persistent efforts to remove his name from the book. Moreover, the ARF aggressively undertook the task of removing any and all references to Shahan Natalie's affiliation with the party, from the day of his second resignation from the party in 1929 (the first was in October of 1919) until after his death in 1983, when he was perceived an asset, once they felt he could no longer threaten the establishment.

SHAHAN: No! No! Against Soghomon ... Do you know what happened? Now, about Soghomon ... that was a loose, loose thing, which was written. But I knew that... I know, that he had written it; he had requested, do you get it? That they not, that they remove my name, but Vahan Navasartian requested there, that if printed elsewhere, because the idea of printing his memoirs had been around for quite a while. The Tashnags of America wanted to publish them. Thinking that in America there were not those, when Soghomon says *"do not remove him"* et cetera, do you know? They don't do anything against Soghomon's will; they don't go, but Vahan Navasartian ... Vahan Navasartian, who regarding Soghomon, get it? [Snickers]. He makes up something. When he talks to Soghomon, he also removes Soghomon. Vahan Navasartian is that kind of character. Well, Soghomon knows that. Contrary to that, regarding his special request, that *"he not be removed"*, they remove my name, my name remains as director. That is what *the man* wrote. And ... And nevertheless, well, what importance does Soghomon have as a **perpetual hero**! But that is not an issue. **His/Theirs/Them** pleasure is what you are subjected to. If you are not, then it is Talaat he assassinated. Do you get it? And other such things, because it has happened a lot.

Four decades later, in our quest to find and document the alleged omissions from Soghomon's memoirs, we discovered something unexpected. My mother obtained the second edition of *Soghomon Tehlirian's Memoirs* (1956) and began painstakingly comparing every word with the original edition (1953) that has

Shahan's marginal notes. On page 192 of the second edition, she stumbled. The following page was numbered 209. The missing 16 pages were not cut out of the book, but rather removed before binding. This was a shocking example of blatant censorship that insults the intelligence of the readership.

Since our attempts to find the exact reason why these very pages were eliminated were unsuccessful, we had to resort to the clues within the text itself. Particularly striking is the ending of the missing chapter that details Soghomon Tehlirian's assassination of Haroutiun Megerdichian, the Armenian traitor who had compiled the infamous list of about 250 prominent Armenian intellectuals, including writers, artists, as well as political and religious leaders. They were to become amoung the first official victims of the Armenian Genocide, arrested on April 24, 1915 and later murdered.

The following are the missing pages from *Soghomon Tehlirian's Memoirs* regarding the hunt of the Armenian traitor (with Shahan Natalie's marginal notes):

P. 193

<u>In Bolis in those days, no one was preoccupied either with the treacherous Haroutiun, nor with Tala'at, and neither with the issues of the other fleeing criminals</u>. The moods / orientations were different. The **keywords** of the day were the Armenian and Armenia. Professed, earthly separations and preferences had become deprived of value. There was a tension, to bring to the forefront a national totality to the remnants of segments. Outside of narrow-hearted political environments, there was at present an amalgamated subject of particular affection, *"Araratian Armenia"*. There, had risen the dawn. From there it would possible to disperse the light upon the dark Armenian horizons and for the nation to be reborn.

These moods flourished in <u>*January 1919 [1918?]*</u>, when the Armenian delegation arrived from Armenia to Bolis, headed by A[vetis] Aharonian. The delegation had come to the Tokatlian hotel, in Pera, where night and day every class of nationals were coming in and out, and were inspired by news of Armenia. I also had occasion to hear A. Aharonian, when he made an appearance at the Armenian club of Pera, and in his elegant and smooth language he made clear, under the applauses of the massive crowd, with what supreme effort the Armenian soldier had thrust out the enemy, and with what heavy contractions *"the child Armenia"* had been born. For those times, indeed, this was a miracle. And both the picturesque words and emotion of the talented orator were inspiring those present. Shortly thereafter, when he was heading toward Paris,

P. 194

an innumerable crowd was gathered on the dock to wish him farewell before the eyes of interminable Turks, and the entourage was thundering with *"long lives"*.

A greater enthusiasm was created at the end of February, when the British battleship *"Caesar"* put ashore on the dock at Galata Patriarch Zaven Der Yeghiayan, who was returning from exile. They were still testing the road to nationalization. The traditional spiritual princedom was still everything. The Patriarch had returned alive and healthy. This means that the nation is still standing and will live. And the multi-thousand Armenians of Bolis were on their feet. The area from the ocean side to the Bank Ottoman was occupied by a crowd. The return of the elderly patriarch symbolized the return of all the exiles . . .

Armenian-Turkish relationships were not bad. From the standpoint of amalgamation, the Armenians of Bolis did not have many reasons for dissatisfaction. And the municipal conditions necessitated the latter's submission. Just in July of the previous year, in the place of the deceased Sultan Reshat, Prince Vahideddin Mouhammed VI had risen to the throne, who was considered a worshipper of British municipality and an Armenophile. Respectable Armenians testified that the enlightened and artistically knowledgeable heir-to-the throne prince Abd-ul-Mejit himself has said to an influential Armenian, that *"our present Sultan is supremely kind and will resolve the Armenian vengeance."* But from whom and how? He did not say. Of the Turkish newspapers *"Igdam"* was writing that *"all the deported Armenians will be returned."* All the respectable Armenians applied to the Armenophile sultan's heir to the throne on that occasion, -- *"Yes! Absolutely, all exiled Armenians, wherever they may be, will be returned"*, he had said.

P. 195

And if they are not? . . . At that time the Armenian people were a child like *"the child Armenia"*.

The relationships of two similarly fated peoples, Armenians and Greeks had received a nature of cordial fraternity during the course of horrors. In those days, the administration of the Greek patriarchate, in the great church of *HagiaTriada* [Holy Trinity] in PeraTaksim, performed a pompous liturgy in memory of the Greek martyrs, with the participation of metropolitans and Fenners, and sang "In heavenly Jerusalem", "Because we bless Thee", "To the spirits of the deceased" and other psalmodies and prayers.

As a matter of course, nation-aiding works were being performed. The patriarchate had succeeded in organizing, with the participation of Catholic, Protestant religious leaders, an inter-faith body, which was to manage the care of orphans, the needs of exiles and to patronize the Armenian Red Cross. Public forces were in motion. Exerting diligent efforts in particular was the Armenian Red Cross, which had hospitals in Shichli, Bankalti, and Beshigtash. The orphan care had feeding stations in various neighborhoods and orphanages, which had been placed on better foundations then in Caucasia. The Armenian Medical Union had opened a short course for nurses, in which hundreds were enrolled. Day to day, former literary clubs were re-established. New societies and unions were organized,

P. 196

such as, for example, the Union of Assistance of Armenia, the General Benevolent Committee, the Activities Home, the Women's Union, and others. Theatrical presentations were again being made as evening events for the benefit of Armenia. For the same purpose, numerous receptions and luncheons, in honor of agreeing governments' generals or foreign newspapers' correspondents, who were already Armenophiles or, according to hypothesis, were affected by that spirit, during the course of wasteful honors.

It was deemed beneficial to the Bolis residents and the municipal system, on March 20 [1920], according to the proposal of [President Woodrow] Wilson, the Versailles Congress [Paris Peace Conference, 18 January 1919 to January 21, 1920] had decided to send to the Near East, a commission composed of representatives from America, France, England and Italy, to examine and consider the condition of the land masses to be separated from the Ottoman empire and the needs of the people. Armenian national municipal areas were striving to interest with the Armenian question the United States of America, whose representatives in Congress, specifically President Wilson himself, as they said, was very closely accepting the Armenians in his heart and showing his disposition of taking on the care of Armenia . . .

With hopes and expectations, passing through blood and fire, the remnants of the Armenian people were everywhere expressing the strongest liveliness and unforeseen determination of living as a nation. In the motives of great nations regarding its consideration, that people only saw the good. But when it understood its mistake, it was already late. Now its survivors were taking everything in hand,

P. 197

which was possible to be useful for living. *There was only one thing lacking - the neutralization of revolutionary dispositions. They took very hard the revolutionary and anti-humanitarian blow, and the amalgamated harvest of former revolutionary workers' positions had remained vacant.*

I already had relatives, friends, who with one voice were testifying about the sad role played by the treacherous Haroutiun [Megerdich]ian. He was the informant to Tala'at regarding the realities that took place in the patriarchate, at the eve of the deportation. He was the one, with the defrocked archimandrite from Armash, Hamazasp [Hovasapian], who had taken under surveillance the members of the delegation of Armenia a year before, during the government of Tala'at. It was he, who had compiled the list of exiled and massacred Armenians revolutionaries and intellectuals. It was he, who until the last possibility had pursued the popular Armenian forces of Bolis, without exception. It was already proven, that the list compiled by the traitor and, by *means of the police chief Bedri, the black list consisting of 250 intellectuals had been delivered to Tala'at.* Of said list, barely ten people had been spared, of whom the majority were those, whose wretchedness was included in the black list by careless misunderstanding. Thus, for example, in lieu of Minas Tcheraz, he had implicated his attorney brother, KasparTcheraz, who had succeeded in confirming the mistake made and was spared from death, not being aware, which one was the revolutionary Megerdich Hovhannesian. At the same time, he implicated, two of them with the same name, of whom one was saved. Aside from the noted revolutionary Haig Tiriakian, he implicated another "Haig", who had succeeded being spared from death, thanks only to

P. 198

the insistence of Tiriakian, who was the actual Haig. He had confused Levon Shamtanjian with Mikael Shamtanjian, who had succeeded in returning from exile, and others.

It was already two weeks that I was seriously tracking that monster. Every day for several hours, at different times, I was in Beshigtash. But the traitor understood that the times were changed and he did not go in and out. It was possible to get him only in his residence, but the entrance door was always closed.

At one time, in that famous neighborhood were left from the past the burned walls of the Tcheghazan palace. The traitor was established in that part of the neighborhood. *Across from the sprawling residence, there was a winery, which belonged to an Armenian. Up and down from there were scattered grocery stores. It was superfluous to look for a residence there, which was ultra-necessary in order to be at close proximity to the traitor.* At the back of the neighborhood were specialized pastry shops, eastern colorful shoes, carpet stores, whose owners, with half-myopic eyes slowly turning the calculator beads, were waiting for customers. In the upper parts, were scattered here and there houses of Armenians. There, were living Levon's parents. In the lower part was a row of coffeehouses, where covered with green and white veils, beards white as snow, majestic-faced elders under the walls, at thresholds, leaning in the shadows of coffeehouses were lazily sucking the *nargile* water pipes and slowly bringing the finger-sized coffee cups to their lips.

One day at the end of March, I made an attempt to become friends with the owner of

P. 199

the winery, but knowing that I am a deportee, he made an unpleasant face. *It was that day, when in the traitor's residential building, a youth appeared, who headed directly to the winery, and purchasing a single bottle of "Margel", he went home. In the evening, I informed Miss Yeranouhi [Danielian], who was my only supporter in this work. Through acquaintances she had established ties with the traitor's relatives and had secured his picture. The youth was the only offspring of the traitor.*

The next day was Sunday. In the Holy Trinity church of Pera there was a *mourning ceremony on the occasion of the martyrdom of Armenian intellectuals*. Present was a dense crowd of both genders. A liturgy of Gomidas was being performed by a four-part choir. The scenario was emotional and heart-rending. Many of those present had suffered losses. *After the liturgy, Patriarch Zaven spoke* of the biblical text [John 12:24], *"Truly, truly, I say to you, Except a corn of wheat fall into the ground and die, it stays alone: but if it die, it brings forth much fruit."* He likened all the martyrs to corns of wheat which would sprout and bring forth much results . . .

In the evening the Pangalti Student Union, in the large hall of the Red Cross, had organized a citizen requiem. When I arrived, all the seats were taken by a male and female throng. I remained under the wall, in a corner of the gathering.

The editor of the satirical magazine *"Gavroche", Y[ervant - F.Y?] Tolayan,* who was one of the deportees, opened the memorial event. In a few words, he raised the value and significance of the martyred intellectual class to a great height, inviting the attention of the youth to the advancing emptiness in the literary, public and revolutionary arenas,

P. 200

and urging them to take the places left empty by the martyred literati.

Of the surviving intellectuals, Doctor Melkon Gulistanian recalled that *evil-shadowed Saturday night, when he and his friends were arrested, when all the notable workers of the Bolis Armenians: congregational, delegate, revolutionary, editorial, instructional, medical, banker, pharmacist, commercial and others, dressed hurriedly, sleep deprived, with slippers, without hats, following each other, were led to prison.*

-- "The newcomers were coming happily, with a condemning smile," he was saying, "but when they saw hundreds of well-known national old and new workers around them afflicted and deep in thought, they also were immersed in ponderous worries . . ."

The dawn is breaking. Everyone is spiritually arming himself with hopes of the aid to come. Expectations, that "misunderstanding" will quickly be revealed. From the nearby minaret is heard the *muezzin's "Allah ekber / God is great"*. In the nearby *"Mehterhane"* central jail, little by little the twilight is thickening and once again the darkness is reigning. Only from outside is heard the thundering echo of British battleships. . .

Now begins the third act of the tragedy: verification of the black lists, investigation, division of groups, with not more than twenty persons in each and every group and toward the outside. *The general chief of police Bedri*, with his special automobile, is here. And departure group by group, from *Hagia Sophia* street toward the ocean front, by way of *Sirkeji*. Sobs. And the *Sarai-Bournou, Kiulhane* orchards. Disturbed ocean with mountain-crested waves.

P. 201

The individual groups are arriving here. Once again seeing each other's face is a divine gift. And the *Shirket* Number 67 ship. 220 persons, the salt of the Armenian nation, and even police officers, and soldiers. Here is *Marmara*, soul-stirring remembrances. Torment of death. *Haydar pasha*. A train with lights turned off. Now the *Senjan-Keöy* station. Obscurity. The central jail chief is reading the list of first group martyrs. Whispers. Those mentioned are hugging, kissing, and alighting. 75 persons toward Ayash: Agnouni, Khajag, Zartarian, Jangulian, Shahrigian, Siamanto, Pashayan, Parseghian, Daghavarian, Varoujan, Atchekpashian, Zakarian, LevonLarents, Tchavoushian, Tomajanian . . .

And the announcer all in one piece is reading the names of 75 persons. A woman is sobbing aloud. In the hall are heard whispers, *"who is it?"*, *"it's the sister"*, *"whose?"* The announcer is continuing, unaffected.

Daybreak. From Kalayjek toward Tchankere . . . Some kind of huge fortress, whose windows are boarded up with wood. A new list of 56 persons. Names that are unfamiliar to me. But where is the huge deserted fortress, whose windows were nailed with wooden boards, I am thinking, now unable to follow the announcer.--*"Bilaterettutvemerhamet, biraylekdandoksaniashenazadaritlafe"*. He is reading in Turkish Tala'at's order . . .

I understand, *"Without exception and without mercy, from one month old until ninety years old are to be annihilated"* . . .

<u>There was a huge crowd, the air was heavy, my head was spinning and I was becoming breathless. I was having difficulty *[SN marginal annotation: Who then wrote the announcer's nearly complete speech? -- Minakhorian]*</u>

P. 202

understanding the announcer. The words were jumping around in my head. *"Jelal-Haleb"* . . . *"Tcherkez Mehmed"* . . . *"Vartkes, Zohrab"* . . . I am tensing up my entire attention.

-- <u>"Vartkes! I will not give you the permission to go to Bulgaria. I know, you want to free your collar, but there is no means. Whatever we are, you are going to be with us"</u> . . .

-- Who said that? I turned to my neighbor.

-- Tala'at, to Vartkes . . .

-- Zohrab, feeling that he is being led to death, applies to the landlord *Mahmoud Nedim,* "*They are taking us to be killed. I beg you to intercede!*" The announcer is continuing monotonously.

Once again, I am unable to understand anything . . . The same man once more, *"Tcherkez Mehmed"* . . . whatever *Khalil* . . . *Dikranakert . . . Karakeöpriv . . .*

It is as if there is a mitre, which is squeezing my head like lead. It is torture, not a requiem . . . Suddenly, my head spun. I smelled cold blood. I was overcome by dread. I was going to fall down. Giving strength to my feet, I was barely able to reach the door. Reeling, I went out . . .

It was cool outside. The sky was clear. I was thinking about going to *[word blacked out]* Levon's parents, to request permission for me to live there for a while, so that I would be close to the traitor's residence. Otherwise, on a tremendous expanse, nothing could be revealed. Perhaps...

P. 203

Levon had already come back. In that instance, the issue would be facilitated. I would be able to express my observation to him.

Going on to the military academy, I entered the main street of *Nshantash,* from the heights of which, under the lamps of which were scintillating the waters of *Bosphorus.* Not having yet reach *Okhlamour Keöshke,* from afar I see the white marble *Hamidye* mosque, near which the sharp-pointed minaret is playing under the reflections of stars. It was here that, 14 years before, was sealed the mortality of Tala'at's spiritual father *Hamid,* but the fire spewing carriage came out in the air under the nose of *"the Great murderer".* Who could have imagined that comparatively greater murderers would be born in this land? A little lower, toward the interior, perched on the height *"Yeldezi Keöshke"* is sleeping in the nightly black shadows of trees . . .

Having reached the traitor *H[aroutiun]*'s building, I remained nailed in my place. There was light. The window curtains of the windows overlooking the street were not drawn. In the hall, around a wide table covered with a cloth white as snow, a woman was going around. She was laying plates, spoons, knives, and forks on the four sides of the table. I immediately disappeared upward, crossed over to the other sidewalk, and turning back, I entered the winery across from the house. The owner, who was sitting at a round table with two elderly men, stretched his neck questioningly in my direction.

-- "A bottle of beer . . ."

-- "If *Boghos Noubar* were not here, who knows what the issue would be," said one of the two old men sitting under the wall, folding the notebook placed in front of him.

P. 204

"*Mashallah [Praised be Allah]*, seven *vilayets*, that is world-sized land, for goodness' sake," said the other, filling the brandy glasses.

-- "Is Cilicia included in that?" asked the winery owner.

-- "What kind of man are you? They are telling you they are giving to us seven *vilayets*, of *Marash, Gozan, Jebel-Bereket*, the *sanjaks of Adana*, together with the port of *Alexandretta*,. And you still say *'Cilicia'?"* roared the one wearing glasses with indignation, like someone who feels deep personal insult.

-- "So, that's what I am saying also, *Hamedos agha*," said the winery owner apologetically, and coughed as if to clear his throat.

--"Fine, the land of lakes without a population is the same as a waterless garden. Who is going to go there to live?" said the second one, smoking.

--"Brother, first we should get hold of the land. After that, it's easy. Does a man first think of his house? Or of the rent? . . ."

<u>All of a sudden, with a signal from the winery owner, they became silent. A bareheaded young man came in, whom they seemed to have seen before.</u>

-- <u>*"Five bottles of Martel"*. . .</u>

<u>He paid, took the bottles, and left.</u>

<u>"Who was he?" asked the man wearing glasses.</u>

-- <u>"He was the dog's son."</u>

Suddenly I remembered that the young man was the traitor's son.

--"What was that revelation? Five bottles of Martel," muttered the other man.

P. 205

"He has guests…"

The confusion affected me. Wasn't it possible that I could become imprisoned with that young man?

--"Alas! Nobody was found to wipe out the dog and wipe the mire from the nation's brow!" roared the man wearing glasses.

--"It is not the time, *Hamedos agha*. First let the nation recover itself," the other man said.

--"*It's not time"*, what it he like the one from *Armash* also takes a powder . . .

Wherever he goes, *Judah's* fate is bound to be hell.

All of a sudden, as if from a spring, they threw me up. But until I paid,

I overcame. It was too late. The entrance door was closed. Disappointed, I ran toward the window. And what did I see! More than ten women and men are gathered around a table. At the head of the table, right in front of the window, the traitor is sitting with goblet in hand, and is making a speech. A horrible rage overcame me. Should I drag him out, throw him directly from the window like an arrow? . . .

--"Shall I drag him out?". . .

--"Drag him out!". . .

--"Straight from the window?" . . . !

--"Straight! Straight!" . . .

My whole being is stormy.

--"To the head!" . . .

--"To the heart!" . . .

All of a sudden, with a creaking noise and dreadful tumult,

P.206

the window glasses fell. The traitor, trembling with death throes, fell backwards and folded up where he was sitting.

In the morning early, I learned from the newspapers, that the traitor was merely wounded. Everything was destroyed. I should have nailed the bullet to his head. The realization of my clumsiness was as heavy as death itself. . .

A little later, Miss Yeranouhi appeared before me. More sleepless than usual, confused, but smiling, she shook my hand. *"I congratulate you, my brother. What a coincidence! How marvelous!".* . .And she looked at me, befuddled.

--"Are you ill?"

--"Are you mocking me?"

--"What are you saying. Why would I mock you?"

--"Don't you know that the traitor remained alive?"

--"Oh, don't worry. I already visited the hospital, where he is in bed. A Greek doctor friend of mine said that his hours are numbered . . ."

The next day, the traitor was dead.

Chapter 26

Lausanne Treaties

On, July 24, 1923, Turkey, France, Great Briton, Italy, Japan, Greece, Romania, and the Kingdom of Serbs, Croats, and Slovenes signed a peace document known as the Treaty of Lausanne. It allegedly nullified the territorial claims of Armenia under the Treaty of Sèvres (August 10, 1920) and the arbitral award of United States President, Woodrow Wilson (November 22, 1920).

De jure, nonetheless, Armenia retained ownership of what has been deemed 'Wilsonian Armenia,' since no representation, internationally or otherwise recognized, had signed the Treaty of Lausanne on behalf of the Armenian people, the rightful owners of the territories under question, as guaranteed by the Treaty of Sèvres. Thus, the terms of the Lausanne Treaty have no legal weight for surrendering ownership of what is currently Eastern Turkey, which hereon I will refer to as "Occupied Armenia."

By signing the Lausanne Treaty in absence of Armenian representation, the countries listed above aided the Turks to take what didn't belong to them and, thus, they betrayed the Armenian people.

After being ratified by Turkey, Greece, Italy, Japan, and Great Britain, it came into force on August 6, 1924, when the instruments of ratification were officially deposited in Paris, France.

The Turkish delegation at the Treaty of Lausanne

Prior to the Treaty of Lausanne, the Treaty of Sèvres had been signed, on August 10, 1920, by the Principal Allied Powers (Britain, France, Italy and Japan), other allied powers (Belgium, Czechoslovakia, Greece, Hejaz, Poland,

Portugal and Romania), the Supreme internationally recognized leader of the Ottoman Empire, Sultan Mehmed VI, and the internationally recognized First Republic of Armenia represented by Avetis Aharonian, President of the Armenia's Delegation. The terms of the Treaty of Sèvres paved the way for an independent Armenian nation, awarding it the lands they had inhabited for thousands of years, including what was believed then to be 1/6 of the world's crude oil reserves near Lake Van. The terms of the treaty had enraged the convicted Turkish war criminals, including Talaat and Enver Pashas, who had been sentenced to death for their crimes against humanity during World War One.

With the covert backing of the United States, namely that of retired Rear Admiral Colby M. Chester and the owners of the Ottoman-American Development Company and the awarded concessionaires of the Armenian minerals, this New York-based corporation owned by influential Americans, including the son of President Theodore Roosevelt, Kermit, as well as with support from the French, Italians, and Bolsheviks in Russia, the so-called Turkish War of Independence was ignited. The leader was Mustafa Kemal Pasha. His successful struggle made him the founder of modern day Turkey in 1923.

The Treaty of Lausanne was made effective August 6, 1924, in order to appease Mustafa Kemal Pasha and his Turkish Nationalist Movement, putting an end to the hostilities, which had resulted in the killings of thousands of Greeks and Armenians who had survived the initial wave of the Armenian Genocide.

At the time of the signing of the Treaty of Lausanne by the allied powers, the United States had entered into a separate treaty with Mustafa Kemal Pasha and his Turkish government. The U.S. never ratified this treaty as it faced a great deal of opposition from Americans who were supportive of the Armenians' rights to self-determination and the formation of independent Armenia. One such concerned power had an opportunity to present its case at a forum sponsored by the New York-based Foreign Policy Association (FPA).

At a luncheon meeting held at the Hotel Astor in New York on April 5, 1924, a forum titled, "The Lausanne Treaty – Should the United States Ratify it?" was presented. In order to give a concise pre-history of this treaty, I will share the following text from the pamphlet, which was prepared after the forum. The presentation by Mr. James G. McDonald, Chairman of FPA, provides an overview of what led up to the Treaty of Lausanne:

> The discussion to-day is on the merits and demerits of the Lausanne Treaty, recently negotiated by our [United States] Government with the Government of Turkey. The question is: Should that Treaty be ratified? It is to be an American discussion from the American point of view and with American speakers. I emphasize this, not to suggest that we are not interested in the Greek, the Turkish, and the Armenian viewpoints, but because this problem is for us to-day an American problem. It will be up for decision as soon as the State Department sends the Treaty to the Senate. It will require from us a definite political answer. Therefore, much as we are interested in foreign viewpoints, our discussion to-day is to be primarily

American.

I have been asked to do a very difficult thing, to sketch in three or four minutes the background out of which the Treaty of Lausanne grew. This would be easy were I not laboring under the imperative injunction to be absolutely impartial. How can one avoid the charge of partiality, when almost any statement in reference to Turkey will be characterized by one group or the other as untrue or at least inaccurate? Perhaps, by limiting my remarks to a bare and unadorned narrative of a few of the chief events during the last decade, I may hope to maintain my reputation for impeccable evenhandedness as chairman.

In October, 1914, Turkey entered the Great War on the side of the Central Powers and like them was decisively defeated. As a result, August 10, 1920, she accepted the Treaty of Sevres. This humiliating peace gave an international status to the Straits and to Constantinople, handed over Smyrna and the immediate hinterland to Greece, created the Armenian Republic and divided the rest of the Turkish Empire, except a portion of Anatolia, among the various Powers as mandated territories, or into semi-independent states.

A few months earlier, January 28, 1920, a group of Nationalist leaders in the Parliament at Constantinople signed what they called the National Pact, a virtual Declaration of Independence. This document formally repudiated: (1) the Capitulations under which the representatives of the Great Powers had exercised extraterritorial jurisdiction in Turkey; (2) the Ottoman Public Debt Administration; and (3) all other "judicial or financial restrictions of any nature which would arrest our national development." Recognizing this, that the most important Turkish imperial possessions were lost permanently, the authors of the Pact demanded that Cilicia, Mosul and Western Thrace, together with complete control of Constantinople and the Straits, be restored.

Within three months the Grand National Assembly set up its government at Angora and began to exercise jurisdiction over the unoccupied portion of Anatolia. Then under the leadership of Mustapha Kemal Pasha, the Nationalists began active military operations against the forces of the Allies. By October, 1920, the Armenian Republic was Over-run and crushed, the British had returned to the Ismid Peninsula, the Italians to Adalia, while the French were withdrawing from Cilicia.

During the spring of 1921, separate treaties with Russia, Italy and France ended most of the military operations, gave formal diplomatic recognition to the Nationalist Government and legalized most of its territorial gains. Now followed the long-drawn-out struggle with the Greeks, which culminated in the destruction of a large part of the Greek forces, the evacuation of Smyrna, and finally, the Armistice of Mudania, October 10, 1922.

Three weeks later the Sultanate was abolished and a republic declared. Thus, in little more than two years the military and political victories of the Angora Government — I purposely have omitted any reference to the part said to have been played by some of the European powers in abetting these successes — tore up the Treaty of Sevres. Recognizing this fact, the Allies consented to negotiate for a new treaty at the first Lausanne Conference which opened November 20, 1922. This effort failed after a few months because of differences of opinion about economic, fiscal and judicial terms. It was followed by the second Lausanne Conference beginning April 22, 1923. Out of these negotiations, often enlivened by peremptory, but usually empty and futile ultimatums, came the Treaty of Lausanne between the Allies and Turkey. A few weeks later our Government signed a similar but not identical treaty with the Angora Government. It is this Treaty which we are to discuss today; and at this point I leave the discussion for the speakers.

(The full text of the pamphlet can be found in Appendix XI)

By 1927, the Congress abandoned the process of ratification of the Treaty of Lausanne. In its place, a friendship and extradition treaty was signed into in order to establish formal commercial relationship between the United States and Turkey.

On April 23, 1923, former Ambassador to Turkey, Henry Morgenthau lectured at Bowdoin College Institute of Modern History in Brunswick, Maine, of why the victors of World War I would sign into the Treaty of Lausanne. Most revealing in Morgenthau's lecture was his pointing out the fact that the "New" Turkish Government led by Mustapha Kemal was in fact those who had lead the country for the last 15 years, the perpatrators of the Armenians Genocide, the Young Turks.

> The Philadelphia Inquirer
> April 24, 1923
>
> MORGENTHAU FLAYS GREED THAT REVIVED POWER OF THE TURK
> ------------
> Declares British Policy Saved World From Incalculable Bloodshed
> ------------
> Deplores Success of Malevolent Forces in Smashing Treaty of Serves
> ------------
> BRUNSWIK, ME., April 23.—There is no solution of the Turkish problem, "uncles there is first change in fundamental purpose," said Henry Morgenthau, former Ambassador to Turkey, in a lecture at the Bowdoin College Institute of Modern History tonight.
> So long as the European Powers regard Turkey as a field for the exploitation of their own selfish purposes, Turkey will continue to be a scene of unending misery and injustice, he said.
> Through five centuries, said Mr. Morgenthau, the Turk "has been nothing but a destructive force; he has been a killing frost to whatever he has touched. The underlying fact is that the Turk is not a nation. He is simply a nomadic tribe."

The Treaty of Serves, he said, seemed to have accomplished the result of putting an end to Turkish outrages on non-Moslem populations, leaving to turkey on the region of Anatolia, where there lived four million of the five million Turks in the world—a region which could support its population in comfort because of its agricultural and mineral resources.

Kemal's Dream of Empire

"But certain malevolent forces," he continued, "now began to gain headway. The group of politicians which has really governed Turkey in the last fifteen years is an absolutely close corporation which calls itself the Union and Progress Party. I was this committee which engineered the massacre of more than a million Armenians and more than half a million Greeks.

"Most people imagine that the authority of the committee fell with the collapse of the Turkish power in 1918. Nothing could be further from the truth. Another chieftain seized control. This was a man whose name has recently figured so conspicuously in print, Mustapha Kemal Pasha. He was brave, audacious, cleaver and unscrupulous. Progress Committee, transformed into the Nationalist Party, now undertook a new task. That was to destroy the Treaty of Serves and attempt to restore Turkey to the position it had held in 1914.

"Probably the imagination of Kemal and his associates reached for beyond this. In a hundred years turkey had lost by several stages the great European Empire which the conquerors of the fifteenth and sixteenth centuries had added to the crown of Osman. Kemal's ultimate ambition was to reverse all this inglorious history, to extend the crescent again over the last territories, to rejuvenate the old Turkish Empire."

Lauds British Policy

Mr. Morgenthau said that practically all of European Powers except Great Britain dislike the Treaty of Serves almost as cordially as did the Turkish Nationalist themselves. France and Italy dislike the advantages given Greece, and Russian still coveted Constantinople. The Turks, he said, took advantage of this situation to bring about the secret treaties whereby France and Italy withdrew their troops from Turkish territory.

The disaster to the Greek army in Asia Minor followed.

"For the policy which Great Britain pursued," said Mr. Morgenthau, "I have only the warmest admiration. Indeed the world does not realize the extent of this obligation to Lloyd George's government. Probably this is because the world does not completely understand the danger which Great Britain forestalled. The rapid conquest of the Greeks was a tragedy, for a deeper reason than the mere fact that it enabled the Turk to regain great areas in which his rule will be restored. Perhaps its most deplorable aspect is its inevitable effect upon the Turkish mind. The Turkish army now produced a state of exultation in the Turkish mind. The Turkish army now had its eyes upon Constantinople. England played the part in September, 1922 that Poland played in the seventeenth century; she stopped the Turkish armies at the threshold of Europe and saved the world from an incalculable amount of bloodshed and misery."

Played Powers Against Each Other

"At the Lausanne conference," he said, "the same old rivalries prevailed, the same greedy desire for concessions and the wily Turks were again permitted to play the various Powers against each other.

"The encouragement given by the various Powers was only a question of degree. Even the observers of the United States gave as much or more attention to the division of the oil wells at Mosul and the Chester project than to the protection of the Christian minorities in Turkey.

"In the meantime the Turks completed his plan to expel the Greeks, Armenians and other Christians and to Turkify Turkey, so that today, outside of Constantinople, there are only about 300,000 Christians in Turkey, while there are over 1,000,000 shelterless, ragged and starving refugees in Greece who have recently been notified by our State Department that after June 30 the American Red Cross would withdraw her support and leave them to shift for themselves and starve."

Chapter 27

Chester Concessions

On April 20, 1923, Retired U.S. Naval Rear Admiral, Colby M. Chester (1844-1932) gave a speech to 100 members of the Federated American Chambers of Commerce of the Near East during a dinner in the heart of New York's Time Square, at the world-famous Hotel Astor. Chester gave a detailed description of the Chester Concession, which, ten days earlier, had been approved by the newly established Turkish Government, led by Mustafa Kemal.[93]

Chester's belligerent tone and wholesale attacks upon other nations did not make it easier for the U.S. State Department to deal with the subject. The Government was bound to support the rights of its nationals' seeking concessions in Turkey and elsewhere, but where there was controversy, as in this instance, tact and ordinary diplomatic courtesy were not out of place.

Former U.S. Ambassador to Germany (1913-1917) James W. Gerard's protest to U.S. Secretary of State Charles Evans Hughes (1921-1925) was against his government sanctioning any part of the Chester Concession in Turkey, which violated Armenia's rights. The U.S. could not become a party to any scheme that would further enslave the Armenian people. Admiral Chester did not touch on this question raised by Mr. Gerard.

U.S. Naval Rear Admiral, Colby M. Chester

The abandonment of the Armenians by the U.S. brought forth some of the tragic consequences of the policy of aloofness inaugurated by the Warren G. Harding Administration from 1921 to 1923. It came close both to U.S. President Harding and Secretary Hughes, who had repeatedly indicated their friendship for the cause of Armenian independence. However, that friendship yielded largely negative outcome. At the Lausanne Conference

---
93 Brooklyn Daily Eagle, *Ready to Fight for Concession – Admiral Chester*, (Brooklyn, NY, Brooklyn Daily Eagle, April 21, 1921)

earlier that year, U.S. Ambassador to Italy, Richard Washburn Child (1921-1924) mildly urged the Turks to treat the Armenians fairly, but this was the extent of the U.S. Government's activities on behalf of the Armenians.

For the U.S. to fight for the Chester concessions, which called for the exploitation of Armenia, was worse than forsaking an oppressed people, it also made the U.S. a party to their continued oppression.

In 1908, President Theodore Roosevelt sent retired Rear Admiral Colby M. Chester to Asia Minor to arrange for America to be awarded oil concessions. The navy had been converting their ships from coal to oil, and America's supply, which provided the majority of oil to the world at that time, was believed to be running out.[94]

Chester had met Sultan Abdul Hamid of the Ottoman Empire back in 1900, as the Captain of the U.S.S. Kentucky battle ship, in order to collect $100,000 for the losses the United States missionaries had sustained during the 1895 Hamidian massacres of the Armenians. In 1908, Chester was able to secure the deal. However, later that year the Sultan was deposed by the Young Turks. The new Ottoman government, nonetheless, agreed to honor the deal approved by the Sultan and, better yet, expand on it.

U.S.S. Kentucky battle ship - 1900

A comprehensive plan was drawn up by James Wood Colt, Esq., of New York. Mr. Colt, who in later years worked for J.P. Morgan, was part of a special commission to study mines in Armenia, sent on behalf of the investment bank, Kuhn, Loeb & Co., of New York. This bank was run by German-born banker, Jacob H. Schiff, who made a financial contribution to the Bolshevik Movement (see Chapter 10, "Russians Turned Bolshevik").[95]

The initial focus of interest was the Arghana-Maden Copper Mines, which were found in the vilayet of Diarbekir, 53 km south-east of the town of Kharpout and 66 km north-west of the town of Diarbekir, the capital of the vilayet.

In a confidential report written in June of 1912, Colt noted that the mine extracted 1,500 tons of black copper annually, which was exported to Europe.

---

94 El Paso Herald, *United States Oil Supply To Be Ended In 16 Years, Belif,* (El Paso, TX, El Paso Herald, June 2, 1921) 1.

95 Committee on Foreign Relations, *Maintenance of Peace in Armenia Hearings Before a Subcommittee on Foreign Relations United States Senate, S.J.R. 106,* (Washington, D.C., Washington Government Printing Office, 1919) Page 21.

In his *Confidential Report on the Copper Mines of Arghana – Maden (Turkey)*, Colt wrote:

> Reestablishing the legendary history of the Chalypes and the Telchines, the ancient inhabitants of Armenia, before the apparition of Armenians who played such a great part of the development of primitive metallurgy, one arrives at the conclusion that there must have existed an important center of copper production at Arghana at a very remote epoch, and the copper produced was directed towards two centers of consumption: on one side towards Babylon going down the Tigres on these primitive rafts which still work; on the other side towards Kyprus to be worked there and them exported to the Mediterranean ports; this explains the antique fame of Kyprus as an important center of the production of articles of copper. It is certain, that according to the Assyrian chronicles, 20 centuries before J.C. [Jesus Christ], there was already at Arghana – at the source of the Tigris – a great center for the extraction of copper, and, if one adds to these historical indications the legend of the pretended invention of work of copper and iron by the Chalypes in Armenia, it can be easily presumed that the art of casting the copper and probably also bronze must have been produced at Arghana itself.[96]

The Arghana copper mines were estimated to have a minimum value that was at least double the entire cost of the concessions. The estimated 4 to 8 billion barrels of oil found in the Armenian-inhabited lands of Bitlis, Van, Erzerum, and Trebizond were valued at a billion dollars.

In 1921, the concessions fit right in with the vigorous claims the Harding administration had been making to Britain, France, Italy, and Japan with regard to the American rights to mandate territories and, particularly, so far as Mesopotamia was concerned, maintain an open-door policy.

Assured by Republican leaders of ardent support, Secretary of State Bainbridge Colby (1920-1921) took the first steps in demanding American rights in Mesopotamia, protesting against the intention of the British and the French to exclude nationals of other countries from the opportunity to develop the tremendous natural resources of the country.

More than a year prior, Herbert Hoover told some friends at a dinner that by attempting to give the United States a mandate over Armenia, the allies were handing America a poorhouse surrounded by three treasure houses.[97] Among these treasure houses were the Mesopotamian oil fields, from which the U.S. would be excluded unless the protests made by the U.S. government were heeded. Hoover had neglected to acknowledge that Armenia had not only large oil deposits, but also coal, asphalt, gold, silver, platinum, copper, iron, chrome, zinc, lead, emery, and many other sought-after valuable mineral deposits.

The heightened interest in the concessions necessitated a conference between the Secretary Hughes and Admiral Chester, attended also by the latter's son, Clarence Chester.

The concessions obtained by admiral Chester for the United States

---

96 James Wood Colt, *Confidential Report on the Copper Mines of Arghana – Maden (Turkey)*, (University of Rochester's River Campus Libraries, folder number 1, titled "Arghana Copper Mines, 1908-1911", July, 1912) 2-3.

97 Carter Field, *U.S. to Demand Oil Concessios in Mesopotamia*, (Buffalo, NY, Buffalo Evening News, April 9, 1921)

included not only the rich oil field in Western Armenia, with at least a billion dollars' worth of oil, but also the right to build a pipeline and a railroad over the cross country stretch of about 60 miles separating the oil fields from the Mediterranean Sea. The admiral told Mr. Hughes that the total cost of the pipeline and the railroad would be from $50-60,000,000. He was sure there would be incidental benefits exceeding the cost of the railroad and the pipeline.

The tensions between the world powers over the concessions were coming to a boil. It was clear that failure to reach a compromise might trigger yet another world war. Reported by *The Evening Times*, on May 4, 1923, Chester believed he could have prevented the previous world war had he only shared the concessions he possessed:

> "CHESTER SAYS HE HAD A CHANCE TO AVERT WORLD WAR – Tells Newspaperman How He Unwittingly Contributed to Bringing on Great Conflict by Refusing to Develop Concession."
>
> WASHINGTON, May 4—Rear Admiral Colby M. Chester had a chance to prevent the great world-war—but, he did not know the consequences of his refusal, he says, he did not take it.
>
> Chester told Washington newspaperman in a speech at the National Press club how he unwittingly contributed to bring on the great conflict, and how, later on, he was prevented from taking a step he believes would have kept the United States out of what he called the "most nonsensical war ever fought."
>
> Chester said that in 1911 when he was in Rome, an American capitalist tried to arrange with him for development of Tripolitan sulphur concession which he held. Chester refused, and is ashamed now that he did.
>
> "I believe this was the prime cause of the Italian-Tripolitan war" said Chester. "This led immediately into the first Balkan war, that led to the second, and that in turn caused the world war."
>
> Explaining how he might have prevented America's entrance into the world war, Chester said he tried to buy 100 German ships [for the Ottoman Empire] interned in American harbors in 1914, but was prevented by the United States Government.
>
> "I feel that was a mistake, for I am sure if I had been permitted to buy these ships the United States would have been kept out of the war," Chester said. [98]

For a while, the newspapers were reporting on deals being made with the European powers. Chester was allowing them to take part in the concessions, claiming that it was beneficial to him and his partners, especially in those regions where the construction of railroad was difficult and almost cost-prohibitive. Was this the way the United States would prevent another world war?

On September 6, 1923, *The Elizabethville Echo* newspaper reported on a deal in an article titled "Canadians Get Chester Right – Arbitrators Award Admiral $300,000 and 10 Per Cent of Profit":

> "New York – The two groups of financiers, gambling for versioned

---

98 Dunkirk Evening Observer, *Rear Adm. Chester Blames Himself for the World War,* (Dunkirk, NY, May 4, 1923) 1.

profits of billions of dollars by the exploitation of the vast Mosul oil fields in Turkey through the Chester concessions have stopped fighting. The financial associates of Rear Admiral Colby M. Chester, retired, agreed to accept $300,00 in cash and 10 per cent interest in the profits of the concessions."[99]

There was, however, an obvious way out of this difficulty — The Lausanne Conference. The United States had an opportunity to send a fully empowered delegation to the conference to represent U.S. interests and to let the American Government assume the obligations and responsibilities involved in a settlement that would protect those interests and cement peace in the Near East. In such a settlement, the U.S. was to ensure justice was served in Armenia and also nurture an opportunity to foster a relationship with the rightful owners of the minerals they desired.

On April 6, 1924, *The Brooklyn Daily Eagle* newspaper ran a story on page A5 titled "Gerard Charges Hughes Betrayed U.S. at Lausanne – Flag Trailed in Mire to Aid Oil Speculators, He Declares."

> Charges that Secretary of State Charles E. Hughes "betrayed Christian Armenia and his own country" at Lausanne and that "the Stars and Stripes were trailed in the mire in the interest of a group of oil speculators [Chester]" were made by James W. Gerard, former Ambassador to Germany, at a luncheon of the Foreign Policy Association at the Hotel Astor yesterday. At the same time he characterized the Lausanne Treaty as "immoral and purposeless" and predicted the fall of the Turkish Angora regime.
>
> The question before the members of the Foreign Policy Association was that of weather the United States should or should not ratify the Lausanne Treaty. The speaker included Profs. Edward M. Earle and A. D. F. Famlin of Columbia University; Dr. James Barton, secretary of the foreign department of the American Board of Commissioners for Foreign Missions, and Albert W. Staub, American director of Near East colleges, Prof. Albert Bushnell Heart of Harvard was unable to attend but outlined his views in a paper which was read to the gathering. James G. McDonald presided.
>
> **Says He Betrayed Country.**
>
> After asserting that "Christian civilization was crucified at Lausanne," Mr. Gerard continued by saying:
>
> "Let us examine the facts of the case a little more closely. The conference met in November, 1923. In December Secretary Hughes, speaking through Ambassador Child, our unofficial observer, advised the conference that the United States would not trust American lives and property—our missionaries and educators—to the caprice of corrupt and oppressive Turkish courts and laws. It would insist upon the retention of its century-old right to maintain its own consular courts, its capitulatory jurisdiction, for the protection of its nationals and, further, he sought in a perfunctory way, albeit, some recognition for the rights of Armenia which President Harding, on the eve of the conference, had solemnly promised to defend.
>
> "Four months thereafter, in April 1923, Secretary Hughes made a hurried and inglorious retreat from the position which he took in December, 1922. He accepted the Turkish views on the capitulations and upon the

---

99 Elizabethville Echo, *Canadians Get Chester Right – Arbitrators Award Admiral $300,000 and 10 Per Cent of Profit,* (Elizabethville, PA, Elizabethvill Echo, September 6, 1923)

Armenian case. In other words, in consideration of the Chester concessions, he surrendered to the Turks the rights which he claimed for American nationals and for Armenia before the granting of that concession. Obviously, he went to Lausanne fully prepared to make any and all sacrifice to clinch this oil concession, and he betrayed Christian Armenia and his own country to attain his purpose.

Puts Questions to Hughes.

"There is still another equally sordid aspect to this melancholy affair. It is this: The most important part of the Chester concession lies in that part of Armenia allotted to her by the President of the United States—the Armenia oil deposits. Secretary Hughes, by leading support to the Chester concessions in July, 1923, a month before the adjudication of the Armenian case and the signing of the treaty, prejudged and condemned the Armenian case which President Harding had promised to sponsor and defend. By so doing he, in effect, served notice on the Allies and Turkey that this Government considered the Armenian case as having been closed. It now remains for millions of Americans, who have lavishly contributed towards Armenian relief, to register their disapproval of the betrayal of Christian Armenia by their own Government.

"I will now put to Secretary Hughes two pertinent questions:

"Why did he take so active and vigorous a part in behalf of the Chester oil concession, even at the risk of forcing resumption of hostilities, and why does he now deny that he has had anything to do with it?

"Why did he request General Goethals to accept the presidency of the Chester Company, and in what capacity did he direct the reorganization of that company?"

Attack Treaty.

Speaking on the Lausanne Treaty, Mr. Gerard said:

"The treaty accepts the abrogation by the Turks of the capitulations, that is, our right to protect our own nationals—a right which we have enjoyed since 1830. This provision, in effect, is the whole basis of the Lausanne Treaty."

Speaking of the Kemalist government, Mr. Gerard said:

"The Kemalist regime is on the last legs. Fractional armed conflict, widespread banditry and hopeless economic chaos seriously threaten Kemal's regime.

"America stand to gain nothing by resuming relations with a Turkey in this state, and can lose nothing by maintaining the *status quo* and awaiting developments. The downfall of Kemal is inevitable and imminent. By now surrendering our rights to him we shall find it difficult to reassert them against any regime which may overthrow and succeed him. We can well afford to wait."

Other Speakers Differ.

The other speakers differed in their views on the Lausanne Treaty. Mr. Staud declared that the failure to recognize the Turks as a civilized nation and the urging of non-ratification of the treaty would not help the situation. A constructive plan of co-operation is needed if the United States is to be of any service to the people of the Near East, he added. Professor Hart of Harvard, on the other hand, wrote in his letter that it was the duty of the Senate, as representatives of the American people, to refuse ratification of the treaty.

Professor Earle and Dr. Barton expressed themselves as in favor of the ratification. Professor Hamlin took the other side and declared that the treaty was dictated to the United States "by the most pitiable state in the world."

Henry G. Knowles, former minister of Rumania, Bulgaria and Serbia, and counsel for the Ottoman Development Company, holders of the Chester Concessions, denied that the concessions had been sold to Canadians for $300,000 and 10 percent of the profits. This statement was made by Mr. Gerard.

"An effective considerable majority of the shares of the Ottoman American Development are owned by Americans and residents of this city, and the directorate of the company is in their control," said Mr. Knowles. He added that the Turks had granted the concessions through desire to free themselves from the "baneful influence of certain European governments and politicians."[100]

Almost as soon as the concessions were ratified by the National Assembly of modern Turkey founded by Mustafa Kemal, an article appeared with disappointing news — the Ottoman American Development Company (OADC) had lost the concessions as reported by one of the major stock holders, Henry Woodhouse (1884-1970).

Woodhouse, born Mario Terenzio Enrico Casalegno, had immigrated from Turin, Italy, to the United States in 1904. The first job he had in a restaurant kitchen in Troy, NY, ended quickly. He got into a fight with the head chef, killing him with a kitchen knife. Casalegno was found guilty of murder and spent his first 4 years in America in prison. Casalegno became a U.S. citizen supposedly in 1909 (although his naturalization papers are dated May 28, 1917) and began using a new name, Henry Woodhouse.

Henry Woodhouse

Woodhouse was a notorious dealer in false historical artefacts and documents of famous Americans, including Presidents George Washington and Abraham Lincoln. He even partnered with Mr. William Lanier Washington, a descendent of President Washington, to give his forgeries legitimacy.

Had the Chester Concessions truly ended or was the news another one of Woodhouse's forgeries?

In the Henry Woodhouse papers, housed at the Special Collections Research Center of the Syracuse University Libraries, a signed document was discovered among the "Miscellany". This document was an agreement between Chester and Woodhouse, giving the latter 50% interest in the Chester Concession. Surprisingly, the document is dated August 20, 1929, more than

---

100 The Brooklyn Daily Eagle, *Gerard Charges Hughes Betraying U. S. at Lausanne – Flag Trailed in Mire to Aid Oil Speculators, He Declares.*, (Brooklyn, NY, The Brooklyn Daily Eagle, April 6, 1924) A5.

5 years after the concessions had been reported to have ended. The document reads as follows:

> COLBY M. CHESTER
>
> August 20, 1929
>
> Mr. Henry Woodhouse,
> 280 Madison Avenue,
> New York, N.Y.
>
> Dear Mr. Woodhouse:
>
> To commemorate the 20th year of our uninterrupted friendship, I hereby agree to the formation of the Chester Concessions Syndicate, and, for and in consideration of the 50 per cent interest in said Syndicate to be vested in the names of myself and my sons, Arthur T. Chester and C.M.Chester,Jr., I hereby sell, grant and convey to the said Syndicate the following, fully paid and free of debt:
>
> 1. The entire original Concession granted to me by Sultan Abdul Hamid of Turkey in June, 1908 (which I described for the article which you published in the New York Times Current History for March,1922, which description was approved by the Turkish Government, as stated in the Literary Digest for January 20,1923, page 20). Said Concession is intact, except for the section which I granted to the Ottoman American Development Company, and is entirely owned by me. If the Company defaults, that section reverts to me under Article 11, and is hereby conveyed to the Syndicate.
>
> 2. All the Chester rights in the Ottoman American Development Company, including all rights and interests in the Concessions ratified by the Grand National Assembly of Turkey in April, 1923.
>
> 3. All the claims and rights to payments, damages, reversions, contracts and rights whatsoever, in law or in equity which I or my heirs or the original Concession or the Ottoman American Development Company can, shall or may have against any party.
>
> It is understood that you are hereby also assigning your interests to this Syndicate, so that henceforth all our interests will be vested in this Syndicate, ownership of which is by this agreement vested 50 per cent in the Chesters and 50 per cent in you, with equal shares in all outcomes, each reserving full right and freedom to sell, transfer, assign, or incorporate his share, or any part thereof at will. Your acceptance hereto will constitute a contract.
>
> Very sincerely yours,
>
> *[signed] M. Chester*
>
> Dear Admiral Chester:
>
> I hereby accept the foregoing and sell and convey to the Chester Concessions Syndicate all my rights and interests subject to the same conditions as you are conveying the Chester interests, for and in consideration of payment to me of 50 per cent of the said Syndicate, fully paid and non-assessible, which entitles me to 50 per cent of the outcomes from the operations of said Syndicate, reserving right to sell, transfer, assign or incorporate my share at will, or any part. It is gratifying that our friendship and the Chester Concessions have survived the great European empires!
>
> Cordially yours,
>
> *[signed] Henry Woodhouse*

When Retired Rear Admiral Colby M. Chester died at the age of 88 on May 4, 1932, the Chicago Tribune reported that had the Chester Concession carried through successfully, it would have placed Americans virtually in economic control of modern Turkey.

Less than 3 years after the Admiral's demise on February 4, 1935, Chester's son, Arthur Tremaine Chester, unexpectedly died of heart failure. He had been managing the Chester Concession in Turkey since before the Armenian Genocide, through the Turkish Nationalist Movement for independence and thereafter.

Arthur T. Chester's obituary was published in *The Atlanta Constitution* (Atlanta, Georgia) on February 5, 1935 on page 18:

> Arthur T. Chester Passes in New York
>
> NEW YORK. Feb. 4.—(AP)—Arthur T. Chester, 60, who negotiated the "Chester concession" from the Turkish government in 1923, died today at United hospital, Port Chester, N. Y., following an attack of heart disease at his home in Rye.
>
> Chester, a brother of Colby Mitchell Chester, president of General Foods Corporation, was connected with the newly organized General Bank Note Engineering Company, of New York, at the time of his death.
>
> The concession with which his name was connected was a grant by the Ottoman empire to build 2,800 miles of railroad, to exploit oil fiends in Turkey and Mesopotamia, to develop a number of gold mines and also to rebuild several cities, including the area of Mt. Ararat, supposed site of the Garden of Eden.
>
> Chester was the son of the late Rear Admiral Colby Mitchell Chester, and himself was a graduate of United States Naval Academy at Annapolis in 1895.

The Oakland Tribune (Oakland, California) reported, on February 7, 1935, page 12 reported:

> HEART ATTACK KILLS NAVY MAN
>
> NEW YORK, Feb 7.—(U.P.)—Arthur Tremaine Chester, 60, retired naval officer and son of Rear Admiral Chester, U. S. N., died of a heart attack.
>
> After retiring from the Navy in 1906 to enter business, Chester headed the Chester concessions in Turkey for 15 years. Under his direction, the concern built 2800 miles of railroad and developed mines.

Before the death of the Rear Admiral Colby M. Chester, he had been embroiled in litigations by former business associate, Kenneth E. Clayton-Kennedy. Clayton-Kennedy had filed a lawsuit on March 25, 1926 in a New York Supreme Court. He was claiming that the Admiral and his two sons, Chester Jr. and Arthur, had defrauded him of large sums of money and attempted to dispose of him while on a visit to the Ottoman Empire in November of 1922. These damages not only caused him a great deal of financial loss, but almost cost him his life.

On October 7, 1936, Kenneth E. Clayton-Kennedy found himself once again in a New York court room on the witness stand. He was suing Clarence G. Miohalis in a case that didn't have anything to do with the Chesters. At one point, during the hearing, Clayton-Kennedy was asked by his attorney to recall his past business ventures. The Chester Concession came up, and the questions and answers that followed were very revealing as to what really happened to the concessions since Henry Woodhouse's bluff that they had ended:

Q. Let us hear the next thing that you did. A. The next thing of any particular importance was when I went to Turkey to validate a concession.

Q. Who asked you to go there? A. General Goethals, Mr. Blackall, several of their associates.

Q. Now, will you state—by General Goethals do you mean the Goethals who had something to do with the Panama Canal? A. Yes; I understand he was the responsible engineer in charge.

Q. Is that the man? A. That is the man, yes.

Q. And it was he who got you to do what you are going to tell us you did? A. That is correct.

Q. Is that checkable? A. Yes, certainly.

Q. What was it that you were doing? Did you hear Mr. Battle tell the jury that he is still anxious to learn what is this Chester Concession! Will you tell it to him? A. Mr. Battle cannot have read the newspapers at that time, that is all. '

Q. I did not ask that answer. You tell the jury what it is. A. The so-called Chester Concession had its beginning with President Roosevelt, President Theodore Roosevelt, sending a Captain Chester to Turkey—that was long before my time, of course—to get a settlement with the Turkish Government for damages claimed on account of American missionaries and various people of that sort. Abdul Hamid was an absolute monarch and had complete power in running the country, naturally. He promised Admiral Chester various grants and concessions for American capital. Chester came back here and assisted, for instance, Mr. Moore, I understood who built some of the elevated railroads here, Laidlaw Company, Franklin Remington, and many people that I know nothing about personally, except I have read about, and they in turn sent Chester's son and another Remington—I believe an artist, I think a fairly well known man, whose name I cannot recollect offhand—to Turkey; and they there carried on negotiations at a time when several foreign countries, particularly Germany, were trying to get extensions for railroad grants. I believe the Germans—I know the Germans went so far as to have the Kaiser come to Turkey, and they carried on negotiations officially and unofficially. The French intervened. There was a general international scramble for what afterwards became the extension of the Berlin-Bagdad Railway. That involved not only the right to build and operate the railroad, but it involved many kilometric guarantees and the right to take over mineral lands, water powers, timber lands, and so forth. It is a very long and involved affair. I will try to boil it down. Chester and Remington did not secure it. but they got a bill through Parliament. Which came into existence by this time, to the point where it required the signature of the Grand Vizier and two other officials. The Germans were opposed to the thing very, very strongly and the then ambassador, Von Beiberstein or some name of that sort—I may mispronounce—invited the Grand Vizier on his yacht and took him down the Mediterranean and did not come back until after Parliament had prorogued. So the bill was not signed and did not become of legal effect. When I came into the thing through discussion with Admiral Chester—Admiral Chester maintained he had legal rights I could not find the existence of any documents. but I undertook to go to work and find out if could find any prior footnote, in ease of its non-existence to get it validated. I hired Admiral Chester's son, Arthur Chester, the one who had been there previously, at the rate of a thousand dollars a month, and I undertook and did give to Admiral Chester a thousand dollars a month on account of purchase of his rights, and I went to Turkey. Chester, Arthur Chester, appeared there with me, and I spent a matter of a year and a half. By this time Constantinople was in the occupation of the Allied Forces. I was out of the army, but I had been an officer in the Canadian army, and naturally looked upon with a certain amount of suspicion by the Turks. The Nationalist uprising had occurred, Kemal Pasha was in Asia Minor, in opposition to the Khedive Cloyeminent in Constantinople. However, we carried on and in the face of a great deal of opposition and the expenditure of a great deal of money by the French—the Germans were not able to do much—I nevertheless got Parliament to grant a concession to our company headed by General Goethals. I went through a great deal; it in some way or other got in the newspapers; the American High Commissioner, Admiral Bristol, gave me a great deal of assistance, the Secretary of State in Washington sent many cables through for General Goethals. Mr. Herrick, Minister in Paris at that time, assisted me. Mr. Childs at Lausanne gave me some assistance. The matter got a great deal of newspaper headlines owing to more or less foolish attitude of newspaper correspondents, but it did have some relative importance and it was quite a factor in the Lausanne discussions, according to what I am told. Abdul Pasha, who was the Turkish representative, was about as deaf as I am. When we were together I knew what was going on, and when we were not, I did not have this apparatus and did not know anything about it.

Q. The names that you mentioned in this negotiation, did you know these people? A. Necessarily so, yes.

Q. Was your relationship with these people on the footing of you being a man whom they talked with and relied on and had respect fort? A. The best answer to that is the actual documents transmitted to the State Department and back and forward between the different ministers.

Q. Those are in existence? A. Yes.

Q. And those Mr. Battle can find and check if he wants? A. I am sure of that.

Cross-examination by Mr. Battle, attorney of the defendant

[…]

Q. What did you do after that? A. I crossed the Atlantic quite frequently but in course of time I went to Turkey.

Q. Between the time that you left the aviation company in 1921 and the time you went to Turkey what were you doing? A. It was not a very long time.

Q. How long was it! A. A matter of months, I think.

Q. Give us your best recollection. A. I am doing so.

Q. How many months is your best recollection? A. A few months, to the best of my recollection.

Q. Less than six months, would you say? A. I do not know. It is one of those things one gets into gradually. I spent a considerable time here before going to Turkey in discussions with Admiral Chester and traveling between here and Washington to see him, and so forth.

Q. After you had these discussions with Admiral Chester here, then you went to Turkey? A. Then I went to Turkey.

Q. You went to Turkey a few months after you had ceased your connection with the aviation company? A. A reasonable time. I cannot say how many.

Q. I will ask you again to give me your best recollection of how many months? A. I have done so. I have told you one thing gradually merges into another. Where the division point takes place I cannot tell you.

Q. That is the best answer you can give? A. That is the best I can do for you.

Q. Then you went to Turkey. About what time was it you went to Turkey? A. I think it was 1921.

Q. Do you remember the season of the year? A. My first trip to Turkey was in the winter. At least, it was getting cold weather.

Q. In the winter of 1921? A. I think it was the winter or maybe spring. It was not the coldest winter, but it was the cold weather in Constantinople.

Q. In 1921? A. I think in 1921.

Q. How long did you remain in Turkey? A. I was in Turkey on the first trip for—oh, gettine: on a matter of a year or so.

Q. With whom did you, deal in Turkey, Mr. Kennedy? Just answer who it was that you dealt with. A. I dealt with a great number of people.

Q. Who was the chief person that you dealt with? A. I should say—I should say the Premier would be the outstanding man, if you are speaking of native Turks.

Q. How long did you continue in your negotiations with the Premier? A. They were not continued with the Premier; he referred me to the Minister of Public Works.

Q. How long did you continue those negotiations? How long did they last? A. I think approximately a year's time.

Q. You were in Turkey all that time? A. I was in Turkey, I think, all that time. I may have taken a trip or two away, but materially I was there all that time.

Q. That brings you down to 1922. A. That was around somewhere in 1922, if we are starting off the right date.

Q. When did you have your first connection with the Ottoman American Development Company? A. Before I went to Turkey.

Q. Was that a part of the same concession? A. It was. It was the concern that got the concession.

Q. The Ottoman American Development Company was the concern that got the concession? A. Yes.

Q. When did you finally consummate your work on the concession? When did you finish your work on the concession? A. I cannot tell you the date offhand. This crowd pinched all my papers. I think it was a matter

Q. Can you give me your best recollection? A. It was around 1922 when the thing was concluded. I may be nine months out.

Q. And what happened to the concession? A. Nothing happened to it. The grant—the concession passed Parliament—signed by the necessary people, a certain amount of work was done, and owing to political considerations there was a hold-up. The Lausanne conference altered, took away some of the Turkish territory, and just nothing happened.

Q. Mr. Kennedy, I show you this and ask you whether this is your signature (handing paper to witness)? A. I think so—yes.

Q. I am just showing you the signature. A. I think that is my signature.

Q. To the best of your knowledge and belief that is your signature? A.

I think so, yes.

Q. I ask you whether you did not sue Admiral Chester and his sons for false arrest? A. I did not. Most definitely, unequivocally, I did not.

Mr. Battle: I offer this summons and complaint in evidence.

Mr. Schloss: May I see it? I object to this, your Honor, on the ground that is an original complaint which shows nothing on any suit or anything else.

Mr. Battle: I will follow it up.

The Court: It shows nothing of any suit?

Mr. Schloss: It does not show any suit was instituted by verifying a complaint with a lawyer. I also object on the ground it is immaterial, incompetent, irrelevant.

The Court: It is not now because it is offered in contradiction of an alleged statement. I will allow it.

Mr. Schloss: I respectfully except.

(Received in evidence and marked Defendant's Exhibit A.)

Mr. Battle: The summons and complaint are both offered in evidence.

The Court: Yes.

(Mr. Battle read Defendant's Exhibit A to the jury.)

The Court: What is the date of the summons?

Mr. Battle: March 25, 1926.

Q. Mr. Kennedy, did you see the answer to your complaint that was filed by Colby Chester, Colby Chester, Jr., also known as Clarence Chester, and Arthur Chester, through the law firm of Dawes, Abbott & Littlefield! A. I have no knowledge of such a proceeding.

Mr. Battle: I ask that the answer be marked for identification.

(Marked Defendant's Exhibit B for Identification.)

Q. Now, I ask you if this is your signature (handing paper to witness)? A. I think so. I signed a lot of these for him at various times.

Mr. Battle: I offer that in evidence.

Mr. Schloss : I object to that, your Honor, an the--

The Court: Sustained.

Mr. Battle: I except, and ask that it he marked for identification.

(Paper referred to was marked Defendant's Exhibit C for Identification.)

Q. Mr. Kennedy, is this your handwriting, this notation at the top of this paper I show you here (handing paper to witness), A. I think so. I would not swear to it. It looks like it.

Q. To the best of your belief it is? A. If there is anything to support it I would not say the contrary.

Q. Isn't this the notes that you made and gave to your attorney from which to prepare your reply?

Mr. Schloss: I object to that as immaterial, irrelevant, incompetent.

The Court: In relation to what?

Mr. Battle: To relation to the last document.

The Court: The one that is in evidence?

Mr. Battle: No, the one that is excluded.

The Court: Objection sustained.

Mr. Battle: I ask, may I have that marked for identification?

The Court: Certainly.

(The paper referred to was marked Defendant's Exhibit D for Identification.)

Q. Now, Mr. Kennedy, you say you consummated the business of the so-called Chester concession about 1921 A. I am not sure of the date. It was somewhere about it. It was between 1921 and 1922 and 1923.

Q. That is as near as you can come to it? A. It depends on what you call "consummated." There were a lot of negotiations. There was a matter of getting the matter accepted by the different heads.

Q. What I mean by consummated is finishing it, completing it. A. But the thing was never finished, Mr. Battle. That is just it.

Q. It has never been finished up? A. Absolutely. Part of the work was started and never finished yet, but the contract, the grants was secured from the government.

Q. When did you stop working on it? A. Why, strictly speaking, I cannot say it has stopped yet for that matter.

Q. You are still working on it? A. It depends on what you call working on it. The situation is, there is 50,000 pounds on deposit there. The thing has never been legally cancelled as far us I know. There was a certain amount of construction work done.

Q. What was the last amount of work you did? A. That all depends on what you call work. I am still corresponding with banks in Turkey about it.

Q. You are still corresponding! A. Yes, banks that are interested in it, that assisted me when originally got the thing.

Q. After the Chester concession business, what the next business you went into?

While under oath, could Kenneth E. Clayton-Kennedy have uncovered Henry Woodhouse's forgery about the end of the Chester Concession?

The terms of the concessions had a potential life of 99 years. Article 4 of the original Chester concessions found in James Wood Colt's archive that is preserved at Rochester University Library in New York reads:

Art. 4:- For the execution of the engagements which is contracts by the present Convention, the Ottoman American Exploration Co. is held to form at the latest, in the delay of six months reckoned from the moment when the Concession shall become definitive and on the basis of the Statutes usual in such cases, a Limited Ottoman Society, which shall be submitted to all the Ottoman Laws, present and future. The Ottoman American exploration Co. engages itself to reserve <u>one-third</u> of the shares of the Company which it shall issue, and to hold these at the disposition of Ottoman subjects who may wish to subscribe at Constantinople during the 31 days which follow notice which shall be given in the newspapers of the capital.

Could this article in the agreement mean that the concessions secured by the U.S. were not lost, but rather forged into an unrecognizable form? These questions beg further investigation as they may shed some light on certain aspects of even current U.S. foreign policy towards Armenians and their claims against Turkey for reparations, including the occupied territories that had been awarded to the Armenians in 1920, which include minerals covered under the concessions in question.

In recent years, Turkey has been looking for foreign investments in the mining sector. Turkey has ambitions to become one of the top 10 global economies. And they aim to achieve this goal by the 100th anniversary of the Turkish republic in 2023. The mining sector is expected to contribute $15 billion of the targeted $500 billion of exports. Turkey reports that just 10-15% of Turkey's mining operations belong to the public sector. One must wonder who owns the other 85-90%? Could it be the Chester Concession?

Rear Admiral Colby M. Chester and his sons were among the richest men in the United States before World War II. One has to wonder how much of that wealth came from Chester Concession at the expense of the misfortunes of millions of Armenians?

U.S.S. Kentucky Capt. Colby M. Chester in his cabin - 1900
(Edward H. Hart, photographe; Detroit Publishing Co., publisher)

Colby M. Chester's 20th Birthday - February 29, 1924

Arlington National Cemetery, Section 3, Lot 1901

Chapter 28

Confession of a Rear Admiral

Although most everything regarding the Chester Concession and the United States involvement to the detriment of the Armenian nation has been presented in the previous chapter, another layer of the United States involvement in the Armenian Genocide needs to be presented.

At the age of 79, retired Rear Admiral Colby M. Chester gave an interview to Charles G. Ross, Chief Washington Correspondent of the *Post-Dispatch*. Chester's bragging about how clever he was to win a prize from the newly recognized Turkish government, amounts to a confession. To add insult to injury, this same Turkish government was comprised of many officials who had been sentenced to death by an Ottoman courts-martial of 1919-1920 for their crime against the Armenians, including Mustafa Kemal. As highlighted in Chester's confession, the Turkish government then was led by the Grand Vizier, whom Chester himself had groomed at the naval school of Annapolis, in the United States, during Sultan Adbul Hamid's rule over the Ottoman Empire. With this said, it is highly likely that Chester has made his own contributions to the overthrow of the Sultan to end the Ottoman Empire, so he could obtain the mineral concessions for the United States.

The following is the full text of Charles Ross' article that appeared in the editorial section of the *St. Louis Post-Dispatch*, on April 29, 1923 (I have underlined points of importance):

ST. LOUIS POST-DISPATCH
EDITORIAL SECTION
SPEICAL CONTRIBUTION
PART THREE
ST. LOUIS, SUNDAY MORNING, APRIL 29, 1923

The Chester Concession in Turkey
Just What and Where It Is and What It Signifies
PROGRESSIVE AMERICAN ENGINEERS TO DIG MOSLEM
PEOPLE OUT OF THE DUST OF ANTIQUITY

How an Admiral of the U.S. Fleet Won the Sublime Porte's Regard on a Secret Diplomatic Mission During Roosevelt's Administration to Such a Degree He Was Urged to Come to Turkey to Command and Build Up the Fleet, an Honor That Also Was Offered Later to His Son. Likewise and American Naval Officer – Now as a Sequel to This High Regard Comes the Exclusive Privilege to Exploit a Vast Region With Mineral Wealth Estimated at Over $4,000,000,000 While English and French Capitalists Vainly Rave.

By CHARLES G. ROSS.
Chief Washington Correspondent of the Post-Dispatch.

WASHINGTON. April 28. In the beginning, the story of the vast Chester concession which the Turkish Government has granted American interests for the economic development of Turkey is the story of a Connecticut Yankee at the Sultan's court.

Later chapters ramify into world politics. Oil, newest and most virulent of international trouble-makers, becomes the theme. Roosevelt and Root are characters; European diplomatists, keen on the scent of oil, stalk across the pages; in the background are unidentified American financiers and the American State Department.

The leading character throughout is the adventurous American naval officer from whom the concessions takes its name. He is the Connecticut Yankee of the story. At the age of 79, he is watching, with jealous interest, a train of events that he set in motion 23 years ago.

Colby M. Chester, now a Rear Admiral of the United States Navy, on the retired list, went to Turkey in 1900 in command of the U.S.S. Kentucky. His mission was to help collect an American claim for indemnity growing out of the destruction of missionaries' property in 1896, not a mission, it would seem, calculated to win him the favor of the Turks. He got the indemnity and so tactfully and skillfully did he conduct his negotiations he made a warm friend of the Sultan, Abdul Hamid.

Had "Time of His Life"

He had since remarked that during the 10 days he spent in Constantinople as the guest of the Sultan he had the "time of his life." Then and later he was showered with honors by the Turkish

Confession of a Rear Admiral

Government. On one occasion he was offered the command of the Turkish Navy and when he declined, the Sultan told him that the Government would get an order from Roosevelt compelling him to accept. The name of Roosevelt, the Admiral says, was a name to conjure with the Turkey in those days. As a result of the friendly feeling for America engendered by the negotiations of 1900, the Sultan made a contract for the building of a Turkish cruiser at Philadelphia and gave encouragement to Roberts College. The fair policy of the United States, explains Admiral Chester, was an eye-opener to the Sultan, who, during the whole 23 years of his reign up to 1900, had been the constant victim of European intrigues. He let the Admiral know that he would welcome a closer relationship with America and a large increase of the trade between the two countries.

In 1906, after he had filled a number of important posts in the navy, Admiral Chester, being then 62 years old, was retired. The Government, however, recognizing his flair for diplomacy, did not let him go into seclusion, and in 1908 he was sent abroad to represent the United States at an international congress of geographers at Geneva, an aeronautic congress at London, and a convention of navigation experts at St. Petersburg. More important than any of these assignments, which furnished the ostensible reason for his tour, was a commission that he carried from the New York Chamber of Commerce and the Board of Trade and Transportation of New York to go to Turkey and see what could be done to foster trade relations with the Near East.

Roosevelt and Root Supported Move

President Roosevelt and Secretary of State Root were in full sympathy with this effort of American capital to break into the rich Near Eastern field. Admiral Chester was to find the door through which it might enter. The success which had attended his first visit to Turkey made him the right man for the job.

Going to Constantinople, Admiral Chester received a warm greeting from his old friend, the Sultan, and began forthwith the negotiations which have just culminated. 15 years later, in the ratification of the Chester concession by the Turkish National Parliament at Angora.

The Admiral's task was smoothed by the esteem in which the Turks held him, but the Admiral, being the American naval officer, refused. He did decorate a son of the Admiral with one of the highest Ottoman orders.

Coming down to the business in which the admiral was interested, the Sultan suggested that he undertake the direction of all the public works of which Turkey stood in need. Abdul Hamid, the Admiral says, actually proposed that he assume full responsibility for the letting of all contracts for railroad, docks, oil and other development works, with the sole restriction that all the contacts should go to Americans.

Young Turks Overthrew Sultan

The negotiations were in a fair way to come to a happy ending when Abdul Hamid was overthrown by the Young Turks and locked up in the Bosporus Palace. Finally, however, in 1909, the Admiral got sent to a concession base on the scheme of railroad and port construction and mineral development which he had laid down. As its chief feature, the concessions carried the right to construct 1200 miles of railway and develop a strip of territory 20 kilometers wide on each side of the right of way. An incident of the plan is the proposed continuation of the Bagdad Railway eastward to the Persian border, where it is contemplated that Persia, aided by British capital, will continue the construction through that country and thus bring to realization the long-cherished dream of a Constantinople-to-Bagdad road.

This, in brief outline, is the concession which had just been ratified. There is no doubt, according to Admiral Chester, that it would have received parliamentary sanction long ago if a succession of wars had not prevented. When the negotiations were completed in 1909 Turkey was in a turmoil after the revolution. The war between Turkey and Italy, the two Balkan wars, and the World War followed. During all this period it was manifestly impossible for the American promoters of the scheme to operate. Their claim, however, the Admiral insists, validly runs back to the grant of 1909, because the contract, as signed by the Turkish Minister of Public Works, expressly stipulates that operations might be suspended in the event of war, without loss of any of the concessionaires' rights.

Turks Dated Back Concessions

The Admiral points out, moreover, that the Turkish Parliament, in its recent act of ratification, which passed with only 12 dissenting votes in a total of about 350, safeguarded the American's claims by dating the concessions back to 1909.

The companies which have been organized to exploit the concessions are the Ottoman-American Development Co. and the Ottoman-American Petroleum Co. The nature of the financial backing has not been disclosed.

Standard Oil, it is known, is not only not associated with the project, but is antagonistic. At the head of the Ottoman-American Industrial Co., which proposes to build the railroads provided for by the concession, is Major-General George W. Goethals of Panama Canal fame. Kermit Roosevelt, son of the late President, has also been mentioned as one of Admiral Chester's associates. An active assistant in the enterprise is one of the Admiral's sons, Commander Arthur T. Chester, U. S. N., retired, who, after seeing the concession through the Turkish Parliament, is now on his way home with the contracts to arrange financial details prior to the beginning of surveys. An interesting sidelight on the good will of the Turks for the Chesters is the fact that Arthur, like his father before him, was offered command of the Turkish Navy.

In all his dealings with the Turks, the Admiral has seen the return of the bread that he cast upon the waters. For instances, he persuaded President Roosevelt to send the American fleet to Constantinople during its world tour.

The Turkish Government, naturally, was pleased. Going further, Admiral Chester arranged for 12 young Turkish naval officers to return with the fleet and receive instructions at Annapolis.

One of these officers, Rouf Bey, was present when the Turkish Parliament ratified the Chester concession, with only 12 dissenting votes. He happens to be now the Grand Vizier of Turkey.

Not long ago, a representative of the Standard Oil Co. called on the Grand Vizier and said:

"I presume you understand that Standard Oil Co. is not back of this concession?"

"I presume you understand," returned the Grand Vizier, "that the Turkish Government is back of it."

If the story of the Chester concession ended here, it would need only an epilogue telling that American capitalists are getting ready to reap the fruit of Chester's long labors, but oil enters the plot, and oil, in its internal aspect, brings plot and counterplot, claim and counter-claim. No sooner had the Chester concession been ratified than protests from Briton and French sources began to be heard.

If the concession meant only the building of railroads in Turkey, the British and French might view the prospects with comparative equanimity. What galls is the fact that the concession opens up to Americans a territory which according to Admiral Chester, is estimated by experts to contain $4,000,000,000 worth of oil, or about the amount of the British debt to the United States. Just the statement of that fact indicates the dynamite in the situation. Both the British and the French put forth claims in opposition to the Chester grant.

Concession Runs Into Mosul Area.

Briefly, the French Contend that the Chester claim is invalidated by a prior concession granted before the World War for development of harbors and railroads in Northern Anatolia. The French have indicated to Secretary of State Hughes that they will not recognize the Chester concessions in so far as it impinges on what they assert are their own rights.

To understand the British claim, it is necessary to know that the Chester concessions runs into the Mosul area, whose oil fields have made it one of the principal bones of internal contention in the world today. Mosul oil was one of the issues that kept the last Lausanne conference from an agreement. It is a highly contentious issue before the present conference. The Turks claim that the Vallayt (Provence) of Mosul, where the rich oil fields lie, is part of their territory, to do with as they please. The British assert that Mosul is part of the territory of Mesopotamia, or Iraq, which they hold under mandate. At the last Lausanne conference the British asked that the dispute be referred to the League of Nations. The Turks demurred, saying they would have no chance against British influence in the league. They proposed, instead, a plebiscite, which the British declined to accept. There the matter rested, to come anew before the conference now sitting.

The British contend that the Turks not only have no authority over Mosul, but that even if they had, they would have no right to grant a concession in conflict with claims of the Turkish Petroleum Co. Lord Curson set out this view in detail at the last Lausanne conference. He said that just before the war a concession was given for the oil fields of the Mosul and Bagdad Vilayats by the Turkish Government to the Turkish Petroleum Co., in which Germans had an interest with the British. On the defeat of the Germans, he maintained, their interest passed to the British.

"The British Government, after full examination," said Lord Curson, as reported in the official minutes of the proceedings, "were convinced, and remain convinced, of the validity of this concession. They felt, and feel, bound to uphold it."

In a statement declining to admit that Mosul was a part of Iraq, the Turkish delegate, Ismet Pasha, summed up the Turkish position with regard to the Turkish Petroleum Co.'s concession in the following words:

"All the treaties, agreements and conventions which England may have concluded in regard to a country which is still legally part of the Ottoman Empire can have no legal value. The more so because the populations have not been given a chance of expressing their wishes freely and safe from all pressure and foreign occupation."

The attitude of the American Government toward conflicting concessions in the Near East was set forth by Ambassador Child at Lausanne on Jan. 23, as follows:

"Where there are conflicting claims already in existence in respect to legal rights to resources, there should be provided a means for judicial settlement of the rights which would give full and complete assurance of impartiality.

"The American representatives feel in their duty to remind the conference that, without seeking special privileges or favor, the Government of the United States had not assented to the principle that it may be dissociated in the rights of peace from the usual consequence of association in war."

Admiral Chester Would Hold On.

How far the State Department would go in upholding the Chester concession against British and French counter claims remains to be determined.

In the opinion of Admiral Chester, the British and French claimants "have not a leg to stand on." He has announced his determination to hold on to the Chester grant against all comers, while Dr. Gouad Bey, who is now in this country as a special representative of the new Turkish Government, has declared, that no power on earth could induce Turkey to withdraw the concession.

Before continuing with an interview given the writer by Admiral Chester, it is, perhaps, pertinent to say that in some Washington quarters there is a feeling that his failure to name the financial backers of his project maybe be due not to any desire for secrecy but difficulty in interesting American financiers in the scheme. It is estimated that the amount needed for the projected works is $300,000,000. The question is whether American investors will be willing to risk large sums in a disturbed part of the world without any guarantee of permanent protection by the American Government.

However that may be, Admiral Chester appears to be supremely confident that his dream of a Turkey rejuvenated through American capital will be realized. His concession makes possible not only the construction of railroads and the working of mines and oil fields, but the building of canals, factories, banks, hotels, telephone and telegraph lines, and even, it is hinted, a new, model capital city on the site chosen by the Turkish Parliament. The plan goes so far as to contemplate a social welfare program, embracing the establishment of social centers and organized sports, all with a view to the general improvement and Westernizing of the Turkish character.

The American nation, in Admiral Chester's opinion, has much to gain from the commercial development of Turkey.

"After the Revolutionary War, when we were practically bankrupt," said the Admiral, "we went out and developed the West and made a boom. In that way we paid our war debts. A similar process followed the Civil War. We built railroads and continued westward.

"Must Get New Ideas to Develop."

"Now there is nothing left in this country for us to develop. If we keep up with our current requirements we are doing well. To pay our debts, we must get new territory to develop. I've got it for the country. That the thing in a nutshell.

"Lausanne has nothing to do with this. It is not an issue between the Government of the United States and any other Government. The syndicate that I represent had gone into Asia-Minor just as commercial bodies have gone into South America. As American business men, we have the right to go to our Government for protection against any foreign Government that raises to interfere with a legitimate enterprise.

"I want to eradicate the idea that I have carried this country into trouble. This protection was designed under the Roosevelt administration. Wars broke out and prevented our taking over the property. Now we are ready to proceed.

"With materials from America, we're going to build another Denver, another Albuquerque, another Cheyenne. To become prosperous, Turkey waits only on railways to bring out its products. To illustrate, the cost of taking ore from the copper mines at Arghana to the border for smelting is $50 a tone—a prohibitive price. Railways will carry the ore at $2 a ton.

"If as I believe, there is enough oil to pay the British war debt to the United States, there is in the whole concession enough potential commerce to pay all the national debt of the United States.

"American business concerns have been trying to get into South America but have found that they can't compete with European nations in that field. The British and French have covered South America with banks.

Breaking Into Asia by Back Door.

"We've tried for 20 years to break into Asia through China, where John Hay established the principle of the open door, but have been hindered by European spheres of influence. Now we propose to go in through the back door—Asia Minor—which is the nearest door. All trade there is tending toward the West. Turkey is closer to our eastern coast by 5000 miles than China.

"France has forfeited the concession that she got from Turkey. She didn't put in all the money agreed on. Besides, France went to war with Turkey and the United States did not. Our concessions, moreover came first.

"Neither the French nor the English claim has a leg to stand on. I think that in both cases the Governments are being put up to make protests by their citizens, and that when the record is revived it will be found that the claims are not of a nature to cause international controversy. The so-called British concession was granted in 1914 by the Turkish Minister of Finance who shortly afterward was deprived of office. It never was ratified by the Turkish Assembly.

"The Turks are united under Kemal Pasha. If England should try to coerce Turkey, she would lose India. I am for the Young Turks, who are fighting for the freedom of their country just as we fought for ours, against England."

Intriguing European Powers, according to Admiral Chester, have fastened on the Turk, for their own purposes, the reputation of being an "unspeakable" person.

"James Bryce," he said, "declared that the Turks were a lovable and honest people, but that Turkish Governments had been horrible. That is the case. Now the Turks have destroyed despotism. They look on us as their protectors.

"I have sometimes been accused of expressing pro-Turkish views because I am a concessionaire of the Turkish Government. The truth is the other way about. I was willing to become a concessionaire because I believe in the Turks."

Admiral Chester explained that the syndicate is given 18 months in which to make surveys. If at the end of that time it does not find enough minerals to make the project paying venture, it need not go further. The concession runs for 99 years. Turkey having the right to buy at the end of 30 years.

Admiral Chester is an ardent admirer of Roosevelt.

Speaking of a trip he made to Angora last spring in the interest of the Chester concession, the admiral said if Roosevelt had been alive he would have taken his picture out there and done more with it than he could have done on an order from the Sultan.

Although the archive has a great deal more on this subject that could fill a book of its own, I will only share three more very important points involving the Chester Concessions and the United States Government's involvement in the Armenian Genocide.

The estimated value of the overall concession as confessed to by Colby M. Chester was enough to pay the entire war debt of $22 billion dollars. And this a debt that was owed to the bakers in the United States, including that of Jacob H. Schiff, who had sent a special commission in 1909 to the Ottoman Empire to survey for the Chester Concessions.[101]

The other point of importance was the United States and their need for oil, which was believed to be on the verge of exhaustion of their domestic oil reserves in less than 20 years.[102] The estimated 8 billion barrels of oil found in part on Armenian inhabited lands, accounted for 1/6th of the world's known oil reserves.[103] This need for oil resulted in the United States' abandonment of the

---

101 Akron Beacon Journal, *WORLD CONVERT TURK LANDS INTO WORLD'S GARDEN SPOT*, (April 27, 1923, Akron Beacon Journal, Akron, OH) 15.

102 Henry Suydam, *AMERICA, FACING OIL EXHAUSTION IN 18 YEAR, TO DEMAND RIGHT TO UNDEVELOPED WORLD FIELDS*, (December 24, 1922, Brooklyn, NY) 2E.

103 Associated Press, *ASKED TO PARTICIPATE*, (June 28, 1925, Clarion Ledger, Jackson, MS) 1.

Armenians and their rights to lands which were legally awarded to them by the United States President, Woodrow Wilson. The U.S. subsequently partnered with the Young Turks, arming them and then later helping bring to power Mustafa Kemal and his Turkish Nationalist Movement, a relationship which appears to continues until today.

As for mention of the of the concession never materializing by an article written by Henry Woodhouse and then later on during a court case in New York, testimony given under oath the fact came out that the Chester Concessions did continue, to further dispel any doubts, I will present one of the only two newspaper articles of 1925 that were also the last mention in the news of the Chester Concessions. On June 10, 1925, *The Baltimore Sun* printed the following:

Chester Regains Control Of Turkey Concessions
Retired Admiral And Two Sons Will Manage Exploitation Work.

New York, June 9 (AP).—Henry Woodhouse, representing a committee of stockholders of the Ottoman-American Development Company, announced that at a conference today Admiral Colby M. Chester, retired, and his two sons, Colby M. Chester, Jr., and Commander Arthur Chester, accepted and invitation of the committee to assume full control of the Chester concessions in Turkey.

The Chesters and the stockholders' committee, Mr. Woodhouse said, control ninety per cent of the stock of the Ottoman-American Development Company, which was organized to develop the concessions. Disagreements among stockholder which have hitherto prevented work on the concessions have now been settled, Mr. Woodhouse said.

The concessions obtained from Turkey by Admiral Chester gave the holders the right to exploit the oil, gold, silver, platinum, copper and other minerals in an area of more than 50,000 square miles.

Chapter 29

The Bankers

"The hand that gives is above the hand that takes. Money had no motherland; financiers are without patriotism and without decency; their sole object is gain." – Napoleon Bonaparte

The clash of the gargantuan financial and economic interests of the Western powers in different areas of the vast Ottoman Empire at the beginning of the 20th century show that the Armenian Genocide was not merely a hate crime due to cultural and religious differences between Christians and Muslims. There are numerous accounts of Kurdish tribesmen periodically pillaging, with the blessing of the Sultan, hard-working Armenians, Greeks, and Assyrians. However, there is no record of an intent to completely uproot the Armenian population, as documented in 1894-1896 by Sultan Abdul Hamid and then in 1915-1923 by the Young Turk government.

The memoirs of British spy Aubrey Herbert shed light on a possible motive for the genocide of the Armenian people. He dictated his memoirs at the age of 43, bed-ridden in a hospital in the final year of his life. The passage in question is on pages 15-16 in *Ben Kendin: A Record of Eastern Travels* published a year after his death, in 1924:

> Salonika, by the blue sea and amongst the cypresses, is only a poor footstool for Olympus. It is a town of intrigues and persecutions. In the days of my first visit it was more free than Constantinople; there was not the same vigilance, and the Jews, who are the majority of this inhabitants, have always enjoyed a greater liberty than any other subject race in Turkey. They have, indeed, shared with the greatest heartiness in assisting other people to massacre the Greeks and Armenians, who are their commercial rivals.
>
> The coming storm had not yet broken, but already its mutterings were to be heard. The Grand Orient (The Chief Masonic Lodge of the Near East) was at work. There were links between New York and the bootbacks of Salonika, and again between Salonika and the unruly Albanians. Talaat was studying the literature of the French Revolution; Karasso was engaged in Freemasonry; Enver, in the mountains of Macedonia or in a sailing boat in the Gulf, was engrossed in tactics.
>
> The Jews of Salonika, generally known as *Dunmes* (converts), were the real parents of the Turkish revolution. They are a definite people—Hebrews, but indefinable as to creed. The popular verdict was that they were only nominal Moslems and were true followers of the Pentateuch, bowing their heads in the temple of Rimmon for the sake of profit. At that time, only the

most industrious student of the Near East knew of their existence. There was no man to prophesy that the *Dunmes* were to be the chief authors of the revolution whose results were to shake the world.

Who was Herbert referring to in New York? My research has led me to powerful U.S. bankers, most notably Jacob H. Schiff of Kuhn, Loeb & Co. This is the same man who made a financial contribution to the Bolshevik Revolution, the repercussions of which resulted in the retreat of the Russian army in Western Armenia with devasting consequences for the Armenian population. Prior to that, Schiff had financed a survey of the mineral wealth of Armenian-populated lands. This survey was carried out by James W. Colt and Armen Garo. Colt was also working with J.P. Morgan, who, judging by Colt's letters, was also interested in economic opportunities in Western Armenia.

Jacob H. Schiff and wife Teresa Loeb-Schiff (daughter of Solomon Loeb). Circa 1915 or 1920 (Bain News Service, publisher)

Following the promising results of the Colt survey, *The Courier* (Waterloo, Iowa) on May 20, 1909, Page 7, reported:

SCHIFF, ZANGWILL BACK JEW MOVEMENT

New York, May 20. – That Jacob H. Schiff, banker, and Israel Zangwill, author and head of the Jewish Territorialist organization, have come together in an effort to colonize in Mesopotamia, as a compromise of the Zionist colonization plans in Palestine, was the news received yesterday by Jacob Fishman, editor of the Jewish Daily News of this city. The invitations of Ahmed Riza Bey, president of the Turkish chamber of deputies under the new young Turk government, to create a Jewish state in Mesopotamia, was taken under consideration.

The society, the largest and richest Jewish colonization organization in the world, to which $45,000,000 was left in trust by the late Baron de Hirsch, sent a geographical survey commission to investigate conditions. The preliminary reports showed that the land was most fertile and that irrigation was all that was needed to make it prolific. The Zionists readily accepted the scheme, for Mesopotamia is not far from Palestine.

It is thought that through the efforts of Mr. Schiff, who is now touring Europe, the allied Jewish organizations of the world can perfect the plan and the work of settlement can be begun at an early date.

It is estimated that it will take at least $40,000 to irrigate the territory, but with this expenditure and the cost of transportation added, the situation in Russia, where there are between 5,000,000 and 6,000,000 Jews in desperate conditions, not to speak of those of Roumania, numbering about 400,000 will be entirely relieved.

The invitation of Ahmed Riza Bey was extended through the chief rabbi and was sent throughout the entire world with the promise that the Turkish government will allow home rule to the settlers. There will be little or no effect upon the Jewish population of the United States, but a large amount of the necessary capital is expected to come from this country.

On May 27, 1909, *The Union Republican* (Winston-Salem, North Carolina) expanded on the story front page news:

THE ZION MOVEMENT.
JEWISH EYES TURNING TOWARDS MESOPOTAMIA.
PICK VALLEY OF EUPHRATES.

Is it the Beginning of the End?—

The Gospel Preached to Every Nation and the Jews Gathered Again in the Land of Their Patriarch Fathers.

New York, May 20. – That Jacob H. Schiff, banker, and Israel Zangwill, author and head of the Jewish Territorialist Organization, have come together in an effort to colonize in Mesopotamia, as a compromise of the Zionist colonization plans in Palestine, was the news received yesterday by Jacob Fishman, editor of the Jewish Daily News of this city.

The invitation of Ahmed Riza Bey, president of the Turkish chamber of deputies under the new young Turk government, to create a Jewish state in Mesopotamia under home government, was taken under consideration.

$45,000,000 Held in Trust.

The "Ica" Society, the largest and richest Jewish colonization organization in the world, to which $45,000,000 was left in trust by the late Baron de Hirsch, sent a geographical survey commission to investigate conditions. The preliminary reports showed that the land was most fertile and that irrigation was all that was needed to make it prolific.

The Zionists readily accepted the scheme, for Mesopotamia is not far from Palestine.

It is thought that though the efforts of Mr. Schiff, who is now touring Europe, the allied Jewish organizations of the world can perfect the plan and the work of settlement can be begun at an early date.

Will Relieve Russ Situation.

It is estimated that it will take at least $40,000,000 to irrigate the territory, but, with this expenditure and the cost of transportation added, the situation in Russia, where there are between 5,000,000 and 6,000,000 Jews in desperate condition, not to speak of those in Roumania, numbering about 400,000, will be entirely relieved.

The invitation of Ahmed Riza Bey was extended through the chief rabbi and was sent throughout the entire world with the promise that the Turkish government will allow home rule to the settlers.

There will be little or no effect on the Jewish population of the United States, but a large amount of the necessary capital is expected to come from this country.

Private advices from London received in this city yesterday told of a meeting of the Jewish Territorial organization, at which Mr. Zangwill, Sir Andrew Wingate, Meyer Spielman and others declared that in the settlement of Mesopotamia is to be found the solution of the troubles which have beset the Jews since they were dispersed from Palestine.

Mr. Schiff is expected to arrive in London this week to confer with those men who have received assurance from the Turkish government that Mesopotamia will be given to the Jews to develop and govern as they see fit.

50,000 Zionists in U. S.

In the United States there are 330 Zionist organizations, with a total membership of 50,000. Zionists were divided at the last congress between the proposal to accept an offer from the British government to settle in a part of Africa which has since been found to be unacceptable and the proposal to center all energies on the acquisition of Palestine.

It is proposed to send at once an expedition of exploration through Mesopotamia for the purpose of gathering information which will guide the propagandists of the colony idea.

In cable messages from London friends of Mr. Zangwill said today that Mr. Schiff's co-operation will mean that the plan to found a colony in Mesopotamia will have that financial support which no other plan has had.

It seems that Schiff's ambitious plan, which he was carrying out with Henry Morgenthau, near the end of the World War I, to make Palestine the homeland of the Jews, had actually taken off right after the Young Turks rose to power.

The Tennessean (Nashville, Tennessee) published an article on January 19, 1911, page 1, documenting how well-connected Schiff and his cohorts were in the U.S. and what support they had for their plan to colonize the Near East.

HEBREWS HEAR LEADERS TALK
Roosevelt, Gaynor, Straus and Schiff Upon Judaism.

DELEGATES IN NEW YORK GUESTS AT BIG BANQUET

Col. Roosevelt, the Guest of Honor, Is Lauded as the Jew's Greatest American Friend, Who Practices What He Preaches—Immigration Laws.

NEW YORK, Jan. 18.—The delegates to the twenty-second council of the union of the American Hebrew congregations in session here voted unanimously today to hold the next conference in Cincinnati in 1913.

At the banquet tonight the delegates and their guests listened to addresses by Theodore Roosevelt, Mayor Gaynor, Oscar Straus, Dr. David Philipson of Cincinnati and Jacob H. Schiff, who also acted as toastmaster. Gov. Dix sent a telegram of greeting.

Col. Roosevelt, as the guest of honor, was praised by the toastmaster as "one who more than any other American, living or dead, has taught the world the lesson that, equally with any other citizen of this country, the Jew is entitled to the square deal—more than that, he not only preached theories, he turned them into actualities and called on of our co-religionists into the cabinet of the President of the United States, the highest office within his gift. We Jews owe him a debt of gratitude which I hope never will be forgotten."

DR. PHIILIPSON TALKS.

In Introducing Dr. Philipson, of the Hebrew College, Mr. Schiff spoke of the trend of the modern Jewish belief.

"With all the respect—ayer love—," he said, "I have for the old forms as our fathers practiced them, Judaism in American surroundings would soon cease to be a living force without these missionaries—as I have styled them—equipped at and sent out from the American Hebrew Collage."

Gov. Dix wished the delegates "Godspeed in the transcendent work you are doing for the good of mankind."

"The glory of the Jews," he said, "is that from the dawn of history they have revealed and manifested to the world the genius and essence of true religion, based on the worship of the one God, and on the inner spiritual life upon when depends the reality of the eternal and the hope and uplift humanity."

Mayor Gaynor said:

"Israel always has been a growing and advancing religious force. The history of the Jewish race," he continued, "discloses no period in which mere non-essential religious forms were not being gradually changed or abandoned in order to keep pace with the teachings of experience or to conform to the just local or national usages."

IMMIGRATION LAWS.

One of the features of the day was the severe criticism or federal immigration laws and their enforcement by Max J. Kohler and the reply of Charles Nagel, secretary of the department of commerce and labor.

Speaking of exceptional cases of unfortunates and "the stretching" of the letter of the law to help the unfortunates, Secretary Nagel added:

"You may call me a lawbreaker, but I wish to remind you that these exceptions are acts of common justice, of mercy and humanity to save the separation of the members of a family.

"I am absolutely opposed to the illiterate test as a question of fitness for admission of the immigrant. Take a good, healthy uneducated workman; the fact that he does not know how to read and write makes him all the more desirable, as he will the quicker assimilate American ideals and customs and the language of his adopted country"

At the conclusion of Secretary Nagel's address, Chairman Schiff moved a rising vote of thanks to Mr. Nagel, which was given. Mr. Schiff apologized for the unjust criticism of Mr. Nagel and the department of commerce and labor.

"At the same time I want to emphasize this," Mr. Schiff said, "that the Jew, who has come to the United States, has never gone back again voluntarily. He is here to breathe the air of freedom. He comes as did the Pilgrim fathers and the Huguenots, and if he is sent back, particularly to Russia, he is driven back to hell."

MESSAGE FROM TAFT.

President Taft sent the following telegram from the White House:

"I greatly regret my inability to attend the banquet. I should like to be able to testify in my speech to my admiration for the Jewish people, my conviction that they constitute a valuable element in our American citizenship and make most effectively for artistic improvement, educational progress, the extension of charity and the maintenance of law and order.

One thousand diners sat down to tables and 500 of their guests filled the balcony boxes.

Mr. Roosevelt spoke extemporaneously in part as follows:

"Mr. Schiff had praised me in a way that I do not deserve. I've net good Jews and bad Jews just as I've met good Christians and bad Christians, and when I met a good man I stood by him and when I met a bad man I cinched him. A Santiaga, after one of the battles, I promoted eight men in my regiment and found later there were two Protestants, two Catholics and the rest of them Jews. I promoted men on their merits and I knew nothing of their faith previously."

Mr. Roosevelt said he hoped to see the time when the Jew and the Catholic would be equally eligible to the presidency.

STRAUS TRIBUTE

"The republicanism of the United States is the nearest approach to the ideals of the prophets of Israel that has ever been incorporated in the form of a state," declared Useas S. Straus, ambassador to Turkey, in his address. "America is peculiarly a promised land wherein the spirit of the teachings of the ancient prophets inspired the work of the fathers of our country."

Mr. Straus spoke upon "America and the Spirit of American Judaism." His address in part follows:

"The Spirit of American Judaism first asserted itself when Stuyvesant, the Governor of New Amsterdam, would not permit the few Jews who had emigrated from Portugal to unite with the other burghers in standing guard for the protection of their homes. When the tax collector came to Asser Levy to collect a tax on his account, he asked if that tax was imposed on all the residents of New Amsterdam. 'No,' came the reply, 'it is only imposed upon the Jews, because they do not stand guard. 'I have not asked to be exempted,' replied Asser Levy. 'I am not only willing, but I demand the right to stand guard.'

"That right the Jews have asserted and exercised as officers in the ranks of the continental army and in every crisis of our international history from that time until the present day. The American spirit of and the spirit of American Judaism were both nurtured in the same cradle of liberty and united together in origin, in ideals and in historical development. The closing chapter of the chronicles of the Jews on the Iberian Peninsula forms the opening chapter of their history on this continent. It was Luis Sentangel, 'the Beasonfield of his time,' assisted by his kinsman, Gabriel Sanches, the royal treasurer of Aragon, who advanced out of his own purse seventeen thousand florins, which made the voyages of Columbus possible. Luis de Torres, the interpreter, as well as the surgeon and physician of the little fleet, besides several of the sailors who were with Columbus on his first voyage, were Jews.

NEAREST ISRAEL.

"While Zionis mis a child of despair in countries where the victims of oppression are still counted by millions, the republicanism of the United States is the nearest approach to the ideals of the prophets of Israel that has ever been incorporated in the form of a state. The founders of our government converted the dreams of philosophers into a political system, a government by the people, for the people, whereunder the rights of man became the rights of men secured and guaranteed under a written constitution. America is peculiarly a promised land, wherein the spirit of the teachings of the ancient prophets inspired the work of the fathers of our country.

"American liberty demands of no man the abandonment of his conscientious convictions; on the contrary, it had its birth not in the narrowness of uniformity, but in the breadth of diversity which patriotism fuses together into a conscious harmony for the highest welfare of all.

Considering the extent of Jacob H. Schiff's involvement in financing of the conflicts in the region, interest in the mineral wealth and colonizing Jewish settlements, which would eventually become Israel, it is important to get a better understanding of who Jacob H. Schiff is. The American Jewish Year Book (#5682), Volume 23, published in 1921, a year after Schiff's death, an account that offers good insight. It is titled "Jacob Henry Schiff - A Biographical Sketch" written by Cyrus Adler (1863-1940), a prominent educator, religious leader, and scholar (see https://archive.org/details/americanjewishye5682adle/page/n6).

An article published in *The Philadelphia Inquirer* (Philadelphia, Pennsylvania), on July 29, 1907, Page 2, gives a broader picture of Schiff's vision:

AMERICA PROMISED LAND OF THE JEW

Banker Jacob Schiff Makes Telling Address to Big Chautauqua Society

Speaks of Visions of Coming Days and Declares New Arrivals Must Scatter

Special to The Inquirer.

ATLANTIC CITY, N. J., July 28. – Earnest with his theme, positive in his belief, Jacob Schiff, banker and philanthropist of New York, uttered a declaration before the Jewish Chautauqua at its closing session today, which from the spontaneous response with which it was received by the great assembly of leaders of his race, showed that he had echoed the sentiment in their hearts.

"The hope of the restoration of the Jewish nation in Palestine was not the guiding star of Israel's ambition," he said: "The promised land of the Jew it seems to me is America."

"It is in this free land that the Jew drew his inspiration for higher citizenship," he continued, and again did the throngs lend emphasis to his assertion with applause.

He sounded a note of warning to the Jewish people in regard to the evils of tenement house crowding in the great cities and advocated a dispersion of the Jews through the South and West, or he fervently said, as he paused to lend telling effect to his remark:

"Israel would become a curse instead of a blessing to this Nation." He said that a remedy must be found for the overcrowding in the cities and declared his conviction that there must be a scattering of the foreigners if they are not to become a menace to the Nation, and such a condition will be reached when this industrial activity comes to an end, which he hoped would not come for a long time. Whether Jew or Gentile, this tide of immigrants must be diverted into the territory which needs them and where they can found homes and become merged into the Nation as "respected and happy and prosperous industrial units.

Vision of Coming Days

"As I stand before you," said Mr. Schiff, "there arises before me a vision of coming days – the dream of the American Israel of the future, of a generation not yet born, the children's children of the men and women who in this generation have come from all parts of the globe to the blessed shores

– of the thousand who come to free themselves from persecution, oppression, abridged civil rights and limited liberty. The vision which presents itself to me shows me a people of our faith, who have thrown off the shackles, the peculiarities and the prejudices which have handicapped their fathers – a great host, Jews in faith, but in one sentiment with their surroundings, warmly attached to their country, of which they have become part and parcel – a people among the best in the land, proud of their American citizenship, thoroughly imbued with its spirit, with its obligations, with its high privileges, but just as proud of their religion – almost a new type – these descendants of Jewish Pilgrim Fathers, true Americans of the Jewish faith.

"We owe it to ourselves and to those who come after us that we imbue our offspring with the love for our faith our fathers have implanted in us; that we demonstrate to them the beauty of our religion, the moral strength it imparts under all conditions; that we impress upon them the meaning of our faith, not alone to its adherents, but with the value of its teachings to all mankind; that we teach it to our children in the word of the Lawgiver: "When we sit in our houses, when we go on our way, when we rise in the morning and we lie down at night.' Because of the duty of the Jew, thus conceived, we should give our entire support to the Chautauqua, for no other agency is so well adapted to aid in bringing about the Jewish revival which is needed and can so well assure the maintenance of our faith, of its traditions and its spirit throughout the land, and more especially in the small communities now springing up everywhere, in which opportunities for Jewish life and learning are often wanting.

Not Zionism

"Not Zionism, a movement impractical if realization, should be needed to arouse our conscience as Jews; better that we recognize our duty to the Jewish educational institutions, of which I aver the Jewish Chautauqua can be and should be made on of the most efficient agencies. Rapidly the Jewish population of this country is increasing. Before long the newcomers are certain to seek better homes and wider quarters and wider quarters in the great and attractive territory which stretches from the Gulf to our northern boundary, from the Mississippi to the Pacific. Today not quite two millions, at not a distant day double that number are certain to comprise an American population of a Jewish faith. Today looked upon as a foreign element, in times to come, an integral part of a race of Americans yet in the making. Today students, tomorrow teachers; today pilgrims; tomorrow patriots. This is the vision, present, which passes before my eyes. My prayer, my hope, aye, my conviction is, that in due time it becomes a reality."

Thanks were voted to Mr. Schiff and while he was yet still in the hall a compliment was paid him by the adoption of a unanimous vote that 50,000 copies of the address be printed and distributed among the Jews. A fund was raised to carry out the resolution after the meeting closed.

"We should meet in some other place with an atmosphere of less gayety," said Secretary Charles e. Fox, of Philadelphia, after reading his report showing the expansion of the Chautauqua. "We need some place where study should not be subordinated to amusement." The suggestion was referred to the Executive Committee and the next session may go to Chautauqua, N. Y.

Officers Elected

Officers were elected as follows: Chancellor, Rev. Dr. Henry Berkowitz, Philadelphia; president, George W. Ochs, Philadelphia; vice president, Israel Cowen, Chicago; treasurer, Frank Newberger, Philadelphia; secretary and director, Charles E. Fox, Philadelphia; field secretary, Miss Jeanette M. Goldberg, Galveston, Tex.; honorary vice presidents, Adolph S. Ochs, Milton Goldsmith, New York; Albert Hessberg, Albany, N. Y.; Mrs. Jacob H. Hecht, Boston; Max Senior, Cincinnati; Mrs. S. L. Frank, Baltimore; Mrs. August S. Frank, St. Louis; Rev. Dr. I. L. Leucht, New Orleans; Mrs. S. Lesser, Augusta, Ga.; N. Washer, San Antonio, Tex.; William J. Berkowitz, Kansas City, Mo.; Mrs. George Galland, Wilkes-Barre; Abraham Thalmier, Hartford, Conn.; Rev. Dr. William S. Friedman, Denver, Col.; Rabbi Samuel Koch, Seattle, Wash.; Edward Richard, Mobile.

It was shown by the report of Frank Newberger, the treasurer, that the expenses of the Chautauqua work last year was $7346, of which $1698 was for the traveling expenses of the field secretary and the balance for text books and incidentals. There is a balance of $1400.

Aubrey Herbert had made mention of a man named Karasso. Emanuel Karasso Efendi (1862-1934). Was a Sephardic Jew and one of the first non-Muslim members of the Ottoman Freedom Society, which later became part of the Committee of Union and Progress (CUP). Karasu was the Grand Master the Italian "Mecedonia Resurrected" Masonic lodge in Thessaloniki, which many of the Young Turks were members.[104] He was a leading force in establishing "Maşrık-ı Azamı Osmani" (Ottoman Grand Orient), the first Masonic Grand Lodge of Turkey, of which Talaat Pasha was elected Grand Master on August 1, 1909.[105]

Emanuel Karasso Efendi

When Sultan Abdul Hamid II was deposed by the Young Turks in April of 1909, Karasso was among the delegation demanding that the Sultan step down. He would later become the Salonica deputy in the Ottoman parliament.[106]

---

104 David Livingstone, "Black Terror White Soldiers", (Sanilillah Publications, ISBN-13: 978-1481226509, 2013), P. 241

105 http://www.mason.org.tr/en_history.htm

106 Ahsene Gül Tokay, "Macedonian Reforms and Muslim Opposition during the Hamidian Era: 1878–1908", *Islam and Christian–Muslim Relations* **14**:1 (2003)

Karasso was also a leader of the European affiliate of the B'nai B'rith International, a Jewish fraternal organization founded in New York in 1843, having moral, philanthropic, social, educational, and political aims, as well as The Alliance Israélite Universelle (Heb. לְאׇרְשִׂי לְכ_ח״יכ םיִרֵבָח "All Israel are comrades"). U.S. Ambassador Henry Morganthau[107] and Jacob H. Schiff[108] were also members of B'nai B'rith International and The Alliance Israélite Universelle.

Delegation of the Ottoman parliament to depose Abdul Hamid II. Left to right: Rearadmiral Arif Hikmet Pasha, Emanuel Karasu Efendi (Carasso), Esad Pasha Toptani, Aram Efendi and Colonel Galip Bey (Pasiner), April 27, 1909.

---

107 Jewish Activities in the United States, Volume II of The International Jew, "…articles appearing in The Dearborn Independent from Oct. 9, 1920 to March 19, 1921; 'Jewish Rights' to Put Studies Out of Schools", (Dearborn, Mich., The Dearborn Publishing Company, April 1921), P. 174

108 The American Jewish Year Book 5663, October 2, 1902 to September 21, 1903, "National Organizations", (Baltimore, MD, The Jewish Publication Society of America, The Lord Baltimore Press, The Friedenwald Company, 1902), P. 88

Chapter 30

The Colt Memos and Letter

"I feel confident that if the railroad had been constructed in the years immediately following the war by combined American, English and French capital as contemplated by Mr. Harjes and me and with the support of those three government that this whole Armenian massacre might have been avoided" – James W. Colt

As the previous chapters show in detail, James Wood Colt, who worked for the investment bankers of J.P. Morgan and Jacob H. Schiff, aided in the theft of Armenian lands by the Western powers. He shares in the responsibility for some of the most harmful injuries perpetuated against the Armenian people.

When Colt died at the age of 83, the *The Livingston Republican* (Geneseo, Livingston County, New York) wrote about his passing on February 20, 1941.

James W. Colt - Passport photo 1921

JAMES WOOD COLT, PROMINENT GENESEOAN, SUCCUMBS TO ILLNESS

James Wood; Colt, 83, died in his home at 45 Center Street, early Monday morning after a brief illness.

Mr. Colt was born in Geneseo and at the age of 21 left for the West where he settled in St. Paul Minn., and became a partner in the contacting firm of Shepherd Seims & Co. While associated with his firm Mr. Colt played an active part in the rail road construction activities in that section having portions of the Great Northern, Chicago, Milwaukee, St. Paul and Pacific; and Northern Pacific Railroads under his direct charge. Later, in association with A. B. Stickney, he directed the building of portions of what is now know as the Chicago, Great Western Railroad. And still later as Vice President of Mac-Arthur Brothers, New York and Chicago contractors, he directed construction of the parts of, Western Maryland Railroad.

In 1909 Mr. Colt became associated with Admiral Colby M. Chester in a project for the construction of a railroad between Constantinople, Turkey, through Asia Minor to Bagdad. Mr. Colt spent two years in Turkey, laying out the line of the and negotiating for what became known as the Chester Concession. The Turkish Government rejected the plan in 1911, but later adopted it in a modified form, although it has never been carried but.

Returning to New York, Mr. Colt again became associated with Mac-Arthur Brothers and over a period of 15 years he was active in the contracting field in the United states and Europe.

In addition to his business activities Mr. Colt was interested in horses and between 1890 and 1910 his steeplechase horses were among the best known on the American turf. Three times his horses won the American Grand National, the leading steeplechase in the United States. He also owned and raced horses in England and Frances. Mr. Colt was deeply interested in fox hunting and for many years was active in the Genesee Valley Hunt.

His son, James W. Colt, Jr., was also well known in hunting and polo circles having attained membership on the Hurricanes, international polo team, in 1931 at the time of his death in a polo accident.

Surviving Mr. Colt are his widow, Mrs. Frances Bacon Colt, daughters, Mrs. Sylvia colt of Geneseo and Mrs. Howard V. Shattuck, New York City; two sons, Henry F. Colt, Brookline, Mass., and Charles C. Colt, New York City, and 18 grandchildren.

Funeral services were conducted at 12 o'clock noon Wednesday in St. Michael's Episcopal Church, Rev. Milton A. Huggett, pastor.

Within the Colt archive which is housed at the River Campus Library of the University of Rochester, there were four memoranda written by Colt regarding his work in the Ottoman Empire, which, I believe, indicate who may have created furtile ground for the Armenian Genocide to take place. Most of the memoranda are not dated, therefore I have put them in the order, in which I think they were written:

FIRST DOCUMENT

Last week I read as an item of news that the Anglos-Persian Oil Company has decided to build almost immediately the pipe line connecting the Iraq (Mosul) Oil field with the Mediterreranean [sic] Sea.

This brought back vividly to my recollection the incidence of 1910-11 and 1912 which occurred prior to the abandonment of the Turkish concession by the group which I represented and the fact that this concession among other values, included these identical oil fields of Mosul.

Upon my reutnr [sic] from Turkey in 1910 and again in 1911 I reported to my directors that the Arghana Maden Mine alone was proably [sic] worth twice the entire cost of the railroad and that the oil fields were of inestimable value. I was unable however to persuade the monied men connected with the enterprise to do the things necessary to conclude the business with the Turkish government and upon their insistence the cautionment was withdrawn early in 1912. About this time however Mr. Herman Harjes of Paris came to New York and expressed a desire to know the exact status of the enterprise and after several interviews he agreed that upon his return to Paris he would send John Ridgely Carter to Constantinople to discuss with the then Turkish Government the modifications desired by us in the concession and the possibility of obtaining it under such modified terms the principal one of the these being that the government should guarantee one half the series of the bonds until such time as the railroad should earn the entire amount of such service. Three months later I heard from My. Harjes that Carter had been to Constantinople and obtained the assurance of the competent authorities that the concession would be granted at our request and upon the terms stated above and asking me to come at once to Paris with proxies of all the stock and full authority to act. I at once complied with Mr. Harjes request but upon arrival there found that his senior partner Mr. J.P. Morgan had arrived unexpectedly from Rome and upon learning of the business in hand, had forbidden him, Harjes, to proceed further in the matter and so in August 1912 it was definitely abandoned.

Had the monied interests orifinally [sic] connected with the enterprise appreciated the value of the mineral and oil deposits granted by the Turkish government under the concession or had Mr J.P. Morgan, Sr. two years later understood the possibilities of these mineral deposits the group which I represented would now be the owners of these tremendous oil reserves and would be building themselves or in connection with some oil company like the Shell this same pipe line which it is estimated will deliver sufficient oil in the Mediterrenaen [sic] to supply most of the needs of the Near and the Far East.

Armenia

The principal part of the railway contemplated was located in the ancient kingdom of Armenia which after the World War was practically depopulated by the Turks and has become largely unproductive abandoned by its agricultural inhabitants. I feel confident that if the railroad had been constructed in the years immediately following the war by combined American, English and French capital as contemplated by Mr. Harjes and me and with the support of those three government that this whole Armenian massacre might have been avoided; that the country might have been devloped [sic] tremendously agriculturally and that the lives of over two millions industrious and innocent people would probably have been spared to continue their useful avocations in their native homes.

SECOND DOCUMENT

For something over a year past, the Ottoman-American Development Company has carried on negotiations with the Turkish Government for a Railway concession carrying with it the rights to all the mines, known or known, not heretofore granted to third parties, located within a distance of twenty kilometers to the right and twenty kilometers to the left of said railway, the terminal of this system to be fixed at or near the mouth of the Orentes River (the ancient port of Anioch) ahd [sic] the line to extend through the city of Aleppo to a crossing of the Euphrates River at or near Biredjik and to the city of Diarbekir where it joins a second line extending from Sivas, through the city of Harpout, to Diarbekir, and so on to the city of Bitlas and the Lake Van, with a third line extending from a junction point at some convenient location between the cities of Diarbekir and Bitlas to the cities of Mossoul, Kerkook, and Suleymanie, the latter of which is quite near to the Persian boundary. The total length of these lines approximates 1800 kilometers.

At the Sivas terminal, this system will connect with the railway which the Government intends immediately to build between Samsoun and Sivas and by this route make direct connection with the Black Sea. The concession carries with it the right of option to make surveys and geological examination of the regions traversed by the railway in contomplantion [sic], extending over a period of sixteen months from the date of its ratification by parliament and if at the end of this period the concessionaire shall decide not to accept the concession nor to build the railway, it can then withdraw its proposition, giving to the Government the result of its surveys and geological and mineralogical investigations.

During the session of the last parliament, all details were agreed upon with the

Ministry of Public Works, the concession and option were ratified by the General Staff and the Council of State, and were considered by the Council of Ministers and approved by a majority of that body, but owing to objection on the part of the Grand Visier, did not come before the parliament for discussion and ratification. In one or more interviews with members of the Committee of Public Works in parliament, nearly all of which committee is favorable to the granting of this concession to the American group, the Grand Visier has expressed himself as objecting to the concession in its present form because of its giving what he termed rights of monopoly in the mines located withing the zone of the railway, and has said that he would favor the substitution of a kilometric guarantee, similar in form to that given to the German road, and the mines now the property of the Government and such other mines as the Ottoman-American Development Company might itself discover and locate in conformity with the present mining law. From conversations held with the different members of the Committee of Public Works in parliament and with certain leaders of the party of Union and Progress in the House, the agents of the syndicate in Constantinople have become convinced that this proposition of the Grand Visier will meet the approval of the committee and of the majority in the parliament and that when the matter comes up for discussion in parliament at its approaching session, it may be possible to substitute the proposition of the Grand Visier as outlined above for that of the Development Company.

There are certain other minor changes in the terms of the concession desired by the Development Company which the Committee are prepared to discuss and which will undoubtedly be obtained. It is probable, however, that should a kilometric guarantee be given, the optional clause will be withdrawn from the concession and the Development Company will be asked to proceed at once with the construction of the railway. After the adjournment of parliament, two representatives of the Development Company made a hasty reconnaissance of that part of the line between Sivas and the city of Van passing by the way of Divrik, Arabkir, Harpout, Arghana Marden, Diarbekir, Zoch, Bitlas and the south shore of Lake Van, and have reported to the Development Company the results of this hasty examination.

About forty percent of the line is heavy work and the balance can be located in the plains of Harpout and Diarbeker and the valleys leading thereto. These valleys and plains are fertile and produce excellent crops, taking into consideration the antiquated methods employed in their cultivation. The harvest this year, in the vilayets traversed, was fifty percent in excess of the year preceding, and given means for transporting the surplus crop to market, this production might be multiplied several times. The flocks and herds were found in excellent condition and a good business might be expected in transporting their increase to market. The inhabitants are industrious, self-respecting and self-sustaining; there is very little begging and no absolute want was observed. The cities of Harpout, Diarbekir and Sivas were found unexpectedly clean, busy places, well governed and with no evidence of the liability to cholera and typhoid, which the average European expects to find in an oriental city. Diarbekir especially is a most interesting place and might readily become a Mecca for artists and antiquaries. No search for minerals was made beyond observation of the country directly along the line of march and no new mines were discovered. A somewhat hasty examination was made of the copper mines of Arghana from which, and from other data, which has been obtained, it appears that this mine is of great value; and the very rapid inspection of the immediate locality convinced the Engineer of the party that other large copper deposits, possibly of lower grade, exist in in the immediate neighborhood.

The abandoned workings of an iron mine close to Lake Van were examined and the ore upon anaylsis [sic] proved quite valuable, but owing to the caving in of the works and the lack of time, no estimate of quantity could be made at this time. All the indications, however, point to a very large deposit in this locality. No good coal was found along the line examined. It was impossible, during the time at command, to examine that part of the line extending toward Mossoul and Suleymanie, but authentic reports on this region lead one to believe that there are large deposits of Petroleum in the neighborhood of Mossoul and Kirkouk which in the event of no discovery of coal along the line of railway could eventually be employed as fuel for the moving of its trains.

The statistics of the last census and the more recent statistics of the vilayets indicate a population in these regions of thirty to the square mile and this population, taken in connection with the volume of the imports and exports would convince one that the railway, when built, should at least earn operating expenses from its opening without taking into consideration the increase in agricultural and existing activities which is sure to follow the completion of such an important public work and without counting the traffic which would be furnished by the development of mines and such new industries as are sure to spring up along the line of the railway and its branches.

The writer has in mind especially the business which would be furnished by the mines at Arghana and at Lake Van and the possibilities of a great beet sugar industry in the Mousch valley. There is also a probability that upon the completion of this line to Lake Van all the pilgrim traffic to Jerusalem and Mecca from Persia, Russia and Eastern Turkey would choose this route instead of the more tedius [sic] voyage by the Black Sea and this business would add materially to the income of the railway.

The Development Company has fulfilled all of the requirements of the Government in regard to the deposit of caution money and to the form of its proposal so that no other proposition for this system of railways can be considered until that of the Development Company has been submitted to the parliament and there discussed and either rejected or accepted. It has further received assurances from the leaders of the party in power that its proposal shall be forwarded promptly and passed upon during the first half of the approaching session.

J.W. Colt [signed]

THIRD DOCUMENT
Memoir, James W. Colt

Immediately following the failure of the Turkish Parliament to approve the Ottoman American concession I left Constantinople with my family and returned to the United States. We rented a house in Englewood, New Jersey sent the boys to public school and I was retained by the MacArthur Company as business negotiator and was made President of the Ottoman American Development Company in order to keep that company alive. Early in the winter of 1911-12 I was summoned to the Morgan Bank to meet Mr. Herrman Harjes [sic] the active head of the Paris house. Mr. Lamont presented me and Mr. Harjes evidenced a certain interest in our situation vis a vis to the Turkish Government and asked me to state the matter to him briefly which I did. He then told me that former Ambassador to Constantinople, John Ridgely Carter, who had recently joined their house had suggested that he discuss this matter with me and that upon his return to Paris he would consider with Carter what might be done if anything and that Mr. Lamont would keep me advised. Later in the winter or early spring I learned from Mr. Lamont that Harjes has sent Carter to Constantinople where he had conferred with Talaat and the other members of the Government and had received assurance that the concession would be ratified by parliament in terms modified to suit our wishes provided the Morgan House would assume its financing and that Harjes had the matter under consideration. In May or early June I was sent for by Mr. Lamont who gave me a copy of cable from Harjes saying in substance that he was prepared to go forward with the Turkish business provided I would come over at once with proxies for all the stock assigned to me [sic] him. With some difficulty I obtained these proxies and sailed about the 10th. of June called on Harjes the morning after my arrival in Paris only to be told that during the week occupied by my voyage he had conferred with Mr. J.P. Morgan, Sr. and that Mr. Morgan had forbidden him to undertake the business. Harjes was most apologetic and charming as always, but firm and so went glimmering my dreams of Arghana Marden and the Mesopotamians Oil fields. all [sic] of which many other valuable rights were included in the grants given to us by the concession. These oil fields are now the property of the Anglo Persian Oil Company acquired just after the great War.

FOURTH DOCUMENT

I have recent come from Russia, where I spent nearly a year in certain investigations of her resources and possibilities, saw the commencement of of the revolution in March, and the maximilist riots in July, and talked frequently with members of the two Commissions sent out by our Government, and especially with the members of the Railway Commission (several of whom, including the Chairman, Mr. Stevens, I have known for many years). I am convinced that we made a blunder in Russia, and that our present policy of what I might call aloofness is a great mistake. While this policy is the logical sequence to our initial error, it will, if persevered in, result in the most serious consequences to us and our Allies.

When our Commission reached Petrograd, they were met by insistent requests for money and many other necessities, such as : railway equipment, food, etc., and, to practically all these requests they acceded in full; granting among other things, large credits for the purchase of goods in America, and also agreeing to give Russian orders for railway cars, to the number of 40,000, and for locomotives to the number of 2500, preference over those of our own people already placed with our factories: and all this without a semblance of a return to us, merely to help on the new democracy and aid in the prosecution of the war.

This was our first blunder. The Oriental does not understand disinterestedness, and undervalues anything which costs him nothing. He rather scorns his benefactor as a soft sort of a fool whom he has let in. He looks always for the motive, and usually hits upon some explanation so grotesque as to seem unbelievable to us.

In exchange for our assistance, we should have asked and obtained the control and direction of the Russian railways, and of the mines supplying the same with coal and metal, and the direction of her food distribution. At present, her railways function to about 33% of their normal, her mines to about 25%, and her populated centres arennearing [sic] starvation because of her inability to distribute food to her people. I make this statement wittingly as result of an investigation into the grain resources of Russia, undertaken by my Company in association with Stahaef & Co. (a great Russian grain firm, having 900 Agencies) and the Armours of Chicago and others, conducted by experts, selected and sent out by the Armour Firm,. who reported more grain in Russia than in America today: in one district alone, where the average export for the last ten years is 100 million pouds, only 18 million pouds of the 1916 crop have been exported. (A poud is 36 English pounds, or roughly one half bushel).

At the same time, I was intimately conversant with a second investigation made by American associated interests into the steel, iron and coal industries and resources of Russia; and I was told by the Engineer in charge thereof, merely as an instance of what might be done, that one mettallurgical [sic] work on the Sea of Azof and not more than 150 miles from coal, could, if given a train-load a day, turn out a train of freight-cars each day; but they were unable to get the coal with which to start this ceaseless output of railway equipment.

It results from this that, of the 40,000 railway cars promised Russia by us, 10,000 can be produced by one Works within one year, or probably before we can transport that number from America.

Note - The Engineer in charge of this investigation was Mr. Kneeland, former Chief Engineer of the U.S. Steel Corporation, who returned to New York in July last.

Before the arrival in Russia of Mr. Stevens and Commission, and at the request of the Railway Minister and the U.S. Military Attache, I made an investigation of the Mourman Road, then under construction, which connects Petrograd with the open sea to the North, in order to be able to report to Stevens on his arrival the situation in that quarter. The persons in charge of that construction were making demands for additional rolling stock and for food from America, but I found that the engines and cars then on the road were sufficient in number for the completion of the work before winter; much of this equipment was in need of repairs and none of it was functioning to capacity, but that was simply a question of orgainzation [sic]. As to food, I was told by the Purchasing Agent of the road at Archangel that he could get all the cattle and hay necessary if the Ministrev of Agriculture [sic] would keep "hands off", and, as I have stated above, there is plenty of grain in Russia. My conclusions in these matters, affecting the Mourman Road, were afterwards confirmed by Darling, of Steven's Commission, who subsequently went over the road with a mixed Commission of English, French and Russians. I have said above that our initial blunder was in giving Russia something for nothing: our second, and more serious one, consists in continuing that policy so far as material things go, and leaving her without the moral and administrative help she so much needs. Russia is a sick man in delirium, and must have skilled aid, even if it were necessary to force it upon her, and we still have the means of imposing our will upon her, for we have as yet made only trifling deliveries of the goods ordered on the strength of our credit; and, in view of occurrences subsequent to these arrangements, and the general disorganization of everything in Russia, we can with perfect consistency refuse to go further until and unless we are given absolute control of the channels of distribution and the sources of supply. I believe that an offer from us to do this would be hailed with joy by all the better elements in Russia, who comprise 85% of the population, and by the responsible Leaders of every party - except the Bolcheviks. I do not mean a Commission of theorists to go over and talk, but 15 or 20 thousand workingmen, who will go over there and do the trick themselves. They may be all men over military age, but enlisted for the way for the sake of convenience and discipline, and they should be led by some great national figure with a genius for organization, like Roosevelt, whose motives and aim are beyond question. I would joyfully accept service in such an organization under such a Leader, and I believe that tens of thousands of competent Americans would volunteer for this service, especially if they are informed as to the importance of this question, both in its bearing upon the final result of the way, and upon the burning question of ocean transportation.

10 - As to its bearing upon the final result of the war: A proper organization of the resources and transport service of Russia will feed the population, keep them quiet, and relieve the Army and Government Leaders of these harrassing [sic] details, and enable them to reorganize the Army ad make an effective opposition to the further penetration of the Germans in the the country: We might be able to co-operate and assist in this reorganization, and we would certainly obtain the assistance of the Orthodix Church in the propaganda which we should institute against the Bolcheviks and other German sympathisers [sic]. If this is not done, and the Army, through lack of supplies and intelligent reorganization, is allowed to disintigrate [sic] and melt away, the Germans will become possessed of the rich mineral and coal deposits of the Donets Basin, and of the Wheat and Grain-lands of the "Black Coutnry". They will draw upon Russia for forced labour, and possibly for soldiers, and they will be able to continue the war indifinitely [sic]. America can never throw into the scale enough men and food to offset what Germany will obtain from Russia once the back-door is open. To my mind, the

disaster in Italy is a bagatelle as compared with the calamity of opening the Russian border to Germany, for Italy has nothing to give Germany - Russia has everything.

20 - As to its effect upon ocean transportation:

We are straining every nerve to move a million men and their equipment, food, etc., to France, to keep their numbers good, and at the same time we are under contract to transport to Vladivostok large quantities of food, railway equipment, etc., for Russia. the transfer to Russia of 20 or 30 thousand competent men, for the purposes outlined above, would release us from the major part of our transport obligation to her, and leave the shipping necessary to carry it out free for service on the Atlantic in transporting troops to France. Would release it, because we would build the cars in Russia and find and distribute the food now there. And, further, the few ships new employed in this service to Russia - via the Pacific - would run no risk from submarines and could load back with rice from China or from Vladivistok (I am told there are 50 thousand tons of rice at this port).

In order to realize the program which I have roughly outlined, we (Americans) must have the enthusiastic support of our European Allies, who undoubtedly realize the gravity of the situation in Russia, and would welcome any reasonable proposal looking to its amelioration. I feel that the matter should be at once discussed in the proper quarters, but without publicity, and every effort made to send effective help to Russia. But I insist that there should be no talk about it until it be <u>un fait accompli.</u>

(Signed) J. W. Colt.
Paris, Nov. 16th, 1917

Chapter 31

Theodore Roosevelt Letters

Retired U.S. Navy Rear Admiral Colby M. Chester confessed to his crimes against humanity and the Armenian people, and his confession implicated United States President Theodore Roosevelt as an accomplice.

At the time of his confession, President Roosevelt had been dead for over four years and could not defend his good name. For this reason, one must ponder this question: Did President Roosevelt have anything to do with this crime against the Armenian people for the sake of minerals found on Armenian lands?

President Roosevelt had a long history of sympathizing with the plight of the Armenian people going back at least to the Adana massacres of 1909.

To try to find answers to the question of Roosevelt's guilt or innocence, I paid a visit to the Library of Congress in Washington, D.C., to search for evidence. Within the Theodore Roosevelt papers, a collection of almost anything you would want to know about Roosevelt on a personal and professional level, I found letters that were written to him before, during and after he served as the 26th United States President (1901-1909).

The most famous of the Roosevelt letters that has been written about by Armenians is the May 11,1918 letter from Roosevelt to Woodrow Wilson's advisor and financer, Cleveland H. Dodge (1860-1926), where Roosevelt is clearly stating that the Armenians need U.S. intervention. This letter was in fact a response to Dodge, who was against such an intervention. The following is Dodge's letter, which will be followed by the famous May 11, 1918 response:

May 6, 1918.
    Hon. Theodore Roosevelt,
        Oyster Bay, L. I.
    My dear Theodore:
        I have felt, for some time, that I ought to see you and have a good talk with you about conditions in Turkey, and I said to Mr. Perkins yesterday to see if we could arrange for some time to meet this week. He has

just telephoned me of your kind suggestion that we lunch together a week from next Saturday, but hardly feel as if I can wait as long as that to unburden my mind.

I suppose I am somewhat biased in my feelings about Turkey, from the fact that six members of my immediate family are there. My son, Bayard, and his wife,-who is the daughter of Howard Bliss,-and their two babies, in Beirut; and my daughter, Elisabeth, and her husband, at Robert College, Constantinople. My interest in these two great American educational institutions, which have had such a marked influence in the Near East, is an inherited one, but I have become intensely interested not only in the college at Beirut and Robert Collage, but also in the great college in Smyrna, and the other missionary and educational institutions throughout Asia Minor. The great influence to Robert College in Bulgaria you probably know about. Nearly all of the liberal leaders in Bulgaria are graduates of Robert College, and were strongly opposed to Bulgaria joining with Germany and Austria in the War. The pro-German party, led by Emperor Ferdinand, precipitated the war in spite of all the liberal elements in the country, and all the news which I get from Bulgaria indicates that the people are sick of the war, and are afraid of getting into the grip of Germany and that Bulgarian army is not fighting outside of its own border. The State Department has received positive evidence that none of the Bulgarian trips are fighting on the Western front. I can, however, sympathize with you and the others who advocate a declaration of war against both Bulgaria and Turkey. IT certainly seems anomalous that we should not be at war with all of the countries with which our Allies are at war; but, nevertheless, I feel very strongly that in case of both Bulgaria and Turkey, we can be of greater assistance to the Allied cause by keeping on nominally friendly terms with Bulgaria and Turkey, because the work of our missionaries and educational leader in both countries are having an enormous influence in offsetting the strong German propaganda. I have recently read a repot from Mr. Heck, who was First Secretary to Mr. Elkus, and who remained in Constantinople until January fifth of this year, to aid Swedish Minister, who took over our affairs there, and he reports that the Turks hat the Germans, and are mortally afraid of getting into their grip in the future. The Turkish authorities are treating the American and all our institutions there with great consideration, and the work of the college has gone on without interruption. At Beirut there are more students than there are at Oxford and Cambridge combined, and we have nearly five hundred students at Robert College. It is estimated that the value of property owned by these colleges and the different missionary societies in the Turkish Empire, would amount to about twenty million dollars. Of course a declaration of war against Turkey would turn all these properties n to the hands of the Turks, and practically into the hands of the Germans, and all the splendid influences which are being exerted by the Americans would be completely lost. The hundreds of noble American men and woman who have been doing such heroic services in relieving the misery of the Armenians and Syrians and Greeks, and all the Staffs of the different colleges, would either be interned or suffer serious danger. Nevertheless, we all feel that if there was any real reason for our declaring war against turkey, we would sacrifice all that we have been working for the last century. The

Greek Government which is apparently anxious that we should declare war against Bulgaria, fails to realize that if we declared war against Bulgaria, it would be almost necessary to have a war with Turkey also, and in that case the enormous Greek population on the Aegean Littoral would probably be annihilated, because the only thing which is saving them today from starvation is the work our Armenian & Syrian Relief Committee. And that bring me to the principal point in my letter.

The Armenian & Syrian Relief Committee was organized in my office two and one-half years ago, and has raised over ten millions of dollars for the relief of the Armenians and Syrians, and also of the Greeks in Asia Minor, and of Armenians and Assyrians who have fled to the Trans-Caucausus and Persia. This fund has been very ably managed and the distribution of relief has been entirely in the hands of the American missionaries. It is probable that more of the Armenians have been saved than we realize. Many who were reported lost in the various deportations have been scattered throughout the country in the small towns and villages, and the large number safely reached the Caucausus and Persia. Probably a million to a million and a half of the Armenian race are still alive, but they are kept alive only by work of our committee. The sufferings of these poor people have been on my heart and conscience for the last two and a half years, and it has been on of the greatest joys of my life to be able to do something to help them. It is hard to suppress one's indignation at the Turkish authorities who perpetrated the awful deeds which have been done, but it is undeniable that these were instigated, if not supported, by the Germans.

Now, it is absolutely certain, and there is no doubt in the minds of any of us who are in the situation, that the moment this country should get into the war with Turkey, the beautiful Christ-like work which is being done by our people would instantly stop, and just as secure as the sun arrives tomorrow morning will it be that within a comparatively few months, every man, woman and child of the Armenian race, who is today living in the Turkish Empire, will be dead, because all restraining influences will be removed from the Turkish Government, and all possible means of relief will be destroyed. As I think of the awful possibilities involved, I want to appeal to you with all my hear to reconsider the view which you have publicly expressed, and even if you cannot come to my view of this situation, at least to cease your efforts to bring this country into war with Bulgaria and Turkey, remembering that if we wen to war with Bulgaria, would have to go into war with Turkey, Also.

In this connection, I want to tell you that I have known intimately, for many years, Dr. Panaretoff, who is a Bulgarian Minister in Washington. He was one of the first graduates of Robert College, and almost the adopted son of old Dr. Washburn, who had the highest regard for him. Prior to his being appointed Minister here he was, for nearly thirty years, Professor in Robert College, and is thoroughly imbued with American ideas of Democracy. I now how seriously he deprecates the fact that Bulgaria entered the war on the side of Germany. He did all he could to oppose it, and poor man, lost his only don in one of the first battles in which Bulgaria was engaged. His wife is a charming American woman and all his sympathies, I can say confidentially, are on the side of the Allies. He is, of course, in a very embarrassing and difficult situation, and feels terribly the accusation that he is a spy. I would vouch, with my life, that he has done nothing of that kind, and in fact, the poor man has no communication with his own country, and, as Mr. Lansing told Mr. Root and myself on Saturday, even if he wanted to be a spy he would find it impossible.

I have written a much longer letter than intended, but my heart is so full of this whole matter that I can hardly contain myself when I think of the awful horrors which would follow our declaration of war with Turkey.

I should like to very much to see you some day and have a good talk with you about the whole matter, but meanwhile hope you will consider my letter in the spirit in which I have written it, and believe me with warm regards to you all.

Cordially and sincerely yours,

Cleveland H. Dodge

P.S. Hearty congratulations on the splendid work with your boys are doing on the other side. My own sons, who is in the same regiment with young George Perkins, reached France safely last Friday, and I suppose will soon be in the fight.

A week later, Roosevelt responded:

May 11th, 1918.

My dear Cleve:

It is difficult for me to write you because of the very fact that six members of your immediate family are in Turkey. Now, my dear Cleve, kinsfolks of mine are in Germany. They are suffering at present from being there. My feeling has been from the beginning that they had no business to stay there. As regards Turkey my feeling is even stronger. I do not feel that any men should have permitted their wives and daughters to stay in Turkey since we have gone to war with Germany. Indeed, my feeling is that form the time of the sinking of the Lueitania every American in Germany, Austria, Bulgaria or Turkey should have proceeded on the assumption that ultimately this country would go to war with those four embodiments of satanic policies on this globe at this time, and should have governed himself accordingly. Any Americans in Turkey who now suffer will suffer purely from their own fault; and if they plead their presence in Turkey, after the ample warning they have had, as a reason why this nation should not do its duty, they are guilty of grave moral dereliction.

I entirely agree with all that you say about Robert College and Beirut Collage in the past. I have no doubt that you are right when you say that there are Bulgarians and Turks (a few!) who are opposed to what their two countries have done joining Germany. There were Germans and Austrians who felt the same way. But all these men have proven utterly powerless to influence the policies of their countries. They are entitled to no consideration from s in shaping our international policy. It is a good deal worse than silly for us to repeat the worse than silly mistake of those Englishmen who kept insisting that there were Turks and Bulgarians who loved England, and so that England ought not to make active war on Turkey and Bulgaria. I do not for one moment believe that any effective body of Turkish opinion is against Germany, save as it is against all Christians – even against the Christians that let them massacre other Christians. There has been no sign whatever of the existence of any such body of effective opposition to Germany. Foolish person in England kept insisting on its existence, and did much damage by their insistence. In Turkey public opinion is nil and the people always obey any effective executive force, and obey nothing else. The surest way to strengthen the German hold on Turkey is to give the impression that the Allies are in any way divided. The perpetuation of Turkish rule is the perpetuation of infamy, and to perpetuate it on the theory that there are large numbers of Turks who have fine feelings by who never make those feelings in any way manifest, in an absurdity. If Robert and Beirut Colleges are used as props for the Turkish infamy and if they exert directly or indirectly any influence to keep the country from going to war with Turkey, they will more than counterbalance the good they have done in the past, and will make themselves by-words of derision for the future.

So far from "being of assistance to the Allied cause by keeping on nominal terms of friendliness with Bulgaria and Turkey", I am convinced we are of the very greatest damage to the Allied cause by so doing. Moreover, I feel that we are guilty of a peculiarly odious form of hypocrisy when we profess friendship for Armenia and the downtrodden races of Turkey, but don't go to war with Turkey. To allow the Turks to massacre the Americans and then solicit permission to help the survivors, and then to allege the fact that we are helping the survivors as a reason why we should not follow the only policy that will permanently put a stop to such massacres is both foolish and odious.

I have a most interesting letter on the subject from Einstein, formerly with our Embassy in Turkey. I will send it to you by George Perkins. Some suffering would be caused if we went to war with Turkey, just as some suffering was caused when we went to war with Germany. But the Americans now would suffer only as the English and French suffered three years ago, when their nations were doing their duty, and ours was shirking its duty. We have no business to expect the allies to do the fighting which alone will accomplish anything permanent while we play the utterly ignoble part of being neutral and hoping that somehow or other we can thereby both save our own skins and also accomplish something. The arguments advanced against our going to war with Turkey are on a par with those formerly advanced against our going to war with Germany and then with Austria; only they are not quite as good. The Armenian horror is an accomplished fact. Its occurrence was largely due to the policy of pacifism this nation has followed for the last four years. The presence of our missionaries, and our failure to go to war, did not prevent the Turks from massacring between half a million and a million Armenians, Syrians, Greeks and Jews - the overwhelmingly majority being Armenians. Our declaration of war now will certainly not do one one-hundredth part of the damage already done by our failure to go to war in the past; and it will enable us to render service of permanent value for the future, and incidentally to take another step in regaining our self-respect.

We should go to war because not to do so is really to show bad faith towards our allies, and to help Germany; because the Armenian massacre was the greatest crime of the war, and failure to act against Turkey is to condone it; because the failure to deal radically with the Turkish horror means that all talk of guaranteeing the future peace of the world is mischievous nonsense; and because when we now refuse to war with Turkey we show that our announcement that we meant "to make the world safe for democracy" was insincere claptrap.

With regret, my dear Cleve, that I must so radically and so fundamentally disagree with you, I am

Sincerely yours,

Mr. Cleveland H. Dodge,
99 John Street,
New York City.

Dodge acknowledged receipt of the letter from Roosevelt a couple of week later:

May 20, 1918.

Hon. Theodore Roosevelt,
347 Madison Avenue,
New York City.

My dear Theodore:

I want to tell you how much I appreciate your taking so much time to give your full views regarding the Turkish situation. I hardly think it would accomplish anything for us to continue the discussion any longer, but I must say one thing in reference to the remark you made regarding my family staying in Turkey. I think if you and your children had been situated as I and my children have been during the last few years, that you of all men would have felt as I have, - that I would have been ashamed of my children if they had not responded to what was a very definite and direct call to duty. If all of the Americans had left their work a year ago, I do not think we would have been proud of them. Even if I wanted to have them come back, they are of age, and I think would have decided for themselves.

Trusting that you will have an interesting and successful trip in the West, believe me with warn regards to all the family ,

Very sincerely,

CHD.C

Cleveland H. Dodge

A few weeks later Roosevelt received a letter written by a Captain Nushan Der Hagopian. I only found this letter as I was looking to see if Shahan Natalie had ever written to him when he was still legally known as Hagop Der Hagopian.

Captain Der Hagopian, originally from Harpout, Armenia (born 1883), had written to Roosevelt on June 12, 1918, asking for his help to protect the Armenian's who were in desperate need. Captain Der Hagopian wrote:

P.O.Box 35
Berkely
California.
June 12, 1918

Mr. Theodore Roosevelt
Ex-President, U.S.A.

Dear Sir:

I trust you will excuse the great liberty I am taking in writing to you; I have been wanting to do so for some time, but until this moment I have not had the courage to do so.

When we glance through history we find men such as Washington and Garribaldi who sacrificed their lives for the welfare of humanity; this is happening at the present momen. In the midst of this horrible war we need the courage of the heroes in history. At this very moment there are numberless men and woman who are conscientious and humane and who would help but for the fact that they lack the opportunity.

In 1909, during the Armenian massacres by the Turks in Adana, Asia Minor, your noble sympathy for our race stirred the hearts of the Armenian people. No doubt you are doing the same thing to-day, nor more, but it seems to me that, at this time, more definite <u>action</u> is needed than is being given. In the midst of this gigantic struggle of the Armenian nation the people are crying out for Washington or a Garribaldi–for a savior of their nation.

In the battlefield at the Caucasian front where I was an eye-witness in 1915, it was one hundred per cent worse than was represented in the press. It was inuman—unspeakable.

The international policy of Europe and Turkey is so damnable that we can not keep quiet: the conditions in Armenia are unspeakable. There are men who are plotting to influence our U.S. government not to declare war against Bulgaria or Turkey. How can we tolerate such conditions? Armenia to-day is crying out for help against her foes—it is <u>urgently</u> necessary to declare war upon Turkey for Armenia's sake and for the sake of the whole civilized world. Armenia is holding the gate of the East; if this gate falls to the Huns, the devil of Asia will be let loose upon India and it will be hard task for the Allies to finish the game.

From day to day a dispatch comes from the Georgian and Armenian forces at the Caucasian front, saying that they are holding back the Turkish hordes whilst massacres are a daily occurrence.

How long are these conditions to last? Drastic action should start at once. For this reason I wrote recently to Secretary Baker, explaining the facts and telling him that the Armenians in this country are willing to form a volunteer army if war against Turkey was declared. I was advised that the matter would be given special consideration, that it was put on official record, and further communication was promised. Finally I have decided to ask you to act as guide for us in this matter. We are willing to go and fight. Will you help us at this critical moment and be our Washington?

My suggestion to Sec. Baker was for the Armenians to join the American army if war was declared against Turkey; but the plan I am putting before you is different. I suggest that if you take this matter up, you should be free to lead the Armenians to any Turkish front you think necessary. I assure you that not only the twenty-thousand Armenians will stand by you in this venture, but there will be many thousands of noble Americans. In this way we may be led into the light and the coming generation will enjoy our share.

If you will forgive me, at your earliest convenience, with your option upon this matter, I shall be glad to present to you a plan for working out the campaign.

I am enclosing a copy of the "Forum" from July 1917 in which an article of mine appears. Another article upon Armenia will appear in the Century Magazine for July or August 1918. I am also engaged in preparing a book for publication upon conditions in Armenia, which will be out in the Fall; Prof. C.M.Gayley, Dean of the University of Calfiornia has written the Preface.

Your obedient servant,

Ex-President, Theodore Roosevelt was quick to respond on June 22, 1918, reaffirming his commitment the Armenian people.

June 22nd, 1918.

My dear Captain:

You know I have done all I can to get our country to act, and I shall continue do to do.

Faithfully yours,

Capt. N. Der Hagopian,
P.O.Box 35,
Bekeley, Calif.

After reading the letter of support from Roosevelt to Captain Der Hagopian, I started to doubt if the confession of the Rear Admiral, Colby M. Chester. Perhaps it could have been a ruse by an old man who embellished history to give himself more credibility and a feeling of importance.

I then searched for letters to Roosevelt from various other Armenians, finding a few letters from the one man Armenian lobby, Vahan Cardashian.

In the fall of 1911, Cardashian wrote a letter to Roosevelt, similar to that which Captain Der Hagopian had, asking that Roosevelt lend his voice to the cause to defend the rights of the Armenians who were facing oppression and death at the hands of the Turkish government. Cardashian wrote on Ocotber 20, 1911:

VAHAN CARDASIAN
COUNSELOR AT LAW
55 LIBERTY STREET
NEW YORK

TELEPHONE 3402 CORTLANDT

Oct. 20th, 1911.

Col. Theodore Roosevelt: -

My dear Mr. Roosevelt: -

I am taking the liberty to enclose herewith a copy of a letter addressed by me to Dr. Andrew D. White, and a copy of his letter addressed to me, both dealing with the necessity of creating an American Committee, that may help to influence the Turkish Government in its treatment of the Christians, which, of late, has been immeasurably oppressive. In my letter, I state the reasons for the creation of such a Committee, its nature and its purpose.

I know well that your time is amply occupied; but, it is a fact that one who has ample time would not be much service on a Committee such as the one proposed. The Committee, to be effective, must consist of men whose names carry international weight. This committee will hardly make a considerable call upon your time. Perhaps, once in all, a meeting may be held. Thereafter, there may bot be anything else for it to do but to exist, unless, of course, an extraordinary development may call upon it to act.

With the expression of my deepest gratitude for your noble sympathy in my race, I am, sir,

Yours respectfully,

Vahan Cardashian

[Enclosure]

VAHAN CARDASIAN
COUNSELOR AT LAW
55 LIBERTY STREET
NEW YORK

TELEPHONE 3402 CORTLANDT

C O P Y

Oct. 12th, 1911.

Dr. Andrew D. White,
    Ithaca,
        N.Y.

My dear Dr. White: -

After a long and careful deliberation, I decided, very reluctantly, to address myself again to you, depending largely, of course, upon your broad sympathy, your Christian humanity and your statesmanship. The question that has been engaging my anxious thought for some time past has been the necessity of providing some means for the safety of the Armenians in Turkey against the chronic Turkish and Kurdish aggressions.

As you well know, since the accession of the Young Turkey Party to power, the general conditions in Turkey have not changed. The central government has been either unwilling or unable to bring into play its authority in the provinces. The representations of the Armenian Patriarchate have met with the same evasive and dilatory a attitude as practiced by the Old Regime. Under the circumstances, there is actually no reasonable hope for any amelioration or improvement in those conditions. To the contrary, there are frequent alarming reports of threatened Kurdish or Turkish massacres of the Armenians. In fact, each day records a case of kidnapping, forcible conversion, unprovoked murder, desecration of a church or monastery, etc. The unavoidable result of these occurrences is a galling fear in the minds and hearts of the Armenians throughout Turkey of some approaching disaster.

I am not condemning any person or persons for this abnormal situation. I am simply calling your attention to the unavoidable conditions of irrefutable facts which we cannot ignore. Under these circumstances, I see clearly the coming cloud. That is, one or more massacres of the Armenians will take place, unless some preventive measures are adopted. Such measures must necessarily be initiated by an outside agency and such agency, for its weapon and power must depend upon its moral influence and public opinon. So if a number of eminent Americans were to organize a Committee and make a declaration of intention, to the effect, that the Committee is a friend of Turkey; that, in view of the peculiar conditions prevailing in the Turkish Empire, it is solicitous for the protection of Christian life, honor and property; and that, in the event of mob violence against these Christians, the Committee will employ all its moral influence and other reasonable means for their protection; then, I believe, a step forward in the cause shall have been taken. I believe that the Turk in power would be anxious not to create any pretext that may be used by Europe as a justification in invading on his dominions. The Italo-Turkish conflict showed a decided change in their temper and disposition of Europe in its attitude to Turkey.

For such a Committee, I will mention at random the following gentlemen: Theodore Roodevelt, Andrew D. White, Bishop Greer, Gov. Baldwin, of Conn., Andrew Carnegie, Seth Low, Lyman Abbot, Charles Eliot, Arthur Twining Harley, Nicholas Murray Butler, Gen. Horace Porter, Chauncey M. Depew, Rollow Ogden, Willian Randolph Hearst, Henry Clews, etc.

I know that the gentlemen whose names I mentioned are deeply interested in the Armenian race. I also know that they are very busy men. If they wanted or desired (and I know that they do) that the Armenians should be spared the result of the fanaticism of the Turk, they cold, at least, spare a very little part of their time to serve on the Committee itself, as a reserve force, will have its mandator influences upon the polices of the Turkish government in regard to the Armenians.

Will you, at your convenience, look into this matter and let me know as to what you think of such a step, as proposed.

Yours sincerely,

Cardashian

October fourteenth 1911

My dear Mr. Cardashian:

Referring to your letter of October twelfth, I need hardly say that I have the deepest sympathy in the matter to which you refer,- indeed, I hardly know of any great iniquity of modern times at which I feel so indignant, from the bottom of my heart, as the treatment of the Armenians which Turkey has so long allowed, and doubtless to a considerable extent connived at.

I feel that at my age I can be of very little use to you, for, though constantly engaged with more work than I ought to undertake, I am just entering my eightieth year and rarely leave home, - in fact, for the first time in my life, have remained in Ithach through the entire summer.

But should you think that my name and what little I can do under the circumstances will be of use to you, you are at liberty to name me as a member of the committee to which you refer.

With all good wishes for your success in the matter,

I remain,

Very respectfully and

Sincerely yours,
(signed) ANDREW D. WHITE

Vahan Cardashian, Esq.
New York City.

About a week later (October 21, 1911), Roosevelt responded to Cardashian's request:

October 21ˢᵗ, 1911.

My dear Mr. Cardashian:

I thank you for your letter regarding your suggestion of the creation of an American Committee to influence the Turkish Government in the treatment of Christians. You know how cordially I sympathize with any movement to put a stop to the Turkish atrocities in this respect, but I a sure you will realize on thinking it over how impossible it is for me to head such a committee. I am really unable to go into anything further of any kind or sort at present. I am very sorry, and appreciate your writing.

With renewed expression of my sympathy and regret that I am unable to help y heading such a committee, I am.

Very truly yours,

Vahan Cardashian, Esq.,
55 Liberty Street,
New York City.

The next letter I found in 1911, was dated November 15. It was from James W. Colt. It was a very different letter than that of Captain Der Hagopian and Vahan Cardashian. Rather than asking Roosevelt to help the Armenians from oppression and dangers of the Turks, it was a letter to Roosevelt inviting him to help himself to what rightfully belonged to the Armenians and thus support the Turks in their efforts to exterminate the Armenian People. The letter also included a hand-written note documenting a telephonic response to agreeing to a meeting with Colt to further discuss Roosevelt's involvement in the Chester Concessions. The letter read as follows:

MAC ARTHUR BROTHERS COMPANY
HANDOVER BANK BUILDING
NEW YORK

November 15ᵗʰ 1911.

Col. Theodore Roosevelt,
Oyster Bay.
My dear Sir:-

You may recall having met me two or three times at Geneseo where I live, and where I am still a member of the Geneseo Valley Hunt.

For two years past I have been in Constantinople and Asia Minor as a representative of the firm MacArthur Brothers Company, who are members of a certain American Syndicate seeking a Concession for the construction of Railways and the exploitation of Mines located principally in the ancient kingdom of Armenia.

I wish very much to have a few moments talk with you on the subject of this concession, which is of interest, not only financially, but also diplomatically to our own government, and which is now, or very soon, to be considered by the Turkish Parliament.

I am leaving on Saturday for the West Indies, to be absent about six weeks, and I beg, if possible, you will appoint me an interview within the next two or three days. I shall occupy only a few moments of your time and I especially desire your advice.

I am, Sir,
Yours very respectfully,

JWC/F

J.W. Colt

[hand written] Since writing the above, I have had a telephone conversation with your secretary at the office of "The Outlook" who has issue Friday 12:30 as a time that I may wait upon you.

The Roosevelt letters contain hundreds of thousands of documents which were donated to the Library of Congress by Roosevelt's wife, Edith Kermit Roosevelt, following her husband's unexpected death. After extensive research, I want to share a key excerpt from a letter dated December 25, 1911, which written by J. P. Morgan. Knowing the history documented in this book, this reads as a confession to a sinister plan concocted by the ultra-wealthy and powerful whose actions resulted in the theft and murder of the Armenian nation and people:

[...]

Personally, I would like to see you president and I believe that if you should be interested that I could give you the names of the few men who control these two districts so that you could carefully test the sentiment. Appearing as it does that the whole world is facing a crisis which may result in new maps of empires being made, it behooves the people of the United States to have a strong and courageous man at the helm, and the people believe in you.

Trusting that you accept my Christmas wishes in the spirit in which they are sent I get to remain,

Yours sincerely,

J. P. Morgan

It would seem from the letters found within the Theodore Roosevelt papers, what Rear Admiral Colby M. Chester claimed in his confession had some truth to it.

Although Theodore Roosevelt was able to fool the Armenian people for almost a decade with his sympathies, as a Christian, the outcome of his action speaks for itself.

As a Christian, I have to wonder if God had decided to intervene and end these harmful games being played on the Armenian people. Less than a month following what I would suspect was a disingenuous response to Captain Der Hagopian's request, which had the same intentions that Vahan Cardashian has had received 7 years earlier, Theodore Roosevelt's youngest son, Quentin, was killed on July 14, 1918 (Shahan Natalie's 44th birthday), in the theater of battle during World War I, in an aerial fight over German occupied France. Quentin Roosevelt, the youngest son of Theodore Roosevelt had been shot in the head with two bullets by a German pilot, causing him to crash his plane behind enemy lines. In less than 6 months following the loss of his son, on January 4, 1919, at the age of 60, Theodore Roosevelt would die after a blood clot had detached from a vein and traveled to his lungs. As for the interests in the Chester Concessions that Roosevelt had put in the name of his son, Kermit, it would seem that those did not bring enjoyment to him. After a lifelong battle with depression, on June 4, 1943, at the age of 53, while serving in the U.S. Army in Alaska during World War II, far from the theater of battle, Kermit Roosevelt would take his own life with a self-inflicted gunshot wound to the head.

Chapter 32

An Open Letter to President Wilson

With the untimely death of Theodore Roosevelt, it appeared to the general public that the Armenian people lost a powerful fighter for their cause. Roosevelt was a man who was famously known for his foreign policy: "speak softly and carry a big stick, you will go far." Next to Cleveland H. Dodge, Roosevelt was one of the most influential people in the United States and had the ear of President Wilson. It is worth pondering what would have happened if Roosevelt had lived. Would he had been successful in swaying President Wilson to do right by the Armenian people and declared war against Turkey?

With Roosevelt's passing, hopes of the U.S. declaring war against Turkey were rapidly fading. A German soldier and medic who witnessed the Armenian Genocide while serving as a second lieutenant in the German Sanitary Corps, which was attached to the Ottoman Sixth Army, Armin T. Wagner, wrote an open letter to President Woodrow Wilson, appealing to him to help the Armenian people.

Armin T. Wagner -

Wagner's letter was published in the German language newspaper, *Berliner Tageblatt,* in January, 1919, and was submitted to President Wilson at the peace conference of 1919.[109] Although in the end, Wilson appeared to not help the Armenians as Wager had hoped, his open letter remained as witness to what had happened to the Armenian people and how the United States and Europe failed to help the people and nation of Armenia during their most desperate time of need.

---

[109] Balakian, Peter (2003). The Burning Tigris: The Armenian Genocide and America's Response. New York: HarperCollins, p.318

BETRAYAL: The Promise Never Kept
AN OPEN LETTER TO PRESIDENT WILSON
BY
ARMIN T. WEGNER
(A German eye-witness of the Armenian massacres)
Berlin,
January 1919.

Mr. President,

In your message to Congress of January 8, 1918, you made a demand for the liberation of all non-Turkish peoples in the Ottoman Empire. One of these peoples is the Armenian nation. It is on behalf of the Armenian nation that I am addressing you.

As one of the few Europeans who have been eye-witnesses of the dreadful destruction of the Armenian people from its beginning in the fruitful fields of Anatolia up to the wiping out of the mournful remnants of the race on the banks of the Euphrates, I venture to claim the right of setting before you these pictures of misery and terror which passed before my eyes during nearly two years, and which will never be obliterated from my mind. I appeal to you at the moment when the Governments allied to you are carrying on peace negotiations in Paris, which will determine the fate of the world for many decades. But the Armenian people is only a small one among several others; and the future of greater States more prominent in the world's eye is hanging in the balance. And so there is reason to fear that the significance of a small and extremely enfeebled nation may be obscured by the influential and selfish aims of the great European states, and that with regard to Armenia there will be a repetition of the old game of neglect and oblivion of which she has so often been the victim in the course of her history.

But this would be most lamentable, for no people in the world has suffered such wrongs as the Armenian nation. The Armenian Question is a question for Christendom, for the whole human race.

The Armenian people were victims of this War. When the Turkish Government, in the Spring of 1915, set about the execution of its monstrous project of exterminating a million of Armenians, all the nations of Europe were unhappily bleeding to exhaustion, owing to the tragic blindness of their mutual misunderstanding, and there was no one to hinder the lurid tyrants of Turkey from carrying on to the bitter end those revolting atrocities which can only be likened to the acts of a criminal lunatic. And so they drove the whole people—men, women, hoary elders, children, expectant mothers and dumb sucklings—into the Arabian desert, with no other object than to let them starve to death.

For a long time, Europeans had been wont to regard Siberia as one of the most inhospitable regions in the world; to be condemned to live there was regarded as a most severe punishment. And yet, even in that place, there are fertile lands and, despite the cold of its winters, the climate is healthy. But what is Siberia compared with the Mesopotamian Steppes?

There we find a long tract of land without grass, without trees, without cattle, covered with stunted weeds, a country where the only inhabitants are Arab Bedouins, destitute of all pity; a stretch of grey limestone plains several miles in extent, bare wastes of rock and stone, ruined river banks, exposed to the rays of a merciless sun, ceaseless autumn rains, and frosty winter nights, leaving sheets of ice behind them. Except its two large rivers there is no water. The few small villages scarcely suffice to feed a handful of Bedouins, who, in their wretched poverty, regard any traveler as a welcome prey. From the dwellings which their race had held for Armenian women refugees devouring the flesh of dead horses more than two thousand years, from all parts of the Empire, from the stony passes of the mountain region to the shores of the Sea of Marmora and the palmy oases of the South, the Armenians were driven into this desolate waste, with the alleged purpose of forcibly transplanting them from their homes to a strange land—a purpose which, even had it been the real one, is repugnant to every human feeling. The men were struck down in batches, bound together with chains and ropes, and thrown into the river or rolled down the mountain with fettered limbs. The women and children were put on sale in the public market; the old men and boys driven with deadly bastonados to forced labour. Nor was this sufficient; in order to render indelible the stain on their criminal hands, the captors drove the people, after depriving them of their leaders and spokesmen, out of the towns at all hours of the day and night, half-naked, straight out of their beds; plundered their houses, burnt the villages, destroyed the churches or turned them into mosques, carried off the cattle, seized all the vehicles, snatched the bread out of the mouths of their victims, tore the clothes from off their backs, the gold from their hair. Officials—military officers, soldiers, shepherds—vied with one another in their wild orgy of blood, dragging out of the schools delicate orphan girls to serve their bestial lusts, beat with cudgels dying women or women close on childbirth who could scarcely drag themselves along, until the women fell down on the road and died, changing the dust beneath them into bloodstained mire. Travelers passing along the road turned away their eyes in horror from this moving multitude, driven on with devilish cruelty—only to find in their inns new-born babes buried in the dung-heaps of the court-yards, and the roads covered with severed heads of boys, who had raised them in supplication to their torturers. Parties which on their departure from the homeland of High Armenia consisted of thousands, numbered on their arrival in the outskirts of Aleppo only a few hundreds, while the fields were strewed with swollen, blackened corpses, infecting the air with their odours, lying about desecrated, naked, having been robbed of their clothes, or driven, bound back to back, to the Euphrates to provide food for the fishes. Sometimes gendarmes in derision threw into the emaciated hands of the starving people a little meal which they greedily licked off, merely with the result of prolonging their death-agony.

Even before the gates of Aleppo they were allowed no rest. For incomprehensible and utterly unjustifiable reasons of war, the shrunken parties were ceaselessly driven barefooted, hundreds of miles under a burning sun, through stony defiles, over pathless steppes, enfeebled by fever and other maladies, through semi-tropical marshes, into the wilderness of desolation.

Here they died—slain by Kurds, robbed by gendarmes, shot, hanged, poisoned, stabbed, strangled, mown down by epidemics, drowned, frozen, parched with thirst, starved—their bodies left to putrefy or to be devoured by jackals.

Children wept themselves to death, men dashed themselves against the rocks, mothers threw their babes into the brooks, women with child flung themselves, singing, into the Euphrates. They died all the deaths on the earth, the deaths of all the ages.

I have seen maddened deportees eating as food their own clothes and shoes, women cooking the bodies of their new-born babes.

In ruined caravanserais they lay between heaps of corpses and half-rotted bodies, with no one to pity them, waiting for death; for how long would it be possible for them to drag out a miserable existence, searching out grains of com from horse-dung or eating grass? But all this is only a fraction of what I have seen myself, of what I have been told by my acquaintances or by travelers, or of what I have heard from the mouths of the deportees.

Mr. President, if you will look through that dreadful enumeration of horrors compiled by Lord Bryce in England and by Dr. Johannes Lepsius in Germany with regard to these occurrences, you will see that I am not exaggerating. But I may assume that these pictures of horrors of which all the world has heard except Germany, which has been shamefully deceived, are already in your hands. By what right, then, do I make this appeal to you?

I do it by the right of human fellowship, in dutiful fulfilment of a sacred promise.

When in the desert I went through the deportees' camp, when I sat in their tents with the starving and dying, I felt their supplicating hands in mine, and the voices of their priests, who had blessed many of the dead on their last journey to the grave, adjured me to plead for them, if I were ever in Europe again.

But the country to which I have returned is a poor country; Germany is a conquered nation. My own people (the Germans) are near starvation; the streets are full of the poor and wretched. Can I beg help of a people which perhaps will soon not be in a condition to save itself for a people (the Armenians) which is in even more evil case?

The voice of conscience and humanity will never be silenced in me, and therefore I address these words to you.

This document is a request. It is the tongues of a thousand dead that speak in it.

Mr. President, the wrong suffered by this people is immeasurable. I have read everything that has been written about the war. I have carefully made myself acquainted with the horrors in every country on this earth, the fearful slaughters in every battle, the ships sunk by torpedoes, the bombs thrown down on the towns by air-craft, the heartrending slaughters in Belgium, the misery of the French refugees, the fearful sickness and epidemics in Roumania. But here is wrong to be righted such as none of these peoples has suffered—neither the French nation, nor the Belgian, nor the English, nor the Russian, nor the Serbian, nor the Roumanian, nor even the German nation, which has had to suffer so much in this war. The barbarous peoples of ancient times may possibly have endured a similar fate. But here we have a highly civilised nation, with a great and glorious past, which has rendered services that can never be forgotten to art, literature and learning; a nation which has produced many remarkable and intellectual men, profoundly religious, with a noble priesthood; a Christian people, whose members are dispersed over the whole earth, many of whom have lived for many years in your country, Mr. President. Men acquainted with all the languages of the world, men whose wives and daughters have been accustomed to sit in comfortable chairs at a table covered with a clean white cloth, not to crouch in a cave in the wilderness. Sagacious merchants, distinguished doctors, scholars, artists, honest prosperous peasants who made the land fruitful, and whose only fault was that they were defenceless and spoke a different language from that of their persecutors, and were born into a different faith.

Every one who knows the events of this war in Anatolia, who has followed the fortunes of this nation with open eyes, knows that all those accusations which were brought, with great cunning and much diligence, against the Armenian race, are nothing but loathsome slanders fabricated by their unscrupulous tyrants, in order to shield themselves from the consequences of their own mad and brutal acts, and to hide their own incapacity for reconciliation with the spirit of sincerity and humanity.

But even if all these accusations were based on the truth, they would never justify these cruel deeds committed against hundreds of thousands of innocent people.

I am making no accusation against Islam. The spirit of every great religion is noble, and the conduct of many a Mohammedan has made us blush for the deeds of Europe.

I do not accuse the simple people of Turkey, whose souls are full of goodness; but I do not think that the members of the ruling class will ever, in the course of history, be capable of making their country happy, for they have destroyed our belief in their capacity for civilisation.

Turkey has forfeited for all time the right to govern itself.

Mr. President, you will believe in my impartiality if I speak to you on this subject, as a German, one of a nation which was linked with Turkey in bonds of close friendship, a nation which in consequence of this friendship has most unjustly been accused of being an accomplice in these murderous man-hunts. The German people knows nothing of this crime. The German Government erred through ignorance of the Turkish character and its own preoccupation with solicitude for the future of its own people. I do not deny that weakness is a fault in the life of nations. But the bitter reproach of having made possible this unpardonable deportation does not fall on Germany alone.

In the Berlin Treaty of July 1878, all the six European Great Powers gave the most solemn guarantees that they would guard the tranquility and security of the Armenian people. But has this promise ever been kept? Even Abdul

Hamid's massacres failed to bring it to remembrance, and in blind greed the nations pursued selfish aims, not one putting itself forward as the champion of an oppressed people.

In the Armistice between Turkey and your Allies, which the Armenians all over the world awaited with feverish anxiety, the Armenian question is scarcely mentioned. Shall this unworthy game be repeated a second time, and must the Armenians be once more disillusioned?

The future of this small nation must not be relegated to obscurity behind the selfish schemes and plans of the great states. Mr. President, save the honour of Europe.

It would be an irremediable mistake if the Armenian districts of Russia were not joined with the Armenian provinces of Anatolia and Cilicia to form one common country entirely liberated from Turkish rule, with an outlet of its own to the sea. It is not enough, Mr. President, that you should know the sufferings of these people. It is not enough that you should give them a state in which the houses are destroyed, the fields laid waste, the citizens murdered. The exhaustion of this country is such that by its own strength it cannot rise again. Its trade is ruined; its handicrafts and industries have collapsed. The asset of its annihilated population can never be restored.

Many thousands of Armenians were perverted to Islam by force, thousands of children and girls kidnapped, and thousands of women carried away and made slaves in Turkish harems. To all these must be given perfect assurance of their return to freedom. All victims of persecution who are returning to their homes after spending two years and more in the desert must be indemnified for the wealth and goods that they have lost, all orphans must be cared for. What these people need is love, of which they have so long been deprived. This is, for all of us, a confession of guilt.

Mr. President, pride prevents me from pleading for my own people (the Germans). I have no doubt that, out of the plenitude of its sorrow, it will gain power by sacrifice to co-operate in the future redemption of the world. But, on behalf of the Armenian nation, which has suffered such terrible tyranny, I venture to intervene; for if, after this war, it is not given reparation for its fearful sufferings, it will be lost for ever.

With the ardour of one who has experienced unspeakable, humiliating sorrows in his own tortured soul, I utter the voice of those unhappy ones, whose despairing cries I had to hear without being able to still them, whose cruel deaths I could only helplessly mourn, whose bones bestrew the deserts of the Euphrates, and whose limbs once more become alive in my heart and admonish me to speak.

Once already have I knocked at the door of the American people when I brought the petition of the deportees from their camps at Meskene and Aleppo to your Embassy at Constantinople, and I know that this has not been in vain.

If you, Mr. President, have indeed made the sublime idea of championing oppressed nations the guiding principle of your policy, you will not fail to perceive that even in these words a mighty voice speaks, the only voice that has the right to be heard at all times—the voice of humanity.[110]

---

[110] Andonian, Aram (1920). The Memoirs of Naim Bey: Turkish Official Documents relating to the Deportation and Massacres of Armenians. Great Britain: Richard Clay & Sons, Limited, p.72-84

Chapter 33

Still Arming the Enemy

By Ara Manoogian
[published on April 14, 2016]

"The sale of weapons to a government committing genocide is like the sale of weapons to Nazi Germany during World War II"
— Yair Auron, Israeli historian

IAI Harop unmanned combat air vehicle (UCAV) developed by the Israel Aerospace Industries was used in combat for the first time, on April 4, 2016, by the military of Azerbaijan against Nagorno-Karabakh Republic (which Armenians call by its ancient name, Artsakh). The deployment of this UCAV, armed with 23 kg warhead, caused the death of seven Armenians during a ceasefire violation by Azerbaijan.

Israeli Kamikaze drones (photo from socialunderground.com)

In 1921, Soviet dictator Joseph Stalin transferred predominantly Armenian-populated Nagorno-Karabakh to the Soviet Socialist Republic of Azerbaijan. For decades thereafter, Karabakh Armenians tried to restore historical justice and reunite with Armenia to no avail.

Soviet leader Mikhail Gorbachev's Perestroika and Glasnost opened a new phase in the struggle of the Armenian people in Karabakh, in 1988. The local authorities of Nagorno-Karbakh Autonomous Oblast (NKAO) announced their decision to secede from the Azerbaijani SSR and reunite with Armenia. The Soviet government turned down the request. And the Soviet Azerbaijani authorities organized pogroms of ethnic Armenians in Sumgait, Kirovabad (now Ganja), and Baku.

On September 2, 1991, the Council of People's Deputies declared Nagorno-Karabakh an independent Republic within the borders of NKAO and the bordering Shahumyan Region of the Azerbaijani SSR. This declaration was followed by a referendum on the status of the NKR, on December 10, where the absolute majority voted in favor of independence.

As a result of this unrelenting determination, Azerbaijan escalated the conflict to large-scale war against Nagorno-Karabakh.

In February 1992, the Organization for Security and Co-operation in Europe (OSCE), including member states of the United States, France, and Russia, initiated an arms embargo against Armenia and Azerbaijan. This embargo was intended to help the OSCE to seat the opposing sides at the negotiating table.

A ceasefire agreement was eventually reached in 1994, brokered by the OSCE and, particularly, Russia, after Azerbaijan lost control of Nagorno-Karabakh and seven adjacent regions. More than 30,000 people died as a result of the war.

In the 22 years that followed, a peace treaty has not been signed, and the ceasefire has been violated with growing frequency, resulting in hundreds of deaths among the Armenian and Azeri military personnel. These borderline cross shootings are commonly initiated by the Azerbaijani armed forces. For over two decades, unsatisfied with the status quo, the Azerbaijani authorities have been threatening to start a war against Nagorno-Karabakh and take control of the independent republic.

Though the OSCE's request for embargo has never been repealed, Russia supplies arms to both Armenia and Azerbaijan. However, oil rich Azerbaijan has had an additional major arms supplier — Israel. Some of the early purchases took place before the ceasefire agreement, but the majority came later, when the oil prices in the world market skyrocketed. In 2012 alone, Azerbaijan purchased $1.6 billion worth of weapons from Israel, including sophisticated reconnaissance and attack drones from Israel Aerospace Industries.

Many Israelis have raised concerns over their government's arms deal with Azerbaijan. In his article, "Israel Must Not Sell Arms to the Azeris" (Haaretz, October 26, 2014), Israeli historian Yair Auron writes:

> Israel must refrain from such acts also because we are a people of Holocaust survivors. A tragic crime and humanitarian disaster could take place in the centennial year of the Armenian genocide, which continues to go unrecognized by most countries [including Israel].[111]

In mid-August of 2014, at the height of clashes at the line of contact between Nagorno-Karabakh and Azerbaijan, Eitay Mack and Yair Auron submitted an urgent request to the Arms Exports Department of the Israeli Defense Ministry to stop Israel's arms sales to Azerbaijan. They demanded that Dubi Lavi, the head of that department, 'use his authority to revoke or delay the corresponding permits issued by Defense Ministry, at least until the end of the current escalation.'

They received an ambiguous response, which implied undeterred resolution to continue the arms exports: "We have closely examined the statements in your letter. Security export is carefully examined <...> considerations of human rights and conflict zones worldwide are seriously weighed."

On April 2, 2016, Azerbaijan committed the deadliest violation of the armistice since 1994, launching a large-scale offensive all along the line of contact. In a matter of a few days, the death toll among the military forces and the civilians, by different estimates, ranges from 200 to 2,000. Russia managed

---

111 http://www.haaretz.com/opinion/.premium-1.622701

to broker a shaky ceasefire on April 5, 2016, which, nevertheless, has not put an end to Azerbaijani President's war rhetoric.

Two days after this major offensive, Tali Ploskov, Deputy Speaker of Israel's Knesset, paid a visit to Armenia to express support for Armenia and condemn Azerbaijan's deadly attacks against Nagorno Karabakh. At a meeting with her Armenian counterpart Hermine Naghdalyan, Ploskov described Azerbaijan's actions as terrorism against the entire region.[112]

Israeli anti-tank laser missiles (photo from asbarez.com)

In an interview to the Voice of America's Azerbaijani Service, on April 8, 2016, Alexander Murinson, a researcher from the Begin-Sadat Center for Strategic Studies at Bar-Ilan University of Israel, admitted to the pivotal role of Israel's arms supply in the commencement of the Azerbaijan's large-scale offensive. "On March 31, Israel supplied anti-tank laser missiles to Azerbaijan. Azerbaijan is the first country to purchase these missiles, which has, certainly, given advantage to its military capabilities," he said.[113]

"I am ashamed," said Israel Charny, a prominent Israeli historian, executive director of the Institute on the Holocaust and Genocide in Jerusalem, about the 3-day April war in Nagorno-Karabakh and Israel's contribution to the casualties, in his article, "Would Israel Sell a Used Drone to a Hitler?" published in Haaretz.[114]

"If the Nazis were not at all murdering Jews but 'only' were murdering say hated Slavs, Gypsies, and Jehovah's Witnesses; and if our beloved State of Israel were in existence; would you agree to our selling arms to the Nazis?" writes Charny.

On April 24, 2018, Yaniv Konovich wrote an article for Haaretz Daily Newpaper titled "Advanced Israeli Weapons Sold to Azerbaijan Exposed in Army-produced Pop Music Video" (Haaretz, April 24, 2018) in which he discusses the content

Israel Charny (© http://unotes. hartford.edu)

---

112 http://panarmenian.net/m/eng/news/209585

113 see Amerika icmalı - https://www.youtube.com/watch?v=Eqm20FQEpT0 and "Voice of America: On March 31, Israel supplied laser anti-tank missiles to Azerbaijan" - http://news.am/eng/news/321409.html

114 The Armenian Weekly- http://armenianweekly.com/2016/04/12/sassounian-charny/

found in the footage of a music video produced by Azerbaijan's army that showcased Israeli made weapons in action. Israeli technology was not the only noticeable equipment present in this video. Czech military hardware was also present in the form of artillery and rocket launchers. Also, on April 24, 2018, California Courier publisher, Harut Sassounian, wrote an article titled "Czech Republic Sells Weapons to Azerbaijan Illegally via Israel" (The California Courier, April 24, 2018) which details how the Czech Republic went against European Union's recommendation, as well as the U.N. Security Council Resolution 853, which was adopted on July 29, 1999, and managed to sell its arms to Azerbaijan. Sassounian details how exactly these weapons ended up in Azerbaijan. Below is a segment from Harut's article.

> In the meantime, The Slovak Spectator revealed on April 17, 2018 that 'Bratislava [capital of Slovakia] airport is used as a transit point for smuggling Czech rocket launchers and howitzers to Azerbaijan.... The weapons are reportedly produced by the Czechoslovak Group Holding, owned by Czech Jaroslav Strnad, according to Czech Television.... An employee of the Slovak arms factory MSM spoke up and described how the old weapons are rebuilt in the Trenčín-based company and are then transported via Israel to Azerbaijan, the TASR newswire reported.'
>
> The MSM employee further described to the reporters of the Czech Television, as quoted by TASR, according to The Slovak Spectator: 'The whole process starts with bringing the old DANA howitzer that is disassembled directly in the company.... The new facilities, including navigation, camera and communication systems were sent from Israel, the employee added. He also revealed that they signed a contract for distributing 18 howitzers and 15 rocket launchers this year, and the same amount next year, as reported by TASR.... The company confirmed the delivery of DANA-M1 and RM-70 systems to Israel.'
>
> The Slovak Spectator 'even recorded one such transport on camera' confirming the delivery of the weapons to Israel and from there smuggled to Azerbaijan. 'The transport of one rocket launcher started on December 27, 2017, and was carried by a truck from Trenčín to the Bratislava airport, where it was moved to the plane owned by Azerbaijani airlines, Silk Way. It then flew to Tel Aviv in Israel, where the company Elbit, which was described as the end customer, is located. The data then revealed that the plane continued to Baku in Azerbaijan. Nothing is unloaded in Israel; there is only a stop to make sure the papers are correct,' the employee of MSM told the Czech Television. 'The plane flies directly from the Israeli airport to Azerbaijan,' The Slovak Spectator wrote.

Israel made billions of dollars by violating the arms embargo against Azerbaijan. But Israel's lucrative deal with Azerbaijan has cost tiny Nagorno-Karabakh scores of lives and has encouraged Azerbaijan to resume an all-out war.

Since its formation in 1949, Israel has received almost $135 billion of aid from the U.S., of which almost $95 billion is military assistance. As a country that receives more aid from the U.S. taxpayers than any other country, Israel should have honored the U.S. arms embargo against Azerbaijan. In reality, Israel has been working against U.S. interests, by undermining its powerful ally's costly efforts to achieve a peaceful settlement of the conflict.

Pursuant to an understanding signed between the U.S. Department of

Defense and the Israeli Ministry of Defense, the U.S. has the de facto veto power over Israeli third-party arms sales that the U.S. deems harmful to its national security interests.[115]

In order to enforce the embargo ignored by Israel, we, the people of the United States of America, must petition our government to take immediate action against Israel for supplying weapons to Azerbaijan contrary to U.S. interests.

Ironically, the largest arms sales to Azerbaijan today comes from one of the members of the OSCE — Russia that is not only the co-author of the OSCE arms embargo, but also the strategic partner of Armenia (which gets its share of Russian arms at a discounted rate).

---

115 "U.S. Foreign Aid to Israel" by Jeremy M. Sharp
https://www.fas.org/sgp/crs/mideast/RL33222.pdf

Chapter 34

Genocide Recognition

"I think the acknowledgement of the United States of Armenian Genocide is very important and crucial. Not because of the moral aspect of the issue. Because of the legal aspect of that problem. Have you ever heard holocaust gold in Swiss banks? As you know, Nazis put all of gold in Swiss banks and Swiss government denied to pay these to Jewish communities. And Jewish organization filed lawsuits in the United States and according to United States law, you can file any government, if the case related to crime against humanity. And Swiss government didn't have any other choice but to negotiate with claim or the committee this is the Jewish organization, and paid them an important amount of money. There are hundreds, maybe not hundreds, dozens of courts cases waiting in California or other states in the United States and the courts cannot move because they all decided it's a federal issue. Without American government legally considers 1915 as a crime against humanity, there can not be a law case against Turkey. And if United States acknowledged these as a fact, then Turkey had a very difficult time because they can boycott, block Turkish assets in the United States and against Turkish companies and this would at least open the gate of negotiation."

- Dr. Taner Akçam -- June 14, 2018 -- Yerevan, Armenia.

It seems that one of the most costly and time-consuming pastimes of Armenians, is their quest to gain official recognition of the Armenian Genocide by the United States government at a federal level.

As long as I've been alive, I have heard over and over again that the United States won't recognize this crime against my people, a crime that unequivocally is nothing less than a Genocide. This is not just based on historical documents, but what my grandparents witnessed first hand and filled my head with since I was old enough to communicate.

A few months ago, I read Siranush Ghazanchyan's article on Public Radio of Armenia that discussed recognition of the Armenian Genocide by the U.S. State of Indiana. This was quite a big news to Armenians, as this 48th U.S. state to have officially recognized the Armenian Genocide brought the number very close to 50.

In her report, Ghazanchyan quotes Giro Manoyan, leader of the ARF and head of the Armenian Cause Office (*HayTad*) as saying that Indiana's recognition of the Armenian Genocide will not directly affect the U.S. President's stance on the issue.

"According to the U.S. Constitution, the country's foreign policy is determined by the President. There is a court decision in the U.S. that recognition of the Armenian Genocide is a foreign policy affair. Therefore, it's up to the President to make a decision. This does not mean, however, that other authorities cannot take decisions on the Armenian Genocide," Manoyan said in an interview with Public Radio of Armenia.

Manoyan believes, however, that the recognition will establish a generally favorable atmosphere. "At least two resolutions on Armenian Genocide recognition have been submitted to the US House of Representatives at different times. There is another resolution pending in the House today. All of this will create a favorable atmosphere, but will not directly lead to recognition by the President," Giro Manoyan said.

the Armenian lobby in the U.S., according to Manoyan, will keep working in two directions: to press for the passage of a resolution at the House of Representatives, and to build relations with the executive authorities in order to try and persuade that recognition is in the interests of the United States.

"The fact that Turkey is influencing the U.S. President's stance on the Armenian Genocide issue should be disgraceful. This is true not only for the incumbent, but also all previous Presidents besides Ronald Reagan, who used the term "genocide" in one of his April 24 messages," Manoyan said.

What will be the effect of the Armenian Genocide recognition by the U.S. President? According to Giro Manoyan, all these acknowledgements by U.S. States or by different countries are a pressure on Turkey. Recognition by the U.S. President will also be a pressure on Turkey. "The main objective is to force recognition by Turkey itself," he said.[116]

While Giro Manoyan is one of the most powerful Armenians in terms of championing the cause of U.S. recognition of the Armenian Genocide, the non-Armenian champion has to be the Congress Representative in my district of California (the 28th district), Congressman Adam Bennett Schiff (D-California), who has served in Congress for 18 years now.

Adam Schiff was born in Framingham, Massachusetts on June 22, 1960. He received a political science degree from Stanford University and a Juris Doctor degree from Harvard Law School. Not only does he serve as our congressional representative, he currently serves as the Chair of the Permanent Select Committee of Intelligence.

On the eve of the 102nd anniversary of the Armenian Genocide, the *Burbank Leader News* published an article written by Anthony Clark Carpio titled "Rep. Schiff asks Congress to recognize Armenian Genocide."

On previous Wednesday, Schiff and Representative Dave Trott (R-Michigan) introduced a bipartisan resolution (H.R. 220) that recognizes the genocide of Armenians by the Ottoman Empire (modern-day Turkey) that spanned from 1915 to 1923:

> Over 100 years ago, the Ottoman Empire undertook a brutal campaign of murder, rape and displacement against the Armenian people that took the lives of 1.5 million men, women and children in the first genocide of the 20th century," Schiff said in a statement. "Genocide is not a historic relic — even today hundreds of thousands of religious minorities face existential threat from ISIS in Syria and Iraq. It is therefore all the more pressing that the Congress recognize the historical fact of the Armenian Genocide and stand against modern-day genocide and crimes against humanity.[117]

---

116 Siranush Ghazanchyan, *Any recognition of Armenian Genocide adds pressure on Turkey – Giro Manoyan*, (Yerevan, Armenia, Public Radio of Armenia, November 7, 2017)

117 Anthony Clark Carpio, *Rep, Schiff asks Congress to recognize Armenian Genocide,*

To have a better understanding of what could possibly motivate him to champion the cause of official recognition of the Armenian Genocide, I would like to share relate what I heard from a dear friend of mine, Vartkes Yeghiayan, Esq., a man who had devoted most of his adult life to the Armenian cause. Vartkes passed away, on September 30, 2017.

When he worked in Washington, D.C., Vartkes had an opportunity to meet young Adam Schiff who was actively involved in the Armenian Genocide issues. After interacting with him, Vartkes discovered that Adam Schiff was a relation to the prominent New York banker, Jacob H. Schiff. Adam had told Vartkes that part of his motivation to help the Armenian people was to right a wrong done by Jacob Schiff. A kind of family debt he felt he had to settle.

Besides Manoyan and Schiff, there are literally thousands of prominent members of society who have spoken out in favor of the U.S. officially recognizing the Armenian Genocide. Many celebrities parrot what the experts on the subject like Manoyan and Schiff have been discussing in order to ensure official U.S. recognition.

But first, it is worth examining whether theirs is a valid agenda.

The Armenian Genocide has been a subject of contention long before the word Genocide was coined in 1943 by Raphael Lemkin, a lawyer of Polonized Jewish descent.

Before the word Genocide was coined, the crime against the Armenians by the Ottoman government was referred to as a crime against humanity.

The first governments to officially acknowledge this crime were Great Britain, France, and Russia. In their May 24, 1915 joint declaration, these nations accused the Young Turk regime of crimes against humanity and civilization:

> "Such massacres have taken place from mid-April at Erzerum, Terdjan, Egine, Bitlis, Moush, Sasun, Zeitun, and in all of Cilicia. The inhabitants of approximately a hundred villages in the vicinity of Van all have been killed and the Armenian quarter of Van besieged by Kurds. At the same time, the Ottoman Government has acted ruthlessly against the defenseless Armenian population of Constantinople. In view of this new crime of Turkey against humanity and civilization, the Allied Governments make known publicly to the Sublime Porte [Ottoman government] that they will hold all the members of the Turkish Government as well as those officials who have participated in these massacres, personally responsible."[118]

Over the years, many governments have recognized the Armenian Genocide, some in the form of a proclamation and others with resolutions.

One of the most important recognitions of the Armenian Genocide is that made by the post-WWI Turkish Government. This internationally recognized body, led by the Sultan, Mehmed VI, convened courts-martial, which found Talaat Pasha and others guilty of crimes against humanity with regard to Armenian massacres and sentenced the perpetrators to death.

(Burbank, CA, Burbank Leader News, March 24, 2017)

118 Richard G. Hovannisian, *The Armenian Genocide and the Ruse of Protective Dispossession,* (Los Angeles, CA, Southwestern Journal of International Law, February 22, 2017) vol. 23, p206

Although many will argue that the Sultan was a puppet of the Western powers, he was nonetheless internationally recognized as the legitimate leader of the Ottoman Empire. What he did, even if under pressure, was legally binding and internationally recognized. This being said, one of the first to recognize the Armenian Genocide was Turkey itself[119].

Although it should be gratifying for the victims and their descendants that the crimes against the Armenians were actually recognized by Turkey, however, American-Armenians who believe their government refuses to recognize the fact feel offended.

For as long as I can remember, the Armenian lobbying organizations, most notably the Armenian National Committee of America (ANCA), which is the lobbying wing of the ARF, has been supporting politicians who claim to be working towards the U.S. recognition of the Armenian Genocide, including the most prominent champion of the Armenian cause in Congress, Rep. Adam Schiff.

Each year in April, the ANCA speaks out to shame the U.S. government for their denial of the Armenian Genocide, blaming them for not officially recognizing the genocide due to the strategic relationship the U.S. has with Turkey, a fellow NATO member.

The ANCA have been supporters of numerous resolutions that have been presented to the House of Representatives by the politicians they have helped to vote into office in exchange for promises to achieve official recognition of the Armenian Genocide by the U.S.

On March 22, 2017, House Resolution 220 (H.R. 220)[120] was presented. H.R. 220 was co-authored by 16 Congressional representatives and co-sponsored by 108 more (totaling 124). These representatives had promised they would work to gain official recognition of the Armenian Genocide should they remain in office. So, H.R. 220 was their offering to the Armenian voters.

Within the text of H. R. 220, a very accurate and powerful claim is made, one that exposes all those who authored H.R. 220. It reveals the worthlessness of their promise to the Armenian voters and is an admission to have been lying in order to gain the vote and play on the soft emotional vulnerabilities our politicians had implanted in us and our own parents had helped to perpetuate.

HR220's opening paragraph reads:

"Expressing the sense of the House of Representatives regarding past genocides, and for other purposes."

In the 8th paragraph, the 124 representatives claim with accuracy:

"**Whereas the United States is on record as having officially recognized the Armenian Genocide**, in the United States Government's May 28, 1951, written statement to the International Court of Justice regarding the Convention on the Prevention and Punishment of the Crime of Genocide, through President Ronald Reagan's April 22, 1981, Proclamation

---

119 Meline Anumyan, *Acknowledgment and Condemnation: The Trials of Young Turks in 1919-1921 AND 1926*, (Antelias, Lenanon, Printing House of the Armenian Catholicosate of Cilicia, 2017) 223.

120 see appendix XV

No. 4838, and by House Joint Resolution 148, adopted on April 8, 1975, and House Joint Resolution 247, adopted on September 10, 1984; and"

The judicial branch of the U.S. government has recognized the Armenian Genocide, on May 28, 1951. This was followed by the House of Representatives' recognition, on April 8, 1975. Then, on April 22, 1981, President Ronal Reagan officially recognized the Armenian Genocide. If this was not enough, the House of Representatives re-recognized it. What the authors neglected to include is presented by the ANCA on their website (https://anca.org/armenian-genocide/recognition/united-states/), mentioning the 1996 House Resolution 3540, which once again officially re-recognized the Armenian Genocide as a genocide.

If this is the case, as confessed by the 124 elected representatives who had been telling the Armenian voters that no official U.S. recognition of the Armenian Genocide existed, yet co-authored/sponsored H.R. 220, what was their motive in deceiving their constituents?

One thing is certain — they have deceived the voters and, in doing so, have been holding back the Armenians from taking the next logical step of demanding reparations from Turkey.

It is important to note that the information about the U.S. official recognition of the Armenian Genocide was originally reported by a prominent member of the Armenian Diaspora community, Harut Sassounian, Armenian-American writer, public activist and publisher of *The California Courier*. At the time of his disclosure, Sassounian was the President of the United Armenian Fund and Vice Chairman of Armenian billionaire Kirk Kerkorian's Lincy Foundation, which provided close to $1 billion of humanitarian and infrastructure aid to Armenia.

As far back as June 13, 2008, in an article titled "US Recognized Armenian Genocide in 1951, World Court Document Reveals," which was written by Sassounian and published in *Asbarez*, an ARF-controlled news outlet, Sassounian touches upon the U.S. recognition, which H.R. 220 echoes. On June 5, 2012, Sassounian published "All 3 Branches of US Government Recognizes Armenian Genocide" in *The Armenian Weekly*, another pro-ARF publication. Despite these articles, the ANCA, the ARF, and the politicians they continue to claim that we have had no U.S. recognition.[121]

To make matters worse, Schiff and his fellow representatives in Congress continue to introduce resolutions that fortunately until now have not made it to a vote. Harut Sassounian has touched on the dangers of what the likes of Schiff have been doing in an email dated February 15, 2016:

From: Harut Sassounian
Sent: Feb 15, 2016 10:24 AM

---

[121] Harut Sassounian, *US Recognized Armenian Genocide in 1951, World Court Document Reveals,* (Los Angeles, CA, Asbarez, June 13, 2008).

Subject: Re: Is our U.S. Recognition of the Armenian Genocide in danger of being lost?

I have explained this issue a million times in my columns, TV appearances and lectures, for many years.

Here it is one more time:

Has the United States recognized the Armenian Genocide the same way as many of the two dozen countries that we say have recognized it? Yes, absolutely.

If we say that the 2 House resolutions, Pres. Reagan's Proclamation, and the official document submitted by the US government to the World Court in 1951 do not count as "recognition," then most of the countries that we say have recognized it, have not recognized it either! How does such thinking serve our cause? Most of these countries that we say have recognized it, have simply passed a resolution by one of the Houses of their legislature, similar to the US. In fact, the US recognition is much more extensive than most of these countries!

We are confusing genocide recognition with a foreign policy orientation decision. Even the most pro-Armenian countries that we say have recognized the Armenian Genocide (Argentina, Uruguay, Cyprus, Greece), do not take the Armenian Genocide into account in their relations with Turkey.

Finally, continuing our misguided efforts to gain unnecessary recognition can have two major negatives for our cause:

1) all it would take is the one time that by a slim difference we lose a vote in a House or Senate Committee or God forbid in the full House or Senate, we would be doing a lasting damage for our cause, as the Turks would exploit it forever saying that the US Congress decided that the Armenian Genocide is not true! We came very close to such a drastic situation a few years ago when we almost lost the vote in the House International Relations Committee. At the last minute, we managed to win it by one vote!

2) when we continue our misguided efforts to seek unnecessary recognition, we are in fact casting doubt on the veracity of the Genocide and undermining its recognition.

By the way, the ANCA now lists the United States as a country that has recognized the Armenian Genocide. That is why in recent years, the ANCA has proposed congressional resolutions on recovery of Armenian Churches in Turkey or asking the US to pressure Turkey to recognize the Genocide rather than simple US genocide recognition.

Harut Sassounian

Now that we have established that the U.S. and Turkey have recognized the Armenian Genocide, and since the U.S. is therefore morally and legally bound to take action against those governments who have engaged in the act of genocide, it is time for the U.S. government to take appropriate measures to force Turkey to settle its debt with the Armenians.

With elections every other November, it is within our collective power to vote out of office those like Adam Schiff who have lied to us and who give us lip service to get votes.

Most people who have been told by leaders in the Armenian community over and over again that we need to get the U.S. to officially recognize it, struggle with accepting the real facts. Because I know many will be confused in this way, I am including in this chapter the transcript of the video I shot on April 9, 2015, at the invitation of Harut Sassounian, who told me he was going to announce something very important. Besides the transcript and for those who would like to hear Harut Sassounian speak, can find the video on YouTube at https://youtu.be/94O5Vq5fEIw

Quest for Justice or Genocide Recognition?

By Harut Sassounian

(Video presentation can be views at: https://youtu.be/94O5Vq5fEIw)

More than a hundred years after the Armenian Genocide, and its recognition by dozens of countries, 48 US states, international organizations and scholars, Armenians should at long last consider the recognition stage over and turn their full attention to demanding restitution and justice.

Let us quickly review developments of this issue over the past 100 years: In the immediate aftermath of the Genocide, most of the survivors were scattered throughout the Middle East, and other distant lands.

They had no food, no shelter, and barely the clothes on their back!

They vainly hoped to be rescued by Christian European nations, enabling them to return to their ancestral homeland in Western Armenia and Cilicia from which they were so brutally uprooted.

Alas! It was not to be!

On August 10, 1920, the Treaty of Sevres was signed by over a dozen countries, including the British Empire, France, Italy, Japan, Turkey and Armenia.

The leaders of these countries were committed to restore justice to the long-suffering Armenian nation.

The Treaty of Sevres recognized Armenia's independence and asked Pres. Woodrow Wilson to fix the borders between Armenia and Turkey.

Unfortunately, this treaty was never ratified.

The European powers reneged on their commitments to their "Little Ally."

The newly-established Republic of Armenia lasted only two years, before being swallowed up

by the Soviet Union and Turkey.

The destitute Armenian refugees, abandoned to their tragic fate, were forced to settle down in permanent exile.

In those early years, their first priority was survival, fending off starvation and disease.

Gradually, they rebuilt their lives in new homes, churches, and schools.

Engaging in lobbying activities and making political demands were the last things on their minds.

Every April 24, Armenians commemorated the Genocide by gathering in church halls and offering prayers for the souls of the 1.5 million innocent victims.

Successive generations, particularly after 1965, the 50th anniversary of the Armenian Genocide, tried to break the wall of silence surrounding the greatest tragedy that befell the Armenian nation.

Tens of thousands of Armenians in communities throughout the world held protest marches, wrote letters to government officials and petitioned international organizations.

The Turkish government, along with the rest of the world, initially turned a deaf ear to Armenian demands for acknowledgement of the long-forgotten genocide.

But, as media outlets, world leaders, parliaments of various countries, and international organizations began acknowledging the Armenian Genocide, Turkish leaders, astonished that the crimes perpetrated by their forefathers were making headlines after so many decades, pumped massive resources into their campaign of denial, funded foreign scholars to distort the historical facts, engaged the services of powerful lobbying firms, and applied political and economic pressure on countries acknowledging the Genocide.

Since 1965, dozens of countries, including Canada, France, Italy, Switzerland, Germany, Belgium, Greece, Russia, Sweden, Argentina and Uruguay, have recognized the Armenian Genocide.

Even though, it is commonly assumed that the United States has not acknowledged the Armenian Genocide, the fact is that all three branches of the American government—executive, legislative and judiciary—have repeatedly acknowledged the Armenian Genocide.

The first time that the Executive branch made a reference to the Armenian Genocide was all the way back in 1951 in a document filed by the US government with the International Court of Justice (the World Court).

The second reference to the Armenian Genocide by the Executive branch was made by Pres. Ronald Reagan when he issued Presidential Proclamation 4838 on April 22, 1981.

The Legislative branch of the US government adopted two resolutions confirming the historical facts of the Armenian Genocide.

The first resolution, approved by the US House of Representatives on April 8, 1975, designated April 24 "as a day of remembrance for all the victims of genocide, especially those of Armenian ancestry who succumbed to the genocide perpetrated in 1915."

A second resolution was adopted by the House of Representatives on September 10, 1984, designating April 24, 1985 "as a day of remembrance for all the victims of genocide, especially the one and a half million people of Armenian ancestry who were the victims of the genocide perpetrated in Turkey between 1915 and 1923."

Most people are unaware that the Judiciary, the third branch of the US government, has issued three federal court rulings concerning the Armenian Genocide.

Thus, with all three branches of the US government going on record reaffirming the Genocide, the United States has gained its rightful place in the ranks of righteous nations that have recognized the Armenian Genocide.

In fact, in many respects, the United States has compiled a more extensive record of acknowledging the Armenian Genocide than many other countries that have merely adopted a parliamentary resolution on this issue.

International organizations have also acknowledged the Armenian Genocide including the United Nations.

The UN Sub-Commission on Prevention of Discrimination and Protection of Minorities adopted a report in 1985, prepared by Special Rapporteur Benjamin Whitaker, acknowledging that the Armenian Genocide met all the U.N. criteria for genocide.

Two years later, in 1987, the European Parliament adopted a resolution recognizing the Armenian Genocide.

In addition, hundreds of Holocaust and Genocide scholars have issued joint statements confirming the facts of the Armenian Genocide.

After so many acknowledgments, the Armenian Genocide has become a universally recognized historical fact.

Regrettably, despite such widespread acknowledgment, some countries have yet to recognize the Armenian Genocide.

The countries that side with the denialist regime of Turkey, are not doing so due to lack of evidence or conviction, but, sadly, because of political expediency, with the intent of appeasing the denier.

One would hope that these governments would join most of the enlightened world in acknowledging the historical facts as they are, and not as the Turkish government wishes them to be!

Armenians no longer need to convince the world that what took place during the years 1915-1923 was a genocide.

This is why it makes no difference whether Pres. Trump acknowledges the Armenian Genocide

or the Congress passes another Resolution on the Armenian Genocide.

It's all done before. No need to repeat past acknowledgments.

However, the simple acknowledgment of what took place and mere apology would not heal the wounds and undo the consequences of the Genocide.

Armenians are still waiting for justice to be served, restoring their historic rights, and returning their confiscated lands and properties.

In recent years, Armenian-American lawyers have successfully filed lawsuits in U.S. federal courts, securing millions of dollars from New York Life and French AXA insurance companies for unpaid claims to policy-holders who perished in the Genocide.

In 1915, a centrally planned and executed attempt was made to uproot from its ancestral homeland and decimate an entire nation, depriving the survivors of their cultural heritage as well as their homes, lands, houses of worship, and personal properties.

A gross injustice was perpetrated against the Armenian people, entitling them, as in the case of the Jewish Holocaust, to just compensation for their enormous losses.

Restitution can take many forms. As an initial step, the Republic of Turkey should place under the jurisdiction of the Armenian Patriarchate of Istanbul all the Armenian churches and religious monuments which were expropriated and converted to mosques and warehouses or outright destroyed.

In the absence of a voluntary restitution by Turkey, Armenians should resort to litigation,

seeking "restorative justice."

In considering legal recourse, one should keep in mind that the Armenian Genocide did neither start nor end in 1915.

Large-scale killings were committed starting with Sultan Abdul Hamid's massacre of 300,000 Armenians from 1894 to 1896; the subsequent killing by the Young Turk regime of 30,000 Armenians in Adana in 1909; culminating in the Genocide of 1.5 million Armenians from 1915 to 1923; In subsequent decades, tens of thousands of Armenians were forcefully Turkified or deported by the Republic of Turkey.

Most of the early leaders of the Turkish Republic were high-ranking Ottoman officials who had participated in perpetrating the Armenian Genocide.

This unbroken succession in leadership assured the continuity of the Ottomans' anti-Armenian policies.

Today's Republic of Turkey, as the continuation of the Ottoman Empire, which Turkish President Erdogan recently acknowledged, is therefore responsible for the Genocide.

In the 1920's and 30's, thousands of Armenian survivors of the Genocide, were forced out of their homes in Cilicia and Western Armenia and deported to other parts of Turkey or to neighboring countries.

In the 1940's, these racist policies were followed by what in Turkish is called 'Varlik Vergisi,' the imposition of an exorbitant wealth tax on Armenians, Greeks and Jews, bankrupting the remnants of these communities.

During the 1955 Istanbul pogroms, many Greeks as well as Armenians and Jews were killed and injured, and their properties destroyed.

This continuum of massacres, genocide and deportations highlights the existence of a long-term strategy implemented by successive Turkish regimes from the 1890's to more recent times, to solve the Armenian Question with finality.

Consequently, the Republic of Turkey is legally liable for its own crimes against Armenians, as well as those committed by its Ottoman predecessors.

Since the Turkish Republic inherited the assets of the Ottoman Empire; therefore, it also inherited its liabilities.

Finally, since Armenians often refer to their three sequential demands from Turkey:

-- Recognition of the Genocide;

-- Reparations for their losses; and

-- Return of their lands,

Turkish denialists have concluded that once they recognize the Genocide, Armenians will then pursue their two other demands.

This is the main reason why Turkish leaders adamantly refuse to acknowledge the Armenian Genocide, fearing that its acceptance would lead to demands for compensation and lands.

They believe that by denying the first demand—recognition—they would be blocking the next two.

However, the fact is that commemorative resolutions adopted by legislative bodies of various countries, and affirmative statements by world leaders on the Armenian Genocide have no force of law, and therefore, no legal consequence.

Armenians, Turks and others involved in this still unresolved issue, must realize that recognition of the Armenian Genocide or the lack thereof, will neither enable nor deter its consideration by international legal institutions.

Once Turkish officials realize that recognition by itself cannot, and would not, automatically lead to other demands, they may no longer persist in their obsessive denial.

Without waiting for any further recognition, -- one hundred years of waiting is long enough -- Armenians must pursue their historic rights through legal channels, such as the International Court of Justice (where only states have such jurisdiction), the European Court of Human Rights, as well as individual country courts.

Therefore, justice must be pursued by all legal, political and economic means.

After all, who could be opposed to Armenian demands for justice? Not even Turkish President Erdogan, whose ruling political party is called Justice & Development Party.

For Armenians, seeking justice means the recovery of all losses from the Genocide, including communal properties, such as churches, monuments, cemeteries, and schools, confiscated and looted properties, and the occupied territories of Western Armenia.

Therefore, one hundred years after the Genocide, recognition is not the end game, but the long overdue demand for justice, which means the recovery of everything that can be returned and compensation for whatever cannot be returned.

[David Gevorkyan]: ...I'm sure everybody has a number of questions that they would like to ask. I'd like to do one more pass with us and I want to - I really want to talk about, as the old saying goes, the elephant in the room. I want to ask the magic question. Why does the United States not recognize that genocide or other that word... the real reason - real reasons behind it.

[Harut Sassounian]: Uh - well... I hope - I hope you heard my speech.

[laughter]

[David Gevorkyan]: Right, right.

[Harut Sassounian]: I just - I just spent ten minutes explaining that the U.S. has recognized, repeatedly recognized - we just haven't got the news. Let me explain - this is very interesting. There's widespread ignorance in our Armenian community and because we are ignorant we affect the non-Arminian community to think like us. We tell them it's not recognized so the non-Armenians believe us because we ourselves are ignorant about our own issues what we're confusing in fact, it's not a recognition, what's confusing is there is recognition - there's no question about recognition. All the way back in 1951 - talking about the word "genocide" itself, if you go to before the word "genocide" you know you can go all the way to 1915 massacres and mass killings - yeah - crimes against humanity, yes everything but I'm talking - strictly let's use the word genocide it was used in 1951 by the US government in a document submitted to the world court so already in 1951, case closed, genocide is recognized by the United States.

If we did nothing else since 1951 our issue of recognition was already solved 60 years ago, but we keep saying we want recognition. What we really should say, but we don't distinguish, is that we have a president of United States - right now, president Obama - who despite his repeated promises, repeated condemnation of previous presidents, of [the] previous secretary of state, he just refuses to use the word genocide. That's different from not recognizing it. Not recognizing [it is] different from not reaffirming it or not using the term genocide, and in fact he takes the chicken way out of it by saying "I have not changed my mind." In his annual statements if you go back every year on April 24th he says "I have not changed my mind," but does not say what was his mind. You have to go back and find out what is said before, put the two together, it is just silly word games - shameful. But let's not say that it's not recognized, because not only is it not true - let me add something even more serious - when we say it's not recognized we're really doing damage to our cause. We're raising a question in the people's minds, in the public at large, that there's something wrong with the genocide, that's why it's not recognized. In fact, what we should be saying is "It is recognized and anybody who refuses to use the word genocide, shame on them." So we shame them - and not go to politicians and ask them to pass one more resolution. We have plenty of resolutions that were adopted. As I said in my speech. In 1975 the whole House adopted unanimously, there was not one vote against it. '75 vote - if you go back - unanimous vote in the House of Representatives to adopt the resolution saying 'Armenian Genocide, one and half million killed, April 24 to be the day of the commemoration of the Armenian genocide'. '75. Then we go back to 1984 again. Again the House passes a second resolution. Well, how many resolutions are gonna pass before we convince ourselves and others that it was recognized? We should move on.

[David Gevorkyan]: I'm here to play the devil's advocate, that's about it. [To Gevork Nazarian] Give us your thoughts on the subject.

[Gevork Nazarian]: Well I certainly agree, I've been saying it for years, we have to say 'reaffirm' not 'recognize'. I think, exactly, sometimes we don't think too much that terms are important and we just use 'recognize' but it's actually reaffirming because it has been recognized and by -

[David Gevorkyan]: Because I see all over Facebook and Instagram especially, the youth and the activists who might not necessarily be involved everyday with the issue but they every now and then tend to make posts on Facebook and on Instagram and on social media. What - how should they approach it, because they actually are making a bunch of posts and then flooding the internet with evidence and statements and hashtags about the Armenian genocide.

[Gevork Nazarian]: Well, like I said, first of all just educate about the term, which is very important. Educate about these facts that Mister Sassounian also has rightly pointed out that there have been several important crucial resolutions, you know, saying - condemning Turkey for its genocide of the Armenian people and in fact, you know, it's even that 1951 actually the resolution submitted to the ICJ, International Court of Justice in The Hague was actually worked upon by Dr. Raphael Lemkin. So Raphael Lemkin was also the one who insisted that Armenian genocide is a textbook example and this is what was submitted to the United Nations and submitted by the US government to the ICJ in the Hague, citing the Armenian genocide specifically, using those words, 'The Armenian genocide', as a clear example of what constitutes a genocide. So -

[David Gevorkyan]: Agreed. We'd like to open up the floor to any questions anybody would like to ask any one of the panel members. Yes sir - all the way in the back.

[Ara Manoogian]: I have a question which is tonight we established that the genocide has been recognized by the United States. If that's the case then why over the last 20-30 years we've had lobbying groups and we've been supporting politicians for Genocide recognition. Isn't that redundancy and kind of a waste of our time and resources? Thank you. Anybody from the panel can answer that question.

[Dr. Garabet Moumdjian]: That's better for the activists. I'm the historian... [indistinct]

[laughter]

[Harut Sassounian]: Do you want me to answer it? Well, let's be honest and fair - and if we're wrong we're wrong if right or wrong, here's the picture. For a long time there was a need for all of us to struggle to get the genocide recognized. There was a time and a place for that, because a long time ago if you said 'Armenian', they didn't know what an Armenian was. If you said 'genocide' they never heard of the word. And there are still some people like that, but we've come a long way from fifty years ago, seventy years ago - a lot of the people in the world, there's - thank god there's internet - there's TV, there's all this Armenian activism worldwide. Most people who care about the world, unless they're hidden in some village in the middle of China, they're aware now. Even in Turkey millions of Turks now - the public at large I'm talking about, not the leaders. The leaders were aware all along, but the people in the hinterlands, in Anatolia, in villages, even they now have heard on their own TV sets, in Turkish, on the internet, that there was genocide. So we can congratulate ourselves for the fact that we've all done a great job. Our people, our organizations, political parties, the ANCs, and now in recent years the Armenian government with its embassies. No matter how much we criticize each other, let's be honest, we've done [a] relatively good job in spreading the word that there was a genocide. We've published books, there are scholars, there are movies. Can more be done? Yes. Is this necessary to do more? I don't think so. I think we've made our case. In court when you present your case, you've done a good job - that's it. You don't keep on proving your case over and over until you stumble and make a mistake and the whole thing crumbles. So we've made our case. The world knows it. As I said in my remarks, there are a few countries - major countries - and one of them is Israel. The other one is England. They don't want to say Genocide. Is it because they don't know it was genocide? No. Is it because they need more evidence? No. It just because of their relations with Turkey: economic relations, political relations. In fact, there are - you know - Geoffrey Robertson, the famous international lawyer, just published a book. In the book he made a freedom of information request from the British government - this is a similar law that we have in this country, they have it also in England - and he got all the internal documents of recent years. Not 100 years ago, just last few years ago, to see what the British leaders were saying to each other in their private meetings about the Armenian Genocide. And it turns out a lot of them - that they scratched, crossed over, you know, so that you can't read what they said because they're too embarrassed. It's scandalous if the world finds out what they were saying. One of the documents, surprisingly, they forgot to scratch over. It says, 'Well, our position is shameful,' meaning the British government's position, 'but because we have economic and political dealings with Turkey, we have to take this shameful position of denying the genocide, saying it's not really genocide.' So at this point now, so there was a time where we needed to do that. Now in recent years do we want to continue doing this? Absolutely not. It's a complete waste of resources, manpower. We can be spending those funds, those energies that we have in a lot of other ways. Everything from strengthening Armenia economically, politically, militarily, our own communities filing lawsuits in international courts, getting a team of top-notch international lawyers, which costs a lot of money. Set up a fund, hire them. Do a lot of research. Lawyers are not going to get up just because we know it was genocide. You know, just go to court, international court and say it was genocide - or a European court. You need to have documents. You need to have research, and not just emotional statements. It takes a lot of time, it takes years - we haven't done this. We have to start at some point. Recently there are some steps being taken in that direction. So you need to organize this, you need to put money into it, get the experts, put all the documents in front of them and then decide which court you present which of the issues. You don't just go to any court and raise the genocide issue, because not all courts deal with past issues. There are questions about the Genocide Convention because it was in 1948, and they may not consider any issue before 1948. The World Court may not even want to deal with the issue. And then if you don't do proper research for the experts and you just blindly present an issue, and even on the technicality the court says they reject it - on a technicality, not because they rule against it - the Turks will take that, scream about it worldwide from rooftops, saying, "Aha, the World Court rejected the Armenian claims." So this is a very serious thing when it comes to genocide recognition we all get up and protest or do campaigns, we're activists. But when it comes to international law, I don't know if there's anybody here in this hall who's an international expert. I'm not, so you need to be an international legal expert. There are only a few people who qualify. very few among Armenians and even few non-Armenians. So we need to really get these people in a room, fund them, give them time, put all the documents in front of them and then come to the bottom line. That's what would scare the Turks more than anything else like resolutions, protests, lectures, and movies. Turkey has a bigger microphone than we do. They have a bigger loudspeaker than that we do. It's a major country. When they say something, when Erdoğan makes an announcement, the whole world hears it whether they like it or not. If when we say, or even the president of Armenia says something, only our Armenian papers carry it. We hear it. So there's a big difference between their ability to reach out to the world and us. But if you win a court case and there's an actual demand, a lot of people think that even if the court would decide something that Turkey will not comply with. That's another thing that's a falsehood. The European Court of Human Rights where Turkey is a member of European Council, not European Union, and Turkey has been a member of European Council, Council of Europe since the 1950s. There is a something called the European Court of Human Rights that is enforceable to all member states of the Council of Europe, and Turkey is a member. Since 1950 till today, Turkey has lost thousands of lawsuits - thousands of lawsuits - in the European

Court, and believe it or not, they have paid every single fine European Court has placed on Turkey - to the last penny. Why? If they ignore, don't pay a single dollar from the verdict of The European Court, they'll be thrown out of the Council of Europe and they will never ever join the European Union. So we have really important angles. All we have to do is approach it logically, get the help of experts and pursue it in an intelligent way, and I think a Centennial is enough recognition and let's move on to our real demands.

Chapter 35

Talaat's Conclusion

Many conclusions can be drawn from the archival documents found in Shahan Natalie's private archive. I believe that most of them speak for themselves. By studying what's presented, readers can make their own inferences. In the place of a conclusion, I would like to share a secret British document that I believe validates much of what we have presented in this book and gives the reader a better understanding of what was truly happening behind closed doors—where one can find the driving force of the West's secret war for oil and the ongoing Armenian Genocide.

No. 1259   Berlin, **140**
SECRET   5th December, 1920.

My Lord,

I have the honour to enclose a secret Report of a conversation between Talaat Pasha and a private friend of his, which took place in Berlin a few days ago.

Tallat Pasha's statements are not without interest and a good deal that he says is not improbable. I understand that his relations with the German Foreign Office are indirect and that there is dislike and suspicion on both sides.

Talaat Pasha appears to have got through most of the money which he secured during the war and is said not to be at all well off.

I would draw Your Lordship's special attention to the passages describing the nature of the assistance given by Moscow to Kemal Pasha.

Curiously enough another Turk, General Muhmoud Pasha, called at this Embassy to-day and spoke in much the same strain to a member of the Staff. He stated that he had been Minister of Marine and Public Works in 1912, 1913-1914, and had recently been taken to Malta as a hostage subsequently released. He said he was the personal friend of several Ministers in the present Turkish Cabinet. He stated that Djemal Pasha was now in Afghanistan and that Halil Pasha and Sami Bey are at Tashkend.

I have the honour to be with the highest respect,
My Lord,
Your Lordship's most obedient humble servant,
The Right Honourable
The Earl Curzon of Kedleston, K.G.,

Etc., etc., etc.

Enclosure in Lord D'Abernon's dispatch No. 1259 of Dec. 5 1920

BERLIN, **141**
December 2nd, 1920.

INTERVIEW WITH TALAAT PASHA

Talaat prefaced his remarks by a cursory Apologia for the entry of Turkey into the German Alliance in 1914. The efforts of his Government to attain an understanding with England were wain, owing to the opposition of Russia. Russia's interests in the Turkish Empire were more immediate and more vital from the point of view of the integrity and sovereignty of the country, than those of any other European Power. As far back as 1908 he had endeavoured to pacify English opinion by proposing a solution of the Armenian Quesiton. He invited England to nominate an Inspector, who would be furnished with Extraordinary powers in that Province. He visited England and the Government acquiesced, but withdrew their consent shortly afterwards, owing to the protest of the Russian Government.

In Spring, prior to the war he interviewed Sassonoff, and the question of the Dardanelles was exhaustively discussed. Talaat maintained that the Turkish Control of the Straits was after all the best solution of this most difficult problem. They would never be closed to Russia. Sassonoff replied that this held good as long as peace reigned, but in the even of war between Turkey and Greece, for example, the Straits must perforce be closed. Talaat replied that the obvious solution of the whole problem was a Russian-Turkish Alliance, whereupon Sassonoff laughed and the interview terminated.

The building of the Bagdad railway was merely one of the links in the long chain of interference with Turkish affairs of which the Powers were guilty, and which the Turkish financial situation facilitated. Viewed from a patriotic stand-point, Germany's designs in the Near East were the least dangerous, although Germany had estranged sympathy by assenting to the Emos Media Line. Marshall was the ablest of the Corps Diplomatique at the Porte. Neither Wangenheim's influence nor German pressure elicited a declaration in favour of Germany and the Cabinet remained sharply divided during August 1914. Enver and he insisted that Turkey could not remain neutral and demanded a declaration in favour of Germany because the best opinion reckoned with Bulgaria's sympathy with Russia and the intervention of Greece in accordance with her pledge to Servia. He could not assume that Constantine would break his word. To allow Russia free use of the Dardanelles was to violate the agreement with Germany and was equivalent to the loss of the Straits because it assured an Entente victory. Entente supporters in the Cabinet declared that the intervention of England absolved Turkey from her obligation. English sympathy was general among the public. Certain Englishmen knew the Turkish Empire better than the Turks themselves – Fitzmaurice and Aubrey Herbert.

Things drifted. The Cabinet was unaware until 16th of August that Admiral Souchon had telegraphed Berlin for twelve officers and five hundred men to put the defense of the Straits in order. The untimely appearance of the Goeben and Breslau on the 11th August decided the fate of Turkey. The Cabinet had requested their disarmament without success. A fortnight later Souchon promptly bombarded Odessa and Noverossisk flying the Turkish and German flags. The Cabinet found itself with a fait accompli.

The alliance with Bulgaria was unpopular during the war. Talaat viewed Bulgarian intervention with mixed feelings. He was never anxious that Greece should join the Central Powers or that the Central Powers should gain a decisive victory. His visits to German Headquarters were not a pleasant memory. During the Brest Litowsk negotiations Czernin Kuhlmann and he agreed to recognize Turkish interests in the Caucasus but Ludendorff, who was in constant telephonic communication gave General Hoffman instructions to ignore the Turkish view although Enver assisted the Germans in Galicia with two divisions at a critical moment.

He visited Ludendorff in August 1918. He obtained an audience of thirty minutes after waiting two hours. He pointed out the weakness of the Bulgarian position in the event of an attack by the Allies during the Autumn. Ludendorff complained that the settlement of the Maritza Valley and other questions rendered Turkish-Bulgarian relations unsatisfactory. Talaat suggested that the German troops employed on expeditions to Odessa and Batum would be more useful in Macedonia. Their withdrawal would allay Turkish suspicions as to Germany's intentions in the Caucasus. Ludendorff refused.

Loyal co-operation with the astute Ferdinand of Bulgaria was very difficult. Turkish statesmen were not renowned for loyalty but they were honest in comparison with Ferdinand. He recalled an incident at Sofia. Returning to Constantinople his train stopped in Sofia and he observed unusual excitement on the platforms. Malinoff paid him a visit in his saloon and explained that a division had abandoned its post on the front, and was marching on Sofia with an ever-growing army of deserters and that the catastrophe was inevitable. He promptly affered to sear two Turkish [document damaged]

~~Malinoff declined and Talaat gather that~~ Malinoff was not particularly anxious to arrest the course of events. The conversation had lasted an hour when Ferdinand's A.D.C. invited him to an audience. For twenty minutes Ferdinand discussed various political questions. The duplicity angered Talaat who interposed abruptly that Malinoff had just intermewed him for an hour and he was au courant with the situation. Ferdinand merely replied "Interview Malinoff again, impress your point of view on him, as I, too, regard the situation more hopefully."

Reverting to the present situation Tallat said the treaty of Sevres was now driving the Turkish Nationalists into the arms of the Bolshevists. Enver had gone to Moscow and had obtained support for Mustapha Kemal in Armenia. Some two hundred thousand riffles and two and a half million pounds had been delivered and promises of more had been made. Enver's supporters had been given 'carte blanche' to organise Moslems from Turkestan to Asia Minor and incide them to embarrass England everywhere in the East. He did not approve of the conditions which the Soviet Government was anxious to impose. He had no fear of Bolshevist propaganda among Mohomedans. It was doomed to failure, being opposed to their mentality and to the Koran. Talaat regarded the whole adventure skeptically. His influence was sufficient to put an end to the unrest in the East should the occasion arise. Here in Berlin a semblance of an independent Turkish Government was maintained. Thus their Emir Chekkib Arslan was Minister of Foreign Affairs. They lived under false names to obviate embarrassing the German Authorities. He had been to Italy and Switzerland recently. His passport on that occasion (produced) was made out in the name "Monsieur Dupont a Swiss subject." His identity was fairly secure. In Rome a lady remarked his resemblance to Talaat Pasha!

The advantages of a reconciliation with the Turkish Nationalists to Great Britain were obvious. Mesopotamia, Turkestan, and the Caucasus could be readily tranquilized. The oid-fields could be secured to British exploitation. In fact order and peace in the Near East depended on reasonable settlement. An amnesty should be granted to the leaders and to the political prisoners in Malta. The Vilayet of Smyrna might become a free state akin to Danzig. Some Turkish influence should be permitted north of the line Alexandretta-Mosul. He had read Mr. Colby's note from the U.S. State Department on the oil-fields. Turkey was not an industrial country and needed no oil. A settlement in favour of Great Britain was a bagatelle if Turkey secured some financial help.

The struggle of Europe against Bolshevism would be facilitated by the support of the Mahohedan republics bordering on Russia which were a natural barrier against Bolshevism or any other form of Russian penetration. He could count on the support of the twenty million Mahomedan subjects living within Russia. The permission to organise these territories was a weapon which Enver could use more readily against Moscow than with Moscow.

His sojourn in Berlin was disagreeable. Inactivity weighed on him. He could little understanding of the problems of the Near East which were the common stock of the Entente Foreign Offices. He cited with great indignation an invitation by a leading German politician to meet certain alleged Turks at dinner. These turned out to be Constantinople Jews. He concluded by saying that Fate was responsible for the concatenation of events since 1912 which culminated in the destruction of Turkey. Resistance to Fate took the form of adventures of which he was reluctant to approve.

About the Author
Shahan Natalie (1884-1983)

Shahan Natalie (né Hagop Der Hagopian) was born in December 1884, in the village of Husenik, Kharberd province, Western Armenia, the only son of the seven-member family, along with four sisters. He received his primary education in the local St. Varvar Church Armenian School.

His father, mother's brother, and numerous other relatives were among the first of more than 300,000 Armenians who fell victim during the 1894-1896 massacres in Western Armenia.

Separated from his family during the slaughter, Hagop's life was spared thanks to an Armenian neighbor who was a few years old than him. The two of them hid on the plantation of a Turk for whom the older boy worked. The 11-year-old orphaned Hagop remained in hiding for three days before being reunited with the surviving members of his family. He found his mother mourning over his father's corpse, which they dragged together and buried under a walnut tree. He would write about this event later, adding, "The living began to bury the dead." The scene of his mother, sobbing on her husband's lifeless body, left a deep and indelible impression on the young boy at both subconscious and conscious levels.

After studying for a year at the famed Kharberd Euphrates College, together with other orphans, Hagop was sent to the St. James Orphanage in Constantinople. He did not want to stay there, so he himself found an Armenian rug merchant living in New York to adopt him so he could attend the famed Berberian Academy, where he studied until 1900. His teacher was the Academy's director, Reteos Berberian, the noted pedagogue and philosopher. It was out of respect for this great man that Hagop chose the name Shahan as his own, because it was also Reteos' son's first name. The reason for choice of Natalie as a surname is still unknown (it is assumed to be based on the Latin language adjective "natalis", defined as "native-born".

The young Hagop's love of culture, art, beauty, goodness, and truth, as well as the concept of justice were imprinted in his very being. In 1901, he returned to his birthplace, where for three years he served on the local school's teaching staff, at the same time studying the provincial dialect of Kharberd. This philological study earned him special honor in Patriarch Madteos Izmirlian's literary competition.

In 1904, in Kharberd, Hagop joined the Armenian Revolutionary Federation, in whose ranks he would serve with true patriotic spirit for a quarter century. The same year, he immigrated to the United States, where for three years he worked as a laborer in a shoe factory. In 1908, after the proclamation of the Ottoman Constitution, he returned home to Husenik, where he remained barely one year. The 1909 massacres of Armenians in Cilicia drove him back into exile in America. From 1910 to 1912, he attended Boston University, where he studied literature, philosophy (particularly Plato), and theater (particularly Shakespeare).

In 1912, he decided to return home once again and boarded a ship headed for Turkey. However, during that period war had erupted in the Balkans, and the Turkish passport-bearing Shahan Natalie was ejected from the ship by Greek authorities as a citizen of an enemy nation. His attempts to explain his Armenian identity proved fruitless. He was put aboard another ship, leaving for the United States and was deported from the country.

An unwilling returnee to America, he undertook responsible work within the Armenian Revolutionary Federation's United States district. He became a member of the party's "Hairenik" monthly editorial staff, serving as its editor-in-chief from 1912 to 1915. He was also elected a member of the party's United States Central Committee, as an officer of its Executive Body.

During this period, the First World War began, providing an opportunity for the Turkish authorities to finally and totally exterminate the Armenian people. Receiving the news of the Great Atrocity[1], like all exiles, Shahan Natalie experienced nightmarish moments of anguish and rage. And he, the orphaned boy and vengeful youth, made "his vow" not to leave the Genocide perpetrators unpunished, even if the world should choose to ignore their crime.

Shahan Natalie's doubts became reality after the War. The Ottoman military tribunal convened in Constantinople condemned to death the principal perpetrators who had been extradited to Malta by British authorities. However, the British placed no value whatsoever on the sentence and secretly released the enemies of Armenians and humanity.

From September 27 to the end of October 1919, the Armenian Revolutionary

---

[1] On March 23, 1915, one month before the gathering and slaughter of the Armenian intellectuals in Constantinople, Shahan Natalie became a citizen of the United States. On December 27, 1923 the Commonwealth of Massachusetts approved his official name change to "John Mahy"

Federation's 9th General Congress was convened in Yerevan. Shahan Natalie participated as the United States District delegate. On the Congress agenda was also placed the issue of retribution against those Turks principally responsible for the Great Atrocity. Here, Shahan Natalie experienced the first serious embitterment of his political life, when some of the delegates deemed this policy wrong. They rationalized that the newly created Armenian Republic needed Turkey's friendship (such justifications have proliferated today also, within the new Armenian Republic). In opposition to many of the Eastern Armenian delegates' vociferous objections, it was decided by a majority vote to deem the Armenian nation as reconciled with the Turk perpetrators. It is assumed that at this meeting the Responsible Body was also organized to realize the work, known as "Operation Nemesis," whose primary motivator, planner and spirit was Shahan Natalie, with Grigor Merjanov as his principal collaborator. ARF Bureau members, specifically Simon Vratsian, Ruben Ter-Minasian, and Ruben Darbinian, decided to prevent Shahan Natalie's determined efforts. But Natalie had delivered the verdict, on behalf of more than one and a half million martyrs.

The work of eliminating the Turk executioners was organized and the preliminary steps (surveillance, arms-gathering and transport, etc.) were carried out under the most clandestine circumstances. A "black list" of targeted executioners contained approximately 200 names. The executioners of the Armenian people were moving freely and boldly in Berlin, Rome, Baku, Tbilisi and other city streets. They still posed a threat as they had regrouped and were planning their next move to finish the work they had begun — to put an end to the Armenian question once and for all. Their next target was to be the Armenian population of Artsakh (Nargorno-Karabagh) and then Armenia, thus realizing their dream of the all-Turkish state. Some among them were enjoying local secret and overt police protection.

For Shahan Natalie, the primary target was the Armenophobe, Talaat Pasha, whom Shahan called "Number One." The mission of felling Turkey's Minister of the Interior was entrusted to Soghomon Tehlirian.

The Beirut-based *"Nayiri"* weekly, v. 12, nos. 1-6, published Shahan's memoirs about Talaat's assassination. There, Shahan revealed his orders to Tehlirian: *"You blow up the skull of the Number One nation-murderer and you don't try to flee. You stand there, your foot on the corpse and surrender to the police, who will come and handcuff you."* Shahan Natalie's purpose was to turn Soghomon Tehlirian's trial into the political trial of those responsible for the Great Tragedy, which was realized in part. However, there were those in the ARF leadership, Simon Vratsian in particular, who had two chapters, which dealt with Shahan Natalie's leadership role in the assassination of Talaat, deleted from Tehlirian's memoirs before their printing.

The fruits of Shahan Natalie's planning mind were the successive assassinations as follows:

Talaat Pasha, member of the Ittihadist Triumvirate and former Prime Minister, 15 March 1921, Berlin. Executor: Soghomon Tehlirian.

Pipit Jivanshir Khan, former Internal Affairs Minister of Azerbaijan, rabid pan-Turanian, organizer of Armenian massacres, 18 July 1921, Constantinople. Executor: Misak Torlakian.

Saïd Halim Pasha, former Prime Minister, 5 December 1921, Berlin. Organizer: Grigor Merjanov; executor: Arshavir Shiragian.

Behaeddin Shakir Bey, principally responsible organizer and executor of the Ittahadist *"Special Committee,"* 17 April 1922, Berlin. Executor: Aram Yerganian, who in 1919, in Tbilisi, had slain the Azeri Ghasik Bekov; and the following year, Sarafov and Khan Khuysk, also in Tbilisi.

Jemal Azmi, Ittihadist Armenophobe chief, 17 April 1922, Berlin. Executor: T.; collaborator: Aram Yerganian.

Jemal Pasha, Ittihadist Triumvirate member and Defense Minister, 25 July 1922, Tbilisi. Executors, decoys: Stepan Dzaghigian and Bedros D. Boghosian; collaborators: Zareh Melik-Shahnazarian of Artsakh and others.

Enver Pasha, the third member of the Triumvirate, was allegedly killed in 1922 in Turkmenistan (Central Asia) when he was leading the Basmaji Pan-Turanian movement. It is claimed by the ARF that Enver's assassin was an Armenian soldier in the Red Army, Yakov Melkumov aka Hakob Melkumian, a native of Shushi, Artsakh.

Shahan Natalie's avengers also executed several Armenian spies and traitors, who, by denouncing their kinsmen to Turkish authorities, were responsible for their deaths.

The ARF Bureau was against these assassinations because the Bureau, ousted from the homeland, because of their anti-Soviet sentiments, was playing Turkish-spirited politics, which this assassination campaign hindered. And finally, the Bureau succeeded in silencing the sound of the exploding Armenian bullet. Subsequently, when the assassination of Turks proved "profitable" to revitalize party ranks, the Bureau did not hesitate to credit itself alone for the justified assassinations organized by the Armenian Nemesis, Shahan Natalie.

After the Sovietization of Armenia, many of the Armenian Republic's expatriate revolutionary activists were ready to collaborate with Azeri and Turk Armenophobe activists in order to regain governmental control. This policy was contrary to Shahan Natalie's conviction that *"Over and above the Turk, the Armenian has no enemy. Armenian revenge is just and godly."* There were deep dissensions on both sides, but not yet to the point of schism.

In 1924, in Paris, the ARF's 10th General Congress was convened. The revered Western Armenian delegate, Shahan Natalie, was elected as a new Bureau member, along with Shavarsh Misakian and the Jewish "sons-in-law" [their wives were Jews], Ruben Der Minasian and Aram Jamalian. Bureau member Shahan strove in vain to change the party's Turkish-prone mindset, but failed, due to the trio's opposition.

The ultimate collision of these divergent directions became inevitable. In 1925, a group of nationalistic revolutionaries applied to the Bureau to establish relationships with Soviet governments in order to try to find ways of helping the homeland. The leadership tabled the examination and response to this issue.

On 29 December 1926, the ARF Bureau, with four votes in favor and one against (Shahan) decided to join the Promethean Alliance, which declared the Turks as defenders of the Caucasian people.

Shahan Natalie's cup of patience had overflowed. The party's internal power struggle became evident in 1928. From 1920 to 1929, in Paris, *Azadamard* (Freedom Fight) was published under the editorship of Haig Kntouni and Shahan Natalie. *Azadamard* was the expression of outrage of noble revolutionaries toward the anti-national sentiment of the leadership. Shahan Natalie defined the "Freedom Fight" movement thus: *"In Yerevan, in 1919 during the Federation's 9th General Congress, many monuments were going to be destroyed and statues were to crumble within innocent and clean souls ... Before the eyes of the members of the "Freedom Fight," not only was the Revolutionary Federation being horribly transformed, it was also becoming an accomplice against Armenian Revolution. Not only had the Federation, in the person of its leadership, denied the Federation, but by the boorish expression of its traditional feudalism, it had assumed the right to ally itself with the Turk, to plot against Armenian Revolution."*

To forestall the probable victory of the "Freedom Fighters" at the upcoming 11th General Congress (27 March to 2 May 1929), on the eve of the meeting, the Bureau began a *"cleansing campaign.*" The first to be "removed"[2] from the party was Bureau member, Shahan Natalie. "Knowingly" (by his definition) having joined the ARF and unjustly separated from it, Shahan Natalie wrote about this, *"With Shahan began again that which had begun with Antranig; Bureau member Shahan, was 'ousted'"* After Shahan, successively ousted were Haig Kntouni, Armenian Republic army officer Bagrevandian with his group, Glejian and Tartizian with their partisans, General Smpad, Ferrahian with his group, the future *"Mardgots"*-ists (Bastion) Mgrdich Yeretziants, Levon Mozian, Vazgen Shoushanian, Mesrob Kouyoumjian, Levon Kevonian and many others. As a protest to this "cleansing" by the Bureau, some members of the ARF French Central Committee also resigned.

"Freedom Fight" having ceased publication, the "ousted" revolutionaries of France established *"Mardgots"* (Bastion), a semi-weekly newspaper, under

---

2   The contention of the ARF was that Natalie was "ousted". In fact, Natalie resigned the Bureau and the Federation because of his outrage at the leadership's decision to strike a pact with Turkey in an attempt to regain possession of the Anatolian lands seized by the Turks.

the editorship of Mesrob Kouyoumjian and Mgrdich Yeritziants. Contrary to popular belief, Shahan Natalie did not establish or lead the *"Bastion"*-ist movement, because at that time he had returned to America. He learned about the movement from reading the *"Mardgots"* newspaper and acknowledged this Reconstructionist movement. Published in issues of *"Mardgots"* are Shahan's analytical articles, *"Who Ousts Whom?"*, *"Mine and Yours"*, *"Curse, but Listen,"* and *"I Am Inexperienced."*

Generals Dro and Nzhdeh came to Paris for the purpose of defusing the disunion of the party, but they failed. Gradually realizing their inability to control the expanding movement, the Bureau relocated its headquarters from Paris to Cairo.

However, the *"Bastion"*-ist movement was attacked from within. The collaboration of the editor, Mesrob Kouyoumjian, with the Soviet Secret Service was revealed. General Smpad and Shahan Natalie went to Paris to forestall the break-up of the movement. Revolutionaries who had remained loyal to the *"Bastion"*-ists in 1934 established the *"Western Armenian Liberation Alliance"* in Paris and began to publish the *"Amrots"* (Fortress) weekly. *"Alliance"* members were relentlessly persecuted by Bureau killer bandits and by the Secret Service of foreign countries, which wanted to see the ARF as an anti-Soviet tool in their hands. Shahan Natalie relocated *"Amrots"* to Athens, where it was published from 1936 to 1937. ARF Bureau-hired hit men arrived there and killed many loyal revolutionaries with their bullets.

The situation in Europe within the environment of impending war and Bureau-ordered assassinations eroded the "Amrots"-ist movement little by little.[3]

At the eve of the Second World War, Shahan returned to America. Embittered toward Armenian political life, he took up community activism within the Armenian General Benevolent Union. From 1943 to 1953, he directed the Armenian General Benevolent Union's New England District Office Secretariat.[4]

In 1958, for the first time since the Sovietization of Armenia, he visited the homeland, regaining his voice, which had begun to diminish. He experienced spiritual enrichment upon seeing the flowering of Armenia. In Tsaghkadzor, he met schoolchildren at a campground and he saw in them the promise of a new dawn for the Armenian people. in them

Since the 1960s, Shahan Natalie lived almost in seclusion. He preferred to be silent rather than to talk, to remain within the confines of his home, rather than to appear in public.

---

[3] Shahan Natalie was one of those targeted by the ARF. An unsuccessful attempt was made on his life in Boston, in 1929. In the early years of World War II, rumors of subsequent attempts were spread in an effort to harass and disarm his adherents.

[4] In 1954, the Armenian communities in the United States celebrated the 50th Jubilee of Shahan Natalie's community activism and literary career.

Shahan Natalie has bequeathed to us a rich literary legacy. Shahan's literary talents were refined under the canopy of the Berberian Academy. He wrote verses, short stories, dramatic works, as well as national, political analyses and oratorical pages. He used the noms de plume *Posura* (Glow-worm), *Nemesis*, (the goddess of "just anger," [retributive justice], in ancient Greek mythology), and *Shahan*. In private life he used another alias, John Mahy, which he translated as "the darling of death."

Shahan Natalie's published works include:

Օրէնքի և Ընկերութեան Զոհերէն [From the Martyrs of Law and Society]. Boston: Hayrenik, 1909. 63 pages. Short stories.

Ամպեր [Clouds]. Boston: Hayrenik, 1909. Verses.

Մարդը. [The Man]. Smyrna: Keshishian Printing, 1912. Socio-drama in five acts.

Քաւութեան երգեր [Songs of Expiation]. Boston: Hayrenik, 1915. 31 pages. Verses.

Սէրի և ատելութեան երգեր [Songs of Love and Hate]. Boston: Hayrenik, 1915. 165 pages. Verses.

Վրէժի աւետարան [Gospel of Revenge]. New York: Armenia, 1918. 39 pages. Verses.

Ասլան Բէկ [Aslan Bek]. Boston: Hayrenik, 1918. 62 pages. Tragedy in three acts.

Քեզի [To Thee]. Boston: 1920. 116 pages. Verses.

His ethno-political works of public address are:

Թուրքիզմը Անգորայէն Բագու և Թրքական Օրիէնթասիոն ([Turkism from Angora to Baku and Turkish Orientation]). Athens: Nor Or, 1928. 172 pages.

Թուրքերը և Մենք ([The Turks and Us]). Athens: Nor Or, 1928. 70 pages. Second printing, 1931, 93 pages.

Ալեքսանդրապոլի Դաշնագրէն 1930-ի Կովկասեան Ապստամբութիւնները [From the Treaty of Alexandrapol to the 1930 Caucasian Insurgences]. Volumes 1 and 2. Marseilles: Tp. Arabian, 1934-35.

Երեւանի Համաձայնագիրը (The Yerevan Agreement). Boston: 1941. 112 pages.

Գիրք Մատուցման և Հատուցման [Book of Dedication and Compensation]). Contents: Այսպէս Սպաննեցինք [How We Killed]); Յաւելուած [Addendum], illustrated. Beirut: Tp. Onipar, 1949 (first printing). 160 pages. Beirut: Tp Azdarar, 1954 (second printing). 134 pages.

Վերստին Յաւելուած — Ալեքսանդրապոլի Դաշնագրի «Ինչպէ՞սն ու ինչո՞ւն» [Re-Addendum – The Why and How of the Treaty of Alexandrapol]. Boston: Baikar, 1955. 144 pages.

Յաւելուած – Երեք դաշնագրեր. Ալեքսանդրապոլի, Մոսկուայի եւ Կարսի (Բաղդատական Զուգակշիռ) [Three treaties; Alexandrapol, Moscow and Kars (Parallel Comparison)] ԱրարատՄատենաշար Թիւ 25. Beirut: [n.p.] 1957. 157 pages.

He has unpublished literary and ethno-political works and papers, of which «Թալէաթի Դատաստանը Պերլինի Մէջ» [The Trial of Talaat in Berlin] and his «Յուշեր» [Memoirs] are especially significant.

All of Shahan Natalie's publications are out of print and hard to find. The printing facilities of the period, the small print runs, the true patriot's harassment of being the "sought after", and the Bureau clique have worked their ruin and rendered these books unfindable remnants.

Shahan Natalie did not succeed in celebrating his hundredth birthday. The 99-year-old hero closed his eyes forever on the morning of 19 April 1983, in his home in Watertown, Massachusetts. The funeral rites took place on 22 April in Watertown, in the St. James Armenian Church, with the Primate of the Armenian Church of North America, Archbishop Torkom Manoogian (presently the Armenian Patriarch of Jerusalem) officiating. After the reading of the eulogies, the body of the tormented hero was laid to rest in the nearby Mount Auburn Cemetery.

About the Author

Soghomon Tehlirian (1896-1960)

Soghomon Tehlirian's biography is difficult to write as most of what has been written about him are fabrications to support a narrative created by the Armenian Revolutionary Federation (ARF).

In order to present his biography to be most reflective of who he actually was, I turned to Soghomon's younger son, who for the sake of his privacy, I will refer to as Soghomon Jr.

Here is are some biographical facts about Soghomon Tehlirian that I have extracted from a 3-hour face to face visit my family and I had with Soghomon Jr. on May 10, 2015.

Soghomon Tehlirian was born on April 2, 1896 in the village of Nerkin Bagarij, in the Erzurum vilayet. Soghomon was the youngest of five brothers.

In June of 1914, Soghomon moved to Valjevo, Serbia, to live with his father and two brothers. Soghomon's father, Khatchadour, was a coffee merchant and a member of Valjevo's trade union. At the time of the Armenian Genocide, in which Soghomon's mother and oldest brother, Vasken were killed, Soghomon was not in their town of Erzinjan to witness the killing. Soghomon returned to Erzinjan after the massacre and found his 12-year-old niece, Armenouhi, wandering around Western Armenia and learned from her the fate of his mother and eldest brother.

During the Bolshevik Revolution, Soghomon joined General Antranig Ozanian's volunteer army and fought against the Turks.

In 1917, Soghomon would find himself in Tiflis (current day capital city of Georgia) with typhoid fever. He was taken in by an Armenian family who took care of him. Anahit, their youngest daughter, was 14 years old and cared for Soghomon. Soghomon vowed to marry her one day.

In 1919, Soghomon carried out the assassination in Constantinople of an Armenian traitor, Haroutiun Megerdichian, who had provided to Talaat Pasha a list of 250 Armenian intellectuals, the majority of whom were gathered up on April 24, 1915 and murdered. Soghomon had learned about Megerdichian from the niece of General Antranig, Yeranuhi Danielian.

In 1920, when Shahan Natalie was recruiting an assassin to kill Talaat, Yeranuhi Danielian nominated Soghomon. At that time, Soghomon was not a member of the ARF, but rather was introduced as a soldier of General Antranig's.

In 1921, following the assassination of Talaat Pasha, the chief architect of the Armenian Genocide, Soghomon was put on trial. Soghomon Jr. stated: "I'll tell you the story. Most of what was said in the trial was not true. My father didn't have a sister to begin with. I don't think he ever saw his mother slaughtered. He never talked about it. So, I mean they invented things all over the place..."

Following the trial and his acquittal, Soghomon made his way to Manchester, England, where he ws hosted by someone by the name of H. Kamberian, 40 Cooper Street. Soghomon would sail from Southampton, England, on May 31, 1922 on board the *S.S. Homeric* and arrived in New York on June 7th. With $157 in his pocket, the 5 foot 6 inch tall blue-eyed Soghomon entered the U.S., claiming to be a 23- year-old engineering student and a native of Mush, Armenia. He declared his final destination was to be at the home of a friend by the name of Dr. N. Tashjian, at 524 Huntington Avenue, Boston, Massachusetts. Soghomon would eventually end up in Cleveland, Ohio, where a carpet store was opened, using funds that were gifted to him by the Armenian community worldwide.

In 1923, after the attempts to bring Anahit, the girl who had cared for him in Tbilisi and he had vowed to marry, to the United States had failed, Soghomon left his new life in America and went to Marseilles, where Anahit had come on her way to America with her older sister. However, due to the older sister's not having a visa, they were prevented from coming to the U.S. Soghomon and Anahit decided to settle in Belgrade, Yugoslavia (currently Serbia), where they were wed on October 5, 1924. They had two sons, Shahen and Soghomon Jr.

In Belgrade, Soghomon opened a coffee store. He was the official supplier of coffee to the royal family, delivering coffee to the palace in his Ford station wagon.

According to Soghomon Jr., Turks knew that Soghomon had settled in Belgrade: "My father was a hunter. He loved hunting. In 1938 [Mustafa] İsmet İnönü the Turkish premier who succeeded Kemal Ataturk, was coming to Belgrade. The Turks called the police department. They said among the Armenians there is a man who is a killer. They knew my father was in

Belgrade, but they didn't know who he was, because there were maybe only 40 or so people of his generation. And they said that they wanted protection. It's a funny story. The chief of police was a friend of my father's. They were hunting friends. They used to go hunting together. So, they got all the Armenian men together and put them under arrest for two days while the Turkish Prime Minister was there. My father wasn't there. My father was in Zagreb (current day Croatia). When the chief of police noticed that my father was not among the Armenians under arrest, the chief called my mother and asked where he is. She told him he is in Zagreb. He asked that she call him and tell him to come home. So, she called him and he immediately came home. She told him that he must go see the chief of police. He went to see the chief and asked what the hell was going on. He said this was happening and I don't know who the hell they are talking about. My father said, 'It's me [Soghomon].' And Serbs hate Turks. The chief said, 'Why didn't you tell me you killed that son of a bitch!' He told my father to go home and stay home. So my father was the only one who was not under arrest."

In 1948, Josip Broz Tito, came to power and Yugoslavia became a communist country. As a result, Soghomon had lost his business and began his plan for departing with his family to Soviet Armenia. They were granted exit visas to depart Yugoslavia. The documents didn't say how they were to go. In December of 1949, instead of boarding a train heading East, they took a train going West to Italy and managed to escape.

The Tehlirian family ended up in a refugee camp. From there they would go to Casa Blanca: "You know how we got to Casa Blanca? Because we were in a refugee camp for 6 weeks. And those were the days of quota. When you came from an iron curtain country, you had to wait 5 years for a quota [to immigrate to the United States]. Three of my first cousins, my Uncle Misak's children, were stuck in a refugee camp for 5 years. My father was very upset. He literally forced me, well not literally, I agreed to go. I don't know how it started. He [Soghomon] knew this man in Casa Blanca. Khachaturian was his name. He said he was going to bring the whole family to Morocco. Because the only place we could get a visa was Morocco and Brazil. So this guy actually did it. Tickets. Train tickets, ship tickets, all [sent] to the refugee camp. There was an Armenian in Trieste. He was the post office for all Armenians that went in to the refugee camp. And that's how we left the refugee camp after 6 weeks. We went to Marseilles (France), took a ship and landed. Now we thought this man was a divine saviour. He brought us there. To make a long story short, it turned out the guy was a crook. He went all over North Africa and raised money in the name of my father. And then he bought the tickets and when we got there, he put us in his apartment and we had nothing. No place to live, no nothing. He took the money. There were other Armenians there and they found out. Because he advertised how he was going to bring Soghomon Tehlirian. What they didn't know was that he raised all this money in Tunis, in Algeria, everywhere and just paid for the tickets and kept the rest in his pocket. And nobody would come to see us. We knew there were other Armenians, but no one would come to see us, until one day, this man, Azad Surmenian, came. Because now the Armenians spoke to this guy and they knew he was a crook. He [Surmenian] spoke to my father, he took him aside. He said, 'Are you crazy, get out of here. I'll take care of you.' That's how we ended up in the back room of the Surmenian factory. And then eventually, my father worked for his office."

After 10 months in Casablanca, Soghomon Jr. received a visa to go and study in France. They could not afford to send Soghomon Jr., so Soghomon Tehlirian borrowed money to buy a plane ticket. Soghomon's older son, Shahen, found a job working for an American company as an accountant, while Shahen's wife found a job working for Air France. After living in Casablanca for 9 years, Shahen and wife returned to Yugolsavia.

Soghomon and his wife Anahit eventually received visas and immigrated to the United States. On June 6, 1956, they boarded *Flying Tiger* Flight #12320 from Brussels, taking on fuel in Santa Maria, Portugal, and the island of Gander, Newfoundland, arriving in New York on June 7th. They were taken to Boston and then the following day were sent to San Francisco, California.

On October 2, 1956, Soghomon Jr. would arrive in New York, aboard *Flying Tiger* Flight #203.

For the next 3 years, Soghomon worked for George Mardikian Enterprises as a bookkeeper. Soghomon Jr. added: "You know what the ARF did to my father? They schlepped him all over the United States to make speeches. Not one penny, ever!"

On May 23, 1960, at the age of 64, Soghomon died. The cause of death was reported in the newspapers as stroke. According to Soghomon Jr., Soghomon Tehlirian was diabetic, yet that's not what killed him. The actual cause of his death was due to a brain tumor. His wife Anahid would join him in eternal peace on December 27, 1979 at the age of 75. They were both laid to rest in Fresno, California, at the Ararat Armenian cemetery.

About the Author

Garegin Pasdermadjian (1873-1923)

Garegin Pasdermadjian was a native of Erzeroum and a member of a family which has been an object of barbarous persecution at the hands of the Turks. When the Russians in 1829 captured Erzeroum for the first time, 96,000 Armenians, with the encouragement of the Russian government, left that city and the outlying villages with the Russian army, and emigrated towards the Caucasus, where they founded three new cities, Alexandropol, Akhalkalak, and Akhaltsikh. Only 300 Armenian families remained in Erzeroum, refusing to leave their homes, even in face of the Turkish despotism. Among these was the Pasdermadjian family.

In 1872 the Turkish government had Khatchatour Pasdermadjian killed, simply because he was a well-to-do and influential Armenian, and, therefore, undesirable. In 1877 during the Russo-Turkish war, the Pasdermadjian family was subjected to the basest kind of persecution by the Turkish government, which by 1918, still owed the Pasdermadjians 36,000 Turkish liras ($180,000), the value of a quantity of wheat wrested from them by the military authorities. During those same hostilities, taking advantage of the war conditions, the Turkish government planned to hang Haroutiun Pasdermadjian, on the ground that he was in communication with the Russian army; but he was saved through the intervention of the British consul. When the Russian army occupied Erzeroum in 1878, the Pasdermadjians naturally gave a very hospitable reception to the two Armenian Generals, Loris Melikoff and Lazareff. After learning of the family's history, Loris Melikoff asked Haroutiun Pasdermadjian to emigrate to the Caucasus. He promised to bring the influence of the Russian government to bear on Turkey and to claim the family's extensive real estate and various sums of money which the Turkish government owed them. But Haroutiun Pasdermadjian refused the kind offer, saying that he could not leave the country which contained his martyred father's grave. When the Russians, in accordance with the terms of the Berlin Treaty, were forced to evacuate Erzeroum, the Turks came back and began anew to persecute the Pasdermadjians in every possible way. In 1890, the Armenians of Erzeroum made a protest against Turkish despotism and demanded to have the reforms promised in the Berlin Treaty carried out. The first bullet fired by the Turkish soldiers during those disturbances was aimed at Haroutiun Pasdermadjian; but he was saved through the heroism of a group of young Armenians. In the massacres of 1895, the Pasdermadjians were again attacked by an armed Turkish mob, but were saved from plunder and murder through the stubborn resistance of all the members of the household, including the servants. Afterwards, three members of the family, Hovhannes, Tigran, and Setrak, were imprisoned for a long time as revolutionists. In reality, they were imprisoned simply because they had not allowed themselves to be slaughtered like sheep by the Turkish mob. In February 1915, when the present Turkish government began its organized slaughters to eliminate the Armenians from the world, the first victim in Erzeroum was Setrak Pasdermadjian, because he was an influential Armenian and had had the courage several times to protest against the unlawful acts of the government. The remnants of this numerous and ancient Armenian family are now scattered throughout Mesopotamia.

Garegin Pasdermadjian is the son of Haroutiun Pasdermadjian and the grandson of Khatchatour Efendi. He was born in 1873 and received his elementary education at the Sanasarian College of Erzeroum, being one of its first graduates (1891). In 1894 he went to France and studied agriculture in the college at Nancy, intending to return and develop the lands belonging to his family according to the modern agricultural methods of Europe, and in that way give a practical lesson to the Armenian peasants. He had hardly begun his course when the great massacres of 1895 revolutionized the plans of the younger generation of Armenian students. Out of the 26 young Armenians at the University of Nancy, four, Sarkis Srentz, Haik Thirakian, Max Zevrouz, and Garegin Pasdermadjian, left their studies and returned to participate in the effort at vengeance which the Armenian Revolutionary Federation (ARF) had decided to organize in Constantinople. In 1896, Garegin Pasdermadjian and Haik Thirakian, under their assumed names of Armen Garo and Hratch respectively, took part in the seizure of the Ottoman Bank. This European institution, with its 154 inmates and 300 million francs ($60,000,000) of capital, remained in the hands of the Armenian revolutionists for fourteen hours as a pledge that the European ambassadors should immediately stop the Armenian massacre in Constantinople and give assurances that the reforms guaranteed to the Armenians in the Treaty of Berlin should be carried out. On behalf of the six great powers, signatories to the Berlin Treaty, the chief interpreter of the Russian embassy, Mr. Maximoff, made a gentleman's agreement with the young Armenian revolutionists to fulfill their demands. Trusting to Mr. Maximoff's word of honor, the Armenians left Constantinople.

But immediately after their departure, the massacres were resumed with more intensity, while the reforms have remained a dead letter to this day. Such were international morals in 1895.

After these events Garegin Pasdermadjian returned to Europe to continue his unfinished studies. However, Mr. Hanoteau, the French foreign minister at that time, would not allow the Armenians who had been connected with this affair to remain in France, so young Pasdermadjian went to Switzerland and studied the natural sciences at the University of Geneva. In 1900 he completed his course and received the degree of Doctor of Science. Unable to return to Turkish Armenia, as was his desire, Pasdermadjian went to the Caucasus and settled at Tiflis in 1901. There he opened the first chemical laboratory, for the purpose of investigating the rich mines of that region.

National events, however, prevented him from pursuing his research work. Having been a member of the responsible body of the ARF since 1896, he took part in all the movements which aimed to protect the moral and physical well being of the Armenian people from Turkish and Russian despotism. For example, in 1905, when the Caucasian Tartars, with the approval of the Russian government, began to massacre the Armenians in diverse parts of the Caucasus, Pasdermadjian became a member of the Committee created by the ARF to organize defense work among the Armenian people. In November of the same year, when the Armeno-Tartar hostilities began right in Tiflis, under the very nose of the Russian administration, he was entrusted with the command of the Armenian volunteers to protect Tiflis and its environs. During the seven-day struggle which took place in the streets of Tiflis, 500 Armenian volunteers faced nearly 1,400 armed Tartars, and drove them back with heavy losses.

The situation in the Caucasus was almost normal, and Pasdermadjian and his idealistic colleagues were about to resume their main objective, -- to carry arms and ammunition from the Caucasus to the Turkish Armenians in order to prepare them for self-defense, -- when the Turkish revolution came in 1908. The Armenians in Erzeroum, as well as the party to which he was a member, telegraphed to Pasdermadjian and strongly urged him to become their candidate in the coming elections for Representative to the Ottoman Parliament. After seven years of professional studies, Pasdermadjian had been able to create for himself in the Caucasus a life fairly prosperous financially. He had just secured the right to develop a copper mine, and was about to work it in partnership with a large company. His business required that he should stay in the Caucasus to continue his successful enterprise, but he yield to the moral pressure of his comrades and left his personal affairs to go to Constantinople as deputy from Erzeroum.

During his four years in Constantinople as a deputy, Pasdermadjian devoted his entire time to improve the economic conditions of the Armenian vilayets, and especially worked for the railroad bill, of which he was the real author, but which was known to the public as Chester's bill. Its main object was to build railroads as soon as possible in those vilayets of Armenia which were considered to be Russia's future possessions. For that reason neither France nor Germany wished to undertake it, lest they should arouse the enmity of Russia. Another fundamental object was to build those lines with American capital, which would make it possible to counteract the Russo-Franco-German policies and financial intrigues, for the benefit of the Armenian people. But in spite of all his efforts, Pasdermadjian was unable to overcome the German opposition in Constantinople, although, as the outcome of the struggle in connection with that bill, two ministers of public works were forced to resign their post. Both of the ministers were absolute German agents under the name of Turkish ministers. It may also be worth mentioning that during his four years at Constantinople as a deputy from Erzeroum, at three different times, Talaat Bey (who became the butcher of the Armenian people in 1915), on behalf of the "Committee of Union and Progress," offered the portfolio of public works to Pasdermadjian, as the most competent man for the post. Pasdermadjian, however, refused these proposals, for the simple reason that he did not wish to compromise in any way with the leaders of the Turkish government, as long as they continued their chauvinistic and anti-Armenian policy.

In the parliamentary elections of 1914, the "Committee of Union and Progress" used every means to defeat the election of Pasdermadjian in Erzeroum. On account of this attitude of the Turks, all the Armenian inhabitants of the Erzeroum vilayet refused to take part in the last elections. This intense opposition of the Turks to the candidacy of Pasdermadjian was due to the fact that he had taken too active a part in 1913 in the conferences held for the consideration of the Armenian reforms, and especially because, while parliamentary elections were going on in Turkish Armenia during April, 1914, he was in Paris and Holland, as the delegate of the ARF, to meet the inspectors general who were invited to carry out the reforms in Turkish Armenia.

In the autumn of 1914, a month and a half before the beginning of Turco-Russian hostilities, Pasdermadjian went to the Caucasus on a special mission, and joined the committee which had been appointed by the Armenian National Council of the Caucasus to organize the Armenian volunteer movement. In November of the same year, when the Russo-Turkish war had begun, he accompanied the second battalion of the Armenian volunteers, as the representative of the executive committee of Tiflis, to prepare the local inhabitants of Turkish Armenia for self-defense, as the Russian army was about to advance into the captured territories of that country. On November 14, the second battalion of the Armenian volunteers engaged in battle for the first time, near Bayazid, with the Turkish soldiers and the Kurds. In the course of a bloody combat which lasted twenty-four hours, Dro, the brave commander of the battalion, was seriously wounded, and Pasdermadjian was forced immediately to take his place. From that day to March of the following year, he remained at the head of that battalion, and led it into eleven battles in the neighborhood of Alashkert, Toutakh, and Malashkert, until Dro recovered and returned to resume the command. In the summer of 1915, Pasdermadjian (again as a representative of the executive committee of Tiflis) went to Van. He was there when the people migrated en masse to the Caucasus (when the Russian army was forced to retreat to the old Russo-Turkish frontiers) and shared their untold hardships.

In the spring of 1917, when the Russian Revolution turned all the defense work of the Caucasus up-side down, Pasdermadjian, with Zavrieff, was sent from the Caucasus to Petrograd to negotiate with the temporary Russian government concerning Caucasian affairs. From Petrograd he left for America in June of the same year as the representative of the Armenian National Council of Tiflis and as the special Envoy of His Holiness the Catholicos of all the Armenians, to lay before the American public and government the sorrows of the Armenian people with the view of winning their sympathy and protection for the indisputable rights of Armenia.

In October of 1919, Pasdermadjian participated as a witness to a special senatorial hearing in order to win the approval and support of the United States government for the newly independent Armenia. This effort ended in disappointment 7 months later, on May 11, 1920, with U.S. Senate Resolution 359. The request by the Armenian to gather a volunteer force of Armenians living on U.S. soil was denied.

With all viable legal remedies for the preservation of the newly independent Armenian nation exhausted, Pasdermadjian agreed to lend his name and resources to Shahan Natalie to terminate the immediate threat to the Armenian people. His lending his name to this important work, which would later be known as *Operation Nemesis*, played a pivotal role in the success of the operation.

On March 23, 1923, while attending a conference on Russia, in Geneva, Switzerland, 51-year-old, Garegin Pasdermadjian, who had been fighting a bout of depression since the start of the Armenian Genocide in 1915, died of heart disease.

About the Author

Sylva Natalie Manoogian (1937)

SYLVA NATALIE MANOOGIAN
LIBRARY & INFORMATON SCIENCE, PHD

Born in France in 1937, Sylva Natalie Manoogian is the youngest daughter to Shahan Natalie and his wife Angel Kantzabedian Mahy.

At the end of World War II, Sylva, her older sister Etna and her mother were reunited with Shahan, meeting him for the first time face to face after they were separated 7 years earlier due to the war.

Sylva Natalie Manoogian received a B.A. (Classics), from Radcliffe College (1959); M.L.S., University of Southern California (1969); PhD (Library and Information Science, University of California, Los Angeles (2013)

Returning to academia in 2003 as a doctoral student after a 35-year career in public libraries, Dr. Sylva Natalie Manoogian specializes in information institutions, resources, and services to culturally and linguistically diverse communities in dispersion, with particular focus on international librarianship, Armenian culture and identity. Her global linkages, varied professional experiences, and innovative approaches to multilingual library and community services have provided her a distinctive practical and critical lens with which to initiate research, contribute to scholarship, and mentor future generations of information professionals.

Sylva Natalie Manoogian's career as a library professional began in 1964 at the Los Angeles Public Library (LAPL). During her 35 years of employment, she was promoted from intermittent clerk to principal librarian and she "retired" in April 1999. During her 18-year tenure as the Central Library's International Languages Department Manager, she instituted the Language Learning and Literacy Centers, with their independent study and Laubach Way to English tutorial programs. During her last three years as a library administrator, she served as the Northeast Area Manager, with responsibility for the branch libraries where she had been trained and mentored.

Currently, she devotes vast energy as a volunteer consultant to Armenian library projects worldwide, primarily in Jerusalem and Armenia; as a substitute reference librarian at LAPL; and at other Diaspora libraries that serve culturally and linguistically diverse communities, in Armenian language collection development, programming, and reference services.

She has been an active member of the American and California Library Associations since 1968, and was accorded honorary lifetime membership in the Library Association of Armenia for championing its establishment in 1994. She is the chairperson of ALLIC (Armenian Librarians and Libraries Committee) of the American Library Association's Ethnic and Multicultural Information Exchange Round Table.

Dr. Manoogian has published numerous articles and presented papers on international librarianship and Armenian culture and heritage. Her innovative approaches to multilingual library services have earned her recognition, as well as appreciation, reflected by numerous local, state, national, and international awards — most recently the American Library Association International Relations Committee 2006 John Ames Humphry/OCLC/Forest Press Award for her tireless efforts to revitalize the Calouste Gulbenkian Library of the Armenian Patriarchate in Jerusalem, her contributions as a consultant to libraries and librarians in Armenia, and the cooperative spirit she has fostered among librarians from the nations of the Caucasus. An on-line article, dated 29 July 2013, about her academic accomplishments and numerous future research projects is available at www.ampersand.gseis.ucla.edu.

About the Author

Ara Khachig Manoogian (1965)

Ara Khachig Manoogian is a human rights activist, an investigative journalist, Artsakh representative for the *Shahan Natalie Family Foundation* and a member of *Policy Forum Armenia*, a Washington D.C.-based think tank. Human trafficking, illegal adoption practices, army abuse and government corruption in Armenia and Artsakh are among the issues, with which Manoogian is primarily concerned. His activism has been widely covered by *Radio Free Europe/Radio Liberty, Hetq, Keghart, Hraparak* and other media outlets. Ara K. Manoogian is the co-author *Desert Nights* (2006), a book and a documentary, which uncovers a large international human trafficking network functioning in Dubai, involving representatives of the Armenian and UAE law-enforcement agencies.

Ara Khachig Manoogian was born in 1965 in Pasadena, California, to Khachig Evan and Sylva Natalie Manoogian. His maternal grandmother was a direct descendant of the Bagratuni Dynasty, who ruled over the Armenian Nation from the 9th to 11th century. Ara's maternal grandfather is Shahan Natalie, the mastermind behind the executions of the Young Turk leaders responsible for the Armenian Genocide of 1915, and those that conspired with them. He is also the nephew of the late His Beatitude Archbishop Torkom Manoogian (1919-2012), Armenian Patriarch of Jerusalem.

Ara traveled to Armenia for the first time with his parents in 1989 as a videographer to document a project that the Eastern Diocese of the Armenian Church of North America and the American Library Association had undertaken in Armenia's 1988 earthquake zone. Concerned by the hardship of the Armenian citizens, Ara made numerous subsequent fact-finding trips to Armenia and Artsakh from 1992 to 1997. He documented on video, in photographs, and journals, the daily lives of common people to better understand their needs and find ways to make their lives more bearable. Thanks to his active stance in addressing socio-economic issues in Armenia, as well as the long and frequent visits to Armenia, Ara K. Manoogian was elected the President of the Monte Melkonian Fund in 1995 and served until 1997.

In 1998, Ara moved to the town of Martuni, Artsakh, where he coordinated and monitored a number of aid distribution initiatives. At the same time, he has been whistle-blowing on government corruption both in Armenia and Artsakh, helping common citizens benefit from their civil rights without having to pay bribes to public officials.

In 2000, he became the Artsakh representative of *the Shahan Natalie Family Foundation, Inc. (SNFF)*, a California non-profit public benefit corporation, established by the members of the Natalie/Manoogian family in 1999. Dealing with social, economic, cultural, and educational issues in Armenia and Artsakh, the *Shahan Natalie Family Foundation* became the third Non-Governmental Organization (NGO) ever to be registered in Artsakh, following the Red Cross and the *"Hayastan" All-Armenian Fund*, since its independence, proclaimed in 1992. One of the major charitable projects implemented by the Artsakh branch of the SNFF was *Hand-to-Hand* in 2006, intended for the relief of the people of Kashatagh, Artsakh.

His first major initiative was to curb corrupt adoption practices in Armenia. In 2003, posing as a potential adopting parent, Ara was able to uncover an entire mechanism of prospering illicit adoption business. The problem was specifically related the illegal adoptions of Armenian children outside Armenia by U.S.-based companies. Thanks to his findings, the Armenian National Assembly adopted new laws to enhance the adoption process regulation. However, a recent monitoring of the field (2011) has shown that stricter laws have only made the illegal adoption procedure more sophisticated. In March 2011, Ara K. Manoogian embarked on a new phase of his struggle against international child trafficking from Armenia, organized by U.S. based adoption agencies.

In early 2004, joining with the *Hetq Investigative Journalists of Armenia* and the SNFF began an investigation into the trafficking of women and children from Armenia to the United Arab Emirates. This was the operation *Desert Nights*, which ended up becoming one of the most significant projects of the SNFF. Exposing their lives to danger, Ara K. Manoogian of the SNFF and Edik Baghdasaryan, editor-in-chief of *Hetq* weekly eventually succeeded in setting a number of victims of human trafficking free and preventing thousands from treading on the same path by raising awareness through *Desert Nights*, a widely distributed book and a documentary by the two journalists. *"The most important work on human trafficking for sexual exploitation is Desert Nights,"* writes the OSCE in its report on Human Trafficking in Armenia (in Armenian).

As a result of the investigation, numerous criminal cases were filed against pimps and traffickers, more than a dozen were jailed. The investigation also implicated Rafayel Gyulnazaryan, the head of the anti-human trafficking department at the United Nations in Yerevan, as a part of the trafficking ring. With the help of the U.S. State Department, Gyulnazaryan was dismissed from his post. The evidence provided by Ara K. Manoogian and Edik Baghdasaryan about the involvement of the Armenian law-enforcement in the human trafficking network has been denied by the Armenian authorities since 2005. However, on February 18, 2011, *WikiLeaks* released cables of the U.S. Embassy to Armenia, dating back to 2006, which confirmed the evidence.

Ara K. Manoogian has played an active role in resolving the violent murder of Nazareth Berberian, an American-Armenian philanthropist and businessman, in Yerevan, in April 2009. With the intention of getting to the bottom of the truth about the high-profile murder case, Ara dedicated months to a parallel field investigation, which led to uncovering corrupt practices within the Armenian Police system, as well as gaping drawbacks in forensic examination.

In September 2010, after a scandalous *YouTube* video of an Armenian officer's sadistic treatment of two conscripts was removed shortly after the upload under the authorities' pressure, Ara K. Manoogian who had managed to download the video, put it back on *YouTube* through his own channel, which caused a surge of wrath in the Armenian society. Despite calls from the Police Department of Armenia and the Defense Minister of Artsakh, as well as numerous angry emails, death threats, demanding that the video be removed, Manoogian refused to comply. The video went viral and created unprecedented public pressure, resulting in the offender's arrest and conviction.

Ara K. Manoogian's activism has been thoroughly recorded in his blog, *Martuni or Bust!*, established in 2001. Nine years later, he also launched *The Truth Must Be Told*, a web project, where he publishes his reports on key issues concerning government corruption and human rights violations in Armenia and Artsakh. One of them is *"To Donate Or Not to Donate?"* (2011), a white paper on the *"Hayastan" All-Armenian Fund*, which explores how government corruption has been affecting the Fund's efficiency since its establishment.

After Armenian MP Ruben Hayrapetyan's bodyguards' victim, Dr Vahe Avetyan was pronounced dead on June 29, 2012, Ara K. Manoogian played an essential role in consolidating the Los Angeles Armenian community to stage a series of protests in front of the Consulate General of the Republic of Armenia in Los Angeles. During the protest, Ara K. Manoogian handed the Consulate

General a petition demanding termination of MP Ruben Hayrapetyan's powers and involving him as a suspect in Vahe Avetyan's murder case. Manoogian also helped organize the *Los Angeles Candlelight Vigil*, organized in all the major Armenian communities throughout the world in commemoration of Vahe Avetyan on the 40th day of his death on August 7, 2012.

In July 2012, Ara K. Manoogian exposed a Glendale-based self-styled Armenian ultra-nationalist organization called *Armenian Aryan Fist*, which continuously spread hate speech via their TV show broadcast by High Vision TV in Glendale, CA. After publishing a video lambasting the members of this organization, Ara K. Manoogian exposed Armen Shahbazyan, the leader of the phony organization, on Harout Bronozian's *Return to Armenia* TV show. Since then the broadcasting of the *Armenian Aryan Fist* TV show has been discontinued.

Ara K. Manoogian started a hunger strike to March 17, 2013, in protest of U.S. President Obama's congratulatory message to Serzh Sargsyan over his re-election as President of Armenia. Ara K. Manoogian regarded President Obama's message as a validation of widespread and well-documented fraud and demanded that President Obama retract his congratulation for the sake of Democracy and Rule of Law. Ara K. Manoogian carried out his hunger strike in an RV parked in front of U.S. Representative Adam Schiff's headquarters in Burbank, CA. On April 2, 2013, Ara K. Manoogian embarked on a cross-country trip to Washington, D.C., with the purpose of continuing his hunger strike in front of the White House and making stops in different cities to raise awareness about his cause. He ended his hunger strike in front of the White House, on April 9, 2013, the day when Serzh Sargsyan was sworn in as Armenia's President for a second 5-year term in office.

Since 2008, after his mother, Sylva Natalie Manoogian, took possession of Shahan Natalie's private archive from Sylva's oldest sister, Etna Mahy (1927-2017), Ara K. Manoogian has been devoting most of his spare time to archival preservation works, as well as investigative research in order to confirm the validity of the materials found within the archive.

www.ingramcontent.com/pod-product-compliance
Lightning Source LLC
Chambersburg PA
CBHW050328230426
43663CB00010B/1781